English-Dari
Dari-English

Word to Word® Bilingual Dictionary

Compiled by:
C. Sesma, M.A.

Translated & Edited by:
Wali Shearzad

Dari Word to Word® Bilingual Dictionary
1st Edition © Copyright 2022

Published in the United States by:

Bilingual Dictionaries, Inc.
PO Box 1154
Murrieta, CA 92564
T: (951) 296-2445 • F: (951) 296-9911
E: support@bilingualdictionaries.com
www.BilingualDictionaries.com

ISBN13: 978-1-946986-603

Print 221025

Table of Contents

Bilingual Dictionaries, Inc.

We are committed to providing schools, libraries and educators with a great selection of bilingual materials for students. Along with bilingual dictionaries we also publish ESL materials, children's bilingual stories and children's bilingual picture dictionaries.

Sesma's Dari Word to Word® Bilingual Dictionary was created specifically with students in mind to be used for reference and testing. This dictionary contains approximately 19,500 entries targeting common words used in the English language.

Word to Word® Series

Bilingual Dictionaries, Inc. is the publisher of the Word to Word® bilingual dictionary series with over 30 languages that are 100% Word to Word®. The Word to Word® series provides ELL students with standardized bilingual dictionaries approved for state testing. Students with different backgrounds can now use dictionaries from the same series that are specifically designed to create an equal resource that strictly adheres to the guidelines set by districts and states.

entry: our selection of English vocabulary includes common words found in school usage and everyday conversation.

part of speech: part of speech is necessary to ensure the translation is appropriate. Entries can be spelled the same but have different translations and meanings depending on the part of speech.

translation: our translation is Word to Word® meaning no definitions or explanations. Purely the most simple common accurate translation.

List of Irregular Verbs

present - past - past participle

arise - arose - arisen
awake - awoke - awoken, awaked
be - was - been
bear - bore - borne
beat - beat - beaten
become - became - become
begin - began - begun
behold - beheld - beheld
bend - bent - bent
beseech - besought - besought
bet - bet - betted
bid - bade (bid) - bidden (bid)
bind - bound - bound
bite - bit - bitten
bleed - bled - bled
blow - blew - blown
break - broke - broken
breed - bred - bred
bring - brought - brought
build - built - built
burn - burnt - burnt *
burst - burst - burst
buy - bought - bought
cast - cast - cast
catch - caught - caught
choose - chose - chosen
cling - clung - clung
come - came - come
cost - cost - cost

creep - crept - crept
cut - cut - cut
deal - dealt - dealt
dig - dug - dug
do - did - done
draw - drew - drawn
dream - dreamt - dreamed
drink - drank - drunk
drive - drove - driven
dwell - dwelt - dwelt
eat - ate - eaten
fall - fell - fallen
feed - fed - fed
feel - felt - felt
fight - fought - fought
find - found - found
flee - fled - fled
fling - flung - flung
fly - flew - flown
forebear - forbore - forborne
forbid - forbade - forbidden
forecast - forecast - forecast
forget - forgot - forgotten
forgive - forgave - forgiven
forego - forewent - foregone
foresee - foresaw - foreseen
foretell - foretold - foretold
forget - forgot - forgotten
forsake - forsook - forsaken
freeze - froze - frozen

List of Irregular Verbs

get - got - gotten

give - gave - given

go - went - gone

grind - ground - ground

grow - grew - grown

hang - hung * - hung *

have - had - had

hear - heard - heard

hide - hid - hidden

hit - hit - hit

hold - held - held

hurt - hurt - hurt

hit - hit - hit

hold - held - held

keep - kept - kept

kneel - knelt * - knelt *

know - knew - known

lay - laid - laid

lead - led - led

lean - leant * - leant *

leap - lept * - lept *

learn - learnt * - learnt *

leave - left - left

lend - lent - lent

let - let - let

lie - lay - lain

light - lit * - lit *

lose - lost - lost

make - made - made

mean - meant - meant

meet - met - met

mistake - mistook - mistaken

must - had to - had to

pay - paid - paid

plead - pleaded - pled

prove - proved - proven

put - put - put

quit - quit * - quit *

read - read - read

rid - rid - rid

ride - rode - ridden

ring - rang - rung

rise - rose - risen

run - ran - run

saw - sawed - sawn

say - said - said

see - saw - seen

seek - sought - sought

sell - sold - sold

send - sent - sent

set - set - set

sew - sewed - sewn

shake - shook - shaken

shear - sheared - shorn

shed - shed - shed

shine - shone - shone

shoot - shot - shot

show - showed - shown

shrink - shrank - shrunk

shut - shut - shut

List of Irregular Verbs

sing - sang - sung
sink - sank - sunk
sit - sat - sat
slay - slew - slain
sleep - sleep - slept
slide - slid - slid
sling - slung - slung
smell - smelt * - smelt *
sow - sowed - sown *
speak - spoke - spoken
speed - sped * - sped *
spell - spelt * - spelt *
spend - spent - spent
spill - spilt * - spilt *
spin - spun - spun
spit - spat - spat
split - split - split
spread - spread - spread
spring - sprang - sprung
stand - stood - stood
steal - stole - stolen
stick - stuck - stuck
sting - stung - stung
stink - stank - stunk
stride - strode - stridden
strike - struck - struck (stricken)

strive - strove - striven
swear - swore - sworn
sweep - swept - swept
swell - swelled - swollen *
swim - swam - swum
take - took - taken
teach - taught - taught
tear - tore - torn
tell - told - told
think - thought - thought
throw - threw - thrown
thrust - thrust - thrust
tread - trod - trodden
wake - woke - woken
wear - wore - worn
weave - wove * - woven *
wed - wed * - wed *
weep - wept - wept
win - won - won
wind - wound - wound
wring - wrung - wrung
write - wrote - written

**Those tenses with an * also have
   regular forms.**

English-Dari

Abbreviations

a - article - حرف تعریف

adj - adjective - صفت

adv - adverb - قید

conj - conjunction - حرف ربط

e - exclamation - علامت تعجب

n - noun - اسم

prep - preposition - حرف اضافه

pron - pronoun - ضمیر

v - verb - فعل

pv - phrasal verb - فعل مرکب

idiom - idiom - اصطلاح

auxillary v - auxillary verb - فعل کومکی

modal v - modal verb - فعل وجهی

abbr - abbreviation - ففخم

phrase - phrase - عبارت

A

a *a* الف

abandon *v* رها کردن

abandonment *n* ترک، رهایی

abbreviate *v* مختصر کردن

abbreviation *n* اختصار

abdomen *n* بطن

abduct *v* اختطاف کردن

abduction *n* اختطاف

aberration *n* انحراف

abhor *v* تنفر داشتن

abide by *v* اطاعت کردن

ability *n* قابلیت

ablaze *adj* مشتعل، برافروخته

able *adj* توانا

abnormal *adj* غیرعادی

abnormality *n* وضع غیرعادی

abnormally *adv* بطور غیرعادی

aboard *adv* در داخل، سوار بر

abolish *v* لغو کردن

abort *v* سقط کردن

abound *v* زیاد بودن

about *adv* تقریباً

about *prep* در مورد

above *prep* بالای

above *adv* در بالا

abridge *v* مختصر کردن

abroad *adv* خارج

abrogate *v* باطل کردن

abruptly *adv* به سرعت

absence *n* غیابت

absent *adj* غایب

absolute *adj* مطلق

absolutely *adv* مطلقاً

absolve *v* اعلام بی تقصیری کردن

absorb *v* جذب کردن

absorbent *adj* جاذب

abstain *v* خودداری کردن

abstinence *n* اجتناب

abstract *adj* مطلق

absurd *adj* نامعقول

abundance *n* فراوانی

abundant *adj* وافر

abuse *n* سوء استفاده

abuse *v* سوء استفاده کردن

abusive *adj* توهین آمیز

abysmal *adj* عمیق

abyss *n* پرتگاه

academic *adj* علمی

academy *n* اکادمی

accelerate *v* سرعت بخشیدن

accelerator *n* سرعت دهنده

accent *n* لهجه

accept *v* قبول کردن

acceptable *adj* قابل قبول

acceptance *n* قبولی، پذیرش

access *n* دسترسی

access *v* دسترسی داشتن

accessible *adj* قابل دسترس

accident *n* حادثه

accidental *adj* اتفاقی

acclaim v تحسین کردن	acquire v بدست آوردن
acclimatize v عادت کردن	acquisition n حصول، اکتساب
accommodate v جا دادن	acquit v تبرئه کردن
accompany v همراهی کردن	acquittal n برائت
accomplice n همدست، شریک	acre n جریب
accomplish v انجام دادن، ت	acrobat n اکروبات
کمیل کردن	across adv در سراسر
accomplishment n دست آورد	across prep در میان
according to prep نظر به	act v اقدام کردن؛ تمثیل کردن
accordion n اکاردریون	act n عمل؛ تمثیل؛ قانون
account n حساب	action n اقدام
account for v در نظر گرفتن	activate v فعال کردن
accountable adj حسابده، مسوول	active adj فعال
accountant n محاسب	activity n فعالیت
accumulate v جمع شدن	actor n ممثل
accumulation n تجمع	actress n ممثل زن
accuracy n دقت	actual adj واقعی
accurate adj دقیق	actually adv واقعاً
accurately adv دقیقاً	acute adj شدید
accusation n اتهام	adamant adj تزلزل ناپذیر
accuse v متهم کردن	adapt v تطابق داشتن
accustom v عادت کردن	adaptable adj تطابق پذیر
ache n درد	adaptation n تطابق
achieve v بدست آوردن	adapter n تطابق دهنده
achievement n دست آورد	add v اضافه کردن
acid n تیزاب	addicted adj معتاد
acknowledge v تایید کردن	addiction n اعتیاد
acknowledgment n، تصدیق	addictive adj اعتیاد آور
منظوری	addition n جمع
acorn n بلوط	additional adj اضافی
acoustic adj صوتی	address n آدرس
acquaintance n آشنایی	address v آدرس نوشتن؛ خطاب کردن

adequate *adj* کافی	advance *n* پیشرفت
adequately *adv* به اندازه کافی	advance *v* پیشرفت کردن؛
adhere *v* پابند بودن	پیشکی دادن
adhesive *adj* پابند	advanced *adj* پیشرفته
adjacent *adj* همجوار	advantage *n* منفعت
adjective *n* صفت	adventure *n* ماجرا
adjoin *v* پیوستن	adverb *n* قید
adjoining *adj* همجوار	adversary *n* مخالف
adjust *v* عیار کردن	adverse *adj* نامطلوب
adjustable *adj* قابل تنظیم	adversity *n* فلاکت، بدبختی
adjustment *n* تعدیل	advertise *v* اعلان کردن
administer *v* اداره کردن	advertisement *n* اعلان
administration *n* اداره	advice *n* مشوره
administrative *adj* اداری	advise *v* مشوره دادن
administrator *n* اداره کننده	adviser *n* مشاور
admirable *adj* قابل تحسین	advocate *v* وکالت کردن
admiral *n* فرمانده	aesthetic *adj* زیبایی پسند
admiration *n* تحسین	afar *adv* از دور
admire *v* تحسین کردن	affable *adj* خوش برخورد
admirer *n* تحسین کننده	affair *n* رویداد
admission *n* داخله	affect *v* تاثیر کردن
admit *v* داخل کردن؛ اعتراف کردن	affection *n* محبت، عاطفه
admittance *n* پذیرش؛ ورود	affectionate *adj* مهربان
adolescence *n* بلوغ	affiliate *v* تعلق داشتن
adolescent *n* نوجوان	affiliation *n* وابستگی
adopt *v* به فرزندی گرفتن	affirm *v* تایید کردن
adorable *adj* قابل تحسین	affirmative *adj* تایید
adore *v* تحسین کردن	affix *v* اضافه نمودن
adorn *v* آراستن	afflict *v* مبتلا شدن
adulation *n* چاپلوسی	affliction *n* مصیبت
adult *n* بالغ	affluent *adj* ثروتمند
adulthood *n* بلوغ	afford *v* از عهده چیزی برامدن

affordable *adj* قابل استطاعت

affront *n* توهین

afloat *adv* شناور

afraid *adj* ترسیده

after *prep* بعد از؛ در عقب؛ به تعقیب

after *conj* به تعقیب

afternoon *n* بعد از ظهر

afterward *adv* بعد از آن

again *adv* دوباره

against *prep* در مقابل؛ علیه

age *n* سن

aged *adj* سالخورده

agency *n* اداره

agenda *n* آجندا

agent *n* نماینده

aggravate *v* بدتر کردن

aggression *n* خشونت

aggressive *adj* خشونت آمیز

aggressor *n* متجاوز

agile *adj* سریع

ago *adv* قبل

agonize *v* عذاب کشیدن

agonizing *adj* رنج آور

agony *n* رنج

agree *v* توافق کردن

agreeable *adj* توافق پذیر

agreement *n* توافقنامه

agricultural *adj* زراعتی

agriculture *n* زراعت

ahead *adv* روبرو

aid *n* کمک

aid *v* کمک کردن

aide *n* مشاور

ailing *adj* مریض

ailment *n* مریضی

aim *n* هدف

aim *v* هدف قراردادن

aimless *adj* بی هدف، بی اراده

air *v* نشر کردن

air *n* هوا

aircraft *n* طیاره

airfare *n* کرایه طیاره

airfield *n* میدان هوایی

airline *n* شرکت هوانوردی

airmail *n* پُست هوایی

airplane *n* طیاره

airport *n* میدان هوایی

airtight *adj* هوابند

aisle *n* راهرو

ajar *adj* باز

akin *adj* یکسان

alarm *n* زنگ خطر

alarm clock *n* ساعت زنگ دار

alarming *adj* هشدار دهنده

alcohol *n* الکل

alcoholic *adj* الکلی

alert *n* محتاط

alert *v* هشدار دادن

alert *adj* هوشیار

alien *n* بیگانه

align *v* منطبق ساختن

alignment *n* تطابق

alike *adj* مشابه

alive *adj* زنده

all *adv* جمع
all *adj* همه
all right *adj* خوب
all right *adv* درست
allege *v* ادعا کردن
allegedly *adv* ظاهراً
allegiance *n* بیعت، وفاداری
allergic *adj* حساسیتی
allergy *n* حساسیت
alleviate *v* کم کردن
alley *n* کوچه
alliance *n* اتحاد
alligator *n* تمساح
allocate *v* تخصیص دادن
allocation *n* تخصیص
allot *v* اختصاص دادن
allow *v* اجازه دادن
allowance *n* اجازه؛ امتیازات
allure *n* جذابیت
ally *v* پیوستن
ally *n* متحد، همدست
almighty *adj* قادر، توانا
almond *n* بادام
almost *adv* تقریباً
alone *adj* تنها
alone *adv* فقط
along *prep* در امتداد
along *adv* یکجا با
alongside *prep* در کنار
aloof *adj* دور
aloud *adv* بلند
alphabet *n* الفبا

already *adv* قبلاً
alright *adv* درست
also *adv* همچنان
altar *n* محراب
alter *v* تغییر دادن
alteration *n* تغییر
altercation *n* مجادله
alternate *adj* متناوب
alternate *v* متناوب کردن
alternative *n* بدیل
alternative *adj* بدیل
alternatively *adv* متناوباً
although *conj* گرچه
altitude *n* ارتفاع
altogether *adv* باهم یکجا
aluminum *n* المونیم
always *adv* همیشه
amass *v* جمع کردن، گرد آوردن
amateur *adj* آماتور
amaze *v* متحیر ساختن
amazement *n* حیرت
amazing *adj* حیرت انگیز
ambassador *n* سفیر
ambiguous *adj* مبهم
ambition *n* آرزو
ambitious *adj* جاطلب
ambivalent *adj* متضاد
ambulance *n* امبولانس
ambush *v* کمین گرفتن
amend *v* اصلاح کردن
amendment *n* اصلاح، تعدیل
amenities *n* امکانات برای آسایش

American *adj* امریکایی

amicable *adj* دوستانه، صمیمی

amid *prep* در میان

ammunition *n* مهمات جنگی

amnesia *n* فراموشی

among *prep* در میان

amount *n* مبلغ، مقدار

amount to *v* بالغ شدن به

amphibious *adj* ذوحیاتین

ample *adj* فراوان

amplifier *n* تقویت کننده

amplify *v* بزرگ کردن

amputate *v* قطع کردن

amuse *v* سرگرم کردن

amusement *n* سرگرمی

amusing *adj* سرگرم کننده

an *a* یک

analogy *n* قیاس

analysis *n* تحلیل

analyst *n* تحلیلگر

analytic *adj* تحلیلی

analyze *v* تحلیل کردن

anatomy *n* اناتومی

ancestor *n* اجداد

anchor *n* لنگرکشی

ancient *adj* قدیمی

and *conj* و

anecdote *n* حکایت

anesthesia *n* بیهوشی

anew *adv* جدید

angel *n* فرشته

angelic *adj* فرشته ای

anger *n* عصبانیت

angle *n* زاویه

angry *adj* قهر

anguish *n* غم و اندوه

animal *n* حیوان

animate *v* متحرک کردن

animation *n* انگیزش

animosity *n* دشمنی

ankle *n* بجلک پا

annihilate *v* نابود کردن

anniversary *n* سالگرد

annotate *v* یادداشت نوشتن

annotation *n* یادداشت

announce *v* اعلان کردن

announcement *n* اعلامیه

announcer *n* اعلان کننده

annoy *v* اذیت کردن

annoying *adj* اذیت کننده

annual *adj* سالانه

annually *adv* بطور سالانه

anonymity *n* ناشناس، نامعلوم

anonymous *adj* ناشناس

another *adj* دیگر

another *pron* یکی دیگر

answer *n* جواب

answer *v* جواب دادن

ant *n* مرچه

antagonize *v* مخالفت کردن

antelope *n* بز کوهی

antenna *n* آنتن

antibiotic *n* انتیبیتیک

anticipate *v* پیشبینی کردن

anticipation n پیش‌بینی	appealing adj جذاب
antidote n ضد زهر	appear v ظاهر شدن
antiquated adj قدیمی	appearance n ظاهر
antique n عتیقه	appetite n اشتها
anvil n سندان	appetizer n اشتها آور
anxiety n اضطراب	applaud v کف زدن، تقدیر کردن
anxious adj مضطرب	applause n تشویق و تمجید
any adj هر	apple n سیب
any adv هریکی	appliance n وسایل
any pron هیچ	applicable adj قابل اجرا
anybody pron هرکس	applicant n درخواست کننده
anymore adv بیش از این	application n درخواستی
anyone pron هرکسی	apply v درخواست کردن
anything pron هرچیزی	appoint v گماشتن
anyway adv به هر حال	appointment n وعده ملاقات
anywhere adv هرجا	appraisal n ارزیابی
apart adv جدا	appraise v ارزیابی کردن
apartment n اپارتمان	appreciate v قدردانی کردن
apathy n بی تفاوتی	appreciation n قدردانی
ape n بوزینه	apprehend v درک کردن
apiece adv تکه تکه	apprehensive adj درک کننده
apologize v معذرت خواستن	apprentice n شاگرد کار آموز
apology n معذرت	approach n اقدام
apostrophe n علامه اپاستراف	approach v نزدیک شدن
appall v ترساندن	appropriate adj مناسب
appalling adj ترسناک	appropriately adv بطور مناسب
apparel n پوشاک	approval n منظوری
apparent adj آشکار	approve v منظور کردن
apparently adv ظاهراً	approximate adj تخمین کردن
appeal v درخواست کردن؛	approximately adv تقریباً
جذاب بودن	apricot n زردآلو
appeal n درخواست؛ جذبه	April n اپریل

apron *n* پیشبند
aptitude *n* استعداد
aquarium *n* اکواریوم
aquatic *adj* مربوط به آب
aqueduct *n* مجرا
Arabic *adj* عربی
arbitrary *adj* دلخواه
arch *n* کمان
archaeology *n* باستان شناسی
archaic *adj* قدیمی
architect *n* مهندس
architecture *n* مهندسی
archive *n* آرشیف
ardent *adj* مشتاق
area *n* ساحه
arena *n* عرصه
argue *v* مشاجره کردن
argument *n* مشاجره
arise *v* بلند شدن
arithmetic *n* حساب
ark *n* کشتی
arm *n* بازو
arm *v* مسلح کردن
armchair *n* آرام چوکی
armed *adj* مسلح
armor *n* زره
armpit *n* زیربغل
arms *n* آغوش
army *n* اردو
aromatic *adj* معطر
around *prep* در اطراف
around *adv* دور و بر

arrange *v* تنظیم کردن
arrangement *n* ترتیبات
arrest *v* دستگیر کردن
arrival *n* ورود
arrive *v* رسیدن
arrogance *n* غرور
arrogant *adj* مغرور
arrow *n* تیر
arson *n* آتش زدن عمدی
arsonist *n* کسی که عمداً آتش میزند
art *n* هنر
artery *n* شریان
arthritis *n* درد مفاصل
artichoke *n* یکنوع گیاه
article *n* مقاله؛ حرف تعریف
articulate *v* سنجیده حرف زدن
artificial *adj* مصنوعی
artillery *n* توپخانه
artist *n* هنرمند
artistic *adj* هنری
artwork *n* اثرهنری
as *conj* چونکه
as *prep* درنتیجه
as *adv* مانند
ascend *v* صعود
ash *n* خاکستر
ashamed *adj* شرمنده
ashore *adv* درساحل
ashtray *n* خاکستردانی
aside *adv* گذشته از
ask *v* پرسیدن
asleep *adj* خوابیده

asparagus *n* مارچوبه	asteroid *n* شهاب آسمانی
aspect *n* عرصه	asthma *n* نفس تنگی
asphalt *n* قیرشده	asthmatic *adj* دچار نفس تنگی
aspiration *n* تنفس	astonish *v* متعجب ساختن
aspire *v* آرزو کردن	astonishing *adj* تعجب آور
aspirin *n* اسپرین	astound *v* حیران کردن
assassin *n* قاتل	astounding *adj* حیرت انگیز
assassinate *v* ترور کردن	astray *adv* گمراه
assault *v* حمله	astrologer *n* طالع بین
assemble *v* جمع شدن	astrology *n* ستاره شناسی
assembly *n* مجلس	astronaut *n* فضانورد
assert *v* ادعا کردن	astronomer *n* ستاره شناس
assertion *n* ادعا	astronomic *adj* نجومی
assertive *adj* اظهار کننده	astronomy *n* علم نجوم
assess *v* بررسی کردن	astute *adj* زیرک
assessment *n* بررسی	asunder *adv* جدا شده
asset *n* دارایی	asylum *n* پناهند گی
assign *v* واگذار کردن	at *prep* در
assignment *n* وظیفه	athlete *n* ورزشکار
assimilate *v* جذب کردن	athletic *adj* ورزشی
assist *v* کمک کردن	atone *v* جبران کردن
assistance *n* مساعدت	atonement *n* کفاره
assistant *n* معاون	atrocious *adj* وحشیانه
associate *v* همکار	atrocity *n* بی رحمی
association *n* انجمن	atrophy *v* لاغر شدن
assorted *adj* متنوع	attach *v* ضمیمه کردن
assortment *n* دسته بندی	attached *adj* ضمیمه شده
assume *v* فرض کردن	attachment *n* ضمیمه
assumption *n* گمان	attack *n* حمله
assurance *n* اطمینان	attack *v* حمله کردن
assure *v* اطمینان دادن	attacker *n* حمله کننده
asterisk *n* علامه ستاره	attain *v* بدست آوردن

attainable adj قابل دریافت	**authenticate** v تصدیق کردن
attempt v تلاش کردن	**authenticity** n اعتبار
attend v اشتراک کردن	**author** n مؤلف
attendance n حاضری	**authoritarian** adj اقتدارگرا
attendant n ملازم	**authoritative** adj معتبر
attention n توجه	**authority** n صلاحیت؛ متخصص
attentive adj هوشیار	**authorization** n مجوز
attest v تصدیق کردن	**authorize** v اجازه دادن
attic n اتاق کوچک	**auto** n خودکار
attitude n طرز برخورد	**autograph** n امضا
attorney n وکیل مدافع	**automated** adj خودکار
attract v جلب کردن	**automatic** adj خودکار
attraction n جذابیت	**automatically** adv بطور خودکار
attractive adj جذاب	**automobile** n موتر
attribute v نسبت دادن	**autumn** n خزان
auction v به مزایده گذاشتن	**auxiliary** adj کمکی
auction n مزایده	**availability** n قابلیت دسترسی
auctioneer n دلال	**available** adj قابل دسترسی
audacious adj بی باک	**avalanche** n برفکوچ
audacity n جسارت	**avenge** v انتقام گرفتن
audible adj شنیدنی	**avenue** n جاده
audience n حاضرین	**average** adj حد اوسط
audio adj شنیداری	**average** n متوسط
audit v تفتیش کردن	**aviation** n هواپیمایی
audition n آزمون	**aviator** n هوانورد
auditorium n تالار کنفرانس	**avid** adj مشتاق
augment v تقویت کردن	**avocado** n میوه آووکادو
August n ماه آگست	**avoid** v جلوگیری کردن
aunt n خاله، عمه	**avoidable** adj قابل جلوگیری
austere adj تند و تلخ	**await** v منتظر
austerity n ریاضت	**awake** adj بیدار
authentic adj معتبر	**award** v اعطا کردن

award *n* انعام

aware *adj* آگاه

awareness *n* آگاهی

away *adv* دور

awe *n* هیبت، ترس

awesome *adj* عالی

awful *adj* ناخوشایند

awkward *adj* زشت

awning *n* سایه بان

axe *n* تبر

axis *n* محور

axle *n* محور

B

baby *n* طفل

babysit *v* پرستاری طفل

babysitter *n* پرستار طفل

bachelor *n* لیسانسه

back *v* به عقب رفتن؛ پشتی کردن

back *n* پشت؛ عقب

back *adv* عقب

back *adj* عقبی

back away *v* عقب نشینی

back down *v* عقب نشینی کردن

back out *v* عقب برآمدن

back up *v* کاپی گرفتن

backbone *n* ستون فقرات

backdoor *n* دروازه عقبی

backfire *v* نتیجه برعکس گرفتن

background *n* پس منظر؛ سوابق

backing *n* پشتیبانی

backlash *n* واکنش تند

backlog *n* انبار شدن

backpack *n* بکس پشتی

backstage *adv* پشت صحنه

backup *n* کاپی گرفتن

backward *adv* بطرف عقب

backward *adj* عقب مانده

backyard *n* حویلی عقب خانه

bacon *n* گوشت خوک

bacteria *n* باکتریا

bad *adj* بد

badge *n* نشان

badly *adv* شدیداً، بطور بد

baffle *v* گیچ کردن

bag *n* خریطه

baggage *n* بکس سفری

baggy *adj* خریطه یی

bail *n* ضمانت

bail out *v* به ضمانت رها شدن

bait *n* طعمه

bake *v* پختن

baker *n* نانوا

bakery *n* نانوایی

balance *n* توازن

balance *v* متوازن کردن

balanced *adj* متوازن

balcony *n* بالکن

bald *adj* بی مو

bale *n* عدل

ball *n* توپ؛ محفل رقص

ballerina *n* رقاصه

ballet *n* رقص بلیت

balloon *n* پوقانه

ballot *n* ورق رای دهی

ballroom *n* سالون رقص

balm *n* مرهم

bamboo *n* چوب بامبو

ban *n* ممانعت

ban *v* منع کردن

banana *n* کیله

band *n* فیته لاستیکی؛ باند موسیقی

bandage *v* با بانداژ بستن

bandage *n* بانداژ

bandit *n* راهزن

bang *v* با صدای بلند به زمین زدن

bangs *n* موی چتری مانند

banish *v* دور کردن

bank *n* بانک؛ لب دریا

bank account *n* حساب بانکی

bankrupt *adj* ورشکسته

banner *n* لوحه تکه یی، بنر

banquet *n* ضیافت

bar *v* مانع شدن

bar *n* میخانه؛ میله آهنی

barbarian *n* وحشی

barbaric *adj* وحشیانه

barbecue *n* باربی کیو

barber *n* سلمان

barcode *n* بارکود

bare *adj* برهنه

barefoot *adj* پا برهنه

barely *adv* به سختی

bargain *v* چانه زدن

bargain *n* معامله

barge *n* باربری

bark *n* پوست درخت

bark *v* عوعو کردن

barley *n* جو

barn *n* طویله

barracks *n* اتاق موقتی

barrel *n* بُشکه

barren *adj* عقیم

barricade *n* مانع

barrier *n* سد، مانع

bartender *n* میخانه دار

barter *v* معامله تجارتی

base *v* اساس قرار دادن

base *n* بنیاد؛ پایگاه نظامی

baseball *n* بازی بیس بال

baseless *adj* بی اساس

basement *n* زیرخانه

bashful *adj* شرم آور

basic *adj* بنیادی

basically *adv* اساساً

basics *n* اساسات

basin *n* دستشوی

basis *n* مبنا

bask *v* آفتاب دادن

basket *n* سبد

basketball *n* بسکیتبال

bass *adj* بم

bass *n* صدای بم

bat *n* دنده بیسبال؛ شب پرک چرمی

batch *n* بسته

bath n حمام	beautify v زیبا ساختن
bathe v حمام کردن	beauty n زیبایی
bathing suit n لباس حمام	beaver n سگ آبی
bathrobe n چپن حمام	because conj بخاطریکه
bathroom n تشناب	because of prep به علت
bathtub n تب حمام	beckon v اشاره
baton n چوب رهنمای موسیقی	become v شدن
battalion n فرقه	bed n بستر
batter v خمیر	bedroom n اتاق خواب
battery n بطری	bedspread n روجایی
battle v مبارزه کردن	bee n زنبور
battle n نبرد	beef n گوشت گاو
battleship n کشتی جنگی	beehive n خانه زنبود عسل
bay n دریاچه	beep v صدا
be v بودن	beer n بیر
beach n ساحل	beetle n مادرکیک
beacon n چراغ رهنما	beetroot n لبلبو
beak n منقار	before conj پیش
beam n روشنی؛ چوب تیر	before adv قبل
beans n لوبیا	before prep قبل از
bear v تحمل کردن	beforehand adv پیشکی
bear n خرس	befriend v دوست شدن
bearable adj قابل تحمل	beg v تقاضا کردن
beard n ریش	beggar n گدا
bearded adj ریش دار	begin v شروع کردن
bearer n حامل	beginner n تازه کار
beast n حیوان	beginning n آغاز
beat n تپش	behalf n به نماینده گی از
beat v زدن	behave v رویه کردن
beaten adj مورد ضرب و شتم	behavior n برخورد
beating n ضربان	behind prep پشت
beautiful adj زیبا	behind adv در عقب

behold v مشاهده کردن	benign adj بی خطر
beige n رنگ کریمی	bent adj خم شده
being n بودن	berry n توت
belated adj دیرشده	beside prep در پهلوی
belch v آروغ زدن	besides prep علاوه بر
belief n عقیده	besiege v محاصره کردن
believable adj قابل باور	best adv به بهترین شیوه
believe v باور کردن	best adj بهترین
believer n مومن	best n ممتاز
belittle v کوچک شمردن	best man n بهترین مرد
bell n زنگ	bestow v اعطا کردن
bell pepper n مرچ دلمه	bet n شرط
belligerent adj جنگ طلب	bet v شرط بستن
belly n شکم	betray v خیانت کردن
belly button n ناف	betrayal n خیانت
belong v متعلق بودن	better adj بهتر
belongings n متعلقات	better adv بهتر است که
beloved adj دوست داشتنی	between adv در بین
below adv پایین	between prep در میان
below prep در زیر	beverage n نوشابه
belt n کمربند	beware v مطلع بودن
bench n دراز چوکی	bewilder v گیج کردن
bend v خم شدن	bewitch v افسون کردن
bend down v خم شدن	beyond prep آنسو
beneath prep در زیر	beyond adv فراتر
benefactor n نیکوکار	bias n جانبداری
beneficial adj سودمند	biased adj جانبدار
beneficiary n ذینفع	bible n کتاب مقدس
benefit v فایده کردن	biblical adj وابسته به کتاب مقدس
benefit n نفع	bibliography n فهرست کتب
benevolence n خیرخواهی	bicycle n بایسکل
benevolent adj خیرخواه	bid n پیشنهاد

bid v پیشنهاد کردن	**blackmail** n تهدید
big adj بزرگ	**blackout** n خاموشی
bike n بایسکل	**blacksmith** n آهنگر
bikini n لباس آببازی زنانه	**bladder** n مثانه
bile n صفرا	**blade** n تیغ
bilingual adj دو زبانه	**blame** v ملامت کردن
bill v بل دادن	**blame** n ملامتی
bill n بل؛ نوت دالر؛منقار مرغابی	**blameless** adj بی عیب و نقص
billboard n تخته اعلانات تجارتی	**bland** adj نامطلوب
billiards n بلیارد	**blank** adj خالی
billion n میلیارد	**blanket** n کمپل
billionaire n میلیاردر	**blast** n انفجار
bin n صندوقچه	**blaze** v آتش
bind v قات کردن	**bleach** v سفید کردن
binding adj اجباری	**bleach** n سفید کننده
binoculars n دوربین	**bleak** adj غم انگیز
biography n بیوگرافی	**bleed** v خونریزی کردن
bird n پرنده	**blemish** n عیب
birth n تولد	**blend** n ترکیب
birthday n روز تولد	**blend** v مخلوط کردن
biscuit n بسکویت	**blender** n مخلوط کننده
bison n گاومیش	**bless** v دعا کردن
bit n توته	**blessed** adj مبارک
bite v چک زدن	**blessing** n دعا
bite n نیش	**blind** n چشم بند
bitter adj قهر؛ تلخ	**blind** v کور کردن
bitterly adv به تلخی	**blind** adj نابینا
bitterness n تلخی	**blindfold** v چشم بستن
bizarre adj عجیب	**blindfold** n چشم بسته
black n سیاه	**blindness** n نابینایی
black adj سیاهی	**blink** v پلک زدن؛ درخشیدن
blackboard n تخته سیاه	**bliss** n سعادت

blissful *adj* باسعادت	blur *v* خیره کردن
blister *n* آبله	blurred *adj* خیره
blizzard *n* توفان برفی	blush *v* سرخ شدن، شرمنده شدن
bloat *v* باد گرفتن	boar *n* خوک وحشی
bloated *adj* متورم، باد دار	board *n* تخته چوبی؛ تخته بازی
block *v* بسته کردن	board *v* سوار شدن
block *n* خشت کانکریتی؛	boast *v* لاف زدن
بلاک ساختمان؛ بندش سرک	boastful *adj* خودخواه
blockade *n* محاصره	boat *n* کشتی
blockage *n* انسداد	bodily *adj* بدنی
blog *n* وبلاگ	body *n* بدن
blogger *n* وبلاگ نویس	bodyguard *n* محافظ شخصی
blonde *n* طلایی	boil *v* جوشاندن
blonde *adj* موطلایی	boiler *n* آله جوش کننده
blood *n* خون	boiling *adj* جوش
bloodthirsty *adj* خونخوار	boisterous *adj* قوی
bloody *adj* خونین	bold *adj* دلیر
bloom *v* شگوفه کردن	boldness *n* جسارت
blossom *v* شگوفه	bolster *v* تقویه کردن
blot *v* لکه	bolt *n* بولت آهنی؛ الماسک
blouse *n* پیراهن بلوز	bolt *v* پیچاندن
blow *v* پف کردن	bomb *n* بم
blow *n* ضربه	bomb *v* بمبار کردن
blow up *v* منفجر کردن	bond *n* پیوستگی
bludgeon *v* با چوب زدن	bondage *n* برده گی
blue *adj* آبی؛ جگرخون	bone *n* استخوان
blue *n* رنگ آبی	bonfire *n* آتشسوزی
blueprint *n* طرح	bonus *n* انعام
bluff *n* پرتگاه	book *v* ریزرف کردن
bluff *v* فریب دادن	book *n* کتاب
blunder *n* اشتباه بزرگ	bookcase *n* الماری کتاب
blunt *adj* گُند؛ رُک و راست	bookkeeper *n* کتابدار

B

booklet n کتابچه	**boulevard** n جاده
bookstore n کتابفروشی	**bounce** v خیز زدن
boom v توسعه یافتن	**bouncy** adj فنری
boom n رونق	**bound** v محدود کردن
boost v تقویت کردن	**bound** adj مقید
boot n موزه	**boundary** n محدوده
booth n غرفه	**boundless** adj بی حد
border n سرحد؛ مرز	**bounty** n سخاوت
borderline adj خطر مرزی	**bow** v خم شدن
bore v خسته شدن	**bow** n کمان؛ قسمت پیش برامده کشتی
bored adj خسته	**bow out** pv استعفا دادن؛ بیرون شدن
boredom n خستگی	**bowel** n روده
boring adj خسته کن	**bowl** v با توپ بازی کردن
born adj متولد	**bowl** n کاسه
borough n منطقه	**bowling** n بازی بولینگ
borrow v قرض گرفتن	**box** n صندوق
boss n آمر	**box** v ورزش بوکس
boss around v آمرانه رفتار کردن	**box office** n محل خریداری تکت تیاتر
bossy adj آمرانه	**boxer** n بوکسر
botany n گیاه شناسی	**boxing** n بوکسینگ
botch v خراب کردن	**boy** n بچه
both adj هردو	**boycott** v تحریم کردن
both pron هردوی	**boyfriend** n دوست پسر
bother v آزار دادن	**boyhood** n نوجوانی
bothersome adj آزاردهنده	**bra** n سینه بند
bottle n بوتل	**bracelet** n دستبند
bottle v در بوتل ریختن	**braces** n بریس های دندان
bottleneck n مانع	**bracket** n قوس باز و بسته
bottom n زیر	**brag** v لاف زدن
bottom adj قسمت تحتانی	**braid** n چوتی
bottomless adj بدون قسمت تحتانی	**brain** n مغز
boulder n تخته سنگ	**brainwash** v شستشوی مغزی

B

brake v بریک کردن	breathe v نفس کشیدن
brake n بریک موتر	breathtaking adj تعجب آور
branch n شاخه درخت	breed v تولید مثل کردن
branch office n دفتر نماینده گی	breed n نسل
branch out v گسترش دادن	breeze n نسیم
brand v علامه گذاشتن	brevity n کوتاهی
brand n نام تجارتی	brew v تخمیر کردن
brand new adj کاملاً جدید	brewery n کارخانه شراب سازی
brat n شوخ	bribe n رشوه
brave adj شجاع	bribe v رشوه دادن
bravely adv به شجاعت	bribery n رشوه گیری
bravery n شجاعت	brick n خشت
brawl n نزاع	bricklayer n خشتمال
breach n رخنه	bride n عروس
bread n نان	bridegroom n داماد
breadth n وسعت	bridesmaid n نگهبان عروس
break v شکستن	bridge n پُل
break n وقفه	brief v خلاصه کردن
break away v جدا شدن	brief adj مختصر
break down v خراب شدن	briefcase n بکس دستی
break free v آزاد شدن	briefing n ارایه معلومات
break in v به زور داخل شدن	briefly adv بطور مختصر
break off v قطع رابطه کردن	bright adj روشن؛ ذکی
break open v باز شدن	brighten v روشن کردن
break out v شیوع کردن	brightness n روشنایی
break up v جدا شدن	brilliant adj درخشنده؛ خیلی ذکی
breakable adj شکستنی	brim n لبه، حاشیه
breakdown n درهم شکستن	bring v آوردن
breakfast n صبحانه	bring back v دوباره آوردن
breakthrough n پیشرفت ناگهانی	bring down v موجب سقوط شدن
breast n پستان	bring up v مطرح کردن
breath n نفس	brisk adj تیز، چابک

B

brittle *adj* زودشکن	**brush up** *v* مهارت را تقویت کردن
broad *adj* وسیع	**brutal** *adj* وحشی
broadcast *n* نشرات	**brutality** *n* وحشت
broadcast *v* نشرات کردن	**brutalize** *v* وحشی شدن
broadcaster *n* دستگاه نشراتی	**bubble** *n* پوقانه
broaden *v* وسیع ساختن	**bubble gum** *n* پوقانه ساجق
broadly *adv* بطور وسیع	**bucket** *n* سطل
broadminded *adj* روشنفکر	**buckle** *n* بسته کردن
broccoli *n* سبزی براکولی	**buckle up** *v* بسته کردن تسمه یا کمربند
brochure *n* رساله	**bud** *n* پنډک
broil *v* بریان کردن	**Buddhism** *n* مذهب بودا
broiler *n* کوره کباب	**Buddhist** *n* پیرو مذهب بودا
broke *adj* مفلس	**buddy** *n* دوست
broken *adj* شکسته	**budge** *v* جابجا شدن
bronze *n* برونز	**budget** *n* بودجه
broom *n* جاروب	**buffalo** *n* گاومیش
broth *n* یخنی	**buffet** *n* بوفی در رستورانت
brother *n* برادر	**bug** *n* حشره
brother-in-law *n* خسربره، یازنه	**build** *v* اعمار کردن
brotherly *adj* برادرانه	**builder** *n* معمار
brow *n* پیشانی	**building** *n* تعمیر
brown *adj* آفتاب خورده	**built-in** *adj* چارچوب ساخته شده
brown *n* نصواری	**bulb** *n* گل پیاز؛ گروپ چراغ
browse *v* جستجو کردن	**bulge** *n* برامدگی
browser *n* جستجو کننده در کمپیوتر	**bulk** *n* مقدار زیاد، حجم
bruise *n* کبود شده گی پوست	**bulky** *adj* حجیم، بزرگ
bruise *v* کبود کردن	**bull** *n* گاو نر
brunch *n* صبحانه دیر	**bulldoze** *v* زورگویی کردن
brunette *adj* زن یا دختر سبزه	**bulldozer** *n* بلدوزر
brush *n* برس	**bullet** *n* مرمی
brush *v* برس کردن	**bulletin** *n* خبرنامه
brush aside *v* اعتنا نکردن	**bulletproof** *adj* ضدمرمی

B

bully *n* زورگو	**business** *n* تجارت
bump *n* تکان	**businessman** *n* تاجر
bump *v* تکان خوردن	**businesswoman** *n* زن تاجر
bumper *n* بمپر موتر	**bustle** *v* کشمکش کردن
bumpy *adj* تکان دار	**busy** *adj* مصروف
bun *n* نان برگر؛ لاشتک موی	**but** *conj* اما
bunch *n* خوشه	**butcher** *n* قصاب
bundle *n* بسته، بندل	**butler** *n* خدمتگار
bunk bed *n* تخت خواب سفری	**butter** *n* مسکه
bunker *n* زیرزمینی	**butterfly** *n* شب پرک
buoy *n* شناور	**button** *n* دکمه لباس، دکمه ماشین
burden *n* بار، مسوولیت	**buttonhole** *n* سوراخ دکمه
burdensome *adj* پربار	**buy** *v* خریدن
burger *n* برگر	**buy off** *v* با پول جورآمد کردن
burglar *n* دزد	**buyer** *n* خریدار
burglarize *v* دزدی کردن	**buzz** *n* بز بز
burglary *n* دزدی	**buzz** *v* بز بز کردن
burial *n* تدفین	**buzzard** *n* پرنده مانند باشه
burly *adj* تنومند	**buzzer** *n* زنگ
burn *n* سوختگی	**by** *prep* توسط
burn *v* سوختن	**bye** *e* خداحافظ
burp *n* آروغ	**bypass** *v* از راه فرعی گذشتن
burp *v* آروغ زدن	**bypass** *n* راه فرعی
burrito *n* نان چپاتی	**bystander** *n* تماشاچی
burrow *n* سوراخ	**byte** *n* بایت، حجم فایل کمپیوتری
burst *v* ترکیدن	
bury *v* دفن کردن	
bus *n* بس	
bus station *n* استیشن بس	
bus stop *n* ایستگاه بس	
bush *n* بُته	
busily *adv* مشغول	

C

cab n تکسی

cabbage n کرم

cabin n کابین

cabinet n الماری

cable n کیبل

cable television n تلویزیون کیبلی

cactus n کاکتوس

café n قهوه خانه

cafeteria n کفتریا

caffeine n کافیین

cage n قفس

cake n کیک

calamity n مصیبت

calculate v محاسبه کردن

calculation n محاسبه

calculator n ماشین حساب

calendar n جنتری

calf n دلک پا؛ گوساله

caliber n استعداد، کیفیت؛ دیامتر

calibrate v سنجیدن، اندازه کردن

call v تیلفون کردن، صدا کردن

call n فراخوان

call off v لغو کردن

call on v تماس برقرار کردن

call out v به صدای بلند نام کسی را خواندن

calling n تماس تیلفونی

callous adj بی عاطفه

calm adj آرام

calm down v آرام باش

calorie n کالوری

camel n شتر

camera n کمره

camouflage n پوشش

camouflage v مخفی کردن

camp n کمپ

camp v کمپ زدن

campaign n کمپاین

campaign v کمپاین کردن

campfire n آتش کردن در کمپ

campus n صحن مکتب یا پوهنتون

can modal v توانستن

can n قطی

can opener n قطی بازکن

canal n کانال

canary n کنری

cancel v فسخ کردن

cancellation n فسخ

cancer n مرض سرطان

cancerous adj سرطانی

candid adj رُک و پوست کنده

candidate n کاندید

candle n شمع

candlestick n شمعدانی

candor n رُک گویی

candy n شیرینی

cane n نیشکر

canister n قطی کوچک

canned adj در قطی نگهداری شده یا کنسرو

cannibal n ماهی همگون خوار

care for v مراقبت کردن از	cannon n توپ که اتومات فیر میشود
career n شغل، مسلک	cannot v نتوانستن
carefree adj آسوده خاطر	canoe n قایق
careful adj محتاط	cantaloupe n خربوزه یکنوع
carefully adv با احتیاط	canteen n کانتین
careless adj بی احتیاط	canvas n تکه برای نقاشی
carelessly adv به بی احتیاطی	canyon n دره بزرگ
carelessness n بی احتیاطی	cap v پوشاندن
caress v نوازش کردن	cap n سرپوش بوتل
caretaker n مراقبت کننده	capability n قابلیت
cargo n اموال تجارتی	capable adj قادر
caricature n کاریکاتور	capacity n ظرفیت
caring adj دلسوز	cape n یالان، شال سرشانه یی
carnation n گل میخک	capital n پایتخت؛ سرمایه
carpenter n نجار	capital letter n حرف بزرگ
carpentry n نجاری	capitulate v تسلیم دشمن شدن
carpet n قالین	capsize v غرق شدن
carriage n حمل و نقل	capsule n کپسول
carrot n زردک	captain n کپیتان
carry v انتقال دادن	captivate v اسیر گرفتن
carry on v به پیش بردن	captive n اسیر
carry out v انجام دادن	captivity n اسارت
cart n کراچی	capture v دستگیر کردن
cartoon n کارتون	car n موتر
cartridge n رنگ پرنتر	caramel n آب نبات
carve v حک کردن	caravan n کاروان
cascade n شرشره	carcass n شهر کاراکس
case n جعبه؛ قضیه محکمه	card n کارت
cash n پول نقد	cardboard n کاغذ کاک
cashier n صراف	care n مراقبت
casino n قمارخانه	care v مراقبت کردن
casket n صندوقچه جواهرات	care about v پروای چیزی را داشتن

casserole *n* تابه	ceiling *n* سقف اتاق
cast *v* پرتاب کردن	celebrate *v* تجلیل کردن
cast *n* قالب، گچ گیری	celebration *n* جشن
castaway *n* فراری	celebrity *n* هنرمند مشهور
caste *n* طبقه، قبیله	celery *n* سبزی کرفس
castle *n* قصر	celestial *adj* آسمانی
casual *adj* اتفاقی	cell *n* سلول زندان، حجره بدن
casualty *n* جراحات	cell phone *n* تیلفون همراه
cat *n* پشک	cellar *n* انبار
catalog *n* فهرست	cello *n* آله موسیقی ویلون
catalog *v* فهرست بندی کردن	cement *n* سمنت
cataract *n* آبشار بزرگ	cemetery *n* قبرستان
catastrophe *n* فاجعه	censorship *n* سانسور
catch *v* قپیدن	censure *v* سرزنش کردن
catch on *v* درک کردن	census *n* احصائیه
catch up *v* خود را به کسی رساندن	cent *n* سینت
categorize *v* دسته بندی کردن	center *v* در مرکز قرار دادن
category *n* کتگوری	center *n* وسط؛ مرکز
cater *v* غذا تهیه کردن	centimeter *n* سانتی میتر
caterpillar *n* کرم ابریشم	central *adj* مرکزی
cathedral *n* کلیسای جامع	centralize *v* متمرکز کردن
cattle *n* گله گاو	century *n* قرن
cauliflower *n* گلپی	ceramic *n* سنگ سرامیک
cause *v* باعث شدن	cereal *n* حبوبات
cause *n* علت	ceremony *n* مراسم
caution *n* احتیاط	certain *adj* مطمئن
cautious *adj* محتاط	certainly *adv* یقیناً
cave *n* مغاره	certainty *n* قاطعیت، اطمینان
cave in *v* مغاره ساختن	certificate *n* تصدیقنامه
cavern *n* غار	certify *v* تصدیق کردن
cavity *n* گودال	chain *n* زنجیر
cease *v* متوقف ساختن	chain *v* محکم بستن

chainsaw n اره برقی	**charge** v مطالبه پول؛ متهم کردن؛انرژی گرفتن
chair n چوکی	**charge** n مطالبه کردن پول؛ چارج برق
chairman n ریس	**charisma** n جذابیت
chalk n تباشیر	**charismatic** adj جذاب
chalkboard n تخته تباشیری	**charitable** adj خیریه
challenge v به چالش کشیدن	**charity** n خیرات
challenge n چالش	**charm** v شیفته کردن، دل ربودن
challenger n رقیب	**charm** n طلسم؛ خرمهره
challenging adj پرچالش	**charming** adj دلربا
chamber n اتاق	**chart** n جدول
champ n قهرمان	**charter** n اساسنامه
champion n قهرمان، مبارز	**charter** v دربست کرایه کردن
chance n فرصت	**chase** v تعقیب کردن
chancellor n رئیس پوهنتون	**chase away** v بدرقه کردن
chandelier n قندیل	**chasm** n شکاف بزرگ
change v تغییر کردن	**chastise** v مجازات کردن
change n تغییر؛ سکه؛ پول سیاه	**chastisement** n مجازات
channel v انتقال دادن	**chat** v صحبت کردن
channel n چینل تلویزیونی؛ کانال آب	**chauffeur** n راننده موتر
chant n شعار دادن	**cheap** adj ارزان
chaos n هرج و مرج	**cheat** v فریب دادن
chaotic adj وضعیت پر آشوب	**cheater** n فریبکار
chapel n کلیسای کوچک	**check** v تفتیش کردن؛ نشانی کردن؛ متوقف کردن
chapter n فصل کتاب	**check** n چک بانکی؛ چیزی را چک کردن
char v ذغال کردن، سوزاندن	**check in** v تسلیم گرفتن اتاق در هوتل
character n شخصیت؛ قهرمان داستان	**check out** v حساب هوتل را تسویه کردن
characteristic adj مشخصه	**checkbook** n کتابچه چک بانکی
charade n خرابکاری	**checkers** n بازرسی کننده گان
charbroil v روی ذغال بریان کردن	
charcoal n ذغال سنگ	

checkmark n علامت صحه

checkup n معاینه

cheek n گونه

cheekbone n استخوان گونه

cheeky adj گستاخ

cheer v خوشی کردن

cheer up v روحیه دادن

cheerful adj مسرور

cheerleader n تشویق کننده

cheese n پنیر

chef n سرآشپز

chemical adj کیمیاوی

chemical n ماده کیمیاوی

chemist n کیمیادان

chemistry n کیمیا

cherish v گرامی داشتن

cherry n آلوبالو

chess n شطرنج

chest n صندوق سینه؛ صندوق ذخیره گاه

chestnut n شاه بلوط

chew v جویدن

chick n چوچه پرنده

chicken n مرغ

chicken out v ترسیدن، جرأت نکردن

chicken pox n چیچک

chief n آمر

chief adj عمده، مهم

chiefly adv عمدتاً

child n طفل

childcare n کودکستان

childhood n طفولیت

childish adj طفلانه

children n اطفال

chili n مرچ

chill v سرد کردن

chill n سردی، خنک

chill out v آرامش خود را حفظ کردن

chilly adj سرد

chimney n دودکش بخاری

chimpanzee n میمون شامپانزی

chin n زنخ

chip n توته چوب

chisel n اسکنه

chocolate n چاکلیت

choice n انتخاب

choir n آواز خواندن دسته جمعی

choke v خفه کردن

choose v انتخاب کردن

choosy adj مشکل پسند

chop v توته کردن

chopsticks n توته های چوب

chore n کار های روزمره

chorus n آواز خواندن دسته جمعی

Christian adj مسیحی

Christianity n مسیحیت

Christmas n جشن مسیحیان، کریسمس

chronic adj مزمن، شدید

chronological adj به ترتیب زمان

chubby adj چاق و چله

chuckle v خندیدن

chunk n توته

C

church *n* کلیسا

chute *n* ناوه

cider *n* سرکه سیب

cigar *n* سیگار

cigarette *n* سگرت

cinder *n* خاکستر

cinema *n* سینما

cinnamon *n* دارچین

circle *n* حلقه

circle *v* حلقه کردن

circuit *n* دوران

circular *adj* دوره یی

circulate *v* به گردش در آوردن

circulation *n* جریان، گردش

circumstance *n* شرایط، اوضاع

circumstantial *adj* مربوط به شرایط

circus *n* سرکس

cistern *n* مخزن آب

cite *v* اظهار داشتن

citizen *n* تبعه

citizenship *n* تابعیت

citrus *n* مالته

city *n* شهر

city hall *n* سالون شهر

civic *adj* مدنی

civil *adj* داخلی

civilization *n* تمدن

civilize *v* متمدن ساختن

claim *n* ادعا

claim *v* ادعا کردن

clam *n* خاموشی

clamor *v* سروصدا

clamp *n* گیره

clandestine *adj* مخفی

clap *v* کف زدن

clarification *n* وضاحت

clarify *v* وضاحت دادن

clarinet *n* آله موسیقی کلارینیت

clarity *n* وضاحت

clash *v* درگیر شدن

clash *n* سروصدا؛ درگیری

class *n* صنف درسی؛ طبقه بلند مردم

classic *adj* بهترین نمونه

classic *n* کلاسیک، کهن

classical *adj* باستانی

classify *v* دسته بندی کردن

classmate *n* همصنفی

classroom *n* اتاق درسی

classy *adj* درجه یک

claw *n* پنجه

clay *n* گِل

clean *adj* پاک

clean *v* پاک کردن

cleaner *n* صفاکار

cleanliness *n* پاکی، صفایی

cleanser *n* ماده پاک کننده

clear *adj* شفاف؛ واضح

clear *v* صاف کردن

clearance *n* اجازه

clear-cut *adj* صریح

clearly *adv* واضحاً؛ آشکارا

clemency *n* رحمت، شفقت

clench *v* بهم فشردن

clergy *n* روحانی

clergyman *n* کشیش	**cloth** *n* تکه
clerical *adj* دفتری، مربوط به دفتر	**clothe** *v* لباس پوشاندن
clerk *n* کاتب	**clothes** *n* لباسها
clever *adj* هوشیار	**clothing** *n* پوشاک
click *v* کلیک کردن	**cloud** *n* ابر
client *n* مشتری	**cloudy** *adj* ابرآلود
clientele *n* مشتریان	**clown** *n* مداری
cliff *n* صخره	**club** *v* تشکل انجمن دادن
climate *n* اقلیم	**club** *n* کلب؛ چوب برای زدن چیزی
climax *n* اوج	**clue** *n* سرنخ، اثر چیزی
climb *v* بالا شدن	**clumsy** *adj* زمخت، بدشکل
climbing *n* کوهنوردی	**cluster** *n* دسته، گروه
clinch *v* محکم کردن	**clutch** *v* چنگ زدن
cling *v* صدای چسپیدن	**clutch** *n* کلچ موتر
clinic *n* کلینیک	**clutter** *n* بی نظمی
clip *n* گیره، قیدک	**coach** *v* آموزش دادن
clip *v* محکم گرفتن	**coach** *n* کوچ، ترینر ورزش
clipping *n* اصلاح موی	**coal** *n* ذغال
cloak *n* چپن	**coarse** *adj* درشت
clock *n* ساعت دیواری	**coast** *n* ساحل
clockwise *adv* ساعت وار	**coastal** *adj* ساحلی
clog *v* بسته شدن	**coastline** *n* خط ساحلی
clone *v* تکثیر کردن	**coat** *n* بالاپوش
cloning *n* همانند سازی	**coat** *v* پوشاندن
close *v* بسته کردن	**coat hanger** *n* کودبند
close *adv* نزدیک	**coax** *v* ریشخند کردن
close *adj* نزدیک؛ عزیز؛ محتاط	**cobweb** *n* تار جولا
closed *adj* بسته	**cockpit** *n* کابین طیاره
closely *adv* در تماس نزدیک	**cockroach** *n* مادرکیک
closet *n* الماری	**cocky** *adj* ازخود راضی
closure *n* انسداد	**cocoa** *n* کاکاو
clot *n* لخته خون	**coconut** *n* ناریال

C

cod *n* ماهی کاد	colonel *n* دگرمن
code *n* رمز؛ کود نرم افزار	colonization *n* استعمار
coerce *v* وادار کردن	colonize *v* مستعمره کردن
coercion *n* اجبار	colony *n* مستعمره
coexist *v* همزیستی	color *n* رنگ
coffee *n* قهوه	color *v* رنگ کردن
coffin *n* تابوت	colorful *adj* رنگه
coherent *adj* منسجم	colorless *adj* بی رنگ
coherently *adv* بطور منسجم	colossal *adj* عظیم الجثه
coil *n* پیچیدن	colt *n* چوچه اسب
coin *n* سکه	column *n* رکن؛ ستون روزنامه
coincide *v* همزمان بودن	coma *n* کوما
coincidence *n* تصادف	comb *n* شانه
coincidental *adj* تصادفی	comb *v* شانه کردن
cold *adj* سرد	combat *n* مبارزه
cold *n* سردی؛ ریزش	combat *v* مبارزه کردن
collaborate *v* همکاری کردن	combatant *n* جنگجو، مبارز
collaboration *n* همکاری	combination *n* ترکیب
collaborator *n* همکار	combine *v* ترکیب کردن
collage *n* هنر آمیزش رنگها	combustible *n* قابل حریق
collapse *v* سقوط کردن	combustion *n* احتراق
collar *n* یخن؛ تسمه گردن حیوانات	come *v* آمدن
collateral *adj* پهلو به پهلو	come about *v* اتفاق افتادن
colleague *n* همکار	come across *v* مواجه شدن
collect *v* جمع کردن	come apart *v* جدا شدن
collection *n* گردآوری	come back *v* برگشتن
collector *n* جمع کننده	come down *v* پایین آمدن
college *n* دانشکده، کالج	come forward *v* پیش آمدن
collide *v* بهم خوردن	come from *v* آمدن از
collision *n* تصادم	come in *v* داخل آمدن
cologne *n* کلونیا، عطر	come out *v* بیرون آمدن
colon *n* روده	come over *v* سر زدن

C

come up *v* مطرح شدن	**communicate** *v* ارتباط برقرار کردن
comeback *n* بازگشت	**communication** *n* ارتباط
comedian *n* ممثل کمیدی	**communism** *n* کمونیزم
comedy *n* کمیدی	**communist** *adj* کمونیست
comet *n* دنباله دار	**community** *n* جامعه
comfort *n* راحتی	**commute** *v* رفت و برگشت کردن
comfortable *adj* راحت	**compact** *adj* جمع و جور، فشرده
comforter *n* آرامش دهنده	**compact** *v* فشرده کردن
comical *adj* خنده آور	**companion** *n* همراه
coming *adj* آینده	**companionship** *n* همراهی
comma *n* علامه کامه	**company** *n* شرکت؛ رفاقت
command *n* فرمان	**comparable** *adj* قابل مقایسه
command *v* فرمان دادن	**compare** *v* مقایسه کردن
commander *n* فرمانده	**comparison** *n* مقایسه
commemorate *v* بزرگداشت کردن	**compartment** *n* قسمت، بخش
commence *v* آغاز کردن	**compass** *n* قطب نما
commend *v* تقدیر کردن	**compassion** *n* دلسوزی
commendation *n* ستایش	**compassionate** *adj* مهربان
comment *v* نظر دادن	**compatibility** *n* قابلیت تطابق
comment *n* نظریه	**compatible** *adj* قابل تطابق
commentary *n* تفسیر	**compel** *v* وادار کردن
commentator *n* مُفسر	**compelling** *adj* اجباری
commerce *n* تجارت	**compensate** *v* تلافی کردن
commercial *n* اعلان تجارتی	**compensation** *n* تلافی، جبران
commercial *adj* تجارتی	**compete** *v* رقابت کردن
commit *v* مرتکب شدن	**competence** *n* شایستگی
commitment *n* تعهد	**competent** *adj* شایسته
committed *adj* متعهد	**competition** *n* رقابت
committee *n* کمیته	**competitive** *adj* رقابتی
common *adj* معمول	**competitor** *n* رقیب
common sense *n* عقل سلیم	**complain** *v* شکایت کردن
commotion *n* هیاهو	**complaint** *n* شکایت

C

complement *n* تکمیل کردن	compulsive *adj* اجباری
complete *v* تکمیل کردن	compulsory *adj* از روی جبر
complete *adj* مکمل؛ کامل	compute *v* محاسبه کردن
completely *adv* کاملاً	computer *n* کمپیوتر
complex *adj* پیچیده	con *v* مجبور ساختن
complexion *n* رنگ پوست	con man *n* فریبنده
complexity *n* پیچیده گی	conceal *v* پنهان کردن
compliance *n* انطباق	concede *v* قبول کردن
compliant *adj* منطبق	conceited *adj* متکبر
complicate *v* مغلق ساختن	conceive *v* باردار شدن
complicated *adj* مغلق	concentrate *v* تمرکز کردن
complication *n* ابهام	concentration *n* تمرکز
compliment *n* تعریف و تمجید	concept *n* مفهوم، طرح
complimentary *adj* تعارفی	conception *n* حاملگی
comply *v* موافقت کردن، تطابق کردن	concern *v* ربط داشتن
component *n* جزء	concern *n* نگرانی
compose *v* ساختن	concerned *adj* مربوط
composed *adj* ساخته شده	concerning *prep* در رابطه به
composer *n* تنظیم کننده موسیقی	concert *n* کنسرت
composition *n* ترتیب و تنظیم	concession *n* امتیاز
compost *n* کود برای نباتات	concise *adj* مختصر
composure *n* خونسردی	conclude *v* خاتمه بخشیدن
compound *n* مُرکب	conclusion *n* اختتامیه
comprehend *v* درک کردن	conclusive *adj* مشمول
comprehensive *adj* ادراک	concoct *v* ساختن
compress *v* بهم فشردن	concoction *n* ترکیب
compression *n* فشرده سازی	concrete *n* کانکریت
comprise *v* شامل بودن	concrete *adj* مستحکم
compromise *n* مصالحه، جورآمد	concussion *n* ضربه مغزی
compromise *v* مصالحه، جورآمد کردن	condemn *v* محکوم کردن
	condemnation *n* محکومیت
compulsion *n* اجبار	condensation *n* تغلیظ

condense *v* غلیظ ساختن	conform *v* مطابقت داشتن
condescend *v* تحقیر کردن	conformist *adj* سازگار
condiment *n* باب مصالح	conformity *n* تطابق
condition *n* وضعیت	confound *v* گیج کردن
conditional *adj* مشروط	confront *v* مقابله کردن
conditioner *n* نرم کننده	confrontation *n* مقابله
condo *n* آپارتمان	confuse *v* مغشوش کردن
condolences *n* تسلیت	confused *adj* مغشوش
condone *v* بخشیدن	confusing *adj* مغشوش کننده
conducive *adj* سودمند	confusion *n* گیجی
conduct *v* اداره کردن؛ انتقال دادن برق	congenial *adj* مطلوب
	congested *adj* متراکم
conduct *n* رفتار	congestion *n* تراکم
conductor *n* رهبر آرکستر؛ انتقال دهنده برق	congratulate *v* تبریک گفتن
	congratulations *n* تبریکی
cone *n* مخروط	congregate *v* تجمع کردن
conference *n* کنفرانس	congregation *n* تجمع
confess *v* اعتراف کردن	congress *n* کانگریس
confession *n* اعتراف	conjecture *n* حدس
confessor *n* اعتراف کننده	conjunction *n* پیوستگی
confidant *n* محرم	connect *v* وصل کردن
confide *v* اعتماد کردن	connection *n* اتصال
confidence *n* اعتماد	conquer *v* فتح کردن
confident *adj* مطمئن	conqueror *n* فاتح
confidential *adj* محرمانه	conquest *n* تسخیر
confine *v* محدود کردن	conscience *n* هوش، وجدان
confinement *n* زندانی بودن	conscious *adj* باهوش
confirm *v* تأیید کردن	consciousness *n* شعور
confirmation *n* تایید	conscript *n* سربازی اجباری
confiscate *v* ضبط کردن	consecutive *adj* پی در پی
conflict *n* تضاد	consensus *n* توافق
conflicting *adj* متضاد	consent *v* راضی کردن

consent n رضایت	constrain v محدود کردن
consequence n عاقبت	constraint n محدودیت
consequent adj متعاقب	construct v اعمار کردن
consequently adv متعاقباً	construction n کار ساختمانی
conservation n حفاظت	constructive adj مثمر
conservative adj محافظوی	consult v مشوره کردن
conserve v نگهداری کردن	consultant n مشاور
conserve n نگهداشت	consultation n مشوره
consider v مدنظر گرفتن	consume v مصرف کردن
considerable adj قابل ملاحظه	consumer n مصرف کننده
considerably adv بطور قابل ملاحظه	consumption n مصرف
considerate adj مواظب	contact n تماس
consideration n ملاحظه	contact v تماس گرفتن
consignment n محموله	contagious adj ساری
consist v متشکل بودن از	contain v در بر داشتن
consistency n سازگاری	container n ظرف
consistent adj سازگار	contaminate v آلوده کردن
consistently adv بطور سازگار	contamination n آلوده گی
consolation n دلداری	contemplate v اندیشیدن
console n تسلیت	contemporary adj معاصر
console v دلداری دادن	contemporary n معاصر
consolidate v یکی کردن	contempt n تحقیر
consonant n بی صدا	contend v دعوا کردن
conspicuous adj آشکار	contender n مدعی
conspiracy n دسیسه	content adj راضی
constant adj ثابت، پایدار	content n محتوا
constantly adv بطور ثابت	contentious adj بحث برانگیز
constellation n تجمع ستارگان	contest n مسابقه
constipated adj قبض	contestant n مسابقه دهنده
constitution n قانون اساسی	context n متن
constitutional adj وابسته به قانون اساسی	continent n قاره
	continental adj قاره یی

contingency *n* احتمالی	**converse** *v* مکالمه کردن
contingent *adj* محتمل	**conversely** *adv* متقابلاً
continuation *n* ادامه	**conversion** *n* دگرگونی
continue *v* ادامه دادن	**convert** *v* تبدیل کردن
continuity *n* تداوم	**convertible** *n* قابل تبدیل شدن
continuous *adj* جاری	**convey** *v* انتقال دادن
contour *n* کانتور، حد فاصله	**convict** *v* محکوم کردن
contract *n* قرارداد	**conviction** *n* محکومیت
contract *v* قرارداد بستن	**convince** *v* قناعت دادن
contraction *n* اختصار	**convinced** *adj* معتقد
contradict *v* تناقض داشتن	**convincing** *adj* قانع کننده
contradiction *n* تناقض	**convulse** *v* تشنج کردن
contradictory *adj* متناقض	**convulsion** *n* تشنج
contrary *adj* برخلاف	**cook** *n* آشپز
contrast *n* تضاد	**cook** *v* پخته کردن
contrast *v* مقابله کردن	**cooked** *adj* پخته
contribute *v* سهم گرفتن	**cookie** *n* کلچه
contribution *n* اعانه	**cooking** *n* آشپزی
contributor *n* سهم گیرنده	**cool** *v* سرد کردن
control *n* کنترول	**cool** *adj* سرد؛ آرام
control *v* کنترول کردن	**cool down** *v* آرام باش
controversial *adj* بحث برانگیز	**cooler** *n* سرد کننده
controversy *n* جدال	**cooperate** *v* همکاری کردن
convalescent *adj* شفایاب	**cooperation** *n* همکاری
convene *v* تجمع کردن	**cooperative** *adj* تعاونی
convenience *n* راحتی	**coordinate** *n* مختصات
convenient *adj* راحت	**coordinate** *v* همآهنگ کردن
convention *n* معاهده	**coordination** *n* انسجام؛ توازن
conventional *adj* مربوط به معاهده	**coordinator** *n* همآهنگ کننده
converge *v* همگرایی کردن	**cop** *n* پولیس
conversation *n* مکالمه	**cope** *v* مجادله کردن
converse *n* گفتگو	**copier** *n* ماشین کاپی

C

copper *n* مس
copy *v* کاپی کردن
copy *n* نقل؛ نمونه یک نشریه
copyright *n* حق طبع و نشر
coral *n* مرجانی
cord *n* طناب
cordial *adj* صمیمی
cordless *adj* بی سیم
core *n* هسته
cork *n* چوب پنبه
corkscrew *n* پیچ بازکن
corn *n* جواری
corner *v* در کنج گذاشتن
corner *n* کنج
coronation *n* تاج گذاری
corporate *adj* دارای شخصیت حقوقی
corporation *n* شرکت سهامی
corpse *n* جسد
correct *adj* درست
correct *v* درست کردن
correction *n* اصلاح
correctly *adv* به درستی
correlate *v* بهم ارتباط داشتن
correspond *v* مطابقت داشتن
correspondence *n* مکاتبه
correspondent *n* خبرنگار
corresponding *adj*، همخوان
  مطابق
corridor *n* دهلیز
corroborate *v* تأیید کردن
corrode *v* زنگ زدن، پوسیدن
corrupt *v* فاسد کردن

corrupt *adj* مفسد
corruption *n* فساد
cosmetic *n* لوازم آرایشی
cosmic *adj* کیهانی
cost *n* مصرف
cost *v* مصرف داشتن
costly *adj* پرمصرف
costume *n* لباس
cottage *n* کلبه
cotton *n* پنبه
couch *n* کوچ فرنیچر
cough *n* سرفه
cough *v* سرفه کردن
could *modal v* توانستن
council *n* شورا
counsel *v* مشوره دادن
counseling *n* مشوره
counselor *n* مشاور
count *n* شمارش
count *v* شمردن
countdown *n* شمارش معکوس
counter *n* میز
counteract *v* عمل متقابل کردن
counterfeit *adj* تقلبی
counterpart *n* همتا
countless *adj* بی شمار
country *n* کشور
countryside *n* حومه شهر
county *n* ناحیه یک ایالت
coup *n* کودتا
couple *n* زوج
coupon *n* کوپون

courage *n* شجاعت	cram *v* کاملاً پر کردن
courageous *adj* شجاع	cramp *n* گرفتگی عضلات
courier *n* انتقال دهنده	cramped *adj* تنگ، در قید
course *n* مضمون؛ استقامت؛ رشته ورزشی	crane *n* جرثقیل
	crank *n* یک بخش ماشین
court *v* خواستگاری کردن	cranky *adj* بدخو
court *n* محکمه؛ میدان ورزشی	crash *n* تصادم
courteous *adj* مؤدب	crash *v* تصادم کردن
courtesy *n* حسن نیت	crass *adj* خشن
courthouse *n* محکمه	crate *n* صندوق چوبی
courtship *n* خواستگاری	crater *n* دهانه
courtyard *n* صحن حویلی	crave *v* هوس کردن
cousin *n* پسر ماما؛ پسر کاکا	craving *n* میل شدید به
cove *n* دریاچه سرپوشیده	crawl *v* خزیدن
cover *n* پوش	crayon *n* توش رنگه
cover *v* پوشاندن	crazy *adj* دیوانه
coverage *n* پوشش	creak *n* کریک
covering *n* پوش	creak *v* جاری شدن
covert *adj* پنهان	cream *adj* رنگ کریمی
cover-up *n* پوشانیده	cream *n* قیماق
cow *n* گاو	creamy *adj* قیماق دار
coward *n* نامرد	crease *n* چین خوردگی
cowardly *adv* به نامردی	crease *v* چین دادن
cowboy *n* گاوچران	create *v* خلق کردن
cozy *adj* گرم و نرم	creation *n* خلقت
crab *n* خرچنگ	creative *adj* خلاق
crack *v* ترکیدن	creativity *n* خلاقیت
crack *n* شکاف باریک؛ صدای بلند	creator *n* خالق
cracker *n* بسکویت	creature *n* مخلوق
cradle *n* گهواره	credibility *n* قابلیت اعتبار
craft *n* صنایع دستی	credible *adj* قابل اعتبار
craftsman *n* صنعتگر	credit *v* اعتبار کردن

credit *n* کریدیت؛ اعتبار
credit card *n* کریدیت کارت
creditor *n* قرض دهنده
creek *n* نهر
creep *v* خزیدن
creepy *adj* عجیب و غریب
cremate *v* سوزاندن
crest *n* تاج
crevice *n* شکاف
crew *n* عمله طیاره
crib *n* گهواره
cricket *n* جیرجیرک؛ بازی کریکیت
crime *n* جنایت
criminal *n* جنایتکار
criminal *adj* جنایی
cringe *v* خجالت کشیدن
cripple *adj* فلج
cripple *v* فلج کردن
crisis *n* بحران
crisp *adj* نازک
crispy *adj* قاق
criteria *n* معیارها
critic *n* منتقد
critical *adj* بحرانی
criticism *n* انتقاد
criticize *v* انتقاد کردن
crocodile *n* تمساح
crony *n* دوست داشتنی
crook *n* کلاه بردار
crooked *adj* کج؛ متقلب
crop *v* جمع آوری حاصلات
crop *n* حاصلات

cross *n* صلیب
cross *adj* صلیبی، چلیپایی
cross *v* عبور کردن
cross out *v* عبور از
crossing *n* عبور
crossroads *n* چهارراهی
crosswalk *n* پیاده رو
crossword puzzle *n* یکنوع بازی
crouch *v* خم شدن
crow *n* زاغ
crow *v* صدا کردن زاغ
crowbar *n* میله خم شده
crowd *n* ازدحام
crowd *v* بیروبار کردن
crowded *adj* مزدحم، بیروبار
crown *n* تاج
crown *v* تاج گذاری
crucial *adj* حیاتی
crude *adj* خام
cruel *adj* ظالم
cruelty *n* ظلم
cruise *v* کشتی رانی کردن
crumb *n* خرده یا توته
crumble *v* فروریختن
crunchy *adj* قاق
crush *v* توته شدن
crust *n* قشر، پوشت
crusty *adj* سخت، خشن
crutch *n* عصاچوب
cry *n* گریه
cry *v* گریه کردن
crystal *n* شفاف

C

cub *n* خرچنگ	**curl** *n* حلقه
cube *n* مکعب	**curl** *v* حلقه کردن
cubic *adj* مکعبی	**curly** *adj* حلقه یی
cubicle *n* اتاقک	**currency** *n* واحد پول
cucumber *n* بادرنگ	**current** *n* جریان آب؛ جریان برق
cuddle *v* در آغوش گرفتن	**current** *adj* فعلی
cuddly *adj* راحت	**currently** *adv* در حال حاضر
cuff *n* دستبند	**curriculum** *n* نصاب تعلیمی
cuisine *n* غذای متنوع	**curse** *n* لعنت
culminate *v* به اوج رسیدن	**curse** *v* لعنت کردن
culpability *n* تقصیر	**cursor** *n* نشان دهنده موقعیت
culprit *n* مقصر	**curtail** *v* محدود کردن
cult *n* فرقه	**curtain** *n* پرده
cultivate *v* کشت کردن	**curve** *n* منحنی
cultivation *n* کشت	**curved** *adj* کج
cultural *adj* کلتوری	**cushion** *v* با بالش آراستن
culture *n* کلتور	**cushion** *n* بالش
cumbersome *adj* سنگین	**cuss** *v* سروصدا
cunning *adj* حیله گر	**custard** *n* فرنی
cup *n* پیاله	**custodian** *n* ملازم
cupboard *n* الماری ظروف	**custody** *n* توقیف
cupcake *n* کپ کیک	**custom** *n* رسم و رواج
curable *adj* قابل درمان	**customary** *adj* مرسوم
curator *n* نگهبان	**customer** *n* مشتری
curb *n* لبه پیاده رو	**customize** *v* عیار کردن
curb *v* محدود کردن	**custom-made** *adj* سفارشی ساخته شده
curdle *v* سفت شدن	**cut** *n* بریده گی؛ کاهش
cure *n* معالجه	**cut** *v* قطع کردن
cure *v* معالجه کردن	**cut back** *pv* کاهش دادن
curfew *n* قیود شب گردی	**cut down** *pv* کم کردن
curiosity *n* کنجکاوی	**cut off** *pv* قطع کردن
curious *adj* کنجکاو	

C

cut out *pv* جدا کردن
cute *adj* مقبول
cutlery *n* قاشق و پنجه
cyan *n* فیروزه یی
cycle *n* دوران
cycle *v* دوران کردن
cyclical *adj* دورانی
cycling *n* بایسکل رانی
cyclist *n* بایسکل ران
cyclone *n* توفان
cylinder *n* سلندر
cymbal *n* آله موسیقی سمبال
cynic *n* بدبین
cyst *n* مثانه

D

dad *n* پدر
dagger *n* خنجر
daily *adv* روزمره
dairy *n* لبنیات
dairy farm *n* فارم لبنیات
daisy *n* گل مروارید
dam *n* بند آب
damage *n* زیان
damage *v* زیان رساندن
damaging *adj* زیان آور
damp *adj* مرطوب
dampen *v* مرطوب کردن
dance *n* رقص

dance *v* رقصیدن
dancer *n* رقاص
dancing *n* رقاصی
dandruff *n* سبوسک
danger *n* خطر
dangerous *adj* خطرناک
dangle *v* آویزان کردن
dare *v* جرأت کردن
dare *n* شهامت
daring *adj* شجاعانه
dark *adj* تاریک
dark *n* تاریکی
darken *v* تاریک کردن
darkness *n* تاریکی
darling *adj* محبوب
dart *n* نیزه
dart *v* نیزه انداختن
dash *v* به سرعت رفتن
dashing *adj* پرشور
data *n* ارقام
database *n* سیستم ثبت ارقام، دیتابیس
date *n* تاریخ
date *v* وعده ملاقات گذاشتن
daughter *n* دختر
daughter-in-law *n* عروس
daunt *v* ترساندن
daunting *adj* دلهره آور
dawn *n* غروب
day *n* روز
daycare *n* کودکستان
daydream *v* رویا پردازی کردن

daylight n روشنایی روز	**debut** n آغاز کار
daytime n از طرف روز	**decade** n دهه
daze v خیره شدن	**decadence** n زوال
dazed adj خیره	**decaffeinated** adj بدون کافیین
dazzle v خیره کننده	**decay** v پوسیدن
dead adj مرده	**decay** n پوسیده گی
dead end n	**deceased** adj مرده
قسمت آخر کوچه بسته است	**deceit** n فریب
deadline n ضرب الاجل	**deceitful** adj فریبکار
deadly adj کشنده	**deceive** v فریب دادن
deaf adj ناشنوا	**December** n دسمبر
deafen v کر کردن	**decency** n محبوبیت
deafening adj کر کننده	**decent** adj محبوب
deal v	**deception** n فریب
سروکار داشتن با چیزی یا شخصی	**deceptive** adj فریبنده
deal n معامله	**decide** v تصمیم گرفتن
dealer n معامله گر	**deciding** adj تصمیم گیرنده
dean n رئیس	**decimal** adj اعشاری
dear adj عزیز	**decimate** v تلفات وارد کردن
death n مرگ	**decipher** v کشف کردن
deathbed n بستر مرگ	**decision** n تصمیم
debase v تحقیر کردن	**decisive** adj مصمم
debatable adj قابل بحث	**deck** n کف کشتی؛ قطعه بازی
debate n بحث	**declaration** n اعلامیه
debate v بحث کردن	**declare** v اعلام کردن
debit n حساب دهی	**decline** n کاهش
debit card n دیبیت کارت	**decline** v کاهش دادن
debrief v خلاصه کردن	**decompose** v تجزیه کردن
debris n خش و خاشاک	**décor** n دیکور، آرایش
debt n قرض	**decorate** v تزیین کردن
debtor n قرضدار	**decoration** n تزیینات
debunk v خراب کردن	**decorative** adj تزیینی

D

decorum *n* تزیین
decrease *v* کاهش دادن
decree *n* فرمان
decrepit *adj* فرسوده
dedicate *v* وقف کردن
dedicated *adj* وقف شده
dedication *n* پشت کار
deduce *v* نتیجه گیری
deduct *v* کاستن، کسر کردن
deductible *adj* مالیات پذیر
deduction *n* کسر
deed *n* عمل یا کردار
deem *v* فرض کردن
deep *adj* عمیق
deepen *v* عمیق کردن
deeply *adv* عمیقاً
deer *n* آهو
deface *v* بی اعتبار کردن
defame *v* بدنام کردن
defeat *v* مغلوب کردن، شکست دادن
defect *n* عیب
defect *v* عیبی ساختن
defective *adj* معیوب، عیبی
defend *v* دفاع کردن
defendant *n* مدافع
defender *n* مدافع
defense *n* دفاع
defenseless *adj* بی دفاع
defer *v* به تعویق انداختن
defiance *n* سرکشی
defiant *adj* متعصب
deficiency *n* کمبود

deficient *adj* دارای کمبود
deficit *n* کسر، کمبودی
define *v* تعریف کردن
definite *adj* معین
definitely *adv* دقیقاً
definition *n* تعریف
definitive *adj* قطعی، نهایی
deflate *v* باد کردن
deform *v* تغییر شکل دادن
deformity *n* تغییر شکل
defraud *v* فریب دادن
defray *v* دفع کردن
defrost *v* یخ را آب کردن
deft *adj* ماهر، چابک
defuse *v* خنثی کردن
defy *v* سرپیچی کردن
degenerate *adj* فاسد
degenerate *v* فاسد شدن
degradation *n* تنزل
degrade *v* تنزل دادن
degrading *adj* تحقیر آمیز
degree *n* دیپلوم تحصیلی؛ درجه هوا
dehydrate *v* کم آب شدن
dehydrated *adj* کم آب
dejected *adj* دلسرد شده
delay *n* تاخیر
delay *v* تاخیر کردن
delegate *v* محول کردن
delegate *n* نماینده
delegation *n* تفویض صلاحیت، نماینده گی
delete *v* حذف کردن

deli *n* شیرینی	**demonstration** *n* مظاهره
deliberate *v* سنجیدن	**demonstrative** *adj* نمایشی
deliberate *adj* سنجیده	**demoralize** *v* تضعیف روحیه کردن
deliberately *adv* بطور سنجیده شده	**demote** *v* تنزل درجه
delicacy *n* ظرافت	**den** *n* سوراخ حیوانات
delicate *adj* ظریف	**denial** *n* انکار
delicious *adj* خوش مزه	**denigrate** *v* بدنام کردن
delight *v* خوش ساختن	**denim** *n* تکه کاوبای
delight *n* خوشی	**denote** *v* مشخص کردن
delighted *v* مسرور	**denounce** *v* محکوم کردن
delightful *adj* دلپسند	**dense** *adj* غلیظ
delinquent *adj* غفلت کار؛ متخلف	**density** *n* غلظت
deliver *v* تحویل دادن	**dent** *n* فرو رفتگی
delivery *n* تحویلی	**dent** *v* فروبردن
delude *v* فریب دادن	**dental** *adj* دندان
deluge *n* غرق شدن	**dentist** *n* داکتر دندان
delusion *n* توهم، اغفال	**dentures** *n* دندانهای مصنوعی
deluxe *adj* لوکس	**deny** *v* رد کردن
demand *n* تقاضا	**deodorant** *n* خوشبو کننده
demand *v* تقاضا کردن	**depart** *v* حرکت کردن، رفتن
demanding *adj* در تقاضای بلند	**department** *n* شعبه
demean *v* تحقیر کردن	**departure** *n* عزیمت
demeaning *adj* تحقیر آمیز	**depend** *v* مربوط بودن به
demeanor *n* رفتار	**dependable** *adj* قابل اعتماد
demented *adj* بی حوصلگی	**dependence** *n* وابستگی
demise *n* مرگ	**dependent** *adj* وابسته
demo *n* نسخه نمایشی	**depict** *v* تصور کردن
democracy *n* دموکراسی	**deplete** *v* خالی کردن
democratic *adj* دموکراتیک	**deplorable** *adj* تاسف بار
demolish *v* خراب کردن	**deplore** *v* تاسف خوردن
demolition *n* خرابکاری	**deploy** *v* اعزام کردن
demonstrate *v* نشان دادن	**deployment** *n* اعزام

D

deport v رد مرز کردن	desert n صحرا
deportation n رد مرز	deserted adj متروک
depose v عزل کردن؛ خلع کردن	deserter n ترک کننده
deposit v در بانک پول گذاشتن	deserve v سزاوار بودن
deposit n ودیعه؛ بیعانه	deserving adj سزاوار
depot n انبار	design n طرح
deprave v منحرف کردن	design v طرح کردن
depravity n فساد	designate v گماشتن
depreciate v بی ارزش ساختن	designer n طراح
depreciation n بی ارزشی	desirable adj مطلوب
depress v افسرده کردن	desire n آرزو
depressing adj افسرده کننده	desire v آرزو کردن
depression n افسردگی	desist v دست برداشتن
deprivation n محرومیت	desk n میز
deprive v محروم کردن	desolate adj متروک
deprived adj محروم	desolation n ویرانی
depth n عمق	despair n نا امیدی
derail v از خط خارج شدن	desperate adj نا امید
deranged adj آشفته	despicable adj نفرت انگیز
derelict adj متروک	despise v خوار شمردن
derivative adj مشتق	despite prep باوجود
derive v مشتق کردن	despondent adj دلسرد
derogatory adj تحقیر آمیز	despot n مستبد
descend v پایین آمدن؛ فرود آمدن	despotic adj مستبدانه
descendant n نسل	dessert n شیرینی
descent n نزول	destination n مقصد سفر
describe v شرح دادن	destiny n سرنوشت
description n شرح	destitute adj نیازمند
descriptive adj تشریحی	destroy v ویران کردن
desecrate v هتک حرمت کردن	destruction n ویرانی
desegregate v جدا کردن	destructive adj ویرانگر
desert v ترک کردن	detach v جدا کردن

D

D

detachable *adj* قابل جدا شدن	device *n* وسیله
detail *v* با تفصیل بیان کردن	devious *adj* فریبنده
detail *n* تفصیل	devise *v* درست کردن
detailed *adj* با جزئیات	devoid *adj* خالی
detain *v* توقیف کردن	devote *v* وقف کردن
detect *v* کشف کردن	devotion *n* از خودگذری
detective *n* کشفی	devour *v* خوردن
detector *n* کشف کننده	devout *adj* دین دار
detention *n* توقیف	dew *n* شبنم
deter *v* بازداشتن	diabetes *n* مرض شکر
detergent *n* مواد لباس شویی	diabetic *adj* مریض شکر
deteriorate *v* خراب کردن	diagnose *v* تشخیص کردن
deterioration *n* زوال	diagnosis *n* تشخیص
determination *n* عزم و اراده	diagonal *adj* قُطری، مربوط به قُطر
determine *v* تعیین کردن	diagram *n* دیاگرام
determined *adj* مصمم	dial *v* دایر کردن شماره تیلفون
detest *v* نفرت داشتن	dial *n* صفحه شماره ها
detestable *adj* نفرت انگیز	dial tone *n* صدای تیلفون
detonate *v* منفجر کردن	dialect *n* لهجه
detonator *n* منفجر کننده	dialog *n* دیالوگ
detour *n* انحراف	diameter *n* دیامتر
detriment *n* مضر	diamond *n* الماس؛ خشت
detrimental *adj* زیان آور	diaper *n* دایپر
devaluation *n* کاهش ارزش	diarrhea *n* اسهال
devalue *v* تنزیل قیمت دادن	diary *n* کتابچه یادداشت
devastate *v* ویران کردن	dice *v* توته توته کردن
devastating *adj* ویرانگر	dice *n* دانه کمسایی
devastation *n* ویرانی	dictate *v* به صدای بلند خواندن
develop *v* انکشاف کردن	dictator *n* دیکتاتور
development *n* انکشاف	dictatorial *adj* دیکتاتوری
deviate *v* منحرف شدن	dictatorship *n* حکومت استبدادی
deviation *n* انحراف	dictionary *n* دکشنری

die v مردن	**diner** n کسی که غذا میخورد
die out v خاموش شدن	**dining room** n اتاق نان خوری
diesel n دیزل	**dinner** n نان شب
diet v رژیم غذایی گرفتن	**dinosaur** n داینسور
diet n غذا؛ رژیم غذایی	**dip** v پایین آمدن
differ v تفاوت داشتن	**dip** n فرورفتگی
difference n تفاوت	**diploma** n دیپلوم
different adj متفاوت	**diplomacy** n دیپلوماسی
differentiate v فرق گذاشتن	**diplomat** n دیپلومات
differently adv بطور متفاوت	**diplomatic** adj دیپلوماتیک
difficult adj دشوار	**dire** adj وضعیت بغرنج
difficulty n دشواری، سختی	**direct** adv راست
diffuse v منتشر شدن	**direct** adj مستقیم
dig v حفر کردن	**direct** v هدایت دادن
digest v هضم کردن	**direction** n استقامت
digestion n هاضمه	**directions** n هدایات
digit n عدد	**directly** adv مستقیماً
digital adj دیجیتال	**director** n رئیس
dignified adj باعزت	**directory** n فهرست اشیا
dignify v عزت بخشیدن	**dirt** n کثافت
dignity n کرامت، وقار، عزت	**dirty** adj کثیف
digress v منحرف شدن	**disability** n معیوبیت
dilemma n وضعیت دشوار	**disabled** adj معیوب
diligent adj کوشا	**disadvantage** n زیان
dilute v رقیق ساختن	**disagree** v توافق نکردن
dim adj خیره	**disagreement** n اختلاف
dim v خیره ساختن	**disappear** v ناپدید شدن
dime n سکه ده سنتی	**disappearance** n ناپدیدی
dimension n بُعد	**disappoint** v مأیوس کردن
dimensional adj بُعدی	**disappointing** adj مأیوس کننده
diminish v کاهش دادن	**disappointment** n یأس
dine v غذا خوردن	**disapproval** n عدم تایید

D

disapprove v تایید نکردن	**discrimination** n تبعیض
disarm v خلع سلاح کردن	**discuss** v بحث کردن
disaster n فاجعه	**discussion** n بحث
disastrous adj فاجعه بار	**disdain** n بی احترامی
disband v منحل کردن	**disease** n مرض
disbelief n بی اعتباری	**disembark** v پیاده شدن
disburse v پرداخت کردن	**disenchanted** adj دلسرد
disc n دیسک	**disentangle** v جدا کردن
disc jockey (DJ) n سوار بر دیسک	**disfigure** v تغییر شکل دادن
discard v دور انداختن	**disgrace** n رسوایی
discern v	**disgraceful** adj ننگین
تصور و تشخیص کردن چیزی	**disgruntled** adj ناراضی
discharge n تخلیه	**disguise** n تغییر قیافه
discharge v تخلیه کردن	**disguise** v تغییر قیافه دادن
disciple n شاگرد	**disgust** n تنفر
discipline n دسیپلین	**disgusted** adj متنفر
disclose v افشا کردن	**disgusting** adj زشت
discomfort n ناراحتی	**dish** n ظرف
disconnect v قطع شدن	**dishearten** v دلسرد کردن
discontinue v متوقف کردن	**dishonest** adj بی صداقت
discount n تخفیف	**dishonesty** n بی صداقتی
discount v تخفیف دادن	**dishonor** n بی حرمتی
discourage v دلسرد ساختن	**dishonorable** adj بی ناموس
discouragement n دلسردی	**dishwasher** n ماشین ظرف شوی
discouraging adj دلسرد کننده	**disillusion** n
discover v کشف کردن	رهایی از خواب و خیال
discovery n کشفیات	**disinfect** v ضد عفونی کردن
discredit v بی اعتبار کردن	**disinfectant** n
discreet adj محتاط	مواد ضد عفونی کننده
discrepancy n اختلاف	**disintegrate** v از هم پاشیدن
discretion n شرح	**disintegration** n از هم پاشیده گی
discriminate v تبعیض کردن	**disinterested** adj بی علاقه

D

disk *n* دیسک	**disposable** *adj* یکبار مصرف
disk drive *n* دیسک درایف	**dispose** *v* در معرض واقع شدن
dislike *n* تنفر	**disprove** *v* رد کردن
dislike *v* خوش نداشتن	**dispute** *v* دعوی کردن
dislocate *v* بیجا ساختن	**dispute** *n* منازعه
dislodge *v* از جای خود بیرون کردن	**disqualify** *v* سلب صلاحیت کردن
disloyal *adj* بی وفا	**disregard** *v* اعتنا نکردن
dismal *adj* دلخراش	**disrespect** *n* بی احترامی
dismantle *v* از بین بردن	**disrespectful** *adj* بی احترام
dismay *v* بی میل کردن	**disrupt** *v* مختل کردن
dismay *n* بی میلی	**disruption** *n* اختلال
dismiss *v* رخصت کردن	**disruptive** *adj* مختل کننده
dismissal *n* اخراج	**dissatisfied** *adj* ناراضی
dismount *v* پیاده شدن	**disseminate** *v* پخش کردن
disobedience *n* نافرمانی	**dissent** *v* مخالف
disobedient *adj* نافرمان	**dissident** *adj* ناموافق
disobey *v* نافرمانی کردن	**dissipate** *v* از هم پاشیدن
disorder *n* بی نظمی	**dissolve** *v* منحل کردن
disorganized *adj* بی نظم	**dissuade** *v* منصرف کردن
disoriented *adj* منحرف شده	**distance** *n* فاصله
disown *v* عاق کردن	**distant** *adj* دور
disparity *n* نابرابری	**distaste** *n* بی میلی
dispatch *v* ارسال کردن	**distasteful** *adj* بی میل
dispense *v* توزیع کردن	**distill** *v* تقطیر کردن، شراب ساختن
dispenser *n* تلگراف	**distinct** *adj* واضح؛ متمایز
disperse *v* متفرق شدن	**distinction** *n* فرق، تمیز
displace *v* بیجا شدن	**distinctive** *adj* متمایز
displacement *n* بی جایی	**distinctly** *adv* بطور متمایز
display *n* نمایش	**distinguish** *v* تمیز دادن
display *v* نمایش دادن	**distinguished** *adj* ممتاز
displease *v* رنجاندن	**distort** *v* تحریف کردن، کج کردن
displeasing *adj* رنج آور	**distortion** *n* تحریف

distract v تمرکز را بر هم زدن

distraction n بهم زنی تمرکز، گیجی

distraught adj پریشان

distress n پریشانی

distressing adj پریشان کننده

distribute v توزیع کردن

distribution n توزیع

district n ناحیه

distrust n بی اعتمادی

distrust v بی اعتمادی کردن

distrustful adj بی اعتماد

disturb v اذیت کردن

disturbance n مزاحمت

disturbing adj ناراحت کننده

ditch n جوی

dive v دایف کردن در آب؛ از راه دور شدن

diver n آبباز

diverse adj متنوع

diversify v گوناگون کردن

diversion n انحراف

diversity n تنوع

divert v منحرف کردن

divide v تقسیم کردن؛ علامه تقسیم

divine adj الهی

divinity n الهیات

divisible adj قابل تقسیم

division n تقسیم؛ عملیه تقسیم در ریاضی

divorce n طلاق

divorce v طلاق دادن

divulge v افشا کردن

dizzy adj گنس

do v انجام دادن؛ کردن

docile adj مطیع، رام

dock v جا خالی کردن

dock n لنگرگاه

doctor n داکتر

document n سند

documentary n مستند

documentation n مستند سازی

dodge v جلو چیزی را گرفتن

dog n سگ

doll n گُدی

dollar n دالر

dolphin n دولفین

domain n رشته تحصیلی؛ آدرس انترنیتی

dome n گنبد

domestic adj داخلی

domesticate v داخلی ساختن

domesticated adj داخلی شده، اهلی شده

dominant adj غالب

dominate v غلبه کردن

domination n غلبه

domineering adj سلطه گر

donate v اهدا کردن

donation n اهدا

done adj انجام شده

donkey n خر

donor n تمویل کننده

doom n عذاب

D

doomed adj محکوم به	**downtown** n مرکز شهر
door n دروازه	**downturn** adj رکود، کاهش
doorbell n زنگ دروازه	**downward** adv بطرف پایین
doorknob n دستگیر دروازه	**doze** v چرت زدن
doormat n پای پاک دهن دروازه	**dozen** n درجن
doorstep n درب منزل	**draft** v مسوده را ترتیب کردن
doorway n درگاه	**draft** n مسوده؛ سرد کننده هوا
dormitory n لیلیه	**drag** v کش کردن
dosage n مقدار مصرف دوا	**dragon** n اژدها
dot n نقطه	**drain** v خشک شدن
double adj دوتایی	**drainage** n تخلیه آب
double v دوچند ساختن	**drainpipe** n پایپ تخلیه آب
double-check v دوبار بررسی کردن	**drama** n درامه
double-click v دوبار کلیک کردن	**dramatic** adj نمایشی
double-cross v صلیب دوگانه	**dramatically** adv بطور چشمگیر
doubt n شک	**dramatize** v بشکل درامه در آوردن
doubt v شک کردن	**drapes** n پرده
doubtful adj مشکوک	**drastic** adj شدید
dough n خمیر	**draw** v رسم کشیدن؛ کش کردن؛ جلب کردن
dove n کبوتر	**draw** n ریسمان کشی
down adj پایین؛ خفه	**drawback** n مانع
down adv در پایین	**drawer** n روک
down prep در زیر	**drawing** n رسامی
down payment n پیش پرداخت	**dread** v ترساندن
downfall n سقوط	**dreadful** adj ترسناک
downhill adv سرپایینی	**dream** v خواب دیدن؛ آرزو کردن
downpour n بارندگی	**dream** n خواب و خیال هنگام خواب؛ آرزو کردن
downsize v کوچک کردن	**drench** v تر کردن
downstairs adv طبقه پایین	**dress** n لباس
downstairs adj واقع در طبقه پایین	**dress** v لباس پوشیدن
down-to-earth adj واقعبین	

D

dress up *pv* لباس پوشیدن
dresser *n* میز آرایش
dressing *n* تزئین
dribble *v* دریبل زدن
dried *adj* خشکیده
drift *v* جمع شدن
drift apart *pv* کم کم از هم جدا شدن
drill *v* برمه کردن
drill *n* برمه؛ تمرینات
drink *n* نوشابه
drink *v* نوشیدن
drinkable *adj* نوشیدنی
drip *v* چکیدن
drive *v* راندن
drive *n* سفر زمینی؛ تعهد؛ درایف کمپیوتر
driver *n* راننده
driver's license *n* جواز رانندگی
driveway *n* راهرو
drizzle *n* نم نم باران
drizzle *v* نم نم باران باریدن
drool *v* چرت زدن
drop *v* افتادن
drop *n* سقوط
drop in *pv* داخل چیزی افتادن
drop off *pv* بیرون از چیزی افتادن
drop out *pv* رها کردن
dropout *n* ترک تحصیل
drought *n* خشکسالی
drown *v* غرق شدن
drowsy *adj* خواب آلود
drug *n* ادویه؛ مواد مخدر

drug addict *n* معتاد مواد مخدر
drugstore *n* دواخانه
drum *n* دُهل
drunk *adj* نشه
dry *adj* خشک
dry *v* خشک کردن
dry-clean *v* خشکه شویی کردن
dryer *n* خشک کن
dual *adj* دوتایی
dubious *adj* مشکوک
duck *v* غوطه ور شدن
duck *n* مرغابی
duct *n* مجرا
due *adj* ناشی از
duel *n* جنگ تن به تن
dues *n* حق العضویت
duet *n* دونفری نواختن
dull *v* گُند کردن
dull *adj* گُند؛ خسته کن
duly *adv* به درستی، بموقع
dumb *adj* بی عقل، گنگ
dummy *n* آدمک ساختگی
dump *v* در زباله انداختن
dump *n* زباله
dung *n* سرگین
dungeon *n* سیاه چاه
dunk *v* غرق شدن
dupe *v* فریب دادن
duplicate *v* تکثیر کردن، در دو نسخه خوشتن
duplication *n* تکثیر
durable *adj* با دوام

D

duration *n* مدت	**early** *adj* به وقت
during *prep* درجریان	**early** *adv* وقت
dusk *n* غروب	**earn** *v* کمایی کردن
dust *n* خاک	**earnestly** *adv* باجدیت
dust *v* خاک آلود شدن	**earnings** *n* درآمد، عاید
duster *n* خاک پاک کن	**earphones** *n* گوشکی تیلفون
dustpan *n* خاک انداز	**earring** *n* گوشواره
dusty *adj* خاک آلود	**Earth** *n* زمین
duty *n* وظیفه	**earthquake** *n* زلزله
dwarf *n* آدم با اندام کوچک	**earwax** *n* چرک گوش
dwell *v* مسکن گزین شدن	**ease** *v* راحت کردن
dwelling *n* مسکن	**ease** *n* سهولت
dwindle *v* آهسته آهسته خورد شدن	**easily** *adv* به آسانی
dye *n* رنگ	**east** *n* شرق
dye *v* رنگ کردن	**east** *adv* شرقاً
dying *adj* در حال مرگ	**east** *adj* شرقی
dynamic *adj* پویا، پرتحرک	**eastbound** *adj* بطرف شرق
dynamite *n* دینامیت، مواد انفجاری	**Easter** *n* روز مذهبی ایستر
dynasty *n* سلسله	**eastern** *adj* شرقی
	easy *adj* آسان

E

	easygoing *adj* آسان گیر
each *pron* هرکدام	**eat** *v* خوردن
each *adj* هریکی	**eavesdrop** *v* پنهانی گوش کردن
each other *pron* یکی دیگر	**ebb** *v* جاری شدن
eager *adj* مشتاق	**e-book** *n* نسخه الکترونیکی کتاب
eagerness *n* اشتیاق	**eccentric** *adj* غیرعادی
eagle *n* عقاب	**echo** *n* انعکاس
ear *n* گوش	**eclipse** *n* گرفتگی، کسوف و خسوف
earache *n* گوش دردی	**ecology** *n* زیست شناسی
	economic *adj* اقتصادی
	economical *adj* اقتصادی بودن
	economically *adv* بطور اقتصادی

economics *n* علم اقتصاد
economist *n* اقتصاد دان
economize *v* اقتصادی ساختن
economy *n* اقتصاد
ecstatic *adj* وجد زده، به وجد آمده
edge *n* لبه
edgy *adj* لبه دار
edible *adj* خوردنی
edit *v* اصلاح کردن متن
edition *n* نسخه
editor *n* ایدیتور
editorial *n* سرمقاله
educate *v* آموختاندن
educated *adj* تحصیل کرده
education *n* تعلیم و تربیه
educational *adj*
مربوط به تعلیم و تربیه
eerie *adj* ترساننده
effect *n* تاثیر
effective *adj* موثر
effectiveness *n* موثریت
efficiency *n* اثر
efficient *adj* کارا
effort *n* تلاش
egg *n* تخم مرغ
egg white *n* سفیدی تخم
ego *n* نفس
eight *n* هشت
eighteen *n* هجده
eighteenth *adj* هجدهم
eighth *adj* هشتم
eighty *n* هشتاد

either *adj* این و آن
either *adv* هریک
either *pron* یا
eject *v* کشیدن
elapse *v* سپری شدن
elastic *adj* کششی، کش دار
elated *adj* خوشحال
elbow *n* آرنج
elder *n* بزرگتر
elderly *adj* بزرگسال
elect *v* انتخاب کردن
election *n* انتخابات
electric *adj* برقی
electrical *adj* برقی
electrician *n* انجنیر برق
electricity *n* برق
electrify *v* برقی ساختن
electrocute *v* مردن از اثر برق
electronic *adj* الکترونیکی
elegance *n* ظرافت
elegant *adj* ظریف
element *n* عنصر
elementary *adj* ابتدائیه
elementary school *n*
مکتب ابتدائیه
elephant *n* فیل
elevate *v* بلند کردن
elevation *n* ارتفاع
elevator *n* لفت
eleven *n* یازده
eleventh *adj* یازدهم
elf *n* جن

E

eligible *adj* واجد شرايط	emigrant *n* مهاجر
eliminate *v* از بين بردن	emigrate *v* مهاجرت كردن
eloquence *n* فصاحت	emission *n* خروج، دفع مايعات
else *adv* ديگر	emit *v* بيرون ريختن
elsewhere *adv* جای ديگر	emotion *n* احساس
elude *v* فرار كردن، دوری كردن	emotional *adj* عاطفی
elusive *adj* گريزان	empathy *n* همدلی، غمشريكی
e-mail (email) *v* نامه الكترونيكی فرستادن، ايميل كردن	emperor *n* امپراتور
	emphasis *n* تأكيد
e-mail (email) *n*، نامه الكترونيكی، ايميل	emphasize *v* تأكيد كردن
	empire *n* امپراتوری
emancipate *v* از قيد رها كردن	employ *v* استخدام كردن
embalm *v* موميايی كردن	employee *n* كارمند
embark *v* شروع كردن	employer *n* كارفرما
embarrass *v* دست پاچه كردن	employment *n* استخدام، وظيفه
embarrassed *adj* دست پاچه، وارخطا	empress *n* ملكه
	emptiness *n* پوچی
embarrassing *adj* دست پاچه كننده	empty *v* خالی كردن
embarrassment *n* دست پاچگی	empty *adj* خالی، پوچ
embassy *n* سفارت	enable *v* قادر ساختن
embellish *v* آراستن	enchant *v* به دام عشق انداختن
embers *n* خاكستر ذغال نيم سوز	enchanting *adj* دلربا
embezzle *v* اختلاس كردن	encircle *v* احاطه كردن
emblem *n* نشان، علامت	enclose *v* ضميمه كردن
embody *v* مجسم كردن	enclosure *n* ضميمه
emboss *v* مزين كردن	encounter *n* رويارويی
embrace *v* در آغوش گرفتن	encounter *v* مواجه شدن
embroider *v* گلدوزی كردن	encourage *v* تشويق كردن
embroidery *n* گلدوزی	encouraging *adj* دلگرم كننده
emerald *n* زمرد	encroach *v* تجاوز كردن
emerge *v* ظهور كردن	encyclopedia *n* دايرة المعارف
emergency *n* اضطراری، عاجل	end *n* خاتمه

end v ختم کردن	enough adv کافی
end up pv خاتمه بخشیدن	enrage v خشمگین کردن
endanger v به خطر انداختن	enrich v غنی ساختن
endangered adj در معرض خطر	enroll v ثبت نام کردن
ending n خاتمه	ensure v اطمینان حاصل کردن
endless adj بی پایان	entail v شامل بودن
endorse v تأیید و امضا کردن	entangle v گرفتار شدن، گیر انداختن
endorsement n تأیید و امضا	enter v داخل شدن
endure v تحمل کردن	enterprise n تصدی، شرکت
enemy n دشمن	entertain v سرگرم ساختن
energetic adj با انرژی	entertainer n شخص سرگرم کننده
energy n انرژی	entertaining adj سرگرم کننده
enforce v تطبیق کردن	entertainment n سرگرمی
engage v دخیل بودن	enthusiasm n شوق و علاقه
engaged adj نامزد	enthusiastic adj علاقمند
engagement n نامزدی	entice v فریب دادن
engine n ماشین	enticement n فریب
engineer n انجنیر	enticing adj فریبنده
English n انگلیسی	entire adj تمام، کل
engrave v حکاکی کردن	entirely adv کلاً
engraving n حکاکی	entrance n دروازه دخولی
enhance v افزایش دادن	entree n غذای اصلی
enjoy v لذت بردن	entrenched adj جا افتاده
enjoyable adj لذت بخش	entrepreneur n تاجر
enjoyment n لذت	entrust v واگذار کردن، سپردن
enlarge v بزرگ ساختن	entry n دخول؛ ثبت در کتاب
enlighten v روشن کردن	envelope n پاکت خط
enlist v نام نویسی کردن	envious adj حسود
enormous adj عظیم	environment n محیط زیست، ماحول
enormously adv به بزرگی	environmental adj مربوط به محیط زیست
enough adj بسنده	
enough pron به اندازه	

E

environmentalist n
کارشناس محیط زیست

envy n حسادت

envy v حسادت کردن

epidemic n ساری

episode n قسمت سریال

equal adj برابر، مساوی

equality n مساوات

equate v برابر کردن

equation n برابری

equator n خط استوا

equilibrium n تعادل

equip v مجهز ساختن

equipment n تجهیزات

equivalent adj معادل

era n عصر، زمان

eradicate v از بین بردن

erase v پاک کردن

eraser n تخته پاک

erect adj راست شده، عمودی

erect v نصب کردن

erode v فرسودن

erosion n فرسایش

errand n کار های محوله

erroneous adj غلط

error n اشتباه

erupt v فوران کردن

eruption n فوران

escalate v بالا بردن

escalator n لفت

escape v فرار کردن

esophagus n مری

especially adv خاصتأ؛ بسیار زیاد

espionage n جاسوسی

espresso n قهوه تیره سیاه

essay n مقاله

essence n ماهیت

essential adj ضروری

establish v تاسیس کردن

establishment n تاسیس

estate n املاک

esteem v محترم شمردن

estimate n تخمین

estimate v تخمین کردن

estranged adj بیگانه شده

etcetera adv و غیره

eternity n ابدیت

ethical adj اخلاقی

ethics n اخلاق

ethnic adj نژادی، قومی

etiquette n آداب معاشرت

euphoria n رضایت

euro n پول یورو

Europe n اروپا

European adj اروپایی

evacuate v تخلیه کردن

evade v فراربخاطر نجات

evaluate v ارزیابی کردن

evaluation n ارزیابی

evaporate v تبخیر شدن

evasive adj گریزان

eve n شب عید

even adv حتی

even adj هموار؛ برابر؛ عدد جفت

even if *adv* حتی اگر
even though *adv* گرچه
evening *n* شام
evenly *adv* بطور برابر
event *n* رویداد؛
مسابقه ورزشی یا سرگرمی
eventual *adj* تدریجی
eventually *adv* تدریجاً
ever *adv* گاهی
everlasting *adj* دوامدار
every *adj* هر
everybody *pron* هرشخص
everyday *adj* هرروز
everyone *pron* هرکس
everything *pron* هرچیز
everywhere *adv* هرجا
evict *v* بیرون کردن
evidence *n* شواهد
evident *adj* آشکار
evidently *adv* بطور آشکار
evil *adj* بد
evil *n* بدی، زیان
evoke *v* برانگیختن
evolution *n* سیر تکامل
evolutionary *adj* تکاملی
evolve *v* تکامل یافتن
exact *adj* دقیق
exactly *adv* دقیقاً
exaggerate *v* مبالغه کردن
exam *n* امتحان
examination *n* معاینه
examine *v* معاینه کردن

example *n* مثال
exasperate *v* خشمگین کردن
excavate *v* حفر کردن
exceed *v* از حد تجاوز کردن
exceedingly *adv* بیش از حد
excel *v* برتری داشتن
excellence *n* برتری
excellent *adj* عالی
except *prep* بجز از
exception *n* استثنا
exceptional *adj* استثنایی
excerpt *n* برگزیدن
excess *n* افراط، زیادی
excessive *adj* بیش از اندازه
exchange *v* تبادله کردن
excite *v* هیجانی کردن
excited *adj* هیجانی
excitement *n* هیجان
exciting *adj* هیجان آور
exclaim *v* به همه اعلام کردن
exclamation *n* علامه ندائیه،
علامت تعجب
exclude *v* بیرون کردن
excluding *prep* به استثنای
excruciating *adj* عذاب آور
excursion *n* گشت و گذار
excuse *v* بخشیدن؛
غیرحاضر را حاضر شمردن
excuse *n* بهانه
execute *v* اجرا کردن
executive *n* اجرایی
exemplary *adj* قابل تقلید

E

E

exemplify *v* با مثال واضح کردن	experience *n* تجربه
exempt *adj* معاف	experience *v* تجربه کردن
exemption *n* معافیت	experienced *adj* با تجربه
exercise *v* ورزش کردن	experiment *n* آزمایش
exercise *n* ورزش؛ مشق	expert *n* کارشناس
exert *v* بکار بردن	expert *adj* ماهر
exertion *n* اعمال زور	expertise *n* تجربه و تخصص
exhale *v* نفس بیرون کشیدن	expiration *n* انقضا
exhaust *n* خروج	expire *v* منقضی شدن
exhaust *v* خسته کردن	explain *v* تشریح کردن
exhausting *adj* خسته کننده	explanation *n* تشریح
exhaustion *n* خستگی	explicit *adj* روشن، واضح
exhibit *v* نمایش دادن	explicitly *adv* بطور واضح
exhibition *n* نمایشگاه	explode *v* منفجر شدن
exhilarating *adj* نشاط آور	exploit *v* استثمار کردن
exile *n* تبعید	exploration *n* اکتشاف
exile *v* تبعید کردن	explore *v* سیاحت کردن؛
exist *v* وجود داشتن	بصورت کلی آزمایش کردن
existence *n* موجودیت	explorer *n* جستجوگر
exit *n* خروج	explosion *n* انفجار
exotic *adj* عجیب و غریب	explosive *adj* مواد منفجره
expand *v* وسعت دادن	export *v* صادر کردن
expansion *n* وسعت	exporter *n* صادر کننده
expect *v* توقع داشتن	expose *v* درمعرض قرار گرفتن
expectancy *n* توقع، انتظار	exposed *adj* افشا شده
expectation *n* توقع	exposure *n* افشا، در معرض گذاری
expedient *adj* مناسب	express *v* بیان کردن
expedition *n* سفر، اردوکشی	express *adj* سریع السیر
expel *v* اخراج کردن	expression *n* بیان با چهره؛
expenditure *n* مصارف	اصطلاح
expense *n* هزینه	expressly *adv* به صراحت
expensive *adj* قیمتی	expulsion *n* اخراج

exquisite *adj* نفیس، عالی
extend *v* تمدید کردن
extended family *n* خانواده بزرگ
extension *n* تمدید
extensive *adj* وسیع
extent *n* وسعت
exterior *adj* بیرونی
exterminate *v* نابود کردن
external *adj* بیرونی
extinct *adj* خاموش شده
extinguish *v* خاموش کردن حریق
extort *v* اخاذی کردن، به زور گرفتن
extortion *n* اخاذی
extra *adv* اضافی
extra *adj* زائد
extract *v* استخراج کردن
extract *n* عصاره
extraordinary *adj* خارق العاده
extravagant *adj* عجیب
extreme *adj* مفرط، بینهایت
extremely *adv* بینهایت
extremist *adj* افراطی
extroverted *adj* بیرون گرا
exult *v* خوشی کردن
eye *n* چشم
eyebrow *n* ابرو
eye-catching *adj* به ساده گی قابل دید
eyeglasses *n* عینک
eyelash *n* مژه
eyelid *n* پلک
eyeshadow *n* سایه چشم
eyesight *n* دید چشم

eyewitness *n* شاهد عینی

F

fable *n* افسانه
fabric *n* تکه
fabricate *v* ساختن
fabulous *adj* شگفت آور
face *v* روبرو شدن
face *n* صورت، روی
facet *n* جنبه
facial *adj* مربوط به صورت
facilitate *v* تسهیل کردن
facilities *n* تسهیلات
facility *n* سهل
fact *n* حقیقت
factor *n* عامل، فکتور
factory *n* فابریکه
factual *adj* حقیقی
faculty *n* استادان پوهنتون
fad *n* هوس
fade *v* پژمرده شدن؛ محو شدن
faded *adj* پژمرده
fail *v* ناکام شدن
failure *n* ناکامی
faint *v* ضعف کردن
faint *adj* ضعیف
fair *adj* عادلانه؛ خفیف
fair *n* نمایشگاه
fairly *adv* منصفانه

fairness n انصاف، عدالت	**far** adj بسیار
fairy n پری	**far** adv دور
fairy tale n افسانه	**faraway** adj بسیار دور
faith n اعتقاد	**farce** n نمایش کمیدی
faithful adj با ایمان	**fare** n کرایه موتر
fake v جعل کردن	**farewell** n خداحافظی
fake adj جعلی	**farm** n مزرعه
fake n ساختگی	**farmer** n دهقان
fall v افتادن	**farming** n فارمداری
fall n خزان؛ سقوط	**farmyard** n صحن مزرعه
fall apart pv از هم پاشیدن	**farther** adv دورتر
fall asleep pv بخواب رفتن	**fascinate** v مجذوب کردن
fall back pv عقب افتادن	**fashion** n فیشن، مُد
fall behind pv عقب ماندن	**fashionable** adj مُد روز
fall down pv پایین افتادن	**fast** adv به سرعت
fall through pv سقوط کردن	**fast** adj تیز
fallacy n مغالطه، استدلال غلط	**fast** v روزه گرفتن
fallout n عواقب	**fast food** n غذای آماده
false adj غلط	**fasten** v بسته کردن کمربند
falsify v جعل کردن	**fat** adj چاق
falter v لکنت زبان پیدا کردن	**fat** n چربی
fame n شهرت	**fatal** adj کشنده
familiar adj آشنا	**fate** n سرنوشت
family n فامیل	**fateful** adj سرنوشت ساز
famine n قحطی	**father** n پدر
famous adj مشهور	**fatherhood** n پدری
fan n هواداران؛ بادپکه	**father-in-law** n خسر
fanatic adj متعصب	**fatherly** adj پدرانه
fancy adj تجملی	**fatigue** n خستگی
fang n نیش	**fatten** v چاق کردن
fantastic adj عالی	**fatty** adj چربی دار
fantasy n تمایل	**faucet** n شیردهن نل

fault *n* اشتباه	**felon** *n* جنایتکار
faulty *adj* ناقص	**felony** *n* جنایت
favor *n* لطف	**felt** *n* نمد ساخته شده از پشم
favorable *adj* مطلوب	**female** *adj* زنانه
favorite *adj* برگزیده	**female** *n* مؤنث
favorite *n* دلخواه	**feminine** *adj* زنانه گی
fear *n* ترس	**fence** *n* حصار، دیوار
fear *v* ترسیدن	**fencing** *n* حصار کشی؛
fearful *adj* ترسناک	بازی شمشیر زنی
fearless *adj* بی ترس	**fend** *v* دفع کردن
feasible *adj* شدنی، امکانپذیر	**fender** *n* گلگیر
feast *n* جشن	**ferocious** *adj* وحشی
feat *n* شاهکار	**ferry** *n* کشتی
feather *n* پَر	**fertile** *adj* بارور، حاصلخیز
feature *v* نمایان کردن، نشان دادن	**fertility** *n* باروری، حاصلخیزی
feature *n* ویژه گی	**fertilize** *v* کود دادن
February *n* ماه فبروری	**fertilizer** *n* کودکیمیاوی
fed up *adj* بیزار	**fervent** *adj* مشتاق
federal *adj* فدرال	**fester** *v* گندیدن
federation *n* فدراسیون	**festival** *n* جشن، فستیوال
fee *n* فیس	**festive** *adj* شاد
feeble *adj* ضعیف	**festivity** *n* خوشی
feed *v* تغذیه کردن	**fetch** *v* آوردن
feedback *n* نظریه	**feud** *n* دشمنی
feel *v* احساس کردن؛ لمس کردن	**fever** *n* تب
feeling *n* احساس	**few** *pron* چند
feelings *n* احساسات	**few** *adj* چند دانه
feet *n* پاها	**fewer** *adj* کمتر
feign *v* جعل کردن	**fiancé** *n* نامزد
fellow *n* دوست	**fib** *n* دروغ
fellow *adj* همکار	**fiber** *n* فایبر
fellowship *n* بورس تحصیلی	**fickle** *adj* بی ثبات

F

F

fiction n افسانه	filter n فلتر
fictitious adj افسانوی	filter v فلتر کردن
fiddle n آله موسیقی وایلون	filth n آلودگی، کثافت
fidelity n وفاداری	filthy adj کثیف
field n مزرعه؛ میدان ورزشی؛ رشته تحصیلی	fin n بال
	final n خاتمه
field trip n سیر علمی	final adj نهایی
fierce adj خشمگین	finalist n فینالیست
fiery adj آتش مزاج	finalize v نهایی کردن
fifteen n پانزده	finally adv بالاخره
fifteenth adj پانزدهم	finance n دارای
fifth adj پنجم	finance v سرمایه گذاری کردن
fiftieth adj پنجاهم	financial adj مالی
fifty n پنجاه	financially adv از لحاظ مالی
fifty-fifty adv پنجاه پنجاه	find v یافتن
fig n انجیر	find out pv پی بردن
fight v جنگ کردن	fine n جریمه
fight n مبارزه	fine adj خوب
fighter n رزمنده	fine print n چاپ خوب
figure v تصویر کشیدن	finger n انگشت
figure n شکل؛ رقم، عدد	fingernail n ناخن انگشت
figure of speech n طرز بیان؛ استعاره	fingerprint n چاپ انگشت
	fingertip n نوک انگشت
figure out pv فهمیدن، تنظیم کردن	finish v ختم کردن
figure skating n اسکیت بازی	finished adj تمام شده
file v درج کردن؛ سوهان کردن ناخن	finite adj محدود
file n فایل کمپیوتر؛ دوسیه کاغذی؛ سوهان ناخن	fire n آتش
	fire v آتش زدن
fill v پُر کردن	fire alarm n زنگ خطر آتش
filling n پُرکاری	fire department n اطفائیه
film n فلم	fire extinguisher n خاموش کننده حریق
film v فلمبرداری کردن	

fire hydrant *n* نل آب آتش نشانی	**flame** *n* شعله آتش
firearm *n* اسلحه گرم	**flammable** *adj* قابل سوخت
firecracker *n* آتشبازی	**flap** *n* ضربه
firefighter *n* کارمند اطفائیه	**flare** *n* شعله ور شدن
fireman *n* کارمند اطفائیه	**flare up** *pv* شعله ور شدن
fireplace *n* دیگدان	**flash** *v* جرقه کردن
fireproof *adj* ضد آتش	**flash** *n* فلش کمره
firewood *n* چوب سوخت	**flash drive** *n* فلش درایف
fireworks *n* آتشبازی	**flashlight** *n* گروپ دستی
firm *n* شرکت	**flashy** *adj* درخشان
firm *adj* محکم، سفت	**flat** *adj* هموار؛ مسطح
firmly *adv* به سفتی	**flatten** *v* هموار کردن
first *adj* اولی	**flatter** *v* چاپلوسی کردن
first *adv* نخست	**flattery** *n* چاپلوسی
first class *adj* صنف اول	**flaunt** *v* خودنمایی
first name *n* نام اول	**flavor** *n* ذائقه، مزه
fish *n* ماهی	**flaw** *n* نقص، عیب
fish *v* ماهیگیری کردن	**flawed** *adj* با عیب، معیوب
fisherman *n* ماهیگیر	**flawless** *adj* بی عیب
fishy *adj* مشکوک؛ ماهی بوی	**flea** *n* خسک
fist *n* مشت	**flee** *v* فرار کردن
fit *v* برابر بودن	**fleece** *n* پشم گوسفند
fit *adj* مناسب	**fleet** *n* بحریه
fitness *n* تناسب اندام	**fleeting** *adj* زودگذر
fitting *adj* برابر اندام	**flesh** *n* گوشت
fitting room *n* اتاق امتحان کردن لباس	**flex** *v* انعطاف داشتن
five *n* پنج	**flexibility** *n* انطاف پذیری
fix *v* درست کردن	**flexible** *adj* انطاف پذیر
fixed *adj* درست، ثابت	**flick** *v* تکان دادن
flag *n* بیرق	**flicker** *v* لرزیدن
flagpole *n* میله بیرق	**flier** *n* آگاهی روی کاغذ
flamboyant *adj* پر زرق و برق	**flight** *n* پرواز

F

flight attendant *n* زبان طیاره	**fog** *n* غبار
flimsy *adj* لاغر	**foggy** *adj* غبارآلود
flip *v* روی چیز را دور دادن	**foil** *n* ورق المونیمی
flirt *v* معاشقه کردن	**foil** *v* دفع کردن
float *v* شناورشدن	**fold** *v* قات کردن
flock *n* گله	**folder** *n* دوسیه
flood *v* سیل بردن	**folks** *n* مردم
flood *n* سیلاب	**folksy** *adj* شخص اجتماعی،
floor *n* فرش اتاق؛ طرح ساختمان	خوش برخورد
florist *n* گلساز	**follow** *v* تعقیب کردن
floss *n* نخ دندان	**follower** *n* پیرو
flour *n* آرد	**following** *adj* بعدی
flourish *v* رشد کردن	**fond** *adj* علاقمند
flow *v* جاری شدن	**fondness** *n* علاقمندی
flow *n* جریان	**food** *n* غذا
flower *n* گل	**fool** *n* احمق
flowerpot *n* گلدان	**fool** *v* احمق ساختن
flu *n* ریزش	**foolish** *adj* احمق
fluctuate *v* نوسان کردن	**foolproof** *adj* بی عیب و نقص
fluent *adj* فصیح	**foot** *n* پا؛ واحد اندازه گیری فوت
fluently *adv* به فصاحت	**football** *n* فتبال
fluffy *adj* نرم	**footnote** *n* پا ورقی
fluid *n* مایع	**footprint** *n* رد پا
flush *v* شستشو کردن	**footstep** *n* قدم
flute *n* توله	**footwear** *n* بوت
flutter *v* بال بال زدن	**for** *prep* برای
fly *v* پرواز کردن	**forbid** *v* منع کردن
fly *n* مگس	**force** *n* قوه
foam *n* کف دریا	**force** *v* مجبور کردن
focus *n* تمرکز	**forceful** *adj* قوی
focus *v* تمرکز کردن؛	**forcibly** *adv* به زور
لینز کمره را عیار کردن	**forearm** *n* بازو

forecast v پیشبینی کردن	formerly adv قبلاً
foreground n پیش زمینه	formidable adj وحشتناک
forehead n پیشانی	formula n فورمول
foreign adj خارجی	forsake v رها کردن
foreigner n شخص خارجی	fort n دژ، قلعه
foreman n سرپرست	forthcoming adj آینده
foremost adj در درجه نخست	forthright adj دو هفته
foresee v پیشبینی کردن	fortify v مستحکم کردن
foreshadow v از پیش خبر کردن	fortitude n استحکام
foresight n آینده نگری	fortress n قلعه نظامی
forest n جنگل	fortunate adj خوشبخت
foretell v پیشگویی کردن	fortune n بخت، اقبال
forever adv برای همیشه	forty n چهل
forewarn v از پیش اخطار دادن	forward v ارسال کردن
foreword n پیشگفتار	forward adv پیشرو
forfeit v ضبط کردن	fossil n فسیل
forge v ساختن	foster v ارتقا دادن؛ پرورش کردن،
forgery n جعل اسناد	بزرگ کردن
forget v فراموش کردن	foul adj خطا
forgetful adj فراموشکار	foul n خطا در ورزش
forgivable adj قابل بخشش	foundation n بنیاد؛ تهداب
forgive v بخشیدن	founder n موسس
forgiveness n بخشش	fountain n فواره
fork n پنجه	four n چهار
form v تشکیل دادن	fourteen n چهارده
form n نوع؛ شکل؛ فورمه	fourth adj چهارم
formal adj رسمی؛ تفصیلی	fox n روبا
formality n رسمیات	foxy adj حیله باز
formally adv رسماً	fraction n کسر
format n قالب بندی	fracture n شکستگی
formation n تشکیل	fragile adj شکننده
former adj قبلی	fragment n قطعه

fragrance *n* خوشبویی
fragrant *adj* خوشبو
frail *adj* سست، شکننده
frailty *n* سستی
frame *n* چوکات
frame *v* چوکات کردن
framework *n* چارچوب
frank *adj* رُک، واضح
frankly *adv* رُک و راست
frantic *adj* عصبانی
fraternity *n* برادری
fraud *n* تقلب؛ فریبکاری
fraudulent *adj* جعلی
freckle *n* خال های سیاه بر صورت
freckled *adj*
دارای خال های سیاه روی صورت
free *v* آزاد کردن
free *adj* رایگان؛ آزاد؛ قابل دسترس
freedom *n* آزادی
freely *adv* بطور آزاد؛ بدون قید
freeway *n* شاهراه
freeze *v* یخ بستن
freezer *n* یخچال
freezing *adj* یخ زده
freight *n* حمل و نقل
frenzy *n* دیوانگی
frequency *n* تناوب، تکرار
frequent *v* تکرار کردن،
رفت و آمد زیاد کردن
frequent *adj* مکرر
fresh *adj* تازه
freshen *v* تازه کردن

freshman *n* محصل سال اول
freshwater *adj* آب تازه
friction *n* اختلاف، اصطکاک
Friday *n* روز جمعه
fried *adj* بریان شده
friend *n* دوست
friendly *adj* دوستانه
friendship *n* دوستی
fries *n* چیپس
fright *n* ترس
frighten *v* ترساندن
frightened *adj* ترسیده
frightening *adj* ترسناک
frigid *adj* یخ زده
fringe *n* حاشیه؛ لبه
frivolous *adj* بی پروا
frog *n* بقه
from *prep* از
front *n* جبهه
front *adj* قسمت پیشرو
frontier *n* مرز
frost *n* یخبندان
frostbite *n* سرمازدگی
frosty *adj* بیخ زده
frown *v* پیشانی ترشی کردن
frozen *adj* یخ زده
frugal *adj* صرفه جویی
fruit *n* میوه
fruitful *adj* مثمر
fruity *adj* میوه یی
frustrate *v* ناراحت ساختن
frustration *n* ناراحتی

fry *v* بریان کردن
frying pan *n* تخم پزی
fuel *n* مواد سوخت
fugitive *n* فراری
fulfill *v* برآورده کردن
fulfillment *n* تحقق
full *adj* پُر
fully *adv* بطور کامل
fumes *n* بخار
fumigate *v* بخار دادن
fun *adj* سرگرم کننده
fun *n* شوخی
function *n* عملکرد
function *v* فعالیت کردن
fund *n* بودجه
fund *v* تمویل کردن
fundamental *adj* بنیادی
funds *n* وجوه
funeral *n* جنازه
fungus *n* یکنوع سمارق
funny *adj* خنده آور
fur *n* پوستین
furious *adj* خشمگین
furiously *adv* خشمگینانه
furnace *n* تنور
furnish *v* فرش کردن اتاق
furniture *n* فرنیچر
furry *adj* پوستین دار
further *adj* بعلاوه
further *adv* بیشتر
furthermore *adv* علاوتاً
fury *n* خشم

fuse *n* فیوز برق
fusion *n* ادغام
fuss *n* سروصدا
fuss *v* سروصدا کردن
fussy *adj* پر سروصدا
futile *adj* بیهوده
future *n* آینده
future *adj* بعدی
fuzzy *adj* پشمی

G

gadget *n* ابزار
gag *v* دهان بستن
gag *n* دهان بند
gain *v* حاصل کردن
gain *n* منفعت
gal *n* دختر
galaxy *n* کهکشان
gallant *adj* شجاع
gallery *n* نمایشگاه
gallon *n* گیلن
gallop *v* پرش کردن، پریدن
galvanize *v* تکان دادن، هیجانی ساختن
gamble *v* قمار زدن
game *n* بازی
gang *n* دسته، گروه
gangster *n* بدمعاش
gap *n* خلا

garage *n* گاراج موتر	generic *adj* کلی
garbage *n* کثافات	generosity *n* سخاوتمندی
garbage can *n* سطل کثافات	generous *adj* سخاوتمند
garden *n* باغ	genetic *adj* ژنیتیکی، مربوط به نسل
gardener *n* باغبان	genial *adj* جنسی
garlic *n* سیر	genius *n* نابغه
garment *n* لباس	gentle *adj* ملایم
gas *n* گاز	gentleman *n* آقا، شخص محترم
gas station *n* تانک تیل	gently *adv* به نرمی، به ملایمت
gash *n* بریدگی	genuine *adj* خالص
gasoline *n* تیل	geography *n* جغرافیه
gasp *v* نفسک زدن	geology *n* زمین شناسی
gate *n* دروازه	geometry *n* هندسه
gather *v* جمع شدن	germ *n* مکروب
gathering *n* تجمع	gesture *n* اشاره
gauge *v* پیمانه کردن	get *v* بدست آوردن
gauge *n* پیمانه، اندازه	get along *pv* کنار آمدن
gauze *n* گاز پانسمان	get away *pv* فرار کردن
gaze *v* خیره شدن	get back *pv* برگشتن
gear *n* گیر موتر؛	get behind *pv* عقب ماندن
وسایل خاص سپورتی و کاری	get by *pv* کنار آمدن
gel *n* ژل	get down *pv* پایین آمدن
gem *n* گوهر	get down to *pv*
gender *n* جنسیت	کاری را شروع کردن
gene *n* ژن، نسل شناسی	get in *pv* داخل شدن
general *n* جنرال	get off *pv* پیاده شدن
general *adj* عمومی	get out *pv* بیرون شدن
generalize *v* عمومی ساختن	get over *pv* پشت سر گذاشتن
generally *adv* عموماً	get together *pv* یکجا شدن
generate *v* تولید کردن	get up *pv* بلند شدن
generation *n* نسل	geyser *n* چشمه آب گرم
generator *n* تولید کننده	ghastly *adj* غم انگیز

G

ghetto *n* یهودی نشین	**glimmer** *n* روشنایی خیره
ghost *n* جن	**glimpse** *n* نگاه سریع
giant *n* دیو	**glitch** *n* قطع موقت جریان برق
giant *adj* عظیم	**glitter** *v* تابش
gift *n* تحفه	**global** *adj* جهانی
gifted *adj* با استعداد	**globalization** *n* جهانی شدن
gigantic *adj* غول پیکر	**globally** *adv* در سراسر دنیا
giggle *v* خندیدن	**globe** *n* کره زمین
gill *n* سیستم تنفسی ماهی	**gloom** *n* غم و اندوه
gimmick *n* فریب	**gloomy** *adj* غمگین
ginger *n* زنجبیل	**glorify** *v* تجلیل کردن
gingerly *adv* به آرامی	**glorious** *adj* باشکوه
giraffe *n* زرافه	**glory** *n* شکوه، جلال
girl *n* دختر	**gloss** *n* شرح، تفسیر
girlfriend *n* دوست دختر	**glossary** *n* فهرست لغات
give *v* دادن	**glossy** *adj* صاف، براق
give away *pv* هدیه دادن	**glove** *n* دستکش
give back *pv* دوباره دادن	**glow** *v* تابیدن
give in *pv* بخشیدن	**glowing** *adj* درخشان
give out *pv* واگذار کردن	**glue** *n* سرش
give up *pv* دست کشیدن از	**glue** *v* سرش کردن
glacier *n* کنده یخ	**gnaw** *v* ساییدن
glad *adj* خوشحال	**go** *v* رفتن
gladiator *n* سلحشور	**go ahead** *pv* پیش رفتن
glamorous *adj* دلکش	**go around** *pv* دور زدن
glance *n* نگاه	**go away** *pv* دور شدن
glance *v* نگاه انداختن	**go back** *pv* دوباره رفتن
glare *n* نگاه خیره؛ نگاه قهر آمیز	**go down** *pv* پایین رفتن
glass *n* گیلاس؛ شیشه	**go in** *pv* داخل رفتن
glasses *n* عینک	**go on** *pv* ادامه دادن
gleam *n* نور، درخشش	**go out** *pv* بیرون شدن
glide *v* سرخوردن	**go over** *pv* مرور کردن

G

طی کردن **go through** *pv*	شایعه پراکنی **gossip** *n*
ناکام شدن **go under** *pv*	شایعه پراکنی کردن **gossip** *v*
ارتقا کردن **go up** *pv*	حکمرانی کردن **govern** *v*
هدف؛ گول در فتبال **goal** *n*	حکومت **government** *n*
گول کیپر **goalkeeper** *n*	والی **governor** *n*
بُز **goat** *n*	چین **gown** *n*
حریصانه خوردن **gobble** *v*	قپیدن، گرفتن **grab** *v*
خداوند **God** *n*	رحمت **grace** *n*
الهه **goddess** *n*	برازنده **graceful** *adj*
بی خدا **godless** *adj*	به برازندگی **gracefully** *adv*
عینک آببازی **goggles** *n*	بخشنده **gracious** *adj*
رنگ طلایی **gold** *adj*	درجه بندی کردن **grade** *v*
طلا **gold** *n*	درجه؛ نمره **grade** *n*
طلایی **golden** *adj*	تدریجی **gradual** *adj*
بازی گلف **golf** *n*	فارغ شدن **graduate** *v*
میدان بازی گلف **golf course** *n*	فراغت **graduation** *n*
بازیکن گلف **golfer** *n*	دیوار نویسی **graffiti** *n*
درست؛ خوب **good** *adj*	غله **grain** *n*
شی، جنس **good** *n*	گرام **gram** *n*
شب بخیر **good night** *e*	گرامر **grammar** *n*
خدا حافظ **goodbye** *e*	بزرگ **grand** *adj*
خوش نما **good-looking** *adj*	نواسه **grandchild** *n*
خوبی، نیکی **goodness** *n*	نواسه دختر **granddaughter** *n*
اموال، اجناس **goods** *n*	پدرکلان **grandfather** *n*
حسن نیت **goodwill** *n*	مادرکلان **grandmother** *n*
احمق **goof** *n*	پدرکلان و مادرکلان **grandparents** *n*
حماقت کردن **goof** *v*	نواسه پسر **grandson** *n*
قاز **goose** *n*	غرفه بزرگ **grandstand** *n*
تنگه **gorge** *n*	استحکام **granite** *n*
جذاب **gorgeous** *adj*	گرانولا، **granola** *n*
گوریلا؛ چریکی **gorilla** *n*	یکنوع خوراک در صبحانه
غم انگیز **gory** *adj*	اعطا کردن **grant** *v*

G

grant n کمک بلاعوض	**greatness** n بزرگی
grape n انگور	**greed** n حرص
grapefruit n گریپ فروت	**greedy** adj حریص
grapevine n تاک انگور	**green** adj سبز؛ سبز و خُرم
graph n گراف	**green** n رنگ سبز
graphic adj هنر گرافیک؛ واضح و پرقدرت	**green bean** n فاصلیه
	greenhouse n گلخانه
grasp v محکم گرفتن؛ فهمیدن	**greet** v سلام دادن؛ احوالپرسی کردن
grass n سبزه	**greeting** n احوالپرسی
grasshopper n ملخ	**gregarious** adj گروهی
grassroots adj مردمی	**grenade** n بم دستی
grateful adj شکرگذار	**grief** n اندوه
gratefully adv باسپاس	**grievance** n شکایت
gratifying adj خوشحال کننده	**grieve** v غصه خوردن
gratitude n سپاسگزاری	**grill** v کباب کردن
gratuity n بخششی	**grill** n کوره کباب
grave adj بزرگ، سنگین	**grim** adj جدی؛ شدید؛ ناخوشایند
grave n قبر	**grimace** n دهن کجی
gravel n سنگ ریزه	**grime** n سیاهی
gravestone n سنگ قبر	**grin** n پوزخند
graveyard n قبرستان	**grin** v پوزخند زدن
gravitate v متمایل شدن، گرویدن	**grind** v آسیاب کردن
gravity n قوه جاذبه	**grip** n گیرا
gravy n یخنی گوشت	**grip** v محکم گرفتن
gray adj رنگ خاکستری	**gripping** adj چنگال دار
gray n کبود	**grisly** adj وحشتناک
graze v چریدن؛ خراشیدگی	**groan** n ناله
grease v چرب کردن	**groan** v ناله کردن
grease n چربی، گریس	**groceries** n مواد غذایی
greasy adj چرب	**grocery store** n مغازه مواد غذایی
great adj بسیار بزرگ؛ بسیار مهم؛ بسیار خوب	**groin** n قسمت کشالهٔ ران
	groom v آرایش کردن

groom *n* داماد
groove *n* خط باریک دراز
gross *adj* بد، زشت
grotesque *adj* چیز عجیب و غریب
grouch *v* لجاجت کردن
grouchy *adj* لجوج، بد خلق
ground *n* زمین
ground floor *n* منزل اول
group *n* گروه
grow *v* روییدن، رشد کردن
grow up *pv* بزرگ شدن
growl *v* غُر زدن
grown *adj* بزرگ شده
grown-up *adj* بزرگ شده، بالغ
grudge *n* کینه
grueling *adj* طاقت فرسا
gruesome *adj* نفرت انگیز
grumble *v* غُرغُر کردن
grumpy *adj* بد خلق
grunt *v* غُرغُر کردن
guacamole *n* یکنوع غذا
guarantee *n* تضمین
guarantee *v* تضمین کردن
guarantor *n* تضمین کننده
guard *n* محافظت
guard *v* محافظت کردن
guardian *n* نگهبان
guerrilla *n* میمون گوریلا
guess *n* حدس
guess *v* حدس زدن
guest *n* مهمان
guidance *n* رهنمود

guidance counselor *n* مشاور رهنما
guide *n* رهنما
guide *v* رهنمایی کردن
guidebook *n* کتاب رهنما
guidelines *n* طرزالعمل ها
guilt *n* تقصیر
guilty *adj* مُقصر
guitar *n* گیتار
gulf *n* خلیج
gullible *adj* زود باور
gulp *n* قورت
gulp *v* قورت کردن
gum *n* ساجق؛ بیره
gun *n* تفنگ
gunfire *n* تیراندازی
gunman *n* تفنگدار
gunpowder *n* باروت
gunshot *n* تیراندازی
gust *n* تند باد
gusto *n* لذت
gut *n* روده
guts *n* روده و شکمبه
gutter *n* جوی
guy *n* مرد
guzzle *v* غرغره کردن، بلعیدن
gymnasium (gym) *n* جمنازیوم
gymnast *n* ورزشکار جمناستیک
gymnastics *n* ورزش جمناستیک
gypsy *n* کوچی

H

habit *n* عادت

habitable *adj* قابل سکونت

habitual *adj* عادتی، همیشگی

hack *v* هک کردن کمپیوتر

hacker *v* هکر

haggle *v* چانه زدن

hair *n* مو

hairbrush *n* برس مو

haircut *n* اصلاح مو

hairdresser *n* سلمان

hairstyle *n* مُدل مو

hairy *adj* مودار

half *adv* بطور ناقص

half *adj* نصف

half *n* نیمه

half-hearted *adj* نیمه دل، دودلی

halftime *n* نیمه کاره

hall *n* سالون

hallucinate *v* هذیان گفتن

hallway *n* راهرو

halt *v* متوقف کردن

halve *v* نصف کردن

ham *n* گوشت خوک

hamburger *n* همبرگر

hammer *n* چکش

hammer *v* چکش زدن

hammock *n* چکش

hamper *n* زنبیل، سبد بزرگ

hand *n* دست

hand down *pv* منتقل کردن

hand in *pv* دادن، سپردن

hand out *pv* تقسیم کردن

hand over *pv* تحویل دادن

handbag *n* دستکول

handbook *n* کتاب رهنما

handcuff *v* دستبند

handcuffs *n* زولانه

handful *n* شمار محدود؛ مقدار کم

handgun *n* تفنگ دستی

handicap *n* معلولیت

handicapped *adj* معلول

handkerchief *n* دستمال

handle *n* دسته

handle *v* رسیدگی کردن

handmade *adj* دست ساخته

handout *n* خیرات؛ جزوه معلوماتی

handrail *n* دستگیره کناره

handshake *n* قول دادن

handsome *adj* مقبول، جذاب

handwriting *n* دست خط

handy *adj* آماده

hang *v* آویزان کرده

hang around *pv* در همانجا باشید

hang on *pv* صبر کن

hang up *pv* بمانید

hanger *n* کودبند لباس

hang-up *n* خوف

happen *v* اتفاق افتادن

happening *n* رویداد

happiness *n* خوشحالی

happy *adj* خوشحال

harass v اذیت کردن	hatch v تخم گذاشتن
harassment n اذیت و آزار	hatchet n تیشه
harbor n بندرگاه	hate n نفرت
hard adv در مضیقه	hate v نفرت داشتن
hard adj سخت؛ مشکل	hateful adj متنفر
harden v سخت کردن	hatred n تنفر
hardly adv به سختی	haul v حمل و نقل
hardship n مشقت، سختی	haunt v مراجعه کردن
hardware n سخت افزار کمپیوتر	haunted adj رفت و آمد زیاد
hard-working adj زحمتکش	have v داشتن
hardy adj مقاوم	haven n پناهگاه
hare n خرگوش	havoc n ویرانی
harm n ضرر	hawk n شاهین
harm v ضرر رساندن	hay n کاه
harmful adj مضر	haystack n انبار کاه
harmless adj بی ضرر	hazard n خطر
harmonize v همآهنگ کردن	hazardous adj خطرناک
harmony n همآهنگی	haze n بخار، غبار
harp n آله موسیقی هارپ	hazelnut n یکنوع خسته
harpoon n نیزه	hazy adj غبار آلود؛ مبهم
harrowing adj ترسناک	he pron آن مرد
harsh adj زشت، خشن	head n سر
harshly adv به زشتی	head for pv روانه شدن
harvest v جمع آوری محصولات	headache n سردرد
harvest n حاصلات	heading n عنوان
hassle n عذاب	headlight n چراغ پیشرو
hassle v عذاب دادن	headphones n گوشکی تیلفون
haste n عجله، شتاب	headquarters n دفتر مرکزی
hasten v شتاب کردن	headset n گوشکی
hastily adv به عجله	heal v شفا یافتن
hasty adj شتاب زده	health n صحت
hat n کلاه	healthcare n مراقبت صحی

H

healthy *adj* صحتمند	**hell** *n* دوزخ
heap *n* انبار	**hello** *e* سلام
heap *v* انبار کردن	**helmet** *n* کلاه آهنی
hear *v* شنیدن	**help** *n* کمک
hearing *n* استماعیه	**help** *v* کمک کردن
hearsay *n* شایعه	**helper** *n* یاور، کمک کننده
heart *n* قلب	**helpful** *adj* مفید
heartbeat *n* ضربان قلب	**helpless** *adj* درمانده، ناامید
heartbreak *n* قلب شکستگی	**hem** *n* لبه، دامنه
heartbroken *adj* قلب شکسته	**hen** *n* مرغ ماکیان
heartfelt *adj* از عمق قلب	**hence** *adv* بنابراین
heartless *adj* بی احساس	**her** *adj* آن زن
hearty *adj* دلچسپ	**her** *pron* آن زن را
heat *n* حرارت	**herb** *n* گیاه
heat *v* حرارت دادن	**herd** *v* جمع شدن
heater *n* بخاری	**herd** *n* گله
heating *n* سیستم گرم کننده	**here** *adv* اینجا
heatstroke *n* گرمازدگی	**hereafter** *adv* بعد ازاین
heaven *n* بهشت	**hereby** *adv* بدینوسیله
heavenly *adj* بهشتی	**hereditary** *adj* ارثی
heaviness *n* سنگینی، وزن زیاد	**heritage** *n* میراث
heavy *adj* سنگین	**hermit** *n* گوشه نشین
hectic *adj* تقسیم اوقات مصروف	**hero** *n* قهرمان
heed *v* توجه	**heroic** *adj* قهرمانانه
heel *n* کوری پا	**heroism** *n* قهرمانی
height *n* بلندی	**hers** *pron* از آن زن
heighten *v* بلند کردن	**herself** *pron* او خودش
heinous *adj* شنیع، زشت	**hesitant** *adj* دو دل
heir *n* وارث	**hesitate** *v* دو دله بودن
heiress *n* وارث زن	**hesitation** *n* تردید
heist *n* سرقت	**hey** *e* هی
helicopter *n* هلیکوپتر	**heyday** *n* روز های اوج خوشبختی

H

hi *e* سلام	hint *n* اشاره، تذكر
hibernate *v* به خواب زمستانی رفتن	hip *n* لگن خاصره
hiccup *n* عکک زدن	hire *v* استخدام کردن
hidden *adj* پنهان	his *adj* از آن مرد
hide *v* پنهان کردن	his *pron* از آن مرد
hideaway *n* مخفیگاه	hiss *v* خش خش کردن
hideous *adj* زشت	historian *n* تاریخ نویس
hierarchy *n* سلسله مراتب	historical *adj* تاریخی
high *adj* بلند؛ بیشتر از حد معمول	history *n* تاریخ
high *adv* به بلندی	hit *n* اصابت؛ آهنگ مشهور
high school *n* لیسه	hit *v* زدن
highlight *n* برجسته	hitch *n* مانع
highlight *v* نکات مهم را نشانی کردن	hitchhike *n* مسافرت رایگان
highly *adv* به شدت	hive *n* محل نگهداری زنبور عسل
high-tech *adj* تکنولوژی بالا	hoard *v* احتکار کردن
highway *n* شاهراه	hoarse *adj* خشن
hijack *v* هواپیما ربایی	hoax *n* شوخی فریب آمیز
hijacker *n* هواپیما ربا	hobby *n* سرگرمی
hike *n* کوهنوردی	hockey *n* بازی هاکی
hike *v* کوهنوردی کردن	hog *n* خوک
hilarious *adj* خنده دار	hoist *v* برافراشتن
hill *n* تپه	hold *v* برگزار کردن
hillside *n* دامنه تپه	hold *n* نگهداری
hilltop *n* سر تپه	hold back *pv* مانع شدن
hilly *adj* تپه ای	hold on to *pv* منتظر چیزی بودن
him *pron* آن مرد	hold out *pv* تحمل کن
himself *pron* او مرد خودش	hold up *pv* صبر کن
hinder *v* مانع شدن	hold-up *n* دزدی؛ عقب مانی
hindrance *n* عقب مانی	hole *n* سوراخ
hindsight *n* واپس نگری	holiday *n* رخصتی
hinge *n* چپراس دروازه	hollow *adj* خالی
hint *v* اشاره کردن، تذکر دادن	holy *adj* مقدس

homage n ادای احترام

home adj بطرف خانه

home n خانه

home adv مسکن

homeland n وطن

homeless adj بی خانه

homely adj خانگی

homemade adj پخته شده در خانه

homesick adj دلتنگ وطن

hometown n زادگاه

homework n کارخانگی

homicide n قتل

honest adj صادق

honestly adv به صداقت

honesty n صداقت

honey n عسل

honeymoon n ماه عسل

honk v صدای هارن موتر

honor n افتخار

hood n بانت موتر؛ پوز پیچ

hoodlum n اوباش

hoof n قسمت برامدگی پای اسب

hook n چنگک

hoop n حلقه

hop v خیز و جست

hope n امید

hope v امید کردن

hopeful adj امیدوار

hopefully adv به امید اینکه

hopeless adj ناامید

horizon n افق

horizontal adj افقی

horn n شاخ حیوان؛ هارن موتر

horrendous adj وحشتناک

horrible adj ترسناک

horrific adj خوفناک

horrify v ترساندن

horror n وحشت

horse n اسب

hose n پایپ آب

hospital n شفاخانه

hospitality n مهمان نوازی

hospitalize v بستری شدن در شفاخانه

host n مهماندار

hostage n اسیر

hostess n مهماندار زن

hostile adj خصومت آمیز

hostility n خصومت

hot adj داغ؛ تند و تیز

hotdog n هات داگ

hotel n هوتل

hour n ساعت

hourly adv ساعت وار

house n خانه

household n خانواده

housekeeper n خانه سامان

housewife n خانم خانه

housework n کارخانه

hover v در هوا گشت زدن

how adv چطور

however adv با آنهم

however conj باوجوداینکه

howl n فریاد

howl v قوله کشیدن

hub *n* مرکز
huddle *v* جمع شدن
hug *n* آغوش
hug *v* در آغوش گرفتن
huge *adj* بزرگ
hull *n* قشر؛ پوست نخود یا لوبیا
hum *v* زمزمه کردن
human *n* انسان
human *adj* انسانی
humane *adj* مهربان، با مروت
humankind *n* بشر
humble *adj* متواضع؛ ساده یا غریب
humbly *adv* به تواضع
humid *adj* مرطوب
humidity *n* رطوبت
humiliate *v* تحقیر کردن
humility *n* تواضع
humor *n* شوخ طبعی
humorous *adj* شوخ طبع
hump *n* برآمده گی
hunch *n* احساس بوقوع پیوستن چیزی
hunchback *n* برامده گی پشت
hunched *adj* برامده
hundred *n* صد
hundredth *adj* صدم
hunger *n* گرسنگی
hungry *adj* گرسنه
hunt *v* شکار کردن
hunter *n* شکارچی
hunting *n* شکار
hurdle *n* مانع
hurl *v* پرتاب کردن

hurricane *n* گردباد
hurriedly *adv* به عجله
hurry *n* عجله
hurry *v* عجله کردن
hurt *adj* زخمی
hurt *v* صدمه رساندن
hurtful *adj* آزار دهنده
husband *n* شوهر
hush *v* ساکت کردن
husky *adj* نیرومند
hustle *v* شتاب
hut *n* کلبه
hyena *n* آدم درنده خو
hygiene *n* حفظ الصحه
hymn *n* سرود
hyphen *n* خط ربط
hypnosis *n* هپنوتیزم، خواب مصنوعی
hypnotize *v* بطور مصنوعی خواب کردن
hypocrisy *n* دورویی
hypocrite *n* منافق
hypothesis *n* فرضیه
hypothetical *adj* فرضی
hysteria *n* تشنج
hysterical *adj* متشنج

I

I *pron* من

ice *n* يخ

ice cream *n* آیسکریم

ice cube *n* توته یخ

ice skate *v* بازی روی یخ

iceberg *n* کنده یخ

icebox *n* صندوق یخ

ice-cold *adj* بسیار سرد

icicle *n* قندیل یخ

icon *n* الگو، آیکن

icy *adj* پوشیده از یخ

idea *n* مفکوره

ideal *adj* دلخواه

identical *adj* مشابه

identification *n* هویت

identify *v* شناسایی کردن

identity *n* هویت

ideology *n* طرز تفکر

idiom *n* اصطلاح

idiot *n* احمق

idiotic *adj* احمقانه

idol *n* بُت

idolize *v* بُت ساختن و پرستیدن

if *conj* اگر

ignite *v* روشن کردن

ignition *n* آتش سوزی

ignorance *n* جهل؛ نادانی

ignorant *adj* جاهل؛ نادان

ignore *v* چشم پوشی کردن

ill *adj* مریض

illegal *adj* غیرقانونی

illegally *adv* بطور غیرقانونی

illegible *adj* غیرقابل خواندن

illicit *adj* نامشروع

illiterate *adj* بیسواد

illness *n* مریضی

illogical *adj* غیرمنطقی

illuminate *v* روشن کردن

illusion *n* خیال

illustrate *v* بیان کردن

illustration *n* شرح با تصویر

illustrious *adj* برجسته

image *n* تصویر

imaginary *adj* خیالی

imagination *n* تخیل

imagine *v* تصور کردن

imbalance *n* عدم توازن

imitate *v* تقلید کردن

imitation *n* تقلید

immaculate *adj* معصوم

immature *adj* نابالغ

immaturity *n* عدم بلوغ

immediate *adj* فوری

immediately *adv* فوراً

immense *adj* بزرگ

immerse *v* غوطه کردن

immersion *n* غوطه وری

immigrant *n* مهاجر

immigrate *v* مهاجرت کردن

immigration *n* مهاجرت

imminent *adj* قریب الوقوع

immobile *adj* بی حرکت	**importance** *n* اهمیت
immobilize *v* بی حرکت کردن	**important** *adj* مهم
immoral *adj* غیراخلاقی	**impose** *v* تحمیل کردن
immortal *adj* جاویدان	**imposing** *adj* تحمیلی
immune *adj* مصون	**impossibility** *n* عدم امکان
immunity *n* معافیت، مصوونیت	**impossible** *adj* غیرممکن
immunize *v* واکسین کردن	**impound** *v* توقیف کردن
impact *n* تاثیر	**impoverished** *adj* فقیر
impact *v* تاثیر کردن	**impractical** *adj* غیرعملی
impair *v* مختل کردن	**imprecise** *adj* مبهم
impartial *adj* بیطرف	**impress** *v* تاثیر گذاشتن
impatience *n* بی حوصلگی	**impression** *n* تاثیر گذاری
impatient *adj* بی حوصله	**impressive** *adj* تاثیر گذار
impeccable *adj* بی عیب و نقص	**imprison** *v* زندانی کردن
impediment *n* مانع	**improbable** *adj* غیر محتمل
impending *adj* قریب الوقوع	**improper** *adj* نامناسب
imperfection *n* نقص	**improve** *v* تقویت کردن
impersonal *adj* غیرشخصی	**improvement** *n* بهبود
impersonate *v* جعل هویت کردن، تقلید کسی را کردن	**improvise** *v* تعبیه کردن
	impulse *n* انگیزه
impertinence *n* بی حیابی	**impulsive** *adj* انگیزه آور
impertinent *adj* بی حیا	**impure** *adj* ناپاک، ناخالص
impetuous *adj* تکان دهنده	**in** *adv* داخل
implant *v* کاشتن	**in** *prep* در داخل
implement *v* تطبیق کردن	**in depth** *adv* در عمق
implicate *v* دلالت کردن	**inability** *n* ناتوانی
implication *n* پیامد	**inaccessible** *adj* غیرقابل دسترس
implicit *adj* ضمنی	**inaccurate** *adj* نادرست
implore *v* التماس کردن	**inactive** *adj* غیرفعال
imply *v* اشاره کردن	**inadequate** *adj* غیرکافی
impolite *adj* بی ادب	**inadequately** *adv* بصورت غیر بسنده
import *v* وارد کردن	

inappropriate *adj* نامناسب	**incompetent** *adj* بی کفایت
inappropriately *adv* بطور نامناسب	**incomplete** *adj* ناتکمیل
inaugurate *v* افتتاح کردن	**inconsiderate** *adj* بی تفاوت
inauguration *n* افتتاح	**inconsistent** *adj* بی ربط
inbox *n* صندوق دریافت پیام	**inconvenient** *adj* ناراحت کننده
incalculable *adj* غیرقابل محاسبه	**incorrect** *adj* نادرست
incapable *adj* ناتوان	**increase** *n* افزایش
incapacitate *v* ناتوان ساختن	**increase** *v* افزایش دادن
incarcerate *v* حبس کردن	**increasing** *adj* روز افزون
incense *n* خوشبویی	**incredible** *adj* عالی، فوق العاده
incentive *n* تشویقی	**increment** *n* افزایش
inception *n* آغاز	**incriminate** *v* متهم کردن
incessant *adj* بی وقفه	**incur** *v* متحمل شدن
inch *n* اینچ	**incurable** *adj* غیرقابل علاج
incident *n* حادثه	**indecency** *n* بی حیایی، بی نزاکتی
incidentally *adv* اتفاقاً	**indecision** *n* تردید، بی تصمیمی
incinerator *n* زباله سوز	**indecisive** *adj* مترددد، بی تصمیم
incite *v* تحریک کردن	**indeed** *adv* واقعاً
incitement *n* تحریک	**indefinite** *adj* نامعین
inclination *n* تمایل	**indefinitely** *adv* بطور نامحدود
incline *v* خم کردن	**indent** *v* برجسته کردن
inclined *adj* شیب دار، خم شده	**independence** *n* استقلال
include *v* شامل ساختن	**independent** *adj* مستقل
including *prep* بشمول	**in-depth** *adj* در عمق
inclusive *adv* مشمول	**index** *n* فهرست مطالب
incoherent *adj* ناسازگار	**indicate** *v* نشان دادن
incoherently *adv* بطور بی ربط	**indication** *n* نشانه
income *n* عاید	**indicator** *n* نشان دهنده
incoming *adj* ورودی، آینده	**indifference** *n* بی تفاوتی
incompatibility *n* عدم تطابق	**indifferent** *adj* بی تفاوت
incompatible *adj* بی تطابق	**indigestion** *n* سوء هاضمه
incompetence *n* بی کفایتی	**indirect** *adj* غیرمستقیم

indiscreet *adj* بی احتیاط	infection *n* عفونت
indispensable *adj* ضروری، حتمی	infectious *adj* عفونی
indisposed *adj* بی اختیار	infer *v* نتیجه گیری کردن
indisputable *adj* بی چون و چرا	inferior *adj* نامرغوب، پست تر
individual *adj* انفرادی	infested *adj* آلوده
individual *n* فرد	infiltrate *v* نفوذ کردن
individually *adv* بصورت انفرادی	infinite *adj* بی انتها
indivisible *adj* غیرقابل تقسیم	infinitely *adv* بی نهایت
indoor *adj* سرپوشیده	inflammation *n* التهاب
indoors *adv* در داخل خانه	inflate *v* باد کردن
induce *v* وادار کردن	inflation *n* تورم
indulge *v* افراط کردن	inflexible *adj* انعطاف ناپذیر
indulgent *adj* زیاده رو	inflict *v* تحمیل کردن
industrious *adj* کوشا	influence *n* نفوذ
industry *n* صنعت	influential *adj* پرنفوذ
ineffective *adj* غیرموثر	inform *v* اطلاع دادن
inefficient *adj* ناکارا	informal *adj* غیررسمی
inequality *n* عدم مساوات	informant *n* مطلع
inevitable *adj* اجتناب ناپذیر، حتمی الوقوع	information *n* معلومات
inevitably *adv* بصورت اجتناب ناپذیر	informer *n* خبررسان
inexcusable *adj* غیرقابل بخشش	infrequent *adj* نادر، کمیاب
inexpensive *adj* ارزان	infuriate *v* خشگین کردن
inexperienced *adj* بی تجربه	ingenious *adj* با هوش
inexplicable *adj* غیرقابل توضیح	ingenuity *n* نبوغ
infallible *adj* مصوون از خطا	ingest *v* خوردن، قورت کردن
infamous *adj* بدنام	ingredient *n* ترکیبات
infancy *n* دوران نوزادی	inhabit *v* ساکن بودن
infant *n* نوزاد	inhabitable *adj* قابل رهایش
infect *v* مکروبی شدن	inhabitant *n* باشنده، ساکن
infected *adj* عفونی شده، مکروبی شده	inhale *v* تنفس کردن
	inherit *v* به میراث بردن
	inheritance *n* وراثت، میراث

inhibit v مانع شدن
inhuman adj غیرانسانی
initial n اولین قسمت
initial v در آغاز قرار دادن
initial adj نخستین
initially adv در ابتدا
initials n حروف اول نام
initiate v آغاز کردن
initiation n آغاز
initiative n ابتکار
inject v پیچکاری کردن
injection n پیچکاری
injure v زخمی کردن
injured adj زخمی
injury n جراحت
injustice n بی عدالتی
ink n رنگ
inland adj داخل کشور
inland adv درون مرزی
in-laws n اعضای فامیل همسر
inn n مسافرخانه
inner adj داخلی
innocence n معصومیت
innocent adj معصوم
innovation n ابتکار
input n پول تحویل داده شده
inquire v جویا شدن
inquiry n استعلام
inquisitive adj کنجکاو
insane adj دیوانه وار
insanity n دیوانگی
insatiable adj سیر نشدنی

inscription n سنگ نوشته
insect n حشره
insecure adj غیرمصوون
insecurity n عدم مصوونیت
insensitive adj بی حس
inseparable adj غیرقابل تجزیه
insert v داخل کردن
insertion n درج، دخول
inside prep در داخل
inside adv درون
inside adj قسمت داخلی
inside out adv پشت و رو
insignificant adj ناچیز
insincere adj غیرصمیمی
insinuate v تلقین کردن، به اشاره فهماندن
insinuation n تلقین
insist v تأکید کردن
insolent adj گستاخ
insomnia n بی خوابی
inspect v تفتیش کردن
inspection n تفتیش
inspector n مفتش
inspiration n الهام
inspire v تشویق کردن
instability n بی ثباتی
install v نصب کردن
installation n تاسیسات
installment n قسط
instance n مثال
instant n فوری
instantly adv فوراً

instead *adv* به عوض	intensity *n* شدت
instead *prep* در عوض	intensive *adj* تشدیدی
instigate *v* تحریک کردن	intensively *adv* بصورت تشدیدی
instill *v* چکاندن	intention *n* قصد، مقصد
instinct *n* غریزه	intentional *adj* قصدی، عمدی
institute *v* تشکیل دادن	interact *v* تعامل داشتن
institution *n* موسسه	interaction *n* عمل متقابل
instruct *v* هدایت دادن	interactive *adj* در تماس بودن
instruction *n* هدایات	intercept *v* قطع کردن، جدا کردن
instructor *n* مربی	interchange *v* معاوضه کردن
instrument *n* وسیله	interest *n* سود؛ علاقمندی
instrumental *adj* سودمند	interest *v* علاقمند ساختن
insufficient *adj* ناکافی	interested *adj* علاقمند
insulate *v* عایق کاری کردن، جلوگیری از آمدن صدا	interesting *adj* جالب
insulation *n* عایق کاری	interfere *v* مداخله کردن
insult *n* توهین	interference *n* مداخله
insult *v* توهین کردن	interior *adj* قسمت داخلی
insurance *n* بیمه	intermediate *adj* متوسطه
insure *v* بیمه کردن	intern *v* کارآموز
intact *adj* سالم	internal *adj* داخلی
integrate *v* مدغم کردن	internally *adv* درونی
integration *n* ادغام	international *adj* بین المللی
integrity *n* یکپارچگی، اتحاد	internet *n* انترنیت
intelligence *n* ذکاوت	interpret *v* ترجمه کردن
intelligent *adj* ذکی	interpretation *n* تفسیر، ترجمه
intelligently *adv* با ذکاوت	interpreter *n* مترجم شفاهی
intend *v* قصد داشتن	interrogate *v* تحقیق کردن
intense *adj* شدید	interrupt *v* گپ کسی را قطع کردن
intensely *adv* به شدت	interruption *n* انقطاع
intensify *v* شدید ساختن، تشدید کردن	intersect *v* از وسط قطع کردن
	intersection *n* چهارراهی
	intertwine *v* درهم تنیده

interval *n* وقفه	invention *n* اختراع
intervene *v* مداخله کردن	inventory *n* لست اجناس
interview *n* مصاحبه	invest *v* سرمایه گذاری کردن
interview *v* مصاحبه کردن	investigate *v* تحقیق کردن
intestine *n* روده	investigation *n* تحقیق
intimacy *n* صمیمیت	investment *n* سرمایه گذاری
intimate *adj* صمیمی	investor *n* سرمایه گذار
intimidate *v* ترساندن	invincible *adj* شکست ناپذیر
into *prep* بداخل	invisible *adj* غیرقابل دید
intolerable *adj* غیرقابل تحمل	invitation *n* دعوتنامه
intolerance *n* عدم تحمل	invite *v* دعوت کردن
intrepid *adj* بی باک	invoice *n* صورت حساب
intricate *adj* پیچیده	invoke *v* دعا کردن، استدعا کردن
intrigue *n* فتنه	involve *v* دخیل بودن
intriguing *adj* جذاب	involved *adj* دخیل
introduce *v* معرفی کردن	involvement *n* سهمگیری
introduction *n* معرفی	inward *adj* بطرف داخل
introvert *adj* خویشتن گرای	inwards *adv* به داخل
intrude *v* مزاحم شدن	irate *adj* خشگمین
intruder *n* مزاحم	iron *v* اطو کردن
intrusion *n* نفوذ	iron *n* آهن؛ اوطو
intuition *n* بینش	ironic *adj* طعنه آمیز
inundate *v* غرق شدن	ironing board *n* تخته اطو کاری
invade *v* حمله کردن	irony *n* طعنه
invader *n* مهاجم	irrational *adj* غیرمنطقی
invalid *adj* بی اعتبار	irrationally *adv* بطور غیر منطقی
invalid *n* ناتوان	irrefutable *adj* ابطال ناپذیر
invalidate *v* بی اعتبار ساختن	irregular *adj* غیرمنظم
invaluable *adj* ارزشمند	irrelevant *adj* بی ربط
invariably *adv* همواره	irresistible *adj* غیرقابل مقاومت
invasion *n* هجوم	irresponsible *adj* غیرمسوول
invent *v* اختراع کردن	irreversible *adj* برگشت ناپذیر

irrigate v آبیاری کردن
irrigation n آبیاری
irritate v ناراحت ساختن
irritating adj ناراحت کننده
Islam n اسلام
Islamic adj اسلامی
island n جزیره
isle n راهرو
isolate v منزوی کردن
isolation n انزوا
issue v صادر کردن
issue n مسئله؛ جلد یا شماره مجله
it pron این
italics adj کج
itch v خاریدن
itchy adj خارش دار
item n جزء، فقره، شی
itemize v جزبه جز نوشتن
itinerary n برنامه سفر
its adj از این
itself pron خودش
ivory n دندان فیل
ivy n یکنوع بته

J

jab v ضربه زدن
jacket n بالاپوش
jackpot n برنده تمام پول
jagged adj ناهموار

jaguar n پلنگ خالدار
jail n زندان
jail v زندانی کردن
jam n مربا؛ راه بندان؛ وضعیت دشوار
jam v مسدود کردن
janitor n خدمتگار
January n جنوری
jar n مرتبان
jasmine n گُل یاسمن
jaw n الاشه
jazz n آله موسیقی جاز
jealous adj حسود
jealousy n حسد
jeans n پتلون کاوبای
jelly n جیلی
jellyfish n عروس دریایی
jeopardize v به خطر انداختن
jerk v تکان دادن
jerk n تکان ناگهانی؛ آدم فریبکار
jersey n پیراهن ورزشی
jet n طیاره جیت
Jew n یهودی
jewel n جواهر
jeweler n جواهر فروش
jewelry n طلا فروشی؛ جواهر
jewelry store n دوکان جواهر فروشی
Jewish adj یهودی
jigsaw n اره کوچک برقی
job n وظیفه
jobless adj بیکار
jog v دویدن

join v پیوستن	**jump** n پرش
joint n مفصل	**jump** v پرش کردن
jointly adv مشترکاً	**jump rope** adj
joke v شوخی کردن	ریسمان برای ریسمان بازی
joke n شوخی، فکاهی	**jumpy** adj پرشی
joker n آدم شوخ	**junction** n اتصال
jokingly adv به شوخی	**June** n ماه جون
jolly adj خوشحال	**jungle** n جنگل
jolt n تکان	**junior** adj پایین رتبه
jolt v تکان دادن	**junk** n اشیای بیکاره
journal n ژورنال صحی؛ کتابچه یادداشت	**junk** v دور انداختن
journalist n ژورنالیست	**Jupiter** n سیاره مشتری
journey n سفر	**jury** n هیئت داوران
jovial adj خوشحال	**just** adj عادلانه
joy n لذت	**just** adv فقط؛ فقط همین حالا
joyful adj لذت بخش	**justice** n عدالت
joyfully adv با خوشحالی	**justification** n توجیه
joystick n جوی ستیک، یکنوع آله بازی	**justify** v توجیه کردن
jubilant adj نشاط آور	**justly** adv بطور عادلانه
Judaism n یهودیت	**juvenile** adj خوردسال
judge n قاضی؛ داور	**juvenile** n نوجوان
judge v قضاوت کردن	
judgment n قضاوت	
jug n جک آب	# K
juggle v شعبده بازی کردن	
juggler n شعبده باز	**kangaroo** n کانگرو
juice n جوس	**karate** n کاراته
juicy adj آبدار	**keep** v نگهداشتن
July n جولای	**keep on** pv ادامه دادن
jumbo adj آدم نیرومند و خشن	**keep out** pv دور نگهداشتن
	keep up pv ادامه دادن

kennel *n* خانه سگ یا پشک

ketchup *v* کیچپ

kettle *n* چاینک

key *n* کلید دروازه؛
کلید وسایل موسیقی؛ راز موفقیت

key ring *n* کلید بند

keyboard *n* کیبورد

kick *n* لگد

kick *v* لگد زدن

kickback *n* بازپرداخت

kickoff *n* شروع

kid *v* شوخی کردن

kid *n* طفل

kidnap *v* اختطاف کردن

kidnapper *n* اختطاف کننده

kidney *n* گُرده

kill *v* کشتن

killer *n* قاتل

killing *n* قتل

kilogram (kilo) *n* کیلوگرام

kilometer *n* کیلومتر

kilowatt *n* کیلووات

kind *adj* مهربان

kind *n* نوع

kindle *v* روشن شدن

kindly *adv* به مهربانی

kindness *n* مهربانی

king *n* پادشاه

kingdom *n* شاهی

kiss *n* بوسه

kiss *v* بوسیدن

kitchen *n* آشپزخانه

kite *n* کاغذپران

kitten *n* چوچه پشک

knead *v* خمیرکردن

knee *n* زانو

kneecap *n* عینک زانو

kneel *v* زانو زدن

knife *n* چاقو

knight *n* قهرمان

knit *v* بافتن

knob *n* دستگیر دروازه

knock *v* تک تک کردن

knock *n* ضربه

knot *n* گره

know *v* فهمیدن

know-how *n* اطلاعات

knowingly *adv* آگاهانه

knowledge *n* دانش

knuckle *n* بند انگشت

L

label *n* لیبل

label *v* لیبل زدن

labor *n* کارگر

laboratory *n* لابراتوار

labyrinth *n* پیچیدگی

lace *n* بند بوت؛ فیته

lack *n* فقدان

lack *v* نبودن

lacrosse *n* نوع بازی

ladder n زینه	**lash** n شلاق
laden adj مملو	**lash** v شلاق زدن
ladle n ملاقه	**lash out** pv شلاق زدن
lady n خانم	**lasso** v با ریسمان زدن
ladylike adj زنانه	**lasso** n ریسمان اسب
lagoon n جهیل کوچک	**last** adj آخر
lake n جهیل بزرگ	**last** adv آخرین
lamb n گوشت بره	**last** v دوام کردن
lame adj لنگ	**last** n طاقت
lament v تأسف خوردن	**last name** n تخلص
lamp n چراغ	**last night** adv شب گذشته
lamppost n چراغ کنار جاده	**lasting** adj با دوام
lampshade n چراغ خواب	**lastly** adv سرانجام
land n زمین	**latch** n قفل دروازه
land v نشست کردن بر زمین	**late** adj دیر
landfill n محل دفن کثافات	**late** adv ناوقت
landing n نشست طیاره	**lately** adv در این اواخر
landlady n خانم صاحب خانه	**later** adv بعد ها
landlord n صاحب خانه	**later** adj بعداً
landscape n منظره	**lateral** adj جانبی، افقی
lane n کوچه؛ سرک فرعی	**latest** adj آخرین، تازه
language n لسان، زبان	**lather** n کف کردن صابون
languish v پژمرده شدن	**latitude** n عرض، وسعت
lantern n اریکین	**latter** adj آخری
lap n دامن؛ دور مسابقه	**laugh** n خنده
lapse n لغزش	**laugh** v خندیدن
laptop n لپ تاپ	**laughable** adj خنده آور
larceny n سرقت، خیانت	**laughing stock** n مضمون خنده
lard n گوشت خوک	**laughter** n خنده
large adj بزرگ	**launch** v شروع کردن، بکار انداختن
largely adv اکثراً	**laundry** n لباس شویی
laser n لایزر	**lavatory** n تشناب

L

lavish *adj* مجلل	**leap** *v* خیز و جست کردن
law *n* قانون	**leap year** *n* سال کبیسه
lawful *adj* قانونی	**learn** *v* آموختن
lawmaker *n* قانونگذار	**learner** *n* دانش آموز
lawn *n* چمن	**learning** *n* آموزش
lawnmower *n* ماشین قطع سبزه	**lease** *n* اجاره
lawsuit *n* دعوی حقوقی	**lease** *v* به کرایه گرفتن
lawyer *n* حقوقدان	**leash** *n* ریسمان سگ
laxative *adj* نرم کننده	**least** *pron* اقلاً
lay *v* دراز کشیدن	**least** *adj* کمترین
lay off *pv* اخراج کردن	**least** *adv* کوچکترین
layer *n* لایه	**leather** *n* چرم
layout *n* طرح؛ طرح بندی	**leave** *v* ترک کردن؛ رها کردن
laziness *n* تنبلی	**leave out** *pv* کنار گذاشتن
lazy *adj* تنبل	**leaves** *n* برگها
lead *v* رهبری کردن؛ پیشتاز	**lecture** *n* لکچر
lead *n* سُرب؛ قسمت نخست	**lecture** *v* لکچر دادن
leader *n* رهبر	**lecturer** *n* استاد پوهنتون
leadership *n* رهبری	**ledge** *n* طاقچه
leading *adj* پیشتاز	**ledger** *n* کتاب ثبت
leaf *n* برگ	**leech** *n* ظالم
leaflet *n* رساله	**left** *adj* باقیمانده
league *n* لیگ، تیم ورزشی	**left** *n* چپ
leak *v* ریختن	**left** *adv* طرف چپ
leak *n* سوراخ	**leftovers** *n* پس مانده غذا
leakage *n* سوراخ	**leg** *n* پای حیوان؛ پایه میز
lean *v* تکیه کردن	**legacy** *n* میراث
lean *adj* لاغر، نازک	**legal** *adj* قانونی
lean back *pv* به پشت تکیه کردن	**legalize** *v* قانونی ساختن
lean on *pv* بالای چیزی تکیه کردن	**legally** *adv* از لحاظ قانونی
leaning *n* تمایل	**legend** *n* افسانه
leap *n* خیز و جست	**legendary** *adj* افسانوی

L

legible adj خوانا، قابل خواندن
legislate v طرح قانون
legislation n قانونگذاری
legislative adj تقنینی
legislature n قوه مقننه
legitimate adj مشروع
leisure n اوقات فراغت
lemon n لیمو
lemonade n آب لیمو
lend v قرض دادن
length n طول
lengthen v طولانی کردن
lengthy adj طویل
leniency n نرمش، ملایمت
lenient adj نرم، ملایم
lens n لینز
Lent n ماه روزه
lentil n عدس
leopard n پلنگ
leper n جذامی
leprosy n مرض جذام
less pron اندک
less adj کمتر
less adv کوچکتر
lessen v کم کردن
lesser adj کوچک
lesson n درس
let v اجازه دادن
let down pv رها کردن
let go pv رهایی
let in pv اجازه دادن به داخل
let out pv رها کردن

lethal adj کشنده
letter n نامه، مکتوب؛ حرف الفبا
lettuce n کاهو
level n دسته
level v هموار کردن
lever n دسته، بازو
leverage n قدرت نفوذ
levy v وضع مالیات
lewd adj بی حیا
liability n مسوولیت
liable adj مسوول
liar adj دروغگو
libel n تهمت، توهین
liberal adj آزادیخواه
liberate v آزاد کردن
liberty n آزادی
librarian n کتابخانه دار
library n کتابخانه
lice n شپش
license v جواز دادن
license n جواز رانندگی، لایسنس
license plate n لایسنس پلیت
lick v لیسیدن
lid n سرپوش
lie v دراز کشیدن؛ دروغ گفتن
lie n دروغ
lieutenant n خورد ضابط
life n زندگی
life jacket n واسکت نجات
lifeguard n
نجات دهنده در حوض آببازی
lifeless adj بی جان

L

lifestyle *n* سبک زندگی	limp *v* لنگیدن
lifetime *adj* حیات، عمر	line *n* خط؛ قطار مردم؛ لین تیلفون
lift *v* بلند کردن	line up *pv* به صف شدن
lift-off *n* از زمین بلند کردن	linen *n* تکه کتان
ligament *n* بند استخوان	linger *v* معطل شدن
light *n* چراغ	lingering *adj* ماندنی، معطل شونده
light *v* روشن کردن	lining *n* استر، پوشش
light *adj* روشن؛ سبک	link *v* رابطه دادن
light bulb *n* گروپ	link *n* رابطه؛ اتصال
lighten *v* روشن ساختن	lion *n* شیر
lighter *n* لایتر سگرت	lip *n* لب
lighthouse *n* برج کنترول کشتی ها	lipstick *n* لبسیرین
lighting *n* روشنایی	liquid *adj* آبگونه
lightly *adv* بطور خفیف	liquid *n* مایع
lightning *n* الماسک	liquor *n* مشروب
lightweight *n* سبک وزن	list *n* لست
likable *adj* دوست داشتنی	list *v* لست نوشتن
like *v* خوش داشتن	listen *v* گوش دادن
like *prep* مانند	listener *n* شنونده
like *adj* مثل	liter *n* لیتر
like *conj* مشابه	literal *adj* تحت اللفظی
likelihood *n* احتمال	literally *adv* لفظاً
likely *adv* احتمالاً	literate *adj* باسواد
likeness *n* شباهت	literature *n* ادبیات
likewise *adv* به همین ترتیب	litter *n* کثافات؛ حیوان کوچک
liking *n* تمایل	little *adv* اندک
limb *n* عضو بدن	little *adj* کم
lime *n* لیموی سبز	little *pron* کوچک
limit *n* حد	live *v* زندگی کردن
limit *v* محدود کردن	live *adj* شخص زنده؛ نشرات زنده
limitation *n* محدوده	live off *pv* زندگی کردن
limp *n* لنگ	livelihood *n* معیشت

L

lively *adj* زنده دل	**log in** *pv* داخل شدن به محل کار
liver *n* جگر	**log off** *pv* رخصت شدن از کار
livestock *n* مالداری	**logic** *n* منطق
livid *adj* سرحال	**logical** *adj* منطقی
living *adj* جاندار	**logically** *adv* از لحاظ منطقی
living room *n* اتاق نشیمن	**logo** *n* نشان
lizard *n* چلپاسه	**loiter** *v* تاخیر کردن
load *n* بار	**lollipop** *n* شیرین چوشک
load *v* بار کردن موتر؛	**loneliness** *n* تنهایی
ثبت معلومات در کمپیوتر	**lonely** *adv* تنها
loaded *adj* بارشده، پُر	**lonesome** *adj* دلتنگ
loaf *n* قرص، قرص نان	**long** *adj* دراز
loan *n* قرضه	**long** *adv* طولانی
loan *v* قرضه دادن	**long for** *pv* معطل کردن چیزی
loathe *v* نفرت داشتن	**long-distance** *adj* فاصله دور
lobby *n* دهلیز	**long-term** *adj* دراز مدت
lobby *v* وادار کردن	**look** *v* دیدن
lobster *n* خرچنگ	**look** *n* نگاه
local *adj* محلی	**look after** *pv* مراقبت کردن
locate *v* تعیین موقعیت	**look at** *pv* بطرف چیزی دیدن
located *adj* واقع در	**look down** *pv* به پایین دیدن
location *n* موقعیت	**look for** *pv* جستجو کردن
lock *n* قفل	**look forward** *pv* چشم به راه بودن
lock *v* قفل کردن	**look into** *pv* غور کردن
lock up *pv* قفل کردن ساختمان	**look out** *pv* مواظب بودن
locker *n* الماری قفل دار	**look over** *pv* ارزیابی کردن
locker room *n*	**look through** *pv* مرور کردن
اتاق الماری های قفل دار	**looking glass** *n* آیینه
locksmith *n* قفل ساز	**looks** *n* نگاه ها
lofty *adj* بلند	**loom** *n* کارگاه بافندگی
log *v* ثبت کردن	**loophole** *n* خلای قانونی
log *n* کنده چوب؛ کتاب ثبت معلومات	**loose** *v* فراخ کردن

L

loose

loose *adj* فراخ، گشاد	**loyal** *adj* وفادار
loosely *adv* به فراخی	**loyalty** *n* وفاداری
loosen *v* شل کردن	**lubricate** *v* چرب کردن
loot *n* غارت	**lubrication** *n* روغن کاری
loot *v* غارت کردن	**lucid** *adj* شفاف
lose *v* گُم کردن؛ باختن	**luck** *n* بخت
loser *n* بازنده	**lucky** *adj* خوشبخت
loss *n* خساره	**lucrative** *adj* پرمنفعت
lost *adj* گُم شده	**ludicrous** *adj* مزخرف
lot *adv* بسیار	**luggage** *n* بکس سفری
lot *pron* خیلی	**lukewarm** *adj* نیمه گرم
lot *n* یک پارچه؛ قطعه زمین	**lull** *n* آرامش
lotion *n* لوشن	**lullaby** *n* لالایی
lottery *n* لاتری	**lumber** *n* چوب
loud *adj* آواز بلند	**luminous** *adj* نورانی
loudly *adv* به آواز بلند	**lump** *n* غُده
loudspeaker *n* بلندگو	**lunacy** *n* دیوانگی
lounge *n* سالون	**lunatic** *adj* دیوانه
louse *n* شپش	**lunch** *n* نان چاشت
lousy *adj* شپشی	**lunchtime** *n* وقت نان چاشت
lovable *adj* دوست داشتنی	**lung** *n* شُش
love *v* عشق ورزیدن	**lunge** *v* حرکت های ورزشی
love *n* محبت	**lure** *v* رام کردن
lovely *adj* دوست داشتنی	**lurid** *adj* رنگ پریده
lover *n* عاشق	**lurk** *v* در کمین بودن
loving *adj* با محبت	**lush** *adj* شاداب
low *adv* پایین	**lust** *n* شهوت
low *adj* پایین؛ کم	**lustful** *adj* شهوتی
lower *adj* پایین تر	**luxurious** *adj* مجلل
lowercase *n* حروف کوچک الفبا	**luxury** *n* لوکس
low-key *adj* کلید پایین	**lyrics** *n* شعر ترانه
lowly *adj* حقیر	

L

M

macaroni n مکرونی
machine n ماشین
machine gun n تفنگ ماشیندار
mad adj دیوانه؛ عصبانی
madam n خانم
madden v عصبانی کردن
madly adv به عصبانیت
madman n دیوانه
madness n دیوانگی
magazine n مجله
magenta n ارغوانی
magic n جادو
magic adj جادویی
magical adj جادوآمیز
magician n جادوگر
magistrate n قاضی
magnet n آهن ربا
magnetic adj مقناطیسی
magnetism n خاصیت مقناطیسی
magnificent adj باشکوه
magnify v بزرگ نمایی کردن
magnitude n بزرگی
maid n خدمتگار
maiden n دوشیزه، باکره
maiden name n نام خانوادگی
mail n نامه
mail v نامه فرستادن
mail order n سفارش پُستی
mailbox n صندوق پُستی

mailman n نامه رسان
maim v جراحت
main adj عمده
mainland n سرزمین اصلی
mainly adv عمدتاً
mainstream n مسیر اصلی
maintain v حفظ کردن
maintenance n حفظ و مراقبت
majestic adj باشکوه
majesty n عظمت، اعلیحضرت
major n رشته تحصیلی؛ افسر اردو
major adj عمده
major in pv در یک رشته تحصیل کردن
majority n اکثریت
make v ساختن
make n مُدل موتر
make up pv تلافی کردن
make up for pv آماده شدن برای
maker n کسی که میسازد
makeup n آرایش
malaria n مرض ملاریا
male n مذکر
male adj مردانه
malfunction n عدم فعالیت
malice n بدخواهی
mall n مرکز خریداری
malnutrition n سوء تغذی
mammal n پستان داران
man n مرد
manage v تنظیم کردن
manageable adj قابل مدیریت

M

management n مدیریت، اداره	march v راهپیمایی کردن
manager n مدیر	March n ماه مارچ
mandate n منشور	mare n تاریکی
mandatory adj اجباری	margin n لبه، حاشیه
maneuver n مانور	marginal adj حاشیه ای
mangle v پاره کردن	marinate v اخته کردن
manhandle v بدرفتاری کردن	marine adj دریایی
maniac adj دیوانه وار	mark n نشانه، علامه
manicure n مانیکور، آرایش	mark v نشانی کردن
manifest v آشکار کردن	mark down pv علامت گذاری کردن
manipulate v دستکاری کردن	marker n قلم توش؛ علامه
manipulation n دستکاری	market n بازار
mankind n بشر	market v بازاریابی کردن
manliness n مردانگی	marmalade n مربای نارنج
manly adj مردانه وار	maroon adj قهوه ای
man-made adj ساخته دست بشر	marriage n ازدواج
manner n شیوه	married adj عروسی شده
mannerism n خوش اخلاقی	marry v عروسی کردن
manners n اخلاق	Mars n مریخ
manpower n نیروی انسانی	marsh n لجن زار
mansion n عمارت بزرگ	marshal n مارشال
manual adj دستی، انجام شده با دست	marvel n تعجب
manual n کتاب رهنما	marvelous adj حیرت آور
manually adv با دست	mascara n ریمل مژه و ابرو
manufacture v تولید کردن	mascot n طلسم
manure n کود زراعتی	masculine adj مردانه
manuscript n نسخه خطی	mash v مخلوط کردن
many pron بسیار	mask n پوزبند
many adj زیاد	mask v پوشانیدن
map n نقشه	masquerade v ماسک پوشیدن
marble n سنگ مرمر؛ تُشله	mass n مقدار زیاد
march n راه پیمایی	massacre n قتل عام

M

massage *n* ماساژ	maybe *adv* شاید
massage *v* ماساژ کردن	mayhem *n* ضرب و شتم
masseuse *n* ماساژ کننده	mayonnaise *n* مایونیز
massive *adj* عظیم	mayor *n* شهردار
mast *n* میله های بزرگ بر سر کشتی	maze *n* پیچ و خم
master *v* خوب یاد گرفتن	me *pron* به من
master *n* ماستر، ماهر	meadow *n* علفزار، چراگاه
masterpiece *n* شاهکار	meager *adj* ضعیف
mat *n* بوریا	meal *n* غذا
match *n* گوگرد؛ مسابقه ورزشی	mean *adj* پست فطرت
match *v* مطابقت داشتن	mean *v* معنی داشتن
matching *adj* منطبق	meaning *n* معنی
mate *n* دوست	meaningful *adj* با معنی
material *n* مواد	meaningless *adj* بی معنی
materialism *n* مادی گرایی	means *n* راه و چاره
maternal *adj* مادری	meantime *adv* درعین زمان
maternity *n* زایمان	meanwhile *adv* در عین زمان
math *n* ریاضی	measles *n* سرخکان
mathematics *n* ریاضیات	measure *n* اقدام
matriculate *v* نام نویسی کردن	measure *v* اندازه کردن، سنجیدن
matrimony *n* ازدواج	measurement *n* سنجش،
matter *v* اهمیت داشتن	اندازه گیری
matter *n* موضوع	meat *n* گوشت
mattress *n* دوشک	meatball *n* کوفته
mature *adj* بالغ	mechanic *n* مستری
mature *v* رشد کردن، به حد بلوغ رسیدن	mechanism *n* میکانیزم، راهکار
maturity *n* بلوغ	medal *n* مدال
maul *v* چکش چوبی	meddle *v* دخالت کردن
maximum *adj* حد اعظمی	media *n* رسانه ها
May *n* ماه می	mediate *v* میانجی گری کردن
may *modal v* ممکن بودن؛	mediator *n* میانجی
اجازه خواستن	medical *adj* طبی

M

medication *n* ادویه	**mentality** *n* ذهنیت
medicinal *adj* مربوط به ادویه	**mentally** *adv* ازنظر ذهنی
medicine *n* ادویه	**mention** *n* تذکر
medieval *adj* قرون وسطی	**mention** *v* تذکر دادن
mediocre *adj* حد متوسط	**menu** *n* مینوی غذا
mediocrity *n* وسطی	**merchandise** *n* کالا، مال تجارتی
meditate *v* تفکر کردن، عبادت کردن	**merchant** *n* تاجر
meditation *n* تفکر، عبادت	**merciful** *adj* رحیم، مهربان
medium *adj* متوسط	**merciless** *adj* بی رحم
meek *adj* باحوصله	**Mercury** *n* سیاره عطارد
meet *v* ملاقات کردن؛ آشنا شدن	**mercy** *n* رحم، شفقت
meeting *n* جلسه	**mere** *adj* محض، صرف
melancholy *n* مالیخولیا	**merely** *adv* صرفاً، فقط
mellow *adj* ملایم، مهربان	**merge** *v* یکجا نمودن
mellow *v* نرم کردن	**merger** *n* ادغام
melodic *adj* مربوط به میلودی یا نغمه	**merit** *n* استعداد
melody *n* نغمه، میلودی	**mermaid** *n* پری دریایی
melon *n* خربوزه	**merry** *adj* شاد، خوش
melt *v* ذوب شدن	**mesh** *n* شبکه
member *n* عضو	**mesmerize** *v* محسور کردن، توجه را جلب کردن
membership *n* عضویت	**mess** *n* بی نظمی؛ وضعیت دشوار
memento *n* یادگاری	**mess around** *pv* برخورد احمقانه کردن
memo *n* یادداشت	
memoirs *n* خاطرات	**mess up** *pv* نامنظم ساختن
memorable *adj* پرخاطره	**message** *n* پیام
memorize *v* به حافظه سپردن	**messenger** *n* پیام رسان
memory *n* حافظه انسان، حافظه کمپیوتر، خاطره	**messy** *adj* بی نظم
men *n* مردها	**metal** *n* فلز
menace *n* تهدید	**metallic** *adj* فلزی
mend *v* درست کردن	**metaphor** *n* کنایه
mental *adj* ذهنی، روانی	**meteor** *n* شهاب سنگ

M

meter *n* واحد طول یا متر؛ میتر برق	**millennium** *n* هزار سال
method *n* شیوه	**milligram** *n* میلی گرام
methodical *adj* میتودی	**millimeter** *n* میلی متر
methodology *n* روش	**million** *n* میلیون
meticulous *adj* دقیق	**millionaire** *adj* میلیونر
metric *adj* متریک، به اساس متر	**mime** *n* تقلید
microchip *n* مایکروچیپ	**mimic** *v* تقلید کردن
microphone *n* مایکروفون	**mince** *v* چرخ کردن گوشت
microscope *n* مایکروسکوب	**mind** *v* اعتنا کردن به
microwave *n* موج ریز، مایکروویف	**mind** *n* فکر، ذهن
midday *n* نیمه روز	**mind-boggling** *adj* گیج کننده ذهن
middle *adj* در وسط	**mindful** *adj* متوجه، مواظب
middle *n* وسط	**mindless** *adj* بی فکر
middleman *n* واسطه، دلال	**mine** *pron* از من
midnight *n* نیمه شب	**mine** *v* استخراج معدن
midwife *n* دایه، قابله	**mine** *n* مین، بم
might *n* قدرت	**miner** *n* کارگر معدن
might *modal v* ممکن	**mineral** *n* معدنی
mighty *adj* پرقدرت	**mingle** *v* آمیختن
migraine *n* میگرین، سردرد	**miniature** *n* میناتوری
migrant *n* مهاجر	**minimal** *adj* کم، حد اقل
migrate *v* مهاجرت کردن	**minimize** *v* کم کردن
mild *adj* غذای بدون مرچ، ملایم	**minimum** *n* کمترین
mile *n* میل، مایل	**miniskirt** *n* دامن کوتاه
mileage *n* فاصله پیموده شده	**minister** *v* خدمت کردن
milestone *n* مرحله	**minister** *n* وزیر
military *n* نظامی	**ministry** *n* وزارت
milk *n* شیر	**minor** *v* در یک رشته تحصیل کردن
milky *adj* شیری	**minor** *n* صغیر، کوچک
mill *n* آسیاب، فابریکه کاغذ، چوب، فولاد وغیره	**minor** *adj* کوچک
	minority *n* اقلیت
	mint *n* نعنا

M

minus n علامت منفی	mist n غبار
minus adj کمتر	mistake n اشتباه
minus prep منفی	mistake v اشتباه کردن
minute n دقیقه	mistaken adj خطا کردن
miracle n معجزه	Mister n آقا
miraculous adj معجزه یی	mistreat v بدرفتاری کردن
mirage n نقش روی آب	mistrust n بی اعتمادی
mirror n آیینه	mistrust v بی اعتمادی کردن
misbehave v بدرفتاری کردن	misty adj غبار آلود
miscalculate v غلط محاسبه کردن	misunderstand v سوء تفاهم شدن
miscellaneous adj متفرقه	misuse n سوء استفاده
mischief n شیطنت	mitigate v کاهش دادن
mischievous adj شیطنت آمیز	mix v مخلوط کردن
misconstrue v غلط	mixer n مخلوط کن
miserable adj بدبخت	mixture n مخلوط
misery n بدبختی	mix-up n درهم و برهمی
misfit n نامناسب	moan v ناله کشیدن
misfortune n بدبختی	mob n گروه، دسته
misguided adj گمراه	mobile adj سیار
misinterpret v غلط تفسیر کردن	mobile phone n تیلفون همراه
misjudge v قضاوت غلط کردن	mobilize v بسیج کردن
mislead v گمراه کردن	mock v تمسخر کردن
misleading adj گمراه کننده	mode n حالت، وضعیت
mismanage v مدیریت غلط کردن	model v شکل دادن
misplace v بیجا کردن	model n مُدل، نمونه
misprint n چاپ غلط	model adj مطلوب و بی عیب
miss v از دست دادن	modem n
missile n میزایل	مودیم، آله وصل کننده انترنیت
missing adj گُم، مفقود	moderate adj معتدل، خفیف
mission n مأموریت	moderation n اعتدال، میانه روی
missionary n مُبلغ مذهبی	modern adj عصری
misspell v غلط هجا کردن	modernize v عصری ساختن

M

modest *adj* فروتن	**monthly** *adv* ماهانه
modesty *n* تواضع	**monument** *n* بنای تاریخی
modification *n* تغییر، اصلاح	**monumental** *adj* بزرگ و مهم
modify *v* اصلاح کردن، تغییر دادن	**mood** *n* مزاج، حوصله
moist *adj* مرطوب	**moody** *adj* بی حوصله، بدخوی
moisture *n* رطوبت	**moon** *n* مهتاب
moisturize *v* مرطوب کردن	**mop** *v* با پاس پاک کردن
molar *n* دندان آسیاب	**mop** *n* پاس پاس
mold *n* پوپنک	**moral** *n* اخلاق
mold *v* قالب	**moral** *adj* اخلاقی
moldy *adj* پوپنک زده	**morally** *adv* اخلاقاً
mole *n* خال سیاه	**more** *adj* بعلاوه
mom *n* مادر	**more** *pron* زیاد
moment *n* لحظه	**more** *adv* زیادتر
momentarily *adv* لحظه به لحظه	**moreover** *adv* علاوه بر این
monarch *n* پادشاه	**morning** *n* صبح
monarchy *n* شاهی	**mortal** *adj* مردنی؛ فانی
monastery *n* خانقاه	**mortality** *n* مرگ و میر
monastic *adj* رهبانی	**mortgage** *n* رهن، گرو
Monday *n* روز دوشنبه	**mortify** *v* فریب دادن
money *n* پول	**mortuary** *n* سرد خانه،
monitor *n* مانیتور کمپیوتر	مرده شوی خانه
monitor *v* نظارت کردن	**mosaic** *n* موزایک
monk *n* راهب، ترک دنیا کرده	**mosque** *n* مسجد
monkey *n* میمون، شادی	**mosquito** *n* پشه
monologue *n* مونولوگ،	**moss** *n* یکنوع گیاه، خزه
صحبت یکنفری	**most** *pron* بیش از همه
monopoly *n* انحصار	**most** *adj* بیشترین
monotonous *adj* یکنواخت	**most** *adv* مقدار زیاد
monster *n* هیولا	**mostly** *adv* بیشترأ
monstrous *adj* هیولایی	**motel** *n* مسافرخانه
month *n* ماه	**moth** *n* پروانه

M

mother n مادر	**much** pron خیلی
motherhood n مادری	**much** adv زیاد
mother-in-law n خشو	**mud** n گِل
motion v تحرک داشتن	**muddy** adj گِل آلود
motion n حرکت	**muffle** v خاموش کردن
motionless adj بی حرکت	**muffler** n خاموش کننده صدا
motivate v تحریک کردن	**mug** v با چوب زدن
motivation n تحریک	**mug** n گیلاس آب
motive n انگیزه	**mugging** n زورگیری کردن
motor n ماشین	**mule** n قاطر
motorcycle n موترسیکل	**multimedia** adj چند رسانه یی
motto n شعار	**multiple** adj متعدد
mound n تپه، انبار	**multiplication** n عملیه ضرب
mount v سوار شدن	**multiply** v ضرب کردن
mountain n کوه	**multitude** n کثرت، بسیاری
mourn v سوگواری کردن	**mumble** v غُر زدن
mourning n عزاداری	**mummy** n مومیایی
mouse n موش؛ موس کمپیوتر	**mumps** n یکنوع عفونت گوش
mouth n دهن	**munch** v جویدن
move v حرکت دادن؛	**murder** n قتل
کوچ کشی کردن	**murder** v کشتن
move n کوچ کشی	**murderer** n قاتل
move back pv دوباره کوچیدن	**murky** adj تیره، تاریک
move forward pv	**murmur** n زمزمه
به پیش حرکت کردن	**murmur** v زمزمه کردن
move out pv بیرون شدن	**muscle** n عضله
move up pv بالا شدن	**museum** n موزیم
movement n جنبش، حرکت	**mushroom** n سمارق
movie n فلم	**music** n موسیقی
movie theater n تیاترسینمایی	**musical** adj مربوط به موسیقی
mow v قطع کردن سبزه	**musician** n موسیقی دان
much adj بسیار	**Muslim** adj مسلمان

M

must *modal v* باید	**nap** *n* خواب، چُرت
mustache *n* بروت	**napkin** *n* دستمال کاغذی
mustard *n* یکنوع چتنی، مستارد	**narrate** *v* حکایت کردن
muster *v* جمع آوری کردن	**narrow** *adj* باریک
mute *adj* خاموش	**nasty** *adj* کثیف
mutual *adj* خاموش کردن صدا	**nation** *n* ملت
mutually *adv* دوجانبه	**national** *adj* ملی
muzzle *n* پوزبند	**nationality** *n* ملیت
my *adj* از من	**native** *adj* اصلی
myopic *adj* نزدیک بینی	**natural** *adj* طبیعی؛ امر عادی
myself *pron* من خودم	**naturally** *adv* طبیعتاً؛ بطور عادی
mysterious *adj* مرموز	**nature** *n* طبیعت
mystery *n* معما، راز	**naughty** *adj* شوخ
mystic *adj* عرفانی	**nausea** *n* دلبدی
mystify *v* رمزی کردن	**navel** *n* ناف
myth *n* اسطوره، افسانه	**navigate** *v* جستجو کردن
	navigation *n* جستجو
	navy *n* نیروی دریایی
# N	**navy blue** *n* سرمه یی
	near *adv* تقریباً
	near *adj* صمیمی
nag *v* نق زدن	**near** *prep* نزدیک
nagging *adj* آزار دهنده	**nearby** *adj* در نزدیکی
nail *v* میخ کوبیدن	**nearby** *adv* درهمین نزدیکی ها
nail *n* ناخن؛ میخ	**nearly** *adv* تقریباً
naive *adj* آدم ساده	**nearsighted** *adj* نزدیک بین
naked *adj* برهنه	**neat** *adj* پاک
name *n* نام	**neatly** *adv* منظم
name *v* نامیدن	**necessary** *adj* ضروری
namely *adv* به نام	**necessity** *n* ضرورت
nanny *n* نگهبان طفل	**neck** *n* گردن
nap *v* چُرت زدن، خواب کوتاه کردن	**necklace** *n* گردنبند

N

necktie n نکتایی
need n ضرورت
need v ضرورت داشتن
needle n سوزن
needless adj بی نیاز
needy adj نیازمند
negative adj منفی
negative n نامثبت
neglect n غفلت
neglect v غفلت کردن
neglected adj غفلت شده
negotiate v مذاکره کردن
negotiation n مذاکره
neighbor n همسایه
neighborhood n همسایگی

N

neither adv هیچ
neither pron هیچ یک
neither adj هیچکدام
nephew n برادر زاده
Neptune n سیاره نپتون
nerve n عصب؛ جرات، متانت
nervous adj عصبی
nest n آشیانه
net n جالی
network n شبکه
neutral adj بیطرف
neutral n بیطرفی
never adv هرگز
nevertheless adv باوجوداینهم
new adj جدید
newborn n نوزاد
newcomer n تازه وارد

newly adv به تازه گی
newlywed n تازه عروسی شده
news n اخبار
newspaper n روزنامه
newsstand n غرفه فروش اخبار
next adv آینده
next adj بعدی
next door adj دروازه بعدی
next to adj پهلوی چیزی
nibble v نیش زدن
nice adj زیبا
nicely adv به زیبایی
nickel n سکه ۵ سنتی؛ فلز
nickname n تخلص
niece n خواهرزاده
night n شب
nightgown n لباس خواب
nightly adj شبانه
nightmare n خواب وحشتناک
nighttime n شب هنگام
nine n نه
nineteen n نزده
ninety n نود
ninth adj نهم
nipple n نوک سینه
no adj نخیر
no adv نه
no e هیچ
no one pron هیچکس
nobility n اصالت، نجابت
noble adj نجیب،
مربوط به خانواده شاهی

nobody *pron* هیچکس
nocturnal *adj* شبانه
nod *v* تکان دادن سر
noise *n* سروصدا
noisily *adv* با سروصدا
noisy *adj* پرسروصدا
nominate *v* نامزد کردن،
انتخاب کردن
none *prep* هیچ
nonetheless *adv* باوجود این
nonsense *n* مزخرف
nonstop *adv* بدون وقفه
noodles *n* آش
noon *n* چاشت
nor *conj* نه
norm *n* نورم، معیار
normal *adj* عادی
normally *adv* معمولاً
north *adv* به سمت شمال
north *n* شمال
north *adj* شمالی
northeast *n* شمال شرق
northern *adj* شمالی
northerner *n* اهل مناطق شمالی
nose *n* بینی
nostalgia *n* نوستالژی
nostril *n* سوراخ بینی
nosy *adj* مداخله گر
not *adv* نخیر
notable *adj* قابل ملاحظه
notably *adv* بطور قابل ملاحظه
notary *n* دفتر اسناد رسمی

notation *n* یادداشت
note *v* یادداشت کردن
note *n* یادداشت مختصر،
نوت های موسیقی
notebook *n* کتابچه
notepaper *n* کاغذ یادداشت
noteworthy *adj* قابل توجه
nothing *n* هیچ
nothing *pron* هیچیک
notice *n* توجه
notice *v* متوجه شدن
noticeable *adj* برجسته
notification *n* آگهی
notify *v* مطلع ساختن
notion *n* نظریه
notorious *adj* بدنام، رسوا
notwithstanding *adv* باوجود
notwithstanding *prep* باوجوداینکه
noun *n* اسم
nourish *v* تغذیه کردن
nourishment *n* تغذیه
novel *n* ناول
novelist *n* ناول نویس
novelty *n* نوآوری
November *n* ماه نومبر
novice *n* تازه کار
now *adv* حالا
nowadays *adv* در این روزها
nowhere *adv* هیچ جا
noxious *adj* مضر
nozzle *n* دهانه، نیزل
nuance *n* ظرافت

N

nuclear *adj* مبهم

nude *adj* برهنه

nuisance *n* مزاحمت

nullify *v* باطل کردن

numb *adj* بی حس

number *n* عدد

numbness *n* بی حسی

numerous *adj* متعدد

nun *n* راهبه

nurse *n* پرستار

nurse *v* پرستاری کردن

nursery *n* شیرخوارگاه؛ گلخانه

nurture *v* پرورش دادن

nut *n* خسته باب؛ نت و بولت

nutrition *n* تغذیه

nutritious *adj* تغذی

nylon *n* نیلون

O

o'clock *adv* بجه

oak *n* بلوط

oar *n* بیل

oasis *n* مرغزار در بیابان

oath *n* سوگند

oatmeal *n* حبوبات

obedience *n* اطاعت

obedient *adj* تابع

obese *adj* چاق

obey *v* اطاعت کردن

object *v* انتقاد کردن

object *n* شی

objection *n* انتقاد

objective *n* هدف، روشن

objectively *adv* بطور عینی

obligate *v* مکلف ساختن

obligated *adj* مکلف

obligation *n* تعهد

obligatory *adj* اجباری

oblige *v* وادار کردن

obliged *adj* محبور، مکلف

obliterate *v* محو کردن

oblivious *adj* بی توجه

oblong *adj* دراز کشیده

obnoxious *adj* ناراحت کننده

obscene *adj* ناپسند

obscure *adj* مبهم

observant *adj* ناظر

observation *n* مشاهده

observatory *n*
محل نصب وسایل نجومی

observe *v* مشاهده کردن

obsess *v* عقده کردن

obsession *n* عقده روحی

obsolete *adj* منسوخ شده

obstacle *n* مانع

obstinate *adj* لجباز

obstruct *v* منع کردن

obstruction *n* مانع

obtain *v* بدست آوردن

obvious *adj* واضح

obviously *adv* واضحاً

occasion *n* مناسبت	officiate *v* رسمی ساختن
occasionally *adv* گاه گاهی	offline *adj* خاموش، آفلاین
occupant *n* ساکن	offset *v* انحراف
occupation *n* شغل	offspring *n* فرزندان
occupied *adj* درحال استفاده شدن؛ اشغال شده	often *adv* اغلب
	oh *e* اوه
occupy *v* اشغال کردن	oil *n* روغن
occur *v* رخ دادن	oily *adj* روغنی
occurrence *n* وقوع	ointment *n* مرهم
ocean *n* بحر	okay *adv* بسیار خوب
October *n* ماه اکتوبر	okay *adj* درست است
octopus *n* هشت پا	old *adj* کهنه
odd *adj* غیرمعمول؛ عدد تاق	old age *n* سالخورده
oddity *n* عجیب و غریب	old-fashioned *adj* سبک قدیمی
odious *adj* نفرت انگیز	olive *n* زیتون
odometer *n* اودومیتر	olive oil *n* روغن زیتون
odor *n* بوی بد	Olympics *n* المپیک
odorless *adj* بی بوی	omelet *n* آملیت، تخم با رومی و پیاز
odyssey *n* سفر زندگی	omen *n* فال، شگون
of *prep* از	ominous *adj* شوم، بد شگون
off *adv* خاموش	omission *n* حذف
off *prep* دور	omit *v* حذف کردن
offend *v* توهین کردن	on *adv* روشن
offense *n* توهین	on *prep* روی
offensive *adj* توهین آمیز	once *conj* به یکباره گی
offer *n* پیشکش	once *adv* یکبار
offer *v* پیشکش کردن	one *n* شخص
office *n* دفتر	one *pron* کسی
officer *n* کارمند	one *adj* یک
official *adj* رسمی	oneself *pron* یک کسی
official *n* کارمند رسمی	ongoing *adj* جاری
officially *adv* بطور رسمی	onion *n* پیاز

O

online *adj* روشن، آنلاین

onlooker *n* بیننده

only *adv* صرف

only *adj* فقط

onto *prep* به سوی

onward *adv* به پیش

opaque *adj* مبهم

open *adj* باز، قابل دسترس

open *v* بازکردن

opening *n* مجرا، خلا؛ افتتاح

open-minded *adj* روشن فکر

openness *n* باز بودن

opera *n* نمایش اوپرا

operate *v* چلاندن؛ عملیات کردن

operation *n* عملیات

opinion *n* مفکوره

opinionated *adj* معتقد

opponent *n* مخالف

opportunity *n* فرصت

oppose *v* مخالف بودن

opposite *adv* برخلاف

opposite *n* ضد

opposite *prep* معکوس

opposite *adj* مقابل، مخالف

opposition *n* طرف مخالف

oppress *v* ظلم کردن

oppressed *adj* مظلوم

oppression *n* ظلم

optical *adj* نوری، بصری

optician *n* عینک فروشی

optimism *n* خوش بینی

optimistic *adj* خوش بین

option *n* گزینه

optional *adj* اختیاری

opulence *n* رفاه

or *conj* یا

oracle *n* پیشگویی

oral *adj* شفاهی

orally *adv* بطور شفاهی

orange *adj* مالته

orange *n* مالته؛ رنگ نارنجی

orbit *n* مدار

orchard *n* باغ

orchestra *n* آرکستر

ordeal *n* مصیبت

order *v* حکم کردن؛ خریداری کردن

order *n* نظم؛ حکم؛ فرمایش خریداری

ordinarily *adv* بطور عادی

ordinary *adj* عادی

ore *n* سنگ معدنی

organ *n* آله موسیقی

organic *adj* طبیعی، بدون مواد کیمیاوی

organization *n* سازمان

organize *v* تنظیم کردن

organized *adj* منظم

orientation *n* آشنایی

oriented *adj* متمایل

origin *n* اصل، بنیاد

original *adj* اصلی؛ جدید

original *n* نسخه اصلی

originally *adv* اصلاً

originate *v* سرچشمه گرفتن

ornament *n* زینتی	outing *n* گردش بیرون از شهر
ornamental *adj* چیز زینتی	outlast *v* زیاد طول کشیدن
orphan *n* یتیم	outlaw *n* قانون شکن
orphanage *n* دارالایتام	outlet *n* مخرج، راه بیرون رفت
orthodox *adj* درست	outline *v* طرح کردن؛
ostentatious *adj* خودنمایی	موضوع را خلاصه بیان کردن
ostrich *n* شترمرغ	outline *n* طرح؛ فشرده موضوع
other *adj* دیگر	outlive *v* بیشتر زنده ماندن
other *pron* سایر	outlook *n* چشم انداز
otherwise *adv* درغیرآن؛	outnumber *v*
درغیرآنصورت	بیشتر از تعداد معین بودن
ought to *modal v* باید	outpatient *n* خارج بستر
ounce *n* اونس؛ برابر به ۰۳ گرام	outperform *v* عملکرد بهتر
our *adj* ازما	outpouring *n* ریزش
ours *pron* ازما	output *n* محصول، نتیجه
ourselves *pron* خودما	outrage *n* خشم
oust *v* بیرون کردن	outrageous *adj* خشمگین
out *adv* بیرون؛ دور	outright *adj* کاملاً
out *adj* خلاص شده؛ خاموش	outrun *v* پیشی گرفتن
outbreak *n* شیوع	outset *n* آغاز
outburst *n* انفجار	outshine *v* بیشتر درخشیدن
outcast *adj* مطرود، رانده	outside *adv* بیرون
outcome *n* نتیجه	outside *prep* خارج از
outcry *n* فریاد	outside *adj* در بیرون
outdated *adj* منسوخ، تاریخ تیر شده	outside *n* ظاهر
outdo *v* پیشی گرفتن	outsider *n* شخص بیرونی، خارجی
outdoor *adv* بیرون از منزل	outskirts *n* حومه های شهر
outdoors *adv* در بیرون از منزل	outspoken *adj* صریح
outer *adj* بیرونی	outstanding *adj* برجسته
outfit *n* لباس	outward *adj* بیرونی
outgoing *adj* بیرون رو	outweigh *v* سنگین تر بودن از
outgrow *v* بزرگ شدن	oval *adj* بیضوی شکل

O

ovation n تشویق، ستایش	**overrun** v تجاوز کردن
oven n داش	**overseas** adv بیرون از کشور
over prep بالای؛ ختم؛ بیش از	**oversee** v نظارت کردن
over adv در بالای؛ بیشتر از	**overshadow** v سایه انداختن،
overall adv در مجموع	تحت تاثیر قرار دادن
overall adj روی هم رفته	**oversight** n نظارت؛ اشتباه
overbearing adj طاقت فرسا	**overstate** v مبالغه کردن
overboard adv در دریا	**overstep** v فراتر رفتن
overcast adj ابری، پوشیده از ابر	**overthrow** v بهم زدن
overcharge v	**overtime** n اضافه کاری
بیش از حد چارج کردن	**overturn** v واژگون کردن
overcoat n بالاپوش	**overview** n نظر اجمالی
overcome v غالب شدن	**overweight** adj اضافه وزن
overdo v افراط کردن	**overwhelm** v دست پاچه شدن
overdone adj بیش از حد	**owe** v قرضدار بودن
overdose n مصرف بیش از حد دوا	**owl** n بوم
overdue adj	**own** pron از خود
تاریخ پرداخت چیزی تیر شده	**own** v دارا بودن
overestimate v	**own** adj شخصی
بیش از حد تخمین کردن	**owner** n مالک
overflow v لبریز شدن	**ownership** n مالکیت
overgrown adj	**ox** n گاو نر
بیش از حد رشد کرده	**oxygen** n آکسیجن
overhaul v مرمت کردن؛	**oyster** n صدف خوراکی
بازسازی کردن	
overhead adj هوایی	
overhear v از دور شنیدن	# P
overlap v روی هم قرار گرفتن	
overlook v از بالا دیدن؛	
نادیده گرفتن	**pace** n گام
overnight adv شب هنگام	**pace** v گام برداشتن
overpower v غلبه کردن	**pacifier** n تسکین دهنده

O

pacify *v* آرام کردن	palm *n* کف دست؛ درخت خرما
pack *n* بسته	palpable *adj* قابل لمس
pack *v* بسته بندی کردن	paltry *adj* ناچیز
package *n* بسته، قوطی	pamper *v* با محبت پروردن
packed *adj* بسته بندی شده	pamphlet *n* رساله معلوماتی
packet *n* پاکت	pan *n* دیگ
pact *n* پیمان	pancake *n* پن کیک، یکنوع کیک
pad *v* با لایه پوشاندن	pancreas *n* پانقراس
pad *n* لایه بالش؛ ورق یادداشت	pander *v* به کار بد راضی کردن
padded *adj* لایه دار	panel *n* هیئت؛ بخشی از ماشین
padding *n* لایه گذاری	pang *n* درد ناگهانی
paddle *n* پایدل	panic *n* دست پاچگی
paddle *v* پایدل زدن	panorama *n* چشم انداز، منظره
padlock *n* قفل	panther *n* پلنگ
page *n* صفحه	pantry *n* پس خانه
pail *n* سطل	pants *n* پطلون
pain *n* درد	paper *n* کاغذ
painful *adj* دردناک	paperback *n* پوش کتاب
painkiller *n* مُسکن درد	paperclip *n* گیرهٔ کاغذ
painless *adj* بی درد	paperwork *n* طی مراحل اداری
paint *n* رنگ	parable *n* مثل
paint *v* نقاشی کردن، رنگ کردن	parachute *n* فراشوت
paintbrush *n*	parade *n* رسم گذشت
برس رنگمالی یا نقاشی	paradise *n* بهشت
painter *n* نقاش، رنگمال	paradox *n* گفتار مغایر
painting *n* نقاشی	paragraph *n* پاراگراف
pair *n* جوره؛ دو شخص مرتبط بهم	parallel *adj* موازی
pajamas *n* لباس خواب	paralysis *n* فلج
pal *n* رفیق	paralyze *v* فلج شدن
palace *n* قصر	parameter *n* پارامیتر،
palate *n* کام	مقدار معلوم و مشخص
pale *adj* رنگ پریده	paramount *adj* مهمترین

P

paranoid *adj*	**partition** *n* ، تقسیم بندی
مبتلا به مرض روانی پارانویا	دیوار کشیدن دراتاق
paraphrase *v* تفسیر، نقل قول	**partly** *adv* تاحدی، قسماً
parasite *n* پارازیت	**partner** *n* شریک
parcel *n* پارسل	**partnership** *n* شراکت
parch *v* بریان کردن	**party** *v* محفل گرفتن
pardon *v* بخشیدن	**party** *n* محفل، حزب
pardon *n* معذرت، عذرخواهی	**pass** *v* عبور کردن؛
parent *n* والدین	توپ را به کسی پرتاب کردن
parenthesis *n* پارانتیز، قوس	**pass** *n* کارت عبور؛
parish *n* محله	کامیاب شدن در امتحان
parishioner *n* مردم یک محله	**pass around** *pv* دست به دست
parity *n* برابری، توازن	کردن چیزی
park *n* پارک	**pass away** *pv* وفات شدن
park *v* پارک کردن موتر	**pass out** *pv* ضُعف کردن،
parking *n* پارکینگ	بیهوش شدن
parking lot *n* محل پارکینگ	**passage** *n* گذر، عبور؛ تصویب
parliament *n* پارلمان	**passenger** *n* مسافر
parrot *n* طوطی	**passer-by** *n* راهگذر
parsley *n* گیاه جعفری	**passion** *n* علاقمندی
part *n* بخش، قسمت؛ نقش در فلم	**passionate** *adj* پرشور، احساساتی
part *v* قسمت کردن	**passive** *adj* مجهول، غیرفعال
partial *adj* جزئی	**passport** *n* پاسپورت
partially *adv* تا اندازه ای	**password** *n* رمز
participant *n* اشتراک کننده	**past** *n* سابقه
participate *v* اشتراک کردن	**past** *adj* گذشته
participation *n* اشتراک، سهمگیری	**past** *prep* گذشته از
participle *n*	**pasta** *n* پاستا، آش یا مکرونی
شرکت کننده، وجه وصفی در گرامر	**paste** *n* خمیر، چسب
particular *adj* مشخص	**paste** *v* نصب کردن، چسپاندن
particularly *adv* بطور مشخص	**pastime** *n* سرگرمی، تفریح
	pastor *n* پیشوای مذهبی

P

pastry n شیرینی باب	**peace** n صلح
pasture n چراگاه	**peaceful** adj صلح آمیز
pat n ضربه	**peach** n شفتالو
patch n قطعه زمین	**peacock** n طاووس
patch v قطعه کردن	**peak** n قُله کوه؛ نقطه اوج
paternity n پدری	**peanut** n بادام زمینی، مپیلی
path n مسیر	**pear** n ناک
pathetic adj تأسفبار	**pearl** n مروارید
patience n حوصله	**peasant** n دهقان
patient adj باحوصله	**pebble** n سنگریزه
patient n مریض	**peck** v نوک زدن،
patio n دروازه بالکن	با نوک سوراخ کردن
patriarch n پدرسالار	**peculiar** adj عجیب و غریب
patriot n وطندوستی	**pedal** n پایدل
patriotic adj وطندوست	**pedestrian** n شخص پیاده، عابر
patrol n گزمه	**peel** n پوست
patron n حامی، پشتیبان	**peel** v پوست کردن
patronize v تشویق کردن	**peep** v چشمک زدن
pattern n الگو، طرح	**peephole** n دیدگاه، روزنه
pause v مکث کردن	**peer** v هم درجه بودن
pave v هموار کردن	**peer** n همتا، هم درجه
pavement n پیاده رو	**pelican** n پرنده ماهیخور
paw n پنجه	**pen** n قلم؛ خانه کوچک برای حیوانات
pawn v پیاده شطرنج	**penalize** v جریمه کردن
pay v پرداختن، تادیه کردن	**penalty** n جریمه
pay n معاش	**pencil** n پنسل
pay back pv دوباره پرداختن	**pendant** n گردنبند
pay off pv قرضه را پرداختن	**pending** adj معلق، در حالت تعلیق
payable adj قابل پرداخت	**pendulum** n پاندول، جسم آویخته
paycheck n چک معاش	**penetrate** v سرایت کردن،
payment n تادیه، معاش	رخنه کردن
pea n نخود	**penguin** n پنگوین

P

penicillin n دوای پنسلین	perjury n شهادت دروغ
peninsula n شبه جزیره	permanent adj دایمی
penniless adj بی پول	permeate v سرایت کردن،
penny n سینت	نفوذ کردن
pension n پول تقاعدی	permission n اجازه
pentagon n پنج ضلعی	permit v اجازه دادن
pent-up adj محدود، معلق	pernicious adj مضر، مخرب
people n مردم	perpetrate v مقصر بودن،
pepper n مرچ	مرتکب شده
per prep مطابق به	persecute v آزار و اذیت کردن
perceive v درک کردن	persevere v استقامت بخرچ دادن
percent n فیصد	persist v اصرار ورزیدن،
percentage n فیصدی	تأکید کردن
perception n درک، ادراک	persistence n پافشاری
perceptive adj حساس، باهوش	persistent adj مداوم، مقاوم
perennial adj همیشگی، دایمی	person n شخص
perfect adj کامل، بی عیب	personal adj شخصی
perfection n کمال، بی عیبی	personality n شخصیت
perforate v سوراخ کردن	personnel n کارمندان، پرسونل
perforation n ایجاد سوراج	perspective n دیدگاه
perform v اجرا کردن؛ فعال بودن	perspiration n تعریق، عرق بدن
performance n اجرای کنسرت؛	perspire v عرق کردن، دفع کردن
عملکرد	persuade v وادار کردن
performer n اجرا کننده	persuasion n قناعت دهی،
perfume n عطر	متقاعد ساختن
perhaps adv شاید	persuasive adj وادار کننده
peril n خطر	pertinent adj مرتبط
perilous adj خطرناک	perturb v ناراحت کردن،
perimeter n محیط، فضا	مزاحمت کردن
period n دوره زمانی؛ مدت	perverse adj گمراه، منحرف
perish v از بین رفتن	pessimism n بدبینی
perishable adj فاسد شدنی	pessimistic adj بدبین

P

pest *n* آفت، طاعون	phrase *n* عبارت
pester *v* چسپیدن، به ستوه آوردن	physical *adj* فزیکی
pesticide *n* حشره کش	physical *n* معاینه داکتر
pet *v* پرورش دادن حیوان خانگی	physically *adv* بطور فزیکی
pet *n* حیوان خانگی	physician *n* داکتر
petal *n* گلبرگ	physics *n* فزیک
petite *adj* ریزه، خورد	pianist *n* پیانو نواز
petition *n* عریضه، درخواستی	piano *n* پیانو
petrified *adj* متحجر شده،	pick *n* انتخاب
حیران شده، تحت تاثیر قرارگرفته	pick *v* برداشتن، انتخاب کردن
petroleum *n* پطرولیم	pick up *pv* برداشتن
petty *adj* جزئی، خرده	pickle *n* ترشی
phantom *n* روح، خیال	pickpocket *n* کیسه بری
pharmacist *n* دواساز	pickup *n* موتر پیکپ
pharmacy *n* دواخانه	picnic *n* میله
phase *n* مرحله	picture *v* به تصویر کشیدن
phenomenal *adj* فوق العاده	picture *n* تصویر
phenomenon *n* پدیده	picturesque *adj* زیبا، خوش منظر
philosopher *n* فیلسوف	pie *n* کلچه مربا دار
philosophical *n* فلسفی	piece *n* توته
philosophy *n* فلسفه	piecemeal *adv* تکه تکه، تدریجی
phobia *n* ترس، خوف	pier *n* پایهٔ پُل
phone *n* تیلفون	pierce *v* سوراخ کردن
phone *v* تیلفون کردن	piercing *n* سوراخ
phony *adj* ساختگی، غلط	pig *n* خوک
photo *n* تصویر	pigeon *n* کبوتر
photocopier *n* ماشین فوتوکاپی	piggy bank *n* دخل پول
photocopy *n* فوتوکاپی	pile *n* انبار
photograph *v* عکس، تصویر	pile *v* انبار کردن
photographer *n* عکاس،	pile up *v* انباشتن
تصویر بردار	pilgrim *n* حاجی، زائر
photography *n* عکاسی	pilgrimage *n* حج، زیارت

P

pill n تابلیت	**pity** n افسوس
pillage v غارت	**pizza** n پیتزا
pillar n ستون، پایه	**placate** v آرام کردن
pillow n بالش	**place** n جای؛ موقف
pillowcase n پوش بالش	**place** v قراردادن
pilot n پیلوت	**placid** adj راحت، آرام
pimple n بخار صورت در جوانی	**plague** n طاعون، سرایت مرض
pin n سنجاق	**plain** adj ساده
pin v سنجاق کردن	**plainly** adv به ساده گی
pinch n تنگنا، جای باریک و تنگ	**plaintiff** n مدعی، شاکی
pinch v در تنگنا قرار گرفتن	**plan** v پلان کردن، طرح کردن
pine n درخت ناجو	**plan** n پلان، برنامه؛ طرح
pineapple n آناناس	**plane** n طیاره
pink n رنگ گلابی	**planet** n سیاره
pink adj گلابی	**plant** v کاشتن
pinpoint v مشخص کردن	**plant** n گیاه، نبات
pint n پینت، واحد پیمایش	**plastic** n پلاستیک
pioneer n پیشگام	**plate** n بشقاب
pipe n پایپ؛ سیگار	**plateau** n زمین هموار
piracy n دزدی ادبی یا هنری	**platform** n طرح، برنامه
pirate n دزد ادبی یا هنری	**platinum** n پلاتین، طلای سفید
pistol n تفنگچه	**plausible** adj باورکردنی، پذیرفتنی
pit n خسته میوه	**play** v بازی کردن؛ نواختن موسیقی
pitch v پرتاب کردن؛ نصب کردن خیمه	**play** n نمایش
pitch n زیر و بمی صدا	**player** n بازیکن
pitch-black adj خیلی سیاه	**playful** adj شوخ، بازیگوش
pitcher n کوزه آب؛ پرتاب کننده توپ	**playground** n میدان بازی
pitchfork n چنگال، پنجه	**plea** n تقاضا، درخواست
pitfall n گودال سرپوشیده	**plead** v درخواست کردن، تقاضا کردن
pitiful adj مهربان	**pleasant** adj خوشایند
	please v خوش ساختن

please *e* لطفاً	**poet** *n* شاعر
pleased *adj* خوشحال	**poetry** *n* شاعری
pleasing *adj* خوشحال کننده	**poignant** *adj* تکان دهنده، تیز
pleasure *n* خوشحالی، مسرت	**point** *v* اشاره کردن
pleat *n* چین خوردگی	**point** *n* نوک تیز؛ دلیل؛ نظریه؛ نکته
pleated *adj* چین خورده	**pointed** *adj* نوک دار
pledge *v* تعهد، سوگند کردن	**pointless** *adj* بیهوده، بی معنی
pledge *n* سوگند، تعهد	**poise** *n* وقار، متانت
plentiful *adj* فراوان	**poison** *n* زهر
plenty *n* فراوانی	**poison** *v* زهری ساختن
pliable *adj* قابل انعطاف	**poisonous** *adj* زهرآلود
pliers *n* انبور، پلاس	**poke** *v* با نوک انگشت به جان کسی زدن
plot *v* توطئه کردن	**polar** *adj* قطبی
plot *n* طرح؛ قطعه زمین؛ توطنه	**pole** *n* قطب
plow *v* قلبه کردن زمین	**police** *n* پولیس
pluck *v* کندن	**police station** *n* استیشن پولیس
plug *v* پُر کردن سوراخ	**policeman** *n* افسر پولیس
plug *n* سرپوش بوتل واین؛ پلک برق	**policy** *n* پالیسی
plum *n* آلو	**polish** *v* پالش کردن، صیقل کردن
plumber *n* نلدوان	**polish** *n* صیقل
plumbing *n* نلدوانی	**polite** *adj* با ادب
plummet *v* سرنگون شدن، افتادن	**politely** *adv* مودبانه
plump *adj* چاق	**politeness** *n* ادب
plunder *v* غارت کردن	**political** *adj* سیاسی
plunge *v* غوطه خوردن، فرورفتن	**politician** *n* سیاستمدار
plural *n* جمع	**politics** *n* علم سیاست
plus *adj* اضافی	**poll** *n* نظرسنجی، رای
plus *n* بعلاوه	**pollen** *n* گردِ گل
plus *prep* علامه جمع	**pollute** *v* آلوده کردن
plush *adj* مخملی	**pollution** *n* آلودگی
pocket *n* جیب	**pond** *n* حوض
poem *n* شعر	**ponder** *v* اندیشیدن

P

pony *n* اسب کوچک

pool *n* حوض آببازی؛ بازی پول

pool *v* شریک شدن، ائتلاف کردن

poor *adj* غریب

poorly *adv* غریبانه، بطور ضعیف

pop *v* ترق ترق کردن

popcorn *n* جواری پُله

popsicle *n* یکنوع آیسکریم

popular *adj* محبوب

populate *v* پرنفوس ساختن، جمع آوری کردن

population *n* نفوس

porcelain *n* ظروف چینی

porch *n* کتاره پیشروی خانه

porcupine *n* خارپشت کوهی

pore *n* سوراخ های روی صورت

pork *n* گوشت خوک

porous *adj* جلد سوراخ سوراخ

port *n* بندرگاه

portable *adj* حمل شدنی

porter *n* جوالی، بارکش

portion *n* قسمت، بخش

portrait *n* تصویر

portray *v* به تصویر کشیدن

pose *v* قراردادن

pose *n* وضع، حالت

posh *adj* شیک و عصری

position *n* موقف؛ وظیفه

positive *adj* مثبت

positively *adv* بطور مثبت

possess *v* مالک بودن

possession *n* ملکیت

possibility *n* امکان

possible *adj* ممکن

possibly *adv* احتمالاً

post *n* پایه چوبی یا آهنی؛ موقف، وظیفه

post *v* منتشر کردن

post office *n* پُسته خانه

postage *n* تکت پوستی

postcard *n* پُست کارت

poster *n* پوستر

posterity *n* اولاد

postman *n* پُسته رسان

postpone *v* به تعلیق آوردن، معطل کردن

posture *n* حالت، وضعیت

pot *n* ظرف

potato *n* کچالو

potato chip *n* چیپس

potent *adj* قوی، نیرومند

potential *adj* احتمالی

potentially *adv* به احتمال زیاد

pottery *n* کلالی

pouch *n* بسته، خریطه

poultry *n* مرغ خانگی

pound *n* پوند

pound *v* کوبیدن

pour *v* ریختن

poverty *n* فقر

powder *n* پودر

power *n* قدرت؛ انرژی

powerful *adj* قوی، نیرومند

powerless *adj* بی قدرت، ضعیف

P

practical *adj* عملی	**predictable** *adj* قابل پیشبینی
practice *v* تمرین کردن	**prediction** *n* پیشبینی
practice *n* تمرین، عمل	**predisposed** *adj* متمایل
prairie *n* چمن زار	**preempt** *v* پیشدستی کردن
praise *n* ستایش	**preface** *n* مقدمه
praise *v* ستایش کردن	**prefer** *v* ترجیح دادن
praiseworthy *adj* قابل ستایش،	**preference** *n* برتری
ستودنی	**prefix** *n* پیشوند
prank *n* شوخی	**pregnancy** *n* حاملگی، بارداری
prawn *n* حیوان دریایی ده پا	**pregnant** *adj* باردار، حامله
pray *v* نماز خواندن، دعا کردن	**prehistoric** *adj* ماقبل تاریخ
prayer *n* نماز	**prejudice** *n* تعصب، تبعیض
preach *v* وعظ دینی کردن	**preliminary** *adj* مقدماتی
preacher *n* واعظ	**premeditate** *v* از قبل تعیین کردن
precarious *adj* مشکوک، پرخطر	**premier** *adj* برتر
precaution *n* احتیاط	**premise** *n* فرضیه، بنیاد
precede *v* مقدم بودن،	**premises** *n* احاطه، محوطه
قبل از چیزی واقع شدن	**premonition** *n* پیشگویی، اخطار
precedent *n* سابقه	**preoccupation** *n* تمایل، مشغله
preceding *adj* ماقبل، قبلی	**preparation** *n* آمادگی
precious *adj* باارزش	**prepare** *v* آماده کردن
precipice *n* سراشیبی	**prepared** *adj* آماده
precipitate *v* ناگهان واقع شدن	**preposition** *n* حرف اضافی در گرامر
precipitation *n* بارش	**prerogative** *n* امتیاز
precise *adj* مختصر	**prescribe** *v* توصیه کردن
precisely *adv* بطور مختصر	**prescription** *n* نسخه داکتر
precision *n* دقت، درستی	**presence** *n* حضور
precocious *adj* زود رس	**present** *v* پیشکش کردن
predecessor *n* اسبق،	**present** *n* تحفه
کسی که قبل از شما وظیفه داشت	**present** *adj* حاضر
predicament *n* وضع خطرناک	**presentation** *n* ارایه معلومات
predict *v* پیشبینی کردن	**preserve** *v* نگهداشتن

P

preside v نظارت کردن	primarily adv در ابتدا
president n رئیس جمهور	primary adj مقدماتی
press v فشردن	prime adj مهمترین؛ باکیفیت
press n مطبوعات؛ ماشین چاپ	primitive adj قدیمی، باستانی
pressing adj مبرم، عاجل	prince n شهزاده
pressure v فشار دادن	princess n شاهدخت
pressure n فشار؛ تشویش	principal adj اساسی، عمده
prestige n حیثیت، اعتبار	principal n سرمعلم
prestigious adj با اعتبار	principally adv بطور عمده
presumably adv احتمالاً	principle n اساس، بنیاد
presume v فرض کردن	print v چاپ کردن
presuppose v از پیش فرض کردن	print n نسخه چاپی؛ چاپ پا
pretend v وانمود کردن	printer n ماشین چاپ
pretense n بهانه، تظاهر	prior adj قبلی
pretension n تظاهر	prioritize v اولویت بندی کردن
pretentious adj ظاهری	priority n اولویت
pretty adv زیاد	prison n زندان
pretty adj زیبا	prisoner n زندانی
prevalent adj حاکم، مسلط	privacy n خلوت، محرمیت
prevent v جلوگیری کردن	private adj شخصی
prevention n جلوگیری	privilege n امتیاز
preventive adj پیشگیرانه	privileged adj ممتاز، خاص
preview n نمایش از قبل	prize n جایزه
previous adj قبلی	probability n احتمال
previously adv قبلاً	probable adj محتمل
prey n طعمه، شکار	probably adv احتمالاً، شاید
price n قیمت	probe v تحقیق کردن
priceless adj بی بها	problem n مشکل، معضله
pricey adj قیمتی	problematic adj مشکل برانگیز
prick v نیش زدن	procedure n طرزالعمل
pride n افتخار	proceed v به پیش رفتن،
priest n مُلا	حرکت کردن

P

proceeds *n* عاید	program *v* عیار کردن، برنامه ساختن
process *n* پروسه	programmer *n* برنامه ساز
process *v* طی مراحل کردن	progress *n* پیشرفت
procession *n* راهپیمایی	progress *v* پیشرفت کردن
proclaim *v* اعلام کردن	progressive *adj* مترقی، ترقی خواه
proclamation *n* اعلامیه	prohibit *v* منع کردن
procrastinate *v* به تعویق انداختن	prohibition *n* ممنوعیت
procreate *v* تولید مثل کردن	project *n* پروژه
procure *v* تدارک کردن، فراهم نمودن	project *v* طرح کردن، نشان دادن روی دیوار
prod *v* تولید کردن	projector *n* پروجیکتور
prodigious *adj* شگفت انگیز، حیرت آور	prologue *n* مقدمه
prodigy *n* حیرت، چیز غیرعادی	prolong *v* طولانی کردن
produce *n* تولید	promenade *n* گردشگاه
produce *v* تولید کردن	prominent *adj* برجسته، والا
product *n* محصول	promise *v* وعده کردن، تعهد کردن
production *n* تولیدات	promise *n* وعده، تعهد
productive *adj* مثمر	promote *v* ارتقا کردن؛ ترویج کردن
profession *n* مسلک	promotion *n* ارتقا؛ ترویج؛ اعلان تجارتی
professional *n* کارا، مسلکی	prompt *adj* سریع
professional *adj* مسلکی، حرفه ای	prone *adj* متمایل
professionally *adv* از نظر مسلکی	pronoun *n* ضمیر در گرامر
professor *n* پروفیسور، استاد	pronounce *v* تلفظ کردن
proficiency *n* موثریت	pronunciation *n* تلفظ
proficient *adj* موثر، کارا	proof *n* ثبوت
profile *n* مشخصات یک شخص	propaganda *n* تبلیغات
profit *n* نفع	propel *v* سوق دادن
profitable *adj* مفید، پرمنفعت	propeller *n* پروانه طیاره
profound *adj* عمیق	propensity *n* تمایل
program *n* برنامه، پلان، برنامه کمپیوتر	proper *adj* مناسب

properly adv به درستی	**prowler** n جستجو گر
property n جایداد، ملکیت	**proximity** n نزدیکی، مجاورت
proportion n تناسب، قسمت	**prudent** adj با احتیاط
proposal n پیشنهاد	**prune** v آراستن
propose v پیشنهاد کردن	**prune** n آلوبخارا
propose to pv خواستگاری کردن	**pseudonym** n نام مستعار، تخلص
proposition n قضیه، پیشنهاد	**psychiatrist** n داکتر امراض روانی
prose n پیشنهاد کردن	**psychiatry** n تداوی امراض روانی
prosecute v پیگرد قانونی کردن	**psychic** adj روانی
prosecutor n څارنوال	**psychological** adj از لحاظ روانی
prospect n منظره	**psychologist** n روانشناس
prosper v موفق شدن	**psychology** n روانشناسی
prosperity n سعادت، کامیابی	**psychopath** n مریض روانی
prosperous adj کامیاب	**puberty** n بلوغ
protect v حفاظت کردن	**public** adj عامه
protection n حفاظت	**public** n مردم عام
protein n پروتین	**publication** n نشریه
protest n اعتراض	**publicity** n تبلیغات
protest v اعتراض کردن	**publicly** adv درمحضر عام
protrude v تحمیل کردن	**publish** v نشر کردن
proud adj مغرور	**publisher** n ناشر
proudly adv با افتخار	**pudding** n پودینگ، فرنی
prove v ثبوت کردن	**puddle** n آب باران
proven adj ثبوت شده	**puff** n پف کردن
provide v تهیه کردن	**puffy** adj باد شده، باددار
provided conj تهیه شده	**pull** v کش کردن
providence n صرفه جویی	**pull ahead** v پیشرو کش کردن
province n ولایت	**pull up** v پیدا کردن
provision n تهیه، تدارک	**pulley** n قرقره
provisional adj موقت	**pulp** n گوشت میوه
provoke v تحریک کردن	**pulsate** v تکان دادن
prowl v جستجو کردن	**pulse** n نبض

P

pulverize v ساییدن، پودر کردن	put up with pv تحمل کردن
pump n پمپ	putrid adj پوسیده، فاسد
pump v پمپ کردن	puzzle n معما
pumpkin n کدو	puzzled adj گیج شده
punch v مشت زدن، سوراخ کردن	puzzling adj گیج کننده
punctual adj وقت شناس	pyramid n هرم
puncture n سوراخ	python n یک نوع مار بزرگ
punish v جزا دادن	
punishment n جزا	

Q

pupil n شاگرد؛ مردمک چشم	quack v صدای مرغابی کشیدن
puppet n دست نشانده	quagmire n جبه زار، باتلاق
puppy n سگ کوچک، پاپی	quail n بودنه
purchase n خریداری	quaint adj عجیب و جالب
purchase v خریداری کردن	quake v تکان دادن
pure adj خالص، پاک	qualification n
puree n چیز مخلوط شده	سوابق تحصیلی و کاری
purge v پاک سازی	qualified adj واجد شرایط
purify v تصفیه کردن	qualify v واجد شرایط بودن
purity n پاکی، خلوص	quality n کیفیت، مشخصه
purple n ارغوانی	quandary n سردرگمی
purple adj رنگ ارغوانی	quantity n کمیت، مقدار
purpose n هدف	quarantine n انزوا، قرنطین
purposely adv قصداً، عمداً	quarrel v دعوی کردن
purse n دستکول زنانه	quarrel n نزاع، دعوی
pursue v تعقیب کردن	quarrelsome adj ستیزه جو،
push v فشار دادن، فشار آوردن	دعوی یی
push n فشار، زور	quarry n معدن سنگ
pushy adj تحمیل کننده	quart n یک چهارم حصه
put v گذاشتن	
put aside pv کنار گذاشتن	
put away pv علیحده کردن	
put off pv به تعویق انداختن	

Q

quarter n سکه ۵۲ سنتی؛ یک چهارم حصه

quarterly adj در هر سه ماه یکبار

quash v لغو کردن، باطل کردن

queen n ملکه

quell v فرو ریختن

quench v فرونشاندن

query v سوال

quest n تلاش

question n سوال

question v سوال کردن

questionable adj سوال برانگیز

questionnaire n پرسشنامه

queue n صف، ردیف

quick adj سریع، تیز

quickly adv به سرعت

quicksand n ریگ روان

quiet adj خاموش

quietly adv به خاموشی، به آرامی

quilt n لحاف

quit v ترک کردن

quite adv کاملاً

quiver v لرزش

quiz v امتحان دادن

quiz n امتحان مختصر

quota n سهمیه، سهم

quotation n نرخ دادن، نرخ تخمینی دادن

quote v نرخ دادن، نقل قول کردن

quote v نقل قول

quotient n ضریب، خارج قسمت

R

rabbi n عالم یهودی

rabbit n خرگوش

rabies n مرض سگ دیوانه

raccoon n راکون، یکنوع حیوان شبه موش خرما

race v مسابقه دادن، دویدن

race n مسابقه؛ نژاد

racetrack n خط دوش

racing n مسابقه

racism n نژاد پرستی

racist adj نژاد پرست

rack n طاقچه

racket n صدای بلند، جالی بازی تینیس

radar n رادار

radiation n تابش، تشعشع

radiator n رادیاتور، سرد کننده

radical adj افراطی

radio n رادیو

radish n ملی سرخک

radius n شعاع

raffle n قرعه کشی

raft n کشتی یا قایق

rag n کهنه

rage n خشم

ragged adj ناهموار، سرک ناهموار

raid n حمله

raid v حمله کردن

rail n ریل

railroad n خط ریل	rapid adj سریع، تیز
railway n مسیر عبور ریل	rapport n رابطه نزدیک
rain n باران	rare adj نادر، کمیاب؛ نیم پخته
rain v باریدن	rarely adv ندرتاً
rainbow n کمان رستم	rash adj بی پروا
raincoat n بالاپوش بارانی	rash n خارش، بخار
raindrop n قطره باران	raspberry n یکنوع توت سرخ
rainfall n باران شدید	rat n موش
rainforest n جنگل بارانی	rate v برآورد کردن، سنجیدن
rainy adj بارانی	rate n نرخ، سرعت
raise v افزایش دادن؛ بزرگ کردن	rather adv نسبتاً
پرورش کردن	rating n رتبه بندی
raise n ترفیع، افزایش	ratio n نسبت
raisin n کشمش	ration n مزد روزانه
rake n جمع کن برگها	ration v مزد روزانه دادن
rally n تجمع	rational adj منطقی، عقلانی
ram v فروبردن	rationale n بنیاد، اساس
ram n قوچ	rationalize v توجیه کردن
ramification n انشعاب، چند دستگی	rattle v لرزاندن
ramp n سطح شیب دار	ravage v ویران کردن
rampage v خشم، دادوبیداد	rave v غُریدن
rampant adj شایع، حکمفرما	raw adj خام
ranch n فارم بزرگ	ray n شعاع
rancor n کینه، بدخواهی	razor n تیغ، پل ریش
random adj تصادفی	reach n دسترسی
randomly adv بطور تصادفی	reach v رسیدن؛ رسیدگی کردن
range v در صف آوردن	react v عکس العمل کردن
range n صف، رده؛ سلسله کوه ها	reaction n عکس العمل
rank n رتبه	read v خواندن
rank v رتبه بندی کردن	reader n خواننده
ransack v غارت کردن	readily adv بطور آماده
ransom n خون بها	reading n قابلیت خواندن؛ خوانش

R

ready *adj* آماده؛ تیار	**recent** *adj* تازه، اخیر
real *adj* واقعی	**recently** *adv* در این اواخر
realistic *adj* واقعبینانه	**reception** *n* تشریفات رسمی؛
reality *n* واقعیت	میز پذیرش
realize *v* درک کردن	**receptionist** *n* مسوول پذیرش
really *adv* واقعا؛ بسیار زیاد	**receptive** *adj* پذیرا
reap *v* درو کردن حاصلات	**recess** *n* وقفه، عقب نشینی
reappear *v* دوباره ظاهر شدن	**recession** *n* بحران اقتصادی
rear *v* پرورش کردن	**recharge** *v* دوباره چارج کردن
rear *n* پشت	**recipe** *n* برنامه آشپزی
rear *adj* عقبی	**reciprocal** *adj* متقابل، دوجانبه
rearrange *v* دوباره تنظیم کردن	**recital** *n* از یاد خوانی
reason *v* استدلال کردن	**recite** *v* قرائت کردن
reason *n* دلیل	**reckless** *adj* بی احتیاط
reasonable *adj* مناسب	**reckon** *v* فرض کردن
reassure *v* اطمینان دادن	**recline** *v* خم شدن
rebate *n* تخفیف	**recognition** *n* تشخیص؛
rebel *v* شوریدن، شورش کردن	به رسمیت شناختن
rebel *n* یاغی، شورشی	**recognize** *v* تشخیص کردن،
rebellion *n* شورش	به رسمیت شناختن
reboot *v* دوباره روشن کردن	**recollect** *v* دوباره جمع آوری کردن
rebound *v* برگشت	**recollection** *n* جمع آوری مجدد
rebuff *v* رد کردن	**recommend** *v* سفارش کردن
rebuild *v* دوباره ساختن	**recommendation** *n* سفارشنامه
rebuke *v* سرزنش کردن	**recompense** *v* جبران کردن
rebut *v* رد کردن	**reconsider** *v* تجدید نظر کردن
recall *v* به خاطر آوردن	**reconstruct** *v* بازسازی کردن
recant *v* انکار کردن	**record** *v* ثبت کردن رویداد ها؛
recap *v* خلاصه کردن	ثبت موسیقی
recede *v* عقب نشینی کردن	**record** *n* یادداشت؛ ریکارد ورزشی؛
receipt *n* رسید	ثبت موسیقی
receive *v* دریافت کردن	**record player** *n* پخش کننده موسیقی

R

آله ثبت کننده صدا recorder *n*	مأخذ؛ ارجاع reference *n*
ثبت صدا recording *n*	دوباره پر کردن refill *v*
شمارش مجدد recount *n*	تصفیه کردن refine *v*
جبران کردن recoup *v*	تصفیه شده refined *adj*
مراجعه، توسل recourse *n*	تصفیه خانه refinery *n*
شفایافتن، بازیافتن recover *v*	منعکس کردن reflect *v*
تفریح کردن، recreate *v*	انعکاس؛ تفکر reflection *n*
دوباره خلق کردن	اصلاح کردن reform *v*
تفریح recreation *n*	اصلاحات reform *n*
استخدام recruit *n*	اجتناب کردن refrain *v*
استخدام کردن recruit *v*	تازه کردن refresh *v*
مستطیل rectangle *n*	طراوت بخش refreshing *adj*
مستطیلی rectangular *adj*	طراوت؛ نوشابه refreshment *n*
اصلاح کردن rectify *v*	دریخچال گذاشتن، refrigerate *v*
بهبود یافتن recuperate *v*	منجمد کردن
تکرار شدن recur *v*	یخچال refrigerator *n*
تکرار recurrence *n*	گرفتن مواد سوخت refuel *v*
بازیافتن recycle *v*	مهاجرت refuge *n*
بازیافت شده recycled *adj*	مهاجر refugee *n*
رنگ سرخ red *adj*	پس پرداخت refund *n*
سرخ red *n*	تازه کردن، از نو ساختن refurbish *v*
رها ساختن redeem *v*	رد، امتناع refusal *n*
رستگاری redemption *n*	اشیای بیکاره؛ پس مانده؛ refuse *n*
دوباره انجام دادن redo *v*	فاضله
کاهش دادن reduce *v*	رد کردن refuse *v*
زائد، اضافی redundant *adj*	تکذیب کردن، نپذیرفتن refute *v*
تپه دریایی reef *n*	سلطنتی regal *adj*
حلقه reel *n*	مراعت کردن regard *v*
تصویب مجدد reenactment *n*	ملاحظه regard *n*
دخول مجدد reentry *n*	در رابطه به regarding *prep*
رجوع کردن، راجع کردن refer *v*	بدون در نظرداشت regardless *adv*
داور مسابقات referee *n*	احترامات regards *n*

regime *n* رژیم

regiment *n* فرقه

region *n* منطقه

regional *adj* منطقوی

register *v* ثبت نام کردن

register *n* ثبت نام؛
سیستم ثبت فروشات

registration *n* ثبت، نام نویسی

regret *v* پشیمان شدن، تأسف خوردن

regret *n* پشیمانی

regrettable *adj* تأسف آور

regular *adj* عادی، مکرر، منظم

regularly *adv* بطور منظم

regulate *v* تنظیم کردن

regulation *n* مقرره

rehabilitate *v* احیای مجدد کردن

rehearsal *n* تمرین برای اجرای نمایش

rehearse *v*
تمرین کردن برای اجرای نمایش

reign *n* سلطنت

reign *v* سلطنت کردن

reimburse *v* دوباره تادیه کردن

reimbursement *n* بازپرداخت

reindeer *n* یکنوع حیوان، گوزن

reinforce *v* تقویت کردن

reinforcements *n* تقویت، استحکام

reiterate *v* مجدداً تأکید کردن

reject *v* رد کردن

rejection *n* رد

rejoice *v* شادی کردن، خوشی کردن

rejuvenate *v* دوباره جوان کردن

relate *v* ارتباط دادن، همدردی کردن

related *adj* مرتبط، بهم پیوسته

relation *n* رابطه فامیلی؛
رابطه بین اشیا

relationship *n* قرابت؛
رابطه عاشقانه

relative *n* خویشاوند

relative *adj* ربطی، مرتبط

relax *v* راحت شدن، آرام کردن

relaxation *n* آرامش، راحتی

relaxed *adj* آرام، راحت

relaxing *adj* آرامش بخش،
راحت کننده

relay *v* انتقال دادن، بازپخش کردن

release *n* انتشار

release *v* رها کردن؛ منتشر کردن

relentless *adj* بی رحم

relevance *n* ربط

relevant *adj* مربوط

reliable *adj* قابل اعتبار

reliance *n* اتکا، تکیه

reliant *adj* متکی

relief *n* تسکین، راحتی

relieve *v* تسکین شدن؛
جاگزین در وظیفه

relieved *adj* آسوده

religion *n* مذهب، دین

religious *adj* مذهبی، دینی

relinquish *v* رها کردن، ترک کردن

relish *v* لذت بردن

relocate *v* نقل مکان کردن

reluctant *adj* بی میل

reluctantly *adv* به بی میلی

R

rely v اتکا ورزیدن	**repeat** v تکرار کردن
remain v باقی ماندن	**repel** v دفع کردن
remainder n باقیمانده	**repellant** n دفع کننده
remaining adj متباقی	**repent** v توبه کردن
remains n بقایا	**repetition** n تکرار
remark v اظهار نظر کردن	**repetitive** adj تکراری
remarkable adj قابل توجه	**replace** v عوض کردن
remedy n علاج؛ راه حل	**replacement** n عوض، تعویض
remember v به یاد داشتن	**replay** n دوباره نواختن
remind v به یاد آوردن	**replenish** v دوباره پر کردن
reminder n آگهی	**replica** n المثنی
remnant n بقیه، باقی مانده	**replicate** v تکثیر کردن
remodel v بازسازی کردن،	**reply** n پاسخ
تغییر شکل دادن	**reply** v پاسخ دادن
remorse n پشیمانی	**report** n گزارش
remorseful adj پشیمان	**report** v گزارش دادن
remote adj ازراه دور	**report card** n ورقه نمرات در مکتب
remote control n ریموت،	**reporter** n گزارشگر
آله کنترول از دور	**represent** v از کسی نمایندگی کردن
remove v دور کردن، از بین بردن	**representation** n نمایندگی از کسی
renew v تجدید کردن	**representative** n نماینده
renounce v صرف نظر کردن	**repress** v سرکوب کردن
renovate v تجدید کردن، نو ساختن	**reprint** n دوباره چاپ کردن
renovation n نوسازی	**reprisal** n انتقام جویی
renowned adj مشهور	**reproach** v سرزنش کردن
rent n کرایه	**reproduce** v تولید مجدد کردن؛
rent v کرایه گرفتن، کرایه دادن	تولید نسل کردن
reorganize v دوباره تنظیم کردن	**reproduction** n تولید مجدد؛
repair v ترمیم کردن	تولید نسل
repay v دوباره پرداختن	**reptile** n خزنده
repayment n بازپرداخت	**republic** n جمهوری
repeal v لغو کردن	**repudiate** v رد کردن

R

repugnant *adj* متناقض

repulse *v* دفع کردن

repulsive *adj* تنفر آور

reputation *n* حیثیت، اعتبار

request *n* تقاضا

request *v* تقاضا کردن

require *v* مستلزم بودن، نیاز داشتن

requirement *n* شرط، نیاز

reschedule *v*
دوباره زمان بندی کردن

rescue *v* نجات دادن

research *n* تحقیق

research *v* تحقیق کردن

researcher *n* محقق

resemblance *n* شباهت

resemble *v* شباهت داشتن

resent *v* نفرت کردن، رنجیدن از

resentment *n* رنجش، تنفر

reservation *n* ریزرف؛ شک داشتن

reserve *v* ریزرف کردن

reserved *adj* ریزرف شده

reservoir *n* ذخیره آب

reset *v* دوباره عیار کردن

reside *v* سکونت داشتن

residence *n* محل سکونت

resident *n* باشنده، ساکن

residential *adj* رهایشی

residue *n* باقی مانده

resign *v* استعفا دادن

resignation *n* استعفا

resilient *adj* ارتجاعی

resist *v* مقاومت کردن

resistance *n* مقاومت

resolute *adj* مصمم، ثابت

resolution *n* تصمیم، عزم، تصویب

resolve *v* برطرف کردن

resort *v* پناه بردن، متوسل شدن

resounding *adj* چشمگیر

resource *n* منبع

respect *n* احترام

respect *v* احترام کردن

respectable *adj* قابل احترام

respectful *adj* مودب

respective *adj* مربوطه

respiration *n* تنفس

respond *v* جواب دادن

response *n* جواب

responsibility *n* مسوولیت

responsible *adj* مسوول

responsive *adj* پاسخگو

rest *v* استراحت کردن

rest *n* باقیمانده،استراحت

restaurant *n* رستورانت

restful *adj* مستریح، آرام

restless *adj* بیقرار

restore *v* بازگرداندن

restrain *v* مهار کردن

restraint *n* پرهیز، اجتناب

restrict *v* محدود ساختن

restriction *n* محدودیت

restroom *n* تشناب

result *v* باعث شدن، منتج شدن

result *n* نتیجه

resume *v* دوباره شروع کردن

R

resurface v دوباره هموار کردن	revise v تجدید کردن
retail n خرده فروشی	revision n تجدید نظر
retailer n خرده فروش	revive v احیا کردن
retain v حفظ کردن	revoke v لغو، ابطال
retaliate v انتقام گرفتن	revolt v شورش
retention n حفظ، نگهداری	revolting adj شورشی
retire v تقاعد کردن	revolution n انقلاب
retirement n تقاعد	revolutionary adj انقلابی
retract v عقب نشینی کردن	revolutionize v انقلابی کردن
retreat v کناره گیری کردن	revolve v چرخیدن
retrieve v بازیافتن	revue n نقد و بررسی
retroactive adj	reward v انعام دادن، تقدیر کردن
اعتبار داشتن از یک تاریخ در گذشته	reward n انعام، پاداش
return n بازگشت	rewarding adj پرارزش، پر مزیت
return v بازگشت کردن	rewind v چرخاندن، پیچاندن
reunion n دوباره یکجا شدن	rhinoceros n
reunite v دوباره متحد شدن	یکنوع حیوان بنام کرگدن
reuse v دوباره استفاده کردن	rhyme n قافیه در شعر
reveal v افشا کردن، برملا ساختن	rhyme v قافیه ساختن
revealing adj آشکار کننده	rhythm n ریتم،
revel v شادی کردن	وزن در خواندن آهنگ
revelation n افشاء	rib n قبرغه
revenge n انتقام گرفتن	ribbon n فیته
revenue n عاید	rice n برنج
reverence n احترام، حرمت	rich adj ثروتمند؛ غنی
reversal n برگشت، واژگونی	rid v رهایی یافتن از
reverse v تغییر استقامت دادن	rid of pv رها شدن از
reverse n معکوس، برعکس	riddle n معما، چیستان
reversible adj برگشت پذیر	ride v سوار شدن، راندن
revert v برگرداندن	ride n سواری
review n مرور	ridge n لبه، خط الراس
review v مرور کردن، غور کردن	ridicule v مسخره کردن

R

ridiculous *adj* مسخره، خنده آور	**river** *n* دریا
rifle *n* تفنگچه	**riveting** *adj* چین خورده
rift *n* بریدگی	**road** *n* سرک
right *adj* درست؛ طرف راست	**roam** *v* سیر کردن، حرکت داشتن
right *adv* دقیقاً؛ بدرستی؛ به طرف راست	**roar** *n* غُرش
right *n* طرف راست؛ حق قانونی؛ عادلانه	**roar** *v* غُریدن
rigid *adj* محکم	**roast** *v* کباب کردن
rigor *n* سخت گیری	**rob** *v* دزدیدن
rigorous *adj* سختگیرانه، شدید	**robber** *n* دزد
rim *n* لبه، دیواره	**robbery** *n* دزدی
ring *n* انگشتر؛ حلقه؛ صدا در گوش؛ رنگ مسابقه	**robe** *n* لباس، چین
ring *v* زنگ زدن	**robot** *n* روبات، آدم برقی
ringtone *n* صدای زنگ تیلفون	**robust** *adj* مستحکم
rinse *v* آبکش کردن	**rock** *v* تکان دادن، تکان خوردن
riot *n* شورش	**rock** *n* سنگ، سخره؛ موسیقی راک
riot *v* شورش کردن	**rocket** *n* راکت
rip *v* پاره کردن	**rocky** *adj* سنگی، ناهموار
ripe *adj* پخته	**rod** *n* میله آهنی
ripen *v* پخته شدن، پخته کردن	**rodent** *n* حیوان پستاندار
rip-off *n* پاره کردن	**role** *n* نقش، رول
ripple *n* موج دار	**roll** *v* لوله کردن؛ لول دادن
rise *v* بلند شدن، برخاستن	**roll** *n* لوله؛ چیز لوله شده
rise *n* خیزش	**roll over** *pv* تمدید مدت پرداخت
risk *v* به خطر انداختن	**romance** *n* عاشقانه، داستان عاشقانه
risk *n* خطر	**romantic** *adj* عاشقانه، رومانتیک
risky *adj* خطرناک	**roof** *n* بام
ritual *n* مراسم مذهبی	**rookie** *adj* تازه کار
rival *n* رقیب	**room** *n* اتاق، فضا
rivalry *n* رقابت	**roommate** *n* هم اتاقی
	roomy *adj* وسیع، فراخ
	rooster *n* خروس
	root *n* ریشه

R

rope *n* ریسمان	**rudimentary** *adj* ابتدایی
rose *n* گل سرخ	**rug** *n* قالیچه
rosy *adj* گلگون	**rugged** *adj* ناهوار
rot *v* فرسوده شدن، پوسیدن	**ruin** *v* ویران کردن
rotate *v* چرخاندن، چرخیدن	**ruin** *n* ویرانی
rotation *n* چرخش	**rule** *v* حکومت کردن
rotten *adj* پوسیده، فرسوده	**rule** *n* قانون
rough *adj* درشت؛ خشن	**ruler** *n* خط کش؛ حاکم منطقه
roughly *adv* تقریباً؛ تخمینی؛	**rumble** *v* غُرش
به درشتی	**rumor** *n* شایعه، آوازه
round *adj* گِرد	**run** *n* دوش
round-trip *adj* سفر دوطرفه	**run** *v* دویدن، به کار انداختن،
rouse *v* بیدار کردن	پیش بردن تجارت
rousing *adj* تحریک کننده	**run away** *pv* فرار کردن
route *n* مسیر، خط سیر	**run into** *pv* مواجه شدن، برخوردن
routine *n* جریان عادی	**run out** *pv* تمام شدن
routine *adj* روزمره	**run over** *pv* لگد مال کردن
row *n* ردیف	**run up** *pv* اجرا کردن
row *v* کشتی رانی کردن،	**runner** *n* دونده، ورزشکار دوش
پایدل زدن کشتی	**runway** *n* فرار
rowdy *adj* دادوبیداد	**rupture** *n* پاره گی
royal *adj* شاهی، شاهانه	**rupture** *v* گسستن، از هم جدا کردن
royalty *n* اعضای خانواده شاهی	**rural** *adj* دهاتی
rub *v* مالیدن	**ruse** *n* نیرنگ، مکر
rubber *n* رابر	**rush** *v* عجله کردن
rubber band *n* فیته رابری	**rust** *n* زنگ زدگی
rubble *n* خرده سنگ	**rust** *v* زنگ زدن آهن
ruby *n* یاقوت	**rustic** *adj* دهاتی
rudder *n* وسیله هدایت طیاره	**rust-proof** *adj* ضد زنگ زدگی
rude *adj* گستاخ	**rusty** *adj* زنگ زده
rudely *adv* به گستاخی	**ruthless** *adj* بی رحم، ظالم
rudeness *n* گستاخی	**rye** *n* یکنوع غله، جَو

R

S

sabotage *n* خرابکاری قصدی

sabotage *v* خرابکاری کردن،
قصداً خراب کردن

sack *n* خریطه

sacred *adj* مقدس

sacrifice *n* قربانی دادن؛
قربانی کردن حیوان

sad *adj* غمگین

sadden *v* غمگین کردن

saddle *n* زین اسب

sadly *adv* به غمگینی

sadness *n* غمگینی

safe *n* سیف،
صندوق مصوون برای پول

safe *adj* مصوون

safeguard *n* حفاظت

safely *adv* بدون خطر، بطور مصوون

safety *n* مصوونیت

safety belt *adv* کمربند ایمنی

sail *n* کشتی رانی

sail *v* کشتی رانی کردن

sailboat *n* کشتی بادی

sailor *n* کشتی ران

saint *n* مقدس

salad *n* سلاد

salary *n* معاش

sale *n* فروش؛ لیلام

salesman *n* فروشنده مرد

saleswoman *n* فروشنده زن

saliva *n* آب دهن

salmon *n* ماهی سلمون

salon *n* سالون، آرایشگاه

salsa *n* سالسا، سلاته

salt *n* نمک

salty *adj* شور، نمکی

salvage *v* نجات دادن

salvation *n* نجات، رهایی

same *adj* مشابه

same *pron* مشابه

sample *n* نمونه

sanction *n* تحریم

sanction *v* تحریم کردن

sanctity *n* حرمت، تقدس

sanctuary *n* جایگاه مقدس

sand *n* ریگ

sandal *n* چپلک

sandpaper *n* ریگمال

sandwich *n* ساندویچ

sane *adj* عاقل، سالم

sanity *n* سلامت عقل

sap *n* شیره، عصاره

sapphire *n* یکنوع یاقوت کبود

sarcasm *n* طعنه

sarcastic *adj* طعنه آمیز

sardine *n* ماهی ساردین

satellite *n* ستلایت

satire *n* طعنه

satisfaction *n* رضایت، خوشنودی

satisfactory *adj* قناعت بخش

satisfied *adj* قانع، راضی

satisfy *v* قانع ساختن، راضی ساختن

satisfying adj ،قانع کننده رضایت بخش	**scarcely** adv به ندرت
saturate v اشباع کردن	**scarcity** n ندرت، کمبود
Saturday n روز شنبه	**scare** v ترساندن
Saturn n سیاره زحل	**scare away** pv فراردادن، ترساندن
sauce n ساس، چاشنی	**scared** adj ترسیده
saucepan n تخم پزی	**scarf** n دستمال گردن
saucer n بشقاب	**scary** adj ترسناک
sausage n ساسج	**scatter** v پاشیدن، پراگنده شدن
savage adj وحشی	**scenario** n سناریو
save v نجات دادن؛ پس انداز کردن؛ ذخیره کردن	**scene** n صحنه
savings n پس انداز	**scenery** n منظره
savior n نجات دهنده	**scenic** adj خوش منظر
savor v مزه، ذائقه	**scent** n عطر
saw n اره	**scented** adj معطر
saw v اره کردن	**schedule** n تقسیم اوقات
saxophone n آله موسیقی سکسافون	**schedule** v زمان بندی کردن
say v گفتن	**scheme** v طرح کردن
saying n گفته، اظهار	**scheme** n نقشه، طرح
scab n زخم خشک شده	**scholar** n محقق، پژوهشگر
scaffolding n بسته کاری چوب	**scholarship** n بورس تحصیلی
scald v سوزاندن	**school** n مکتب
scale n ترازو؛ مقیاس، اندازه	**science** n ساینس، علم
scalp n جمجمه	**scientific** adj علمی
scam n کلاهبرداری	**scientist** n ساینس دان
scan v اسکن کردن	**scissors** n قیچی
scandal n رسوایی	**scoff** v تمسخر کردن
scanner n ماشین اسکنر	**scold** v سرزنش کردن
scapegoat n بزغاله	**scooter** n اسکوتر اطفال
scar n جای زخم	**scope** n حد، وسعت
scarce adj کمیاب	**scorch** v سوزاندن
	score n نمره
	score v نمره گرفتن در بازی

S

تخته نمرات scoreboard n	غذای بحری seafood n
تمسخر کردن scorn v	مرغ دریایی seagull n
تمسخر آمیز scornful adj	خوک آبی، مُهر یا تاپه seal n
گژدم scorpion n	مُهر کردن، تاپه کردن seal v
پستی، رزالت scoundrel n	درز، شکاف seam n
پاک کاری کردن scour v	بدون درز seamless adj
پیشآهنگ scout n	خیاط، دوزنده seamstress n
مخلوط کردن scramble v	جستجو کردن search v
مخلوط شده scrambled adj	جستجو، بازرسی search n
توته، تکه scrap n	صدف دریایی seashell n
دور انداختن scrap v	ساحل دریا seashore n
تراش کردن scrape v	دریا زده seasick adj
خراش، خراشیدگی scratch n	اخته کردن، مخلوط کردن season v
خراشیدن scratch v	فصل، وقت معین در سال season n
فریاد زدن scream v	فصلی، موسمی seasonal adj
فریاد، چیغ scream n	مصالح جات seasoning n
چیغ زدن screech v	چوکی seat n
ارزیابی کردن، تفتیش کردن screen v	کمربند چوکی seat belt n
پرده تلویزیون و کمپیوتر screen n	منزوی secluded adj
پیچاندن screw n	ثانیه second n
پیچ کش screwdriver n	دوم second adj
خط ناخوانا scribble v	دومی second adv
دستخط script n	ثانوی، فرعی secondary adj
در کمپیوتر از یک متن به scroll v متن دیگر رفتن	رازداری secrecy n
پیچش، پایین و بالا رفتن scroll n	راز secret n
تراش کردن scrub v	مخفی secret adj
دقیق scrupulous adj	سکرتر، منشی secretary n
موشگافی، دقت scrutiny n	مخفیانه secretive adj
مجسمه ساز sculptor n	بطور مخفیانه secretly adv
مجسمه sculpture n	بخش، قسمت section n
دریا sea n	سکتور، بخش sector n
	مصوون نگهداشتن secure v

S

secure adj مصوون، محکم	**sellout** n فروش
securely adv بطور مصوون	**semester** n سمستر
security n امنیت	**senate** n سنا، مجلس سنا
sedate v آرام کردن	**senator** n سناتور
seduce v گمراه کردن	**send** v فرستادن
از راه بدر کردن	**sender** n فرستنده
see v دیدن، ملاقات کردن، فهمیدن	**senior** adj ارشد، بزرگسال
seed n تخم زراعتی	**senior citizen** n شهروند ارشد
seedless adj بی تخم	**seniority** n ارشدیت
seedy adj تخم دار	**sensation** n حس، احساس
seek v جستجو کردن	**sense** v حس کردن
seem v معلوم شدن، به نظر رسیدن	**sense** n حس، احساس
see-through adj لباس جالی دار،	**senseless** adj بی معنی،
نیمه شفاف	بدون احساس
segment n بخش، قسمت	**sensible** adj محسوس، حس شدنی
segregate v جدا کردن	**sensitive** adj حساس
segregation n تفکیک، جداسازی	**sentence** n جمله؛ محکومیت
seize v گرفتن، غصب کردن	**sentence** v محکوم کردن
seizure n تصرف	**sentiment** n تمایل، احساسات
seldom adv به ندرت	**sentimental** adj احساساتی
select v انتخاب کردن	**separate** adj جدا
selection n انتخاب	**separate** v جدا کردن
self n خود	**separately** adv بطور جداگانه
self-conscious adj خجل، خود آگاه	**separation** n جدایی، تفکیک
self-defense n دفاع خودی	**September** n ماه سپتمبر
self-employed n شغل آزاد	**sequel** n نتیجه، خاتمه
self-esteem n اعتماد به نفس	**sequence** n ترادف، سلسله
selfish adj خودخواه	**serenade** n قطعه موسیقی عاشقانه
selfishness n خودخواهی	**serene** adj آرام، بدون سروصدا
self-respect n احترام به خود	**sergeant** n خورد ضابط
sell v فروختن	**series** n سلسله؛ سریال تلویزیونی
seller n فروشنده	**serious** adj جدی، مهم

S

موعظه، خُطبه	sermon *n*
مار بزرگ	serpent *n*
خدمتگار	servant *n*
خدمت کردن	serve *v*
خدمت	service *n*
جلسه	session *n*
سیت، بسته اشیا	set *n*
عیار کردن	set *v*
عازم شدن	set off *pv*
شروع به کار کرده	set out *pv*
نصب کردن، برپا کردن	set up *pv*
شکست، عقب گرد	setback *n*
وضعیت؛ حالت؛ جای	setting *n*
مسکن گزین شدن؛ حساب را تسویه کردن	settle *v*
مستقر شدن	settle down *pv*
قانع شدن برای	settle for *pv*
قرارداد؛ مسکن گزینی	settlement *n*
مستقر کننده	settler *n*
ترتیب و تنظیم، برپایی	setup *n*
هفت	seven *n*
هفده	seventeen *n*
هفتم	seventh *adj*
هفتاد	seventy *n*
جدا کردن	sever *v*
چند	several *pron*
چندین	several *adj*
جدایی، قطع	severance *n*
شدید	severe *adj*
دوختن	sew *v*
دوخت	sewage *n*
دوزنده	sewer *n*

دوختن	sewing *n*
جنسیت	sex *n*
کهنه	shabby *adj*
کلبه	shack *n*
سایه رخ	shade *n*
سایه	shadow *n*
سایه دار	shady *adj*
تکان دادن، شور دادن	shake *v*
لرزان	shaky *adj*
باید، خواهد	shall *modal v*
نیمه عمیق	shallow *adj*
ساختگی	sham *n*
شرم	shame *n*
شرمنده ساختن	shame *v*
شرمنده، خجالت	shameful *adj*
بی حیا، بی شرم	shameless *adj*
شامپو	shampoo *n*
شکل دادن	shape *v*
شکل، وضعیت فزیکی	shape *n*
حصه، تقسیم	share *n*
شریک ساختن، تقسیم کردن	share *v*
شریک تجارت	shareholder *n*
نهنگ	shark *n*
تیز، نوک تیز؛ آشکارا	sharp *adj*
تیز کردن	sharpen *v*
تیزکننده	sharpener *n*
توته توته شدن، توته کردن	shatter *v*
شکننده	shattering *adj*
تراشیدن	shave *v*
آن زن	she *pron*
بریدن، قیچی کردن	shear *v*
ریختن، پاشیدن	shed *v*

shed *n* کلبه، خانه خورد چوبی	shoot *v* فیر کردن؛ در فلم تمثیل کردن
sheep *n* گوسفند	shop *v* خریداری کردن
sheet *n* روجایی؛ ورق کاغذ	shop *n* مغازه، دوکان
shelf *n* طاقچه	shoplifting *n* دزدی از فروشگاه
shell *n* قشر	shopping *n* خریداری
shellfish *n* صدف	shopping mall *n* مرکز خریداری، مال
shelter *n* سرپناه	shore *n* ساحل
shelter *v* سرپناه دادن	short *adj* کوتاه؛ قد کوتاه؛ مختصر
shepherd *n* چوپان	shortage *n* کمبود
sheriff *n* آمر حوزه	shortcoming *n* نقص، کمبودی
shield *n* سپر	shortcut *n* میانبر، راه کوتاه
shield *v* سپر شدن، پوشاندن	shorten *v* کوتاه کردن
shift *v* حرکت دادن؛ تصمیم عوض کردن	shorthand *n* مختصر نویسی، کوتاه نویسی
shift *n* شفت کاری؛ تغییر در وضعیت	short-lived *adj* عمر کوتاه
shin *n* ساق پا	shortly *adv* به زودی
shine *v* درخشیدن	shorts *n* نیکر
shiny *adj* درخشنده	shortsighted *adj* نزدیک بین
ship *v* فرستادن	short-term *adj* کوتاه مدت
ship *n* کشتی	shot *n* فیر تفنگ؛ عکس یا فلم؛ پیچکاری
shipment *n* حمل و نقل	shotgun *n* تفنگ ساچمه یی
shipwreck *n* شکستگی در کشتی	should *modal v* باید، خواهد
shipyard *n* کارخانه کشتی سازی	shoulder *n* شانه
shirt *n* پیراهن	shout *n* فریاد
shiver *v* لرزیدن	shout *v* فریاد کشیدن
shock *v* تکان دادن؛ متعجب ساختن	shove *v* پرتاب کردن
shock *n* تکان؛ تعجب؛ برق گرفتگی	shovel *n* بیل
shocking *adj* تکان دهنده؛ تعجب آور	shovel *v* بیل زدن
shoddy *adj* بی کیفیت	show *v* نشان دادن
shoe *n* بوت	
shoe polish *n* پالش بوت	
shoe store *n* بوت فروشی	
shoelace *n* بند بوت	

S

show n نمایش

show off pv خودنمایی کردن

show up pv حاضر شدن، آمدن

showdown n مرحله نهایی مسابقات

shower n شاور

shred v خرد کردن، ریزه کردن

shred n خرده، ریزه

shrewd adj زیرک، زرنگ

shriek v چیغ زدن

shriek n چیغ، فریاد

shrimp n شریم، یکنوع غذای دریایی

shrine n زیارت

shrink v کوچک شدن

shrub n بُته

shrug v شانه بالا انداختن

shudder v لرزیدن

shuffle v مخلوط کردن، آهسته قدم زدن

shun v اجتناب کردن از

shut v بسته کردن

shut off pv خاموش کردن

shut up pv خاموش باش

shuttle v انتقال دادن مامورین

shy adj عاجز، بی جرات

shyness n بی جراتی، احساس شرم داشتن

sibling n برادر یا خواهر

sick adj مریض

sicken v مریض کردن

sickening adj مریض کننده

sickle n داس

sickness n مریضی

side n طرف

side effect n عوارض جانبی

sideburns n شقیقه

sidestep v کنار گذاشتن، کنار رفتن

sidewalk n پیاده رو

sideways adv به پهلو

siege n محاصره

sift v غربال کردن

sigh v آه کشیدن، افسوس کردن

sigh n آه، افسوس

sight n منظره؛ دید چشم

sightseeing n تفریح، دیدن از مناظر

sign v امضا کردن

sign n لوحه، علامه

signal n زگنال تیلفون، وسیله برقی

signal v زگنال دادن

signature n امضا

significance n اهمیت، ویژه گی

significant adj مشخص؛ مهم، بزرگ

signify v دلالت کردن

silence n خاموشی، سکوت

silent adj خاموش

silhouette n تصویر سایه دارد

silk n ابریشم

silly adj احمق، نادان

silver adj رنگ نقره یی

silver n نقره

silverware n ظروف نقره یی

similar adj شبیه، مشابه

similarity n شباهت

simmer *v* جوشیدن، به جوش آمدن	sitting *n* نشست، جلسه
simple *adj* ساده، عام فهم، ظاهراً ساده	situated *adj* واقع در جای
simplicity *n* سادگی	situation *n* وضعیت
simplify *v* ساده کردن	six *n* شش
simply *adv* به ساده گی	sixteen *n* شانزده
simulate *v* شبیه ساختن، تقلید کردن	sixth *adj* ششم
simulation *n* تقلید، تظاهر	sixty *n* شصت
simultaneous *adj* همزمان	sizable *adj* قابل توجه، بزرگ
sin *n* گناه	size *n* اندازه
sin *v* گناه کردن	skate *v* اسکیت بازی کردن
since *adv* از وقتیکه	skate *n* بازی اسکیت
since *prep* ازآنوقت	skateboard *n* تخته بازی اسکیت
since *conj* چونکه	skeleton *n* اسکلیت
sincere *adj* مخلص	skeptic *n* مشکوک
sincerely *adv* خالصانه، با خلوص	skeptical *adj* دیرباور
sincerity *n* خلوص نیت	sketch *v* طرح کردن
sing *v* آواز خواندن	sketch *n* نقشه، طرح
singer *n* آوازخوان	sketchy *adj* دارای طرح و دیزاین
single *adj* مجرد، منفرد	ski *v* اسکی بازی کردن
single-handed *adv* یکدسته	skill *n* مهارت
single-minded *adj* با اراده	skilled *adj* ماهر
sinister *adj* گمراه کننده	skillful *adj* با مهارت
sink *n* دستشوی	skim *v* کف روی آب را گرفتن
sink *v* غرق شدن	skin *n* پوست جلد، پوست میوه
sip *v* شُپ کردن	skin *v* پوست کردن
sir *n* آقا	skinny *adj* لاغر
siren *n* صدای بلند، زنگ خطر	skip *v* جست و خیز کردن؛ انجام نشده گذاشتن
sister *n* خواهر	skirmish *n* تکان خوردن
sister-in-law *n* خیاشنه	skirt *n* دامن
sit *v* نشستن	skull *n* جمجمه
site *n* محل، مکان، سایت انترنیتی	sky *n* آسمان

S

نورگیر، پنجره اتاق skylight *n*	slight *adj* جزئی
آسمان خراش skyscraper *n*	بطور جزئی slightly *adv*
تخته سنگ slab *n*	باریک slim *adj*
سست، ضعیف slack *adj*	توته کاغذ؛ لغزش یا خطا slip *n*
سست کردن، slacken *v*	لغزیدن slip *v*
ضعیف کردن	بوت سلیپر slipper *n*
تنبان کششی slacks *n*	لشم، لغزنده slippery *adj*
محکم زدن slam *v*	شکاف slit *n*
تهمت زدن slander *n*	شکاف کردن slit *v*
زبان عامیانه slang *n*	خزیدن، لغزیدن slither *v*
کج شده، شیب دار slanted *adj*	تنبل، نامرتب slob *n*
سیلی زدن slap *v*	شعار slogan *n*
چاک، شکاف slash *n*	شیب، سراشیبی slope *n*
شکاف کردن slash *v*	درهم و برهم sloppy *adj*
ذبح کردن slaughter *v*	چاک، شکاف slot *n*
غلام slave *n*	آهسته slow *adj*
غلامی slavery *n*	آهسته بروید slow down *pv*
سست، شُل sleazy *adj*	حرکت آهسته slow motion *n*
کراچی که توسط حیوانات کش sled *n*	به آهستگی slowly *adv*
میشود	گُند، تنبل sluggish *adj*
خواب sleep *n*	محله فقیرنشین slum *n*
خوابیدن sleep *v*	رکود، سقوط slump *v*
خواب آلود sleepy *adj*	مطلب را حذف کردن، slur *v*
آستین sleeve *n*	نادیده گرفتن
بی آستین sleeveless *adj*	مکار sly *adj*
کراچی که توسط حیوانات sleigh *n*	با صدا غذا خوردن smack *v*
کش میشود	کوچک small *adj*
بلند و باریک slender *adj*	زرنگ smart *adj*
توته کردن slice *v*	درهم کوبیدن smash *v*
توته، پارچه slice *n*	چرک کردن، لکه کردن smear *v*
لغزیدن، لغزاندن slide *v*	لکه، چرک smear *n*
یخمالک slide *n*	بو smell *n*

S

smell v بوییدن، بو دادن	snow v برف باریدن
smelly adj بدبو	snowfall n بارش برف
smile v تبسم کردن	snowflake n دانه های برف
smile n لبخند، تبسم	snowstorm n توفان برف
smoke n دود	snub v خاموش کردن
smoke v سگرت کشیدن	so conj بنابراین
smooth v لشم کردن	so adv زیاد
smooth adj لشم، هموار	soak v تر کردن
smoothly adv به نرمی	soak up pv تر شدن
smoothness n نرمی، ملایمت	soaked adj تر
smother v خفه کردن،	soap n صابون
خاموش کردن	soar v اوج گرفتن
smug adj ازخود راضی	sob v گریه کردن
smuggle v قاچاق کردن	sober adj هوشیار
smuggler n قاچاقبر	so-called adj به اصطلاح
snack n خوراک سرپایی	soccer n بازی ساکر
snail n حلزون	sociable adj اجتماعی، خوش برخورد
snake n مار	social adj اجتماعی
snap v شکستن؛ باقهر صحبت کردن	social network n شبکه اجتماعی
snapshot n عکس فوری	socialize v اجتماعی کردن،
snare n دام	رابطه اجتماعی تامین کردن
snatch v قپیدن	society n جامعه
sneak v مخفیانه حرکت کردن	sock n جوراب
sneeze v عسطه زدن	socket n ساکت برق
sneeze n عطسه	soda n نوشابه گازدار
sniff v بوییدن	sofa n آرام چوکی، کوچ
sniper n تیرانداز	soft adj نرم، ملایم و مهربان
snitch v دزدیدن	soften v نرم کردن
snob n بلندپروازی	softly adv به نرمی
snooze v چرت زدن	software n نرم افزار کمپیوتر
snore v در خواب غُریدن	soggy adj تر، مرطوب
snow n برف	soil v چرک شدن

S

soil *n* خاک	**somewhere** *adv* در کدام جای
soiled *adj* خاک شده	**son** *n* پسر
solace *n* آرامش، تسکین	**song** *n* آهنگ
solar *adj* خورشیدی	**son-in-law** *n* داماد
solder *v* لحیم کردن، بهم چسپاندن	**soon** *adv* به زودی
soldier *n* عسکر	**soothe** *v* آرام کردن
sold-out *adj* فروخته شده	**soothing** *adj* آرامش بخش
sole *adj* صرف، محض	**sorcerer** *n* جادوگر
sole *n* کف پا	**sorcery** *n* جادوگری
solely *adv* محضاً صرفاً	**sore** *adj* دردناک
solemn *adj* رسمی	**sore** *n* زخم
solicit *v* التماس کردن	**sorrow** *n* اندوه، غم
solid *n* جامد	**sorry** *adj* متاسف
solid *adj* محکم، جامد	**sort** *v* منظم کردن
solidarity *n* همبستگی، اتحاد	**sort** *n* نوع، گونه
solidify *v* محکم کردن، جامد ساختن	**sort out** *v* منظم کردن
solitary *adj* انفرادی	**soul** *n* روح
solitude *n* تنهایی	**sound** *n* صدا
solo *adj* انفرادی، تنها	**sound** *v* صدا دادن
solution *n* راه حل؛ محلول	**soundproof** *adj* ضد صدا
solve *v* حل کردن	**soup** *n* سوپ
somber *adj* غمگین	**sour** *adj* ترش
some *pron* برخی از	**source** *n* منبع
some *adj* یک مقدار	**south** *adv* بطرف جنوب
somebody *pron* کدام کسی	**south** *n* جنوب
someday *adv* یک روز	**south** *adj* جنوبی
somehow *adv* به نحوی	**southbound** *adv* جنوباً
someone *pron* کسی	**southeast** *n* جنوب شرق
something *pron* چیزی	**southern** *adj* جنوبی
sometimes *adv* بعضی اوقات	**southerner** *n* اهل جنوب
someway *adv* به طریقی	**southwest** *n* جنوب غرب
somewhat *adv* تاحدی	**souvenir** *n* سوغات

S

sovereign *adj* بااقتدار	**species** *n* گونه ها، انواع
sovereignty *n* سلطه، حق حاکمیت	**specific** *adj* مشخص
sow *v* کاشتن	**specifically** *adv* مشخصاً
spa *n* آرایشگاه	**specify** *v* مشخص کردن
space *n* فضا، فضای خالی بین اشیا	**specimen** *n* نمونه
space out *pv* در فاصله معین بین هم	**speck** *n* لکه، خال
قرار دادن	**spectacle** *n* نمایش، منظره
spaceship *n* صفینه	**spectacular** *adj* دیدنی، جذاب
spacious *adj* بزرگ	**spectator** *n* تماشاچی
spaghetti *n* آش	**speculate** *v* حدس زدن، گمان کردن
spam *n* نامه هرزه	**speculation** *n* حدس و گمان
span *v* اندازه گرفتن	**speech** *n* سخنرانی
span *n* طول، محدوده زمانی	**speechless** *adj* گنگ، بی حرف
spank *v* زدن	**speed** *n* سرعت
spare *v* دریغ داشتن، چشم پوشیدن از	**speed** *v* سرعت گرفتن
spare *adj* عوضی	**speed limit** *n* حد مجاز سرعت
spare part *n* پرزه اضافی یا عوضی	**speedy** *adj* سریع
sparingly *adv* کم کم	**spell** *n* هجی
spark *n* جرقه	**spell** *v* هجی کردن
sparkle *v* جرقه زدن	**spelling** *n* هجی
sparrow *n* گنجشک	**spend** *v* مصرف کردن؛ سپری کردن
sparse *adj* پراکنده	**sperm** *n* اسپرم، منی، نطفه
spasm *n* تشنج	**sphere** *n* گره، عرصه
speak *v* گپ زدن	**spherical** *adj* گروی
speaker *n* بلند گو	**spice** *n* مصالح جات
spear *n* نیزه	**spicy** *adj* تند، مصالح دار
spearhead *v* نوک نیزه	**spider** *n* جولاگک، عنکبوت
special *adj* خاص، ویژه	**spider web** *n* خانه جولاگک
specialist *n* متخصص، کارشناس	**spike** *n* لبه
specialize *v* تخصص داشتن	**spiky** *adj* لبه دار
specially *adv* خاصتاً	**spill** *v* ریختن، ریختاندن
specialty *n* تخصص	**spill** *n* ریزش

S

spin v چرخیدن، چرخاندن	**sporty** adj سپورتی، مربوط به ورزش
spinach n سبزی پالک	**spot** v متوجه شدن چیزی، چیزی را دیدن
spine n ستون فقرات	**spot** n نقطه؛ محل
spineless adj بدون ستون فقرات	**spotless** adj بی عیب، بدون لکه
spiral adj مارپیچ	**spotlight** n نور افکن
spirit n روحیه	**spouse** n همسر
spiritual adj معنوی	**sprain** v پیچ خوردن
spit v تف انداختن	**sprawl** v پراکندگی
spite n کینه	**spray** n اسپری
spiteful adj کینه دل	**spray** v اسپری کردن
splash v پاشیدن	**spread** v، هموار کردن؛ پخش شدن، منتشر شدن
splendid adj عالی، باشکوه	
splendor n شکوه	**spreadsheet** n صفحه گسترده در کمپیوتر
splint n برامدگی	
splinter n باریکه چوب	**spring** v خیز زدن
splinter v چوب باریک تراش کردن	**spring** n سپرینگ؛ فصل بهار؛ چشمه آب
split n شکاف	**sprinkle** v پاشیدن
split v شکافتن، جدا کردن	**sprout** v جوانه زدن
split up pv جدا شدن	**spur** n تحریک
spoil v خراب شدن، ضایع شدن	**spy** n جاسوس
spoils n غنیمت	**spy** v جاسوسی کردن
sponge n اسفنج	**squalid** adj کثیف، ناپاک
spongy adj اسفنجی، نرم	**squander** v اسراف کردن، ولخرجی کردن
sponsor n حامی، ضامن	
sponsor v ضمانت کردن	**square** n مربع
spontaneous adj بی اختیار	**squash** v کدو
spooky adj ترسناک	**squat** v خم کردن بدن
spoon n قاشق	**squeak** v با چیغ و فریاد صحبت کردن
spoonful n به اندازه یک قاشق	**squeaky** adj جیرجیری
sporadic adj پراگنده، انفرادی	**squeamish** adj سخت گیر
sport n ورزش، سپورت	
sportsman n ورزشکار	

S

squeeze *v* فشردن، شیلیدن	stamp *v* تاپه کردن
squid *n* یکنوع ماهی چهارکنج	stamp *n* تاپه؛ تکت پوستی
squint *v* چشمک زدن	stamp out *pv* مُهر کردن کاغذ
squirrel *n* موش خرما	stampede *n* ازدحام
squirt *v* سرپیچ کردن	stand *v* ایستاد شدن
stab *v* چاقو زدن	stand *n* پایه
stability *n* ثبات	stand for *pv* ایستادگی کردن
stabilize *v* باثبات کردن	stand out *pv* برجسته بودن
stable *adj* ثابت	stand up *pv* بلند شدن
stable *n* باثبات	standard *adj* معیاری
stack *n* انبار	standard *n* معیاری، استندرد
stack *v* انبار کردن	standardize *v* معیاری ساختن
stadium *n* استیدیوم	standstill *n* بدون حرکت
staff *n* کارمندان؛ عصا چوب	staple *v* استبلر کردن
stage *n* مرحله؛ استیج نمایش	staple *n* اصلی، عمده
stagger *v* لنگیدن	stapler *n* استبلر
staggering *adj* متناوب	star *n* ستاره؛ ستاره هنری
stagnant *adj* راکد، ایستاد	starch *n* نشایسته
stain *n* لکه	stare *v* خیره دیدن
stain *v* لکه دار شدن	stark *adj* خشن، قوی
stair *n* پله زینه	start *n* شروع
staircase *n* زینه	start *v* شروع کردن
stairs *n* زینه ها	startle *v* ترساندن
stake *n* میخ چوبی	startled *adj* ترسیده
stale *adj* کهنه، باسی	starvation *n* گرسنگی
stalemate *n* بازی شطرنج	starve *v* از گرسنگی مردن
stalk *v* تعقیب کردن، کمین کردن	state *v* بیان کردن، اظهار داشتن
stalk *n* ساقه، ساقه نبات	state *n* حالت، وضعیت؛ ایالت
stall *n* غرفه؛ آخور حیوانات	statement *n* بیانیه
stall *v* متوقف ساختن	static *n* راکد، ایستاد
stamina *n* استقامت	station *n* استیشن بس، ریل؛
stammer *v* با لکنت گفتن	استیشن تلویزیون و رادیو

S

stationary *adj* ساکن، ایستاد	stepsister *n* خواهر اندر
stationery *n* قرطاسیه	stepson *n* بچه اندر
statistic *n* احصائیه	stereo *n* استیریو
statistical *adj* احصائیوی	stereotype *n* کلیشه
statistician *n* کارشناس احصائیه	sterile *adj* عقیم
statue *n* مجسمه	sterilize *v* عقیم کردن
status *n* حالت	stern *adj* سخت گیر
staunch *adj* استدلال	stern *n* سخت گیری
stay *n* اقامت	sternly *adv* بطور سخت گیرانه
stay *v* ماندن، اقامت کردن	stew *n* یخنی گوشت و سبزیجات
steady *adj* ثابت، پایدار	stick *v* چسپیدن، باقی ماندن
steak *n* کباب	stick *n* چوب
steal *v* دزدی کردن	stick around *pv* منتظر چیزی بودن
stealthy *adj* دزدانه، دزدکی	stick out *pv* تأکید کردن
steam *n* بخار	stick to *pv* روی چیزی متمرکز ماندن
steel *n* فولاد	sticker *n* چسب، ستیکر
steep *adj* سرشیب	sticky *adj* چسبناک
steer *v* چرخیدن، چرخاندن	stiff *adj* محکم، سفت
stem *n* ساقه	stiffen *v* سفت یا محکم کردن
stench *n* بوی تعفن	stiffness *n* سفتی
stencil *n* استینسل	stifle *v* خفه کردن، خاموش کردن
step *v* گام گذاشتن	stifling *adj* خفه کننده
step *n* گام؛ پله زینه؛ مرحله	still *adv* تاهنوز
step down *pv* کناره گیری کردن	still *adj* ساکت، بدون حرکت
step out *pv* بیرون برآمدن	stimulant *n* محرک
step up *pv* برپاکردن، نصب کردن	stimulate *v* تحریک کردن
stepbrother *n* برادر اندر	stimulating *adj* تحریک کننده
step-by-step *adv* گام به گام	stimulus *n* انگیزه
stepdaughter *n* دختر اندر	sting *n* نیش
stepfather *n* پدر اندر	sting *v* نیش زدن، گزیدن
stepladder *n* زینه	stinging *adj* نیش زننده، گزنده
stepmother *n* مادر اندر	stingy *adj* خسیس

بوی بد دادن *v* **stink**	زور، نیرو؛ *n* **strain**
تعفن، بوی بد *n* **stink**	فشار یا جراحت وارد شده
بدبو *adj* **stinking**	کوشش کردن؛ مجروح کردن *v* **strain**
تصریح کردن *v* **stipulate**	خسته، تحت فشار *adj* **strained**
شور دادن *v* **stir**	صافی، صاف کننده *n* **strainer**
به هم زدن *pv* **stir up**	تنگه، تنگنا *n* **strait**
دوختن، کوک زدن، *v* **stitch**	رشته، لایه *n* **strand**
بخیه کردن	سرگردان *adj* **stranded**
کوک، بخیه، دوخت *n* **stitch**	عجیب *adj* **strange**
ذخیره کردن *v* **stock**	بیگانه *n* **stranger**
ذخیره؛ قسمتی از سرمایه شرکت *n* **stock**	خفه کردن، *v* **strangle**
جوراب ساق بلند *n* **stocking**	گلوی کسی را فشردن
انبار کردن *n* **stockpile**	با تسمه بسته کردن *v* **strap**
رواقی، عضو مکتب رواق *adj* **stoic**	بند، تسمه *n* **strap**
معده *n* **stomach**	استراتیژیک *adj* **strategic**
سنگ *n* **stone**	استراتیژی *n* **strategy**
مواد غایطه *n* **stool**	پایپ برای نوشیدن *n* **straw**
ایستگاه *n* **stop**	توت زمینی *n* **strawberry**
توقف کردن *v* **stop**	منحرف شدن *v* **stray**
توقف کردن *pv* **stop by**	ولگرد *adj* **stray**
چراغ توقف *n* **stop light**	نهر آب، جریان *n* **stream**
ذخیره گاه *n* **storage**	سرک *n* **street**
ذخیره کردن *v* **store**	موتر های لینی *n* **streetcar**
مغازه *n* **store**	چراغ جاده *n* **streetlight**
توفان *n* **storm**	قدرت *n* **strength**
توفانی *adj* **stormy**	تقویه کردن *v* **strengthen**
قصه *n* **story**	سخت، شدید *adj* **strenuous**
بخاری *n* **stove**	تأکید کردن *v* **stress**
مستقیم؛ صادق *adj* **straight**	فشار روحی یا فزیکی *n* **stress**
مستقیماً *adv* **straight**	تشویش کردن *pv* **stress out**
راست کردن *v* **straighten**	*adj* **stressful**
رُک و راست *adj* **straightforward**	پر از پریشانی و فشار های روحی

S

stretch v کش کردن	stuff n اشیا، اجناس
stretch n کشش، سفتی عضلات	stuff v پر کردن
stretcher n تسکره برای انتقال مریض	stuffing n پر کردن داخل چیزی
strict adj سخت، سختگیر	stuffy adj بندش، بندش بینی
stride v گام برداشتن	stumble v لغزیدن
strife n نزاع	stun v حیرت زده کردن
strike v اعتصاب کردن، حمله کردن	stunning adj متحیر کننده، حیران کننده
strike n حمله، اعتصاب	stupendous adj شگفت انگیز
striking adj قابل توجه، برجسته	stupid adj احمق
string n ریسمان	stupidity n حماقت
stringent adj سختگیر، دقیق	sturdy adj سفت، محکم
strip v پوش چیزی را دور کردن، کشیدن لباس	stutter v با لکنت حرف زدن
strip n فیته، نوار	style n سبک، شیوه
stripe n خط خط	stylish adj شیک، خوش لباس
striped adj خط دار، رادار	subdue v رام کردن
strive v کوشش کردن	subdued adj رام شده
stroke n سکته، ضربه	subject v تحت کنترل درآوردن
stroll v قدم زدن	subject n مضمون، موضوع
stroller adv ریکشای اطفال	subjective adj درونی، ذهنی
strong adj قوی	sublime adj عالی، والا
strongly adv به شدت، جداً	submarine n زیردریایی، تحت البحری
structure n ساختار؛ ساختمان	submerge v غوطه ور شدن
struggle v تلاش کردن	submissive adj فروتن، حلیم
struggle n تلاش، کوشش	submit v تسلیم دادن، تحویل کردن
stub n باقیمانده چیزی	subscribe v اشتراک کردن
stubborn adj لجوج	subscription n اشتراک
stuck adj بند مانده	subsequent adj متعاقب، بعدی
student n شاگرد	substance n شی، ماده
studio n استدیو	substandard adj عمومی، عام
study v مطالعه کردن	substantial adj اساسی، قابل توجه
study n مطالعه، ارزیابی	

S

substitute *n* جانشین	suit *n* دریشی
substitute *v* جانشین شدن	suitable *adj* مناسب
subtitle *n* زیرنویس فلم	suitcase *n* بکس سفری
subtle *adj* زیرک، دقیق	sullen *adj* عبوس، بدخُلق
subtotal *n* مجموع ارقام فرعی	sum *v* جمع کردن ارقام
subtract *v* تفریق کردن، منفی کردن	sum *n* مجموعه
subtraction *n* منفی، تفریق	summarize *v* خلاصه کردن
suburb *n* حومه شهر	summary *n* خلاصه، فشرده
subway *n* ترانسپورت زیرزمینی	summer *n* تابستان
succeed *v* موفق شدن	summit *n* اجلاس، همآیش
success *n* موفقیت	summon *v* احضار کردن،
successful *adj* موفق	فراخواندن
successfully *adv* موفقانه	sumptuous *adj* مجلل
successor *n* جانشین	sun *n* آفتاب
succulent *adj* شاداب، پر طراوت	sun block *n* کریم ضد آفتاب
succumb *v* تسلیم شدن، از پا درامدن	sunburn *n* آفتاب سوختگی
such *adj* چنین	Sunday *n* روز یکشنبه
such as *idiom* مانند	sundown *n* غروب آفتاب
suck *v* مکیدن	sunglasses *n* عینک آفتابی
sudden *adj* ناگهانی	sunken *adj* غرق شده
suddenly *adv* بصورت ناگهانی	sunlight *n* نور آفتاب
sue *v* تعقیب کردن،	sunny *adj* آفتابی
مورد پیگرد قانونی قرار دادن	sunrise *n* طلوع آفتاب
suffer *v* رنج کشیدن	sunset *n* غروب آفتاب
suffering *n* رنج، عذاب	sunshine *n* درخشش آفتاب
sufficient *adj* کافی، بسنده	suntan *n* پوست آفتاب خوردگی
suffocate *v* خفه کردن،	super *adj* عالی
خاموش کردن	superb *adj* فوق العاده
sugar *n* شکر، بوره	superficial *adj* سطحی، ظاهری
suggest *v* پیشنهاد کردن	superfluous *adj* زیادی، زائد
suggestion *n* پیشنهاد	superior *adj* برتر
suicide *n* خودکشی کردن	supermarket *n* مارکیت بزرگ

S

superpower n ابرقدرت	**surgery** n عملیات جراحی
superstition n خرافات،	**surgical** adj وابسته به جراحی
موهم پرستی	**surname** n تخلص
supervise v نظارت کردن	**surpass** v پیشی گرفتن
supervision n نظارت	**surplus** n اضافه، باقیمانده
supervisor n آمر، ناظر	**surprise** n تعجب
supper n عصریه، غذای عصرانه	**surprise** v متعجب ساختن
supple adj انعطاف پذیر	**surprised** adj متعجب، حیران
supplier n تجهیز کننده، فراهم کننده	**surprising** adj تعجب آور،
supplies n تجهیزات، لوازم	حیرت انگیز
supply v تجهیز کردن، مجهز کردن	**surrender** v تسلیم شدن
supply n تجهیزات، لوازم	**surround** v احاطه کردن
support v حمایت کردن،	**surroundings** n محیط اطراف،
کمک کردن	پیرامون
support n حمایت، پشتیبانی	**surveillance** n نظارت، مراقبت
supporter n حامی، پشتیبان	**survey** n سروی
supportive adj حمایوی	**survey** v سروی کردن
suppose v گمان کردن، فرض کردن	**survival** n بقاء
supposing conj فرضاً،	**survive** v نجات یافتن
به فرض اینکه	**survivor** n بازمانده، نجات یافته
suppress v سرکوب کردن	**susceptible** adj حساس، ظریف
supremacy n برتری	**suspect** v شک کردن
supreme adj عالی، اعلی	**suspect** n فرد مشکوک
surcharge n اضافه بها، جریمه	**suspend** v به تعویق انداختن
sure adj مطمئن	**suspenders** n تسمه پطلون
surely adv یقیناً، مطمئناً	**suspense** n تعلیق، در حالت تعلیق
surf v موج سواری کردن	**suspension** n تعلیق، توقف
surface n سطح	**suspicion** n شک، تردید
surfboard n تخته موج سواری	**suspicious** adj مشکوک
surfing n بازی موج سواری	**sustain** v متحمل شدن، حفظ کردن
surge n موج، بلند رفتن	**sustainable** adj باثبات، پایدار
surgeon n داکتر جراح	**sustenance** n پایداری، ثبات

S

swallow v بلعیدن

swamp n سیاه آب، باتلاق

swamped adj در سیاه آب گیر مانده

swan n قو، یکنوع پرنده

swap v عوض کردن، مبادله کردن

swarm n ازدحام

swarm v ازدحام کردن

sway v اهتزاز کردن، نوسان کردن

swear v قسم خوردن،
سوگند یاد کردن

sweat n عرق

sweat v عرق کردن

sweater n جاکت

sweatpants n برزو، تنبان ورزشی

sweaty adj عرق آلود

sweep v جاروب کردن

sweet adj شیرین، مهربان

sweeten v شیرین ساختن

sweetheart n عزیز، معشوقه

sweets n شیرینی باب

swell v پندیدن

swelling n پندیده گی

swift adj تیز، سریع

swiftly adv به سرعت

swim v آبازی کردن

swim trunks n نیکر آبازی

swimmer n آباز، شناور

swimming n آبازی، شنا

swimming pool n حوض آبازی

swimsuit n لباس آبازی

swindle v فریبکاری، تقلب

swindler n کلاهبردار، فریبکار

swing n گاز تفریحی برای اطفال

swing v گاز خوردن، تاب خوردن

swipe v کارت را در ماشین زدن

switch v تبدیل کردن

switch n سویچ

switch off pv خاموش کردن

switch on pv روشن کردن

swivel v چرخاندن

swollen adj پندیده

sword n شمشیر

syllable n هجا، جزء کلمه

symbol n سمبول، علامه

symbolic adj سمبولیک، نمایشی

symbolize v سمبولیک ساختن

symmetrical adj متوازن

symmetry n تناسب، توازن

sympathetic adj دلسوز

sympathize v همدردی کردن

sympathy n همدردی

symphony n اجرای موسیقی،
سیمفونی

symptom n علامه، نشانه

synagogue n کنیسه، عبادتگاه یهود

synchronize v همزمان ساختن،
همگام ساختن

synonym n مترادف

synthesis n ترکیب

synthetic adj مصنوعی، ترکیبی

syringe n سرنج پیچکاری

syrup n شربت

system n سیستم

systematic adj سیستماتیک

S

tab 162

T

tab *n* صورت حساب	**talk** *v* صحبت کردن
table *n* میز، جدول	**talkative** *adj* پرحرف
tablecloth *n* سرمیزی	**tall** *adj* قد بلند
tablespoon *n* قاشق نان خوری	**tame** *v* رام کردن
tablet *n* تابلیت، کمپیوتر کوچک	**tame** *adj* رام، اهلی
tack *n* گُل میخ	**tan** *v* آفتاب دادن
tackle *v* از عهده برامدن	**tan** *n* رنگ نخودی
tacky *adj* چسبناک	**tangent** *n* خط مماس
taco *n* ساندویچ مکسیکویی	**tangerine** *n* مالته
tact *n* تدبیر، درایت	**tangible** *adj* محسوس، قابل لمس
tactful *adj* باتدبیر، بادرایت	**tangle** *n* درهم پیچیدن
tactic *n* تاکتیک، شیوه جنگ	**tangled** *adj* گره خورده
tactical *adj* تکتیکی	**tank** *n* تانکی، ظرف؛ تانک نظامی
tag *n* لیبل	**tantrum** *n* اوقات تلخی
tail *n* دُم حیوان	**tap** *v* آهسته زدن
tailor *n* خیاط	**tap** *n* ضربه آهسته؛ شیردهن نل
tainted *adj* آلوده	**tape** *v* با تیپ بستن؛ ضبط کردن
take *v* گرفتن	**tape** *n* تیپ چسب دار
take apart *pv* جدا کردن	**tape measure** *n* متر برای اندازه گیری
take away *pv* بردن	**tape recorder** *n* ثبت کننده صدا
take back *pv* دوباره بردن	**tapestry** *n* پرده نقش دار
take in *pv* داخل بردن	**tar** *n* قیر
take off *pv* کشیدن لباس	**tarantula** *n* یکنوع خزنده
take out *pv* بیرون بردن	**tardy** *adj* ترسناک، دیر، ناوقت
take over *pv* جای کسی را گرفتن	**target** *n* هدف
tale *n* داستان، قصه	**tarnish** *v* لکه دار کردن
talent *n* استعداد	**tart** *v* ترش
talented *adj* بااستعداد	**tart** *n* ترش
talk *n* صحبت	**task** *n* وظیفه
	taste *v* مزه کردن
	taste *n* مزه، ذائقه

T

tasteful *adj* با مزه	**telling** *adj* تأثیر گذار
tasteless *adj* بی مزه؛ بی کیفیت	**temper** *n* مزاج، خُلق
tasty *adj* مزه دار	**temperature** *n* درجه حرارت
tattoo *n* تاتو، تاپه روی جلد	**tempest** *n* توفان، جوش و خروش
tavern *n* رستورانت، میخانه	**template** *n* قالب، الگو
tax *n* مالیه	**temple** *n* شقیقه؛ معبد
taxi *n* تکسی	**temporarily** *adv* بطور موقت
tea *n* چای	**temporary** *adj* موقت
teach *v* درس دادن	**tempt** *v* دچار وسوسه کردن
teacher *n* معلم	**temptation** *n* وسوسه
team *n* تیم	**tempting** *adj* وسوسه انگیز
teammate *n* همکار	**ten** *n* ده
teapot *n* چاینک	**tenacity** *n* سختی
tear *n* اشک؛ پارگی	**tenant** *n* کرایه نشین
tear *v* پاره کردن	**tend** *v* تمایل داشتن
tease *v* آزار دادن	**tendency** *n* تمایل
teaspoon *n* قاشق چای خوری	**tender** *adj* حساس، ظریف
technical *adj* تخنیکی	**tenderness** *n* لطافت
technically *adv* از نظر تخنیکی	**tennis** *n* بازی تینیس
technician *n* تخنیکر	**tenor** *n* صدای زیر یا باریک
technique *n* شیوه، تخنیک	**tense** *adj* وخیم؛ سفت
technology *n* تکنالوژی	**tension** *n* تنش، فشار
tedious *adj* خسته کننده	**tent** *n* خیمه
teenage *adj* نوجوان	**tentacle** *n* شاخک
teenager *n* نوجوان	**tentative** *adj* آزمایشی
teeth *n* دندانها	**tenth** *adj* دهم
telephone *n* تیلفون	**tepid** *adj* نیم گرم
telescope *n* تیلیسکوپ	**term** *n* اصطلاح؛ مدت، میعاد
televise *v* پخش و نشر کردن	**terminal** *n* ترمینل
television *n* تلویزیون	**terminate** *v* خاتمه دادن
tell *v* گفتن	**terminology** *n* اصطلاحات
teller *n* گوینده؛ تحویل دار	**terms** *n* شرایط

T

terrace *n* ، تراس	thaw *v* آب شدن، گرم شدن
محل خوابیدن و نشستن در فضای باز	the *a* را؛ حرف تعریف در گرامر
terrain *n* زمین، اراضی	theater *n* تیاتر
terrestrial *adj* زمینی	theft *n* دزدی
terrible *adj* وحشتناک	their *adj* از آنها
terrific *adj* فوق العاده	theirs *pron* از آنها
terrify *v* ترساندن	them *pron* به آنها
terrifying *adj* ترسناک	theme *n* موضوع، مطلب
territory *n* قلمرو	theme park *n* پارک تفریحی
terror *n* دهشت، وحشت	themselves *pron* آنها خودشان
terrorism *n* دهشت افگنی، تروریزم	then *adv* سپس، بعد از آن
terrorist *n* تروریست، دهشت افگن	theory *n* تیوری
terrorize *v* به وحشت انداختن	therapist *n* درمانگر
test *n* امتحان	therapy *n* درمان
test *v* امتحان کردن	there *adv* آنجا
testament *n* وصیت نامه	there *pron* در آنجا
testify *v* شهادت دادن، گواهی دادن	therefore *adv* بنابراین
testimony *n* گواهی، شهادت	thermometer *n* ترمامیتر
text *v* پیام فرستادن از طریق تیلفون	thermostat *n* ترموستات، گرم کننده
text *n* متن	thesaurus *n* اصطلاحنامه، قاموس
text message *n* پیام کتبی	these *pron* اینان
textbook *n* کتاب درسی	these *adj* اینها
texture *n* بافت	thesis *n* ، پایان نامه
than *prep* در مقایسه به	مونوگراف برای دریافت دیپلوم
than *conj* نسبت به	they *pron* آنها
thank *v* تشکری کردن	thick *adj* ضخیم
thank you *n* تشکر	thicken *v* ضخیم ساختن
thankful *adj* شکرگذار	thickness *n* ضخامت
thanks *n* تشکر	thief *n* دزد
that *adj* آن	thigh *n* ران پا
that *pron* آن یکی	thin *adj* باریک، لاغر
that *conj* که	thing *n* شی

T

think *v* فکر کردن	throne *n* تخت پادشاهی
thinly *adv* به باریکی	through *adv* از طریق
third *adj* سوم	through *prep* مستقیم
thirst *v* تشنگی	throughout *prep* درسراسر
thirsty *adj* تشنه	throw *v* انداختن، پرتاب کردن
thirteen *n* سیزده	throw away *pv* دور انداختن
thirty *n* سی	throw up *pv* استفراغ کردن
this *adj* این	thug *n* اوباش، آدم کش
this *pron* این	thumb *n* شست انگشت
thorn *n* خار	thumbtack *n* گل میخ
thorny *adj* خاردار	thunder *n* رعد و برق
thorough *adj* کامل، سراپا	thunderbolt *n* رعد و برق
those *pron* آنان	thunderstorm *n* الماسک
those *adj* آنها	Thursday *n* روز پنجشنبه
though *adv* باوجواینکه	thus *adv* بنابراین
though *conj* گرچه	ticket *n* تکت
thought *n* تفکر، مفکوره، نظریه	tickle *n* قتقتک
thoughtful *adj* متفکر، بااندیشه	tickle *v* قتقتک دادن، خاریدن
thousand *n* هزار	ticklish *adj* قلقلک یا قتقتک
thread *v* نخ کردن	tidal wave *n* موج بزرگ
thread *n* نخ، تار	tide *n* جریان، جزر و مد
threat *n* تهدید	tidy *adj* منظم
threaten *v* تهدید کردن	tie *v* بسته کردن،
three *n* سه	عین نمرات را در بازی داشتن
threshold *n* آستانه	tie *n* نکتایی
thrifty *adj* صرفه جو	tiger *n* پلنگ
thrill *v* به هیجان آوردن	tight *adj* تنگ، ضیق
thrill *n* هیجان، لرزه	tight *adv* سفت، محکم
thrilling *adj* هیجان آور	tighten *v* محکم کردن
thrive *v* پیشرفت کردن، رونق کردن	tile *n* کاشی
throat *n* گلو	till *prep* تا، الی
throb *v* ضربان، تپش	till *v* تازمانیکه

T

tilt *v* کج کردن	**toddler** *n* کودک نوپا
timber *n* چوب	**toe** *n* پنجه پا
time *v* وقت را معین کردن	**toenail** *n* ناخن پنجه پا
time *n* وقت، زمان	**together** *adv* باهم، یکجا
time limit *n* محدوده زمانی، حد زمانی	**toil** *v* زحمت کشیدن
timeless *adj* بی انتها، بی زمان	**toilet** *n* کمود تشناب
timely *adj* به موقع	**toilet paper** *n* کاغذ تشناب
timer *n* زمان سنج	**token** *n* نشانه
times *prep* ضرب	**tolerable** *adj* قابل تحمل
timid *adj* ترسو	**tolerance** *n* تحمل
tin *n* حلبی، قطی	**tolerant** *adj* متحمل، بردبار
tingle *v* سوزن سوزن شدن	**tolerate** *v* تحمل کردن
tiny *adj* کوچک	**toll** *n* حق العبور
tip *n* نوک؛ پول بخششی؛ نظریه، مشوره	**tomato** *n* بادنجان رومی
tiptoe *v* نوک پا	**tomb** *n* مقبره
tire *n* تایر	**tombstone** *n* سنگ مقبره
tire *v* خسته کردن	**tomorrow** *n* روز بعد
tired *adj* خسته	**tomorrow** *adv* فردا
tireless *adj* خستگی ناپذیر	**ton** *n* تُن
tiresome *adj* خسته کننده	**tone** *n* صدا
tissue *n* دستمال کاغذی	**tongs** *n* انبور، گیرا
title *n* نام، لقب	**tongue** *n* زبان
to *prep* به	**tonight** *adv* امشب
toad *n* بقه	**tonight** *n* امشب
toast *n* نان بریان شده	**too** *adv* همچنان، زیاد
toast *v* نوشیدن به سلامتی کسی	**tool** *n* آله، وسیله کار
toaster *n* گرم کننده نان	**tooth** *n* دندان
tobacco *n* تنباکو	**toothache** *n* دندان دردی
today *adv* امروز	**toothbrush** *n* برس دندان
today *n* امروز	**toothpaste** *n* کریم دندان
	toothpick *n* چوبک دندان
	top *adj* بلند

T

top *n* بلندی؛ پوش؛ پیراهن	**toward** *prep* بطرف، به سوی
topic *n* موضوع، مطلب	**towel** *n* روی پاک
topical *adj* موضوعی	**tower** *n* بُرج
topple *v* سرنگون شدن	**towering** *adj* بلند، سر به فلک کشیده
torch *n* مشعل، چراغ	**town** *n* شهر
torment *v* عذاب، شکنجه	**town hall** *n* سالون شهری
tornado *n* گردباد	**toxic** *adj* زهری
torrent *n* باد و سیلاب زودگذر	**toxin** *n* زهریات
torso *n* تنه بدن	**toy** *n* بازیچه
tortoise *n* سنگ پشت	**trace** *n* اثر، ردپا
torture *n* شکنجه	**trace** *v* تعقیب کردن، پیگیری کردن
torture *v* شکنجه کردن	**track** *v* دنبال کردن، پیگیری کردن
toss *v* پرتاب کردن	**track** *n* مسیر، رد پا
total *adj* مجموع	**traction** *n* کشش، انقباض
total *n* مجموعه	**tractor** *n* تراکتور
totally *adv* مجموعاً	**trade** *v* تبادله کردن
touch *n* تماس، لمس	**trade** *n* تجارت
touch *v* لمس کردن، دست زدن	**trader** *n* تاجر
touch on *v* روی چیزی دست زدن	**tradition** *n* عنعنه، رسم و رواج
touch up *v* لمس کردن، دستکاری کردن	**traditional** *adj* عنعنوی، سنتی
touching *adj* تحریک کننده احساسات	**traditionally** *adv* بطور سنتی
tough *adj* مشکل، خشن، قوی	**traffic** *n* ازدحام
toughen *v* سخت کردن	**traffic jam** *n* ازدحام ترافیکی
tour *n* سیاحت، گشت و گذار	**traffic light** *n* چراغ ترافیکی
tourism *n* توریزم، سیاحت	**tragedy** *n* تراژیدی، حادثه غم انگیز
tourist *n* سیاح، جهانگرد	**tragic** *adj* غم انگیز
tournament *n* تورنمینت، مسابقات ورزشی	**trail** *v* دنباله داشتن
tow *v* موتر را با ریسمان کش کردن	**trail** *n* دنباله، مسیر برای گردش
tow truck *n* لاری که موتر را انتقال میدهد	**trailer** *n* تیلر، واسطه نقلیه تیلردار
	train *v* آموزش دادن
	train *n* ریل
	trainee *n* کارآموز

T

trainer *n* آموزگار، ترینر	**traumatic** *adj* حالت بعد از حادثه
training *n* برنامه آموزشی	**traumatize** *v* آسیب رساندن،
trait *n* ویژگی، خصوصیت	زخمی کردن
traitor *n* خائن	**travel** *v* سفر کردن
trajectory *n* خط سیر	**travel** *n* مسافرت
tram *n* سرویس های برقی	**traveler** *n* مسافر
trample *v* پایمال کردن	**tray** *n* پطنوس
trance *n* بیهوشی	**treacherous** *adj* خیانتکار
tranquility *n* آرامش	**treachery** *n* خیانت
transaction *n* معامله	**tread** *v* پاگذاشتن
transcend *v* فراتر رفتن،	**treason** *n* خیانت، بی وفایی
برتری یافتن	**treasure** *n* گنج
transcribe *v* رونویسی کردن	**treat** *v* برخورد کردن با کسی،
transfer *n* انتقال	تداوی کردن
transfer *v* انتقال دادن	**treat** *n* رفتار؛ معالجه
transform *v* تغییر شکل دادن	**treatment** *n* تداوی، معالجه
transformation *n* تغییر شکل	**treaty** *n* پیمان، عهد
transit *n* عبوری، ترانزیت	**tree** *n* درخت
transition *n* عبور، گذار	**tremble** *v* لرزیدن
translate *v* ترجمه کردن	**tremendous** *adj* عظیم
translator *n* ترجمان	**tremor** *n* لرزش
transmit *v* انتقال یافتن	**trench** *n* سنگر
transparent *adj* شفاف، عادلانه	**trend** *n* روند، تمایل
transplant *v* پیوند دادن	**trendy** *adj* مُد روز
transport *v* انتقال دادن	**trespass** *v* تخطی کردن،
transportation *n* انتقالات،	تخلف کردن
ترانسپورت	**trial** *n* آزمایش
trap *v* به دام انداختن	**triangle** *n* سه ضلعی
trap *n* دام	**tribe** *n* قبیله
trash *n* کثافات	**tribulation** *n* مصیبت
trash can *n* قطی کثافات	**tribute** *n* احترام
trashy *n* بی ارزش، مزخرف	**trick** *v* فریب دادن

T

trick n نیرنگ، فریب	**trunk** n تنه درخت؛ تول بکس موتر؛ ذخیره گاه
trickle v چکیدن	**trust** n اعتماد
tricky adj مکار، نیرنگ باز	**trust** v اعتماد کردن
trigger v راه انداختن	**trustworthy** adj قابل اعتماد
trigger n ماشه	**truth** n واقعیت، حقیقت
trim v کوتاه کردن، اصلاح کردن مو	**truthful** adj حقیقی
trip n سفر	**try** v کوشش کردن؛ امتحان کردن
trip v سفر کردن	**T-shirt** n پیراهن سپورتی
triple adj سه گانه	**tub** n تپ حمام
tripod n سه پایه	**tuba** n آله موسیقی توبا
triumph n پیروزی	**tube** n تیوب
triumphant adj پیروز	**tuck** v قات کردن
trivial adj جزئی، ناچیز	**Tuesday** n روز سه شنبه
trivialize v بی اهمیت جلوه دادن	**tug** v کوشیدن
trolley n کراچی دستی	**tuition** n فیس پوهنتون
trombone n آله موسیقی ترومبون	**tulip** n گل لاله
troops n عساکر، نیروها	**tumble** v جست و خیز زدن
trophy n جام قهرمانی	**tummy** n شکم
tropical adj گرمسیر	**tumor** n تومور، غُده
trouble v به زحمت ساختن	**tumult** n غوغا، جنجال
trouble n زحمت	**tumultuous** adj پرسروصدا
troubled adj پرزحمت	**tuna** n ماهی تونا
troublesome adj دردسر ساز	**tune** n آهنگ
trousers n پطلون	**tune** v کوک کردن
truce n آتش بس	**tunnel** n تونل
truck n لاری	**turbulence** n تلاطم، آشفتگی
trucker n راننده لاری	**turf** n چمن
true adj حقیقی	**turkey** n فیلمرغ
truly adv از روی راستی	**turmoil** n آشوب، غوغا
trumped-up adj بی مورد، خلاف واقعیت	**turn** n تغییر جهت؛ نوبت
trumpet n آله موسیقی ترمپیت	**turn** v دور خوردن، دور دادن

T

turn back *pv* دوباره دور دادن
turn down *pv* رد کردن پیشنهاد
turn in *pv* برگرداندن
turn off *pv* خاموش کردن
turn on *pv* روشن کردن
turn over *pv* دور دادن
turn up *pv* نوبت دادن
turtle *n* سنگ پشت
tusk *n* دندان فیل
tutor *n* معلم
tweezers *n* مو چینک
twelfth *adj* دوازدهم
twelve *n* دوازده
twentieth *adj* بیستم
twenty *n* بیست
twice *adv* دوبار، دو مرتبه
twig *n* شاخه کوچک
twilight *n* نیمه روشن
twin *n* دوگانگی
twinkle *v* چشمک زدن
twist *v* پیچ دادن
twist *n* پیچش
twisted *adj* پیچ خورده
twister *n* چرخان، چرخ دهنده
twitch *v* تکان دادن
two *n* دو
tycoon *n* سرمایه دار
type *v* تایپ کردن
type *n* نوع، قسم
type writer *n* ماشین تایپ
typical *adj* معمول
typo *n* اشتباه تایپی

tyranny *n* ستم، استبداد
tyrant *n* مستبد، ظالم

U

ugly *adj* بدشکل
ulcer *n* زخم
ultimate *adj* نهایی، آخری
ultimatum *n* آخرین، پیشنهاد آخر
umbrella *n* چتری
umpire *n* داور
unable *adj* ناتوان
unanimous *adj* به اتفاق آرا
unarmed *adj* خلع سلاح
unassuming *adj* ساده، بی تکلیف
unattached *adj* ضمیمه نشده
unavoidable *adj* اجتناب ناپذیر
unaware *adj* بی خبر
unbearable *adj* غیرقابل تحمل
unbeatable *adj* شکست ناپذیر
unbelievable *adj* باورنکردنی
unbiased *adj* بی طرفانه
unbroken *adj* ناشکسته
unbutton *v* بازکردن دکمه
uncertain *adj* نامعلوم، نامطمئن
uncle *n* کاکا، ماما
unclear *adj* نامعلوم
uncomfortable *adj* ناراحت
uncommon *adj* غیرمعمول
unconscious *adj* بیهوش

uncontrollable *adj* غیرقابل کنترول	**undeserved** *adj* لیاقت چیزی را ندارد
unconventional *adj* خلاف عُرف، غیرمتعارف	**undesirable** *adj* نامطلوب
unconvinced *adj* متقاعد نشده، قناعت داده نشده	**undisputed** *adj* بلامنازعه، روی چیزی نزاع نشده باشد
uncover *v* برملا کردن؛ کشف جرایم	**undo** *v* باطل کردن
undecided *adj* تصمیم نگرفته، غیرمصمم	**undoubtedly** *adv* بدون شک، مسلماً
undeniable *adj* انکار ناپذیر	**undress** *v* لباس کشیدن
under *adv* در زیر	**undue** *adj* بی مورد
under *prep* زیر	**unearth** *v* از زیر خاک بیرون کردن
underage *adj* زیرسن	**uneasy** *adj* ناراحت
undercover *adj* مخفی	**uneducated** *adj* بی سواد
underdog *n* ضعیف	**unemployed** *adj* بیکار
underestimate *v* دست کم گرفتن، ناچیز پنداشتن	**unemployment** *n* بیکاری
undergo *v* متحمل شدن	**unending** *adj* تمام نشدنی
underground *adv* در زیر زمین	**unequal** *adj* نابرابر
underground *adj* زیرزمینی	**unequivocal** *adj* صریح، بدون چون و چرا
underline *v* در زیر چیز خط کشیدن	**uneven** *adj* ناهموار
underlying *adj* در زیر قرار گرفته	**unexpected** *adj* غیرمترقبه
undermine *v* متضرر ساختن	**unfair** *adj* غیرعادلانه
underneath *prep* در زیر چیزی	**unfaithful** *adj* بی وفا
understand *v* فهمیدن، درک کردن	**unfamiliar** *adj* ناآشنا
understandable *adj* قابل درک، قابل فهم	**unfasten** *v* باز کردن کمربند
understanding *adj* تفاهم	**unfavorable** *adj* نامطلوب
undertake *v* بعهده گرفتن	**unfinished** *adj* تمام نشده
underwater *adv* در زیر آب	**unfit** *adj* نامناسب، ناسالم
underwater *adj* زیرآب	**unfold** *v* بازکردن
underwear *n* زیرپوشی	**unforeseen** *adj* غیرقابل پیشبینی
underweight *adj* کم وزن، لاغر	**unforgettable** *adj* فراموش نشدنی
	unfortunately *adv* بدبختانه
	unfounded *adj* بی اساس، بی بنیاد

U

unfriendly *adj* غیرصمیمی	**unlock** *v* باز کردن
ungrateful *adj* ناسپاس، ناشکر	**unlucky** *adj* بدبخت، بد چانش
unhappy *adj* ناخوش، غمگین	**unmarried** *adj* مجرد، عروسی نشده
unharmed *adj* بدون آسب، متضرر نشده	**unmask** *v* رونمایی کردن
unhealthy *adj* غیرصحی	**unmistakable** *adj* غیرقابل اشتباه
unheard-of *adj* از کسی احوال نیامده	**unnecessary** *adj* غیرضروری
uniform *adj* یکسان	**unnoticed** *adj* پنهان، مورد توجه قرار نگرفته
uniform *n* یونیفورم، لباس مخصوص	**unoccupied** *adj* اشغال نشده
uniformity *n* یکسانی، یکنواختی	**unofficial** *adj* غیررسمی
unify *v* متحد کردن، یکی کردن	**unofficially** *adv* بطور غیررسمی
unilateral *adj* یک جانبه	**unpack** *v* بسته را باز کردن
union *n* اتحادیه	**unpleasant** *adj* ناخوشایند
unique *adj* بینظیر، بی مانند	**unplug** *v* پلک را کشیدن
unit *n* واحد، شعبه	**unpopular** *adj* غیر محبوب
unite *v* متحد کردن، یکی کردن	**unpredictable** *adj* غیرقابل پیشبینی
united *adj* متحد	**unprofessional** *adj* غیرمسلکی
unity *n* اتحاد، همبستگی	**unprotected** *adj* حفاظت نشده
universal *adj* جهانی	**unqualified** *adj* واجد شرایط نیست
universe *n* دنیا	**unravel** *v* بازکردن
university *n* پوهنتون	**unreal** *adj* غیرواقعی
unjust *adj* ناعادلانه	**unreasonable** *adj* غیرمنطقی، نامعقول، نامناسب
unjustified *adj* توجیه نشده	**unrelated** *adj* بی ربط
unkind *adj* نامهربان	**unreliable** *adj* غیرقابل اعتماد
unknown *adj* نامعلوم	**unrest** *n* ناراحتی، اضطراب
unlawful *adj* غیرقانونی، حرام	**unsafe** *adj* غیرمصوون
unleash *v* رها کردن	**unscrew** *v* بازکردن پیچ
unless *conj* مگراینکه	**unspeakable** *adj* ناگفتنی
unlike *adj* برعکس	**unstable** *adj* بی ثبات
unlikely *adj* غیرمحتمل	**unsteady** *adj* ناپایا
unlimited *adj* نامحدود	**unsuccessful** *adj* ناموفق
unload *v* تخلیه نمودن بار	

U

unsuitable *adj* نامناسب	uproar *n* آشوب، غوغا
unsure *adj* نامطمئن	uproot *v* ریشه کن کردن
unsuspecting *adj* بی گمان	upset *adj* ناراحت
unthinkable *adj* غیرقابل تصور	upset *v* ناراحت کردن
untie *v* باز کردن گره	upside-down *adv* سرچپه، سراشیب
until *conj* الی	upstairs *adj* قسمت بالا
until *prep* تا	upstairs *adv* منزل بالا
untimely *adj* بیموقع،نابه هنگام	uptight *adj* بالا بردن
untouchable *adj* غیرقابل لمس	up-to-date *adj* به روز، مطابق عصر فعلی
untrue *adj* نادرست	upwards *adv* بطرف بالا
unusual *adj* غیرمعمول	Uranus *n* سیاره اورانوس
unveil *v* آشکار کردن	urban *adj* شهری
unwillingly *adv* به بی میلی	urge *n* پافشاری، اصرار
unwind *v* سیم پیچ را باز کردن	urge *v* تاکید کردن
unwrap *v* کاغذپیچ را باز کردن	urgency *n* ضرورت، حالت عاجل
unzip *v* زنجیرک را باز کردن	urgent *adj* عاجل
up *adv* بالا	urinate *v* ادرار کردن
up *prep* در بلندی	urine *n* ادرار
upbringing *n* پرورش طفل، تربیت طفل	urn *n* کوزه
	us *pron* ما را، برای ما
upcoming *adj* آینده، بعدی	usage *n* استفاده
update *v* تجدید کردن	use *v* استفاده کردن
upgrade *v* ارتقا دادن	use *n* کاربرد
upheaval *n* آشوب، تحول	useable *adj* قابل استفاده
uphill *adv* سربالایی	used *adj* استفاده شده، مستعمل
uphold *v* تقویت کردن، حفظ کردن	used to *idiom* عادت داشتن
upholstery *n* پوش سیت دوزی، پوش فرنیچر دوزی	useful *adj* مفید
	useless *adj* بی ارزش
upon *prep* بمجرد	user *n* استفاده کننده
uppercase *n* حروف بزرگ الفبا	user-friendly *adj* مورد پسند استفاده کننده
upright *adj* راست، مستقیم	
uprising *n* قیام، شورش	

U

رهنمایی کردن usher *n*	وال، وال نل آب valve *n*
معمول usual *adj*	خون آشام vampire *n*
معمولاً usually *adv*	لاری کوچک van *n*
ظروف utensil *n*	خرابکار vandal *n*
استفاده کردن utilize *v*	خرابکاری vandalism *n*
بیشترین utmost *adj*	خراب کردن vandalize *v*
گفتن، ادا کردن utter *v*	ونیلا vanilla *n*
	محو شدن vanish *v*
	غرور vanity *n*

V

	پیروز شدن بر vanquish *v*
	بخار vapor *n*
	متغیر variable *adj*
جای خالی، بست خالی vacancy *n*	تغییر، دگرگونی variation *n*
خالی vacant *adj*	متنوع varied *adj*
خالی کردن vacate *v*	تنوع variety *n*
رخصتی vacation *n*	مختلف various *adj*
واکسین کردن vaccinate *v*	پوهنتون varsity *n*
واکسین vaccine *n*	تفاوت داشتن vary *v*
جاروب برقی vacuum *n*	گلدان vase *n*
جاروب کردن vacuum *v*	وسیع، پهناور vast *adj*
ولگرد vagrant *n*	گوشت گوساله veal *n*
مبهم، گُنگ vague *adj*	منحرف شدن veer *v*
بیهوده vain *adj*	سبزیجات vegetable *n*
بطور بیهوده vainly *adv*	سبزی خور vegetarian *n*
شجاع، دلیر valiant *adj*	رویاندن سبزیجات vegetation *n*
معتبر، قابل اعتبار valid *adj*	واسطه نقلیه vehicle *n*
تصدیق کردن validate *v*	چادر، حجاب veil *n*
اعتبار، درستی validity *n*	رگ vein *n*
دره، وادی valley *n*	سرعت، شتاب velocity *n*
باارزش valuable *adj*	مخمل velvet *n*
ارزش value *n*	انتقام vengeance *n*
ارزش دادن value *v*	زهر venom *n*

U

vent *n* مخرج	vibration *n* لرزه، لرزش
ventilate *v* تبدیل نمودن هوا، هوا دادن	vice *n* معاون
ventilation *n* تبدیلی هوا، هوا دهی	vicinity *n* نزدیکی، مجاورت
venture *v* اقدام به کار پرخطر کردن	vicious *adj* حیوان صفت
venture *n* مخاطره	victim *n* متضرر، قربانی
verb *n* فعل	victimize *v* متضرر ساختن، قربانی کردن
verbal *adj* شفاهی	victor *n* پیروز
verbally *adv* بطور شفاهی	victorious *adj* فاتح، پیروز
verbatim *adv* تحت اللفظی، کلمه به کلمه	victory *n* پیروزی
verdict *n* حُکم، قضاوت	video *n* ویدیو
verge *n* لبه، حاشیه	video game *n* ویدیو گیم
verification *n* تأیید، تصدیق	view *v* دیدن
verify *v* تایید کردن	view *n* منظره؛ نظریه
versatile *adj* همه کاره	viewpoint *n* نقطه نظر
verse *n* آیه، شعر	vigil *n* بیداری، شب زنده داری
versed *adj* ماهر	vigorous *adj* قوی
version *n* نسخه	village *n* قریه
versus *prep* در مقابل، در برابر	villager *n* قریه نشین، دهاتی
vertebra *n* مهره، ستون فقرات	villain *n* تبه کار، شریر
vertical *adj* عمودی	vindicate *v* حمایت کردن، پشتیبانی کردن
very *adj* بسیار	vindictive *adj* کینه جو
very *adv* زیاد	vine *n* تاک
vessel *n* کشتی	vinegar *n* سرکه
vest *n* جلیقه، واسکت نجات	vineyard *n* باغ تاک
veteran *n* سرباز، عسکر سابق	violate *v* تخطی کردن، نقض کردن
veterinarian *n* داکتر حیوانات	violence *n* خشونت
veto *v* رد کردن	violent *adj* خشن
via *prep* از طریق	violet *adj* بنفش رنگ
vibrant *adj* پر جنب و جوش	violet *n* رنگ بنفش؛ گل بنفش
vibrate *v* لرزیدن، به لرزه درآوردن	violin *n* آله موسیقی وایلین

V

violinist *n* نوازنده وایلین

virgin *n* باکره

virile *adj* مردانه

virtual *adj* مجازی، از راه دور

virtually *adv* بصورت مجازی

virtue *n* تقوا

virtuous *adj* باتقوا

virus *n* ویروس

visibility *n* قابلیت دید

visible *adj* قابل دید

vision *n* دید چشم

visit *v* ملاقات کردن، عیادت کردن

visit *n* ملاقات، عیادت

visitor *n* بازدید کننده، مهمان

visual *adj* بصری، دیداری

visualize *v* مجسم کردن

vital *adj* حیاتی

vitality *n* خاصیت حیاتی

vitamin *n* ویتامین

vivacious *adj* بانشاط، سرزنده

vivid *adj* واضح، روشن

vocabulary *n* لغات

vocal *adj* صوتی، مربوط به آواز

voice *n* صدا

voice mail *n* پیام صوتی

void *adj* باطل

volatile *adj* بخارشدنی، رفتنی

volcano *n* آتشفشان

volleyball *n* والیبال

voltage *n* ولتاژ برق

volume *n* درجه صدا؛ جلد کتاب؛ اندازه

voluntary *adj* اختیاری، داوطلبانه

volunteer *n* داوطلب، رضاکار

volunteer *v* رضاکاری کردن، کار داوطلبانه کردن

vomit *v* استفراغ کردن

vote *n* رای

vote *v* رای دادن

vouch for *v* تایید کردن

voucher *n* کوپون

vow *v* تعهد کردن

vowel *n* حروف صدادار

voyage *n* سفر دریایی کردن

voyager *n* مسافر

vulgar *adj* مبتذل

vulnerable *adj* آسیب پذیر

vulture *n* یکنوع پرنده شکارچی

W

wafer *n* وافر، یکنوع بسکویت

waffle *n* وافل، یکنوع کلچه

wag *v* جنباندن

wage *n* حق الزحمه، مزد

wagon *n* واگون

wail *v* ناله، فریاد

waist *n* کمر

wait *v* انتظار کشیدن

waiter *n* پیشخدمت

waitress *n* پیشخدمت

waive *v* مستثنی کردن، معاف کردن

wake (up) v بیدار شدن، بیدار کردن	**wash** v شستن
walk v قدم زدن	**washable** adj قابل شستن
walk n گردش	**washing machine** n
wall n دیوار	ماشین کالاشویی
wallet n بکسک جیبی	**wasp** n زنبور
walnut n چارمغز	**waste** adj باطله
walrus n فیل دریایی	**waste** v ضایع کردن
waltz n موسیقی و رقص	**waste** n ضایعات
wander v سرگردان بودن	**wastebasket** n سطل کثافات
wanderer n آدم سرگردان	**wasteful** adj بی فایده
wane v کمرنگ شدن	**watch** v تماشا کردن
want v خواستن	**watch** n ساعت دستی
war n جنگ	**watch out** pv مواظب باش
ward n بخش، شعبه	**watchful** adj مراقب
warden n نگهبان	**water** n آب
wardrobe n الماری لباس	**water** v آبیاری کردن
warehouse n گُدام، ذخیره گاه	**water heater** n آبگرمی
warfare n جنگ	**waterfall** n آبشار
warm v گرم کردن	**watermelon** n تربوز
warm adj گرم؛ مهربان	**waterproof** adj ضد آب
warm up pv گرمکاری	**watertight** adj مانع دخول آب
warmth n گرما، حرارت	**watery** adj آبدار
warn v اخطار دادن	**wave** v دست تکان دادن
warning n اخطاریه	**wave** n موج
warp v پیچ و تاب دادن	**waver** v دو دل بودن
warped adj تاب خورده	**wavy** adj موجدار
warrant n حُکم	**wax** n موم
warrant v ضمانت کردن	**way** n راه، طریقه
warranty n ضمانت	**way in** n مسیر، راه دخول
warrior n جنگسالار، جنگجو	**way out** n راه بیرون رفت
wart n بخار روی جلد	**we** pron ما
wary adj محتاط	**weak** adj ضعیف

W

weaken v ضعیف کردن	رفاه؛ کمک خیریه دولت n **welfare**
weakness n ضعیفی، ضعف	بسیار زیاد adv **well**
wealth n ثروت	چاه n **well**
wealthy adj ثروتمند	خوب adj **well**
weapon n اسلحه	خوش برخورد adj **well-behaved**
wear v پوشیدن	خوش لباس adj **well-dressed**
wear down pv فرسوده شدن	شناخته شده adj **well-known**
wear out pv کهنه شدن	سعادتمند، بی نیاز adj **well-to-do**
weary adj خسته، بیزار	غرب n **west**
weather n آب و هوا	غرباً adv **west**
weave v بافتن	غربی adj **west**
web n تار عنکبوت	بطرف غرب adv **westbound**
website n صفحه انترنیتی، ویبسایت	غربی adj **western**
wed v عروسی کردن	مردم غرب نشین adj **westerner**
wedding n عروسی	تر، مرطوب adj **wet**
wedge n توته چوب	تمساح n **whale**
Wednesday n روز چهارشنبه	چی adj **what**
weed n علف هرزه	چی را pron **what**
weed v علف هرزه را چیدن	هرآنچه pron **whatever**
week n هفته	هرچه adj **whatever**
weekday n روز هفته، روز کاری	گندم n **wheat**
weekend n رخصتی هفته	چرخ، تایر n **wheel**
weekly adv هفته وار	کراچی دستی n **wheelbarrow**
weep v اشک ریختن	چوکی تایر دار n **wheelchair**
weigh v وزن کردن	نفسک زدن v **wheeze**
weight n وزن، وزن سنج	چه زمانی conj **when**
weird adj عجیب و غریب	چی وقت adv **when**
welcome n خوش آمدید	هرزمانی adv **whenever**
welcome v خوش آمدید گفتن، پذیرایی کردن	هروقت conj **whenever**
	درکجا conj **where**
weld v ویلدینگ کردن	کجا adv **where**
welder n ویلدینگگار	در چاراطراف n **whereabouts**

W

whereas *conj* حال آنکه	why *adv* چرا
whereby *adv* به موجب آن	wicked *adj* بدکار، شریر
wherever *conj* در هرجای	wide *adj* عریض، وسیع
whether *conj* چه، خواه	widely *adv* وسیعاً
which *adj* کدام	widen *v* وسیع ساختن
which *pron* کدام یکی	widespread *adj* شایع، بطور گسترده
while *n* در هنگام	widow *n* زن بیوه
while *conj* هنگام	widower *n* مرد بیوه
whim *n* هوس چیزی کردن	width *n* عرض، پهنا
whine *v* ناله کردن	wield *v* بکار بردن، عملی کردن
whip *n* شلاق	wife *n* خانم
whip *v* شلاق زدن	wig *n* موی مصنوعی
whirl *v* چرخیدن	wiggle *v* تکان دادن
whirlpool *n* چرخش آب	wild *adj* وحشی؛ جنگلی
whiskers *n* بروت های پشک	wild boar *n* جانور وحشی
whisper *n* نجوا	wilderness *n* بیابان
whisper *v* نجوا کردن، در گوش کسی گفتن	wildfire *n* آتش سوزی
whistle *n* شپلاق	wildlife *n* حیات وحش
whistle *v* شپلاق کردن	will *n* اراده، وصیت
white *adj* سفید	will *modal v* خواهد
white *n* سفیدی	willing *adj* مایل، خواستار
whiten *v* سفید کردن	willingly *adv* با کمال میل
who *pron* کی	willingness *n* تمایل
whoever *pron* هرآنکس	willow *n* درخت بید
whole *n* تمام، کل	wily *adj* مکار، حیله گر
whole *adj* مجموع	wimp *n* شخص کم دل، بی جرات
wholehearted *adj* صمیمی	win *v* برنده شدن
wholesome *adj* سالم، بی عیب	win back *pv* بازپس گیری
whom *pron* برای کی	wind *n* باد، شمال
whose *pron* از کسی	wind *v* پیچاندن
whose *adj* از کی	wind up *pv* باد کردن

W

winding *adj* مارپیچ

windmill *n* آسیاب بادی

window *n* کلکین

windshield *n* شیشه پیشروی موتر

windy *adj* بادی، توفانی

wine *n* شراب

winery *n* کارخانه شراب سازی

wing *n* بال

wink *v* چشمک زدن

winner *n* برنده

winter *n* زمستان

wipe *v* پاک کردن

wire *n* سیم، لین

wireless *adj* بی سیم

wisdom *n* دانایی، عقل

wise *adj* عاقل، دانا

wish *n* آرزو

wish *v* آرزو کردن

wit *n* بذله گویی

witch *n* زن جادوگر

witchcraft *n* جادوگری

with *prep* با، همراه با

withdraw *v* عقب نشینی کردن، منصرف شدن

withdrawn *adj* بیرون شده، عقب نشینی کرده

wither *v* پژمرده شدن

withhold *v* نگهداشتن

within *prep* درداخل، درظرف

without *prep* بدون

withstand *v* تحمل کردن

witness *n* شاهد

witty *adj* شوخ، بذله گو

wizard *n* جادوگر

wobble *v* تکان خوردن

wobbly *adj* لرزان، جنبنده

wolf *n* گرگ

woman *n* زن

womb *n* رحم، بطن

women *n* زنان

wonder *n* تعجب

wonder *v* تعجب کردن

wonderful *adj* فوق العاده، عالی

wood *n* چوب

wooden *adj* چوبی

wool *n* پشم

woolen *adj* پشمی

word *n* کلمه، واژه

work *n* کار

work *v* کار کردن، فعال بودن

work out *pv* ورزش کردن

workable *adj* قابل اجرا، شدنی

workbook *n* کتاب رهنما

worker *n* کارگر

workshop *n* ورکشاپ، محل کار

world *n* دنیا

worldly *adj* دنیایی، جهانی

worldwide *adj* در سراسر دنیا

worm *n* کرم

worn-out *adj* فرسوده

worried *adj* پریشان، مضطرب

worry *v* تشویش کردن

worry *n* تشویش، اضطراب

worse *adj* بدتر

W

worse *adv* وخیم تر
worsen *v* بدتر کردن
worship *v* عبادت کردن
worst *adj* بدترین
worst *n* فاسد
worst *adv* وخیم ترین
worth *adj* ارزش داشتن
worthless *adj* بی ارزش
worthwhile *adj* با ارزش، ارزنده
worthy *adj* با ارزش
would *modal v* خواهد شد
would-be *adj* خواهد بود
wound *n* زخم، جراحت
wounded *adj* زخمی، مجروح
woven *adj* بافته شده
wrap *v* پیچاندن
wrapper *n* پیچانده شده
wrapping *n* پوشش
wrath *n* خشم، غضب
wreath *n* گل سر قبر
wreck *v* خراب کردن
wreckage *n* خرابی، شکستگی
wrench *n* رنج و پلاس
wrestle *v* کُشتی گرفتن
wrestler *n* کُشتی گیر
wrestling *n* بازی کُشتی
wretched *adj* بدبخت
wring *v* فشار دادن
wrinkle *n* چملکی
wrinkled *adj* چملک
wrist *n* بند دست
write *v* نوشتن

writer *n* نویسنده
writing *n* نگارش
written *adj* نوشته شده
wrong *adj* غلط
wrong *adv* نادرست

X

X-mas *n* کریسمیس
X-ray *n* ایکسری، عکس برقی

Y

yacht *n* قایق
yam *n* کچالوی شیرین
yard *n* حویلی؛ واحد اندازه گیری یارد
yarn *n* نخ
yawn *v* فاجه کشیدن
year *n* سال
yearly *adv* سالانه
yearn *v* مشتاق بودن
yeast *n* خمیرمایه
yell *v* چیغ زدن
yellow *n* رنگ زرد
yellow *adj* زردی
yes *adv* بلی
yesterday *adv* دیروز
yesterday *n* روز پیش

Y

yet *adv* تاهنوز

yet *conj* هنوز

yield *v* راه دادن، تسلیم کردن

yoga *n* ورزش یوگا

yogurt *n* ماست

yolk *n* زردی تخم

you *pron* شما، تو

young *adj* جوان، خوردسن

youngster *n* جوانتر

your *pron* از شما

your *adj* از شما

yours *pron* از شما

yourself *pron* خود شما

youth *n* جوانی

youthful *adj* جوان

Z

zeal *n* غیرت

zealous *adj* غیرتمند

zebra *n* گوره خر

zero *n* صفر

zest *n* شوق و شور

zip code *n* کود منطقه

zipper *n* زنجیرک

zone *n* ساحه؛ زون

zoo *n* باغ وحش

zoom *v* بزرگ نشان دادن

zucchini *n* کدو سبز

Y
Z

Dari-English

Abbreviations

a - article - حرف تعريف

adj - adjective - صفت

adv - adverb - قيد

conj - conjunction - حرف ربط

e - exclamation - علامت تعجب

n - noun - اسم

prep - preposition - حرف اضافه

pron - pronoun - ضمير

v - verb - فعل

pv - phrasal verb - فعل مركب

idiom - idiom - اصطلاح

auxillary v - auxillary verb - فعل كومكى

modal v - modal verb - فعل وجهى

abbr - abbreviation - فـفخم

phrase - phrase - عبارت

آ

آب water n
آب تازه freshwater adj
آب دهن saliva n
آب شدن thaw v
آب لیمو lemonade n
آب نبات caramel n
آب و هوا weather n
آبباز swimmer; diver n
آببازی swimming n
آببازی کردن swim v
آبدار juicy; watery adj
آبشار waterfall n
آبشار بزرگ cataract n
آبکش کردن rinse v
آبگرمی water heater n
آبگونه liquid adj
آبله blister n
آبی blue adj
آبیاری irrigation n
آبیاری کردن irrigate; water v
آتش blaze v
آتش fire n
آتش بس truce n
آتش زدن fire v
آتش زدن عمدی arson n
آتش سوزی ignition; wildfire n
آتش کردن در کمپ campfire n
آتش مزاج fiery adj
آتشبازی firecracker; fireworks n

آتشسوزی bonfire n
آتشفشان volcano n
آجندا agenda n
آخر last adj
آخری ultimate; latter adj
آخرین last adv
آخرین latest adj
آخرین ultimatum n
آخور حیوانات stall n
آداب معاشرت etiquette n
آدرس address n
آدرس انترنتی domain; URL n
آدرس نوشتن address v
آدم با اندام کوچک dwarf n
آدم برقی robot n
آدم درنده خو hyena n
آدم ساده naive adj
آدم سرگردان wanderer n
آدم شوخ joker n
آدم فریبکار jerk n
آدم کش thug n
آدم نیرومند و خشن jumbo adj
آدمک ساختگی dummy n
آراستن adorn, embellish; v prune
آرام cool, placid, restful, relaxed; serene, calm adj
آرام باش calm down; v cool down
آرام چوکی sofa; armchair n
آرام کردن relax; pacify, placate, soothe; sedate v

آرامش *n* relaxation; solace; lull; tranquility	آسان *adj* easy
آرامش بخش *adj* relaxing; soothing	آسان گیر *adj* easygoing
آرامش خود را حفظ کردن *v* chill out	آستانه *n* threshold
آرامش دهنده *n* comforter	آستین *n* sleeve
آرایش *n* décor; manicure; makeup	آسمان *n* sky
آرایش کردن *v* groom	آسمان خراش *n* skyscraper
آرایشگاه *n* salon; spa	آسمانی *adj* celestial
آرد *n* flour	آسوده *adj* relieved
آرزو *n* ambition, desire, wish	آسوده خاطر *adj* carefree
آرزو کردن *v* dream, aspire, desire, wish	آسیاب *n* mill
آرشیف *n* archive	آسیاب بادی *n* windmill
آرکستر *n* orchestra	آسیاب کردن *v* grind
آرنج *n* elbow	آسیب پذیر *adj* vulnerable
آروغ *n* burp	آسیب رساندن *v* traumatize
آروغ زدن *v* belch, burp	آش *n* noodles, spaghetti
آزاد *adj* free	آش یا مکرونی *n* pasta
آزاد شدن *v* break free	آشپز *n* cook
آزاد کردن *v* free, liberate	آشپزخانه *n* kitchen
آزادی *n* freedom, liberty	آشپزی *n* cooking
آزادیخواه *adj* liberal	آشفتگی *n* turbulence
آزار دادن *v* tease, bother	آشفته *adj* deranged
آزار دهنده *adj* hurtful; nagging	آشکار *adj* apparent, conspicuous, evident
آزار و اذیت کردن *v* persecute	آشکار کردن *v* manifest; unveil
آزاردهنده *adj* bothersome	آشکار کننده *adj* revealing
آزمایش *n* experiment, trial	آشکارا *adv* clearly
آزمایشی *adj* tentative	آشکارا *adj* sharp
آزمون *n* audition	آشنا *adj* familiar
آژیر *n* siren	آشنا شدن *v* meet
	آشنایی *n* acquaintance; orientation
	آشوب *n* upheaval, uproar, turmoil

آمیختن

آله موسیقی کلارینیت clarinet n	nest n آشیانه
آله موسیقی هارپ harp n	beginning, outset, n آغاز
آله موسیقی وایلون fiddle n	inception, initiation
آله موسیقی وایلین violin n	debut n آغاز کار
آله موسیقی ویلون cello n	commence, initiate v آغاز کردن
آله وصل کننده اینترنیت modem n	arms; hug n آغوش
آلو plum n	pest n آفت
آلوبالو cherry n	sun n آفتاب
آلوبخارا prune n	brown adj آفتاب خورده
آلودگی filth; pollution n	bask, tan v آفتاب دادن
آلوده infested; tainted adj	sunburn n آفتاب سوختگی
آلوده کردن contaminate, v	sunny adj آفتابی
pollute	offline adj آفلاین
آلوده گی contamination n	gentleman, Mister, sir n آقا
آماتور amateur adj	oxygen n آکسیژن
آمادگی preparation n	aware adj آگاه
آماده ready, prepared; handy adj	knowingly adv آگاهانه
آماده شدن برای make up for v	awareness n آگاهی
آماده کردن prepare v	flier n آگاهی روی کاغذ
آمدن come; show up v	notification; reminder n آگهی
آمدن از come from v	tool n آله
آمر supervisor, boss, chief n	recorder n آله ثبت کننده صدا
آمر حوزه sheriff n	boiler n آله جوش کننده
آمرانه bossy adj	joystick n آله کنترل بازی
آمرانه رفتار کردن boss around v	remote control n آله کنترول از دور
آملیت omelet n	organ n آله موسیقی
آموختاندن educate v	trumpet n آله موسیقی ترمپیت
آموختن learn v	trombone n آله موسیقی ترومبون
آموزش learning n	tuba n آله موسیقی توبا
آموزش دادن coach, train v	jazz n آله موسیقی جاز
آموزگار trainer n	saxophone n آله موسیقی سکسافون
آمیختن mingle v	cymbal n آله موسیقی سمبال

آن that *adj*	آوازخوان singer *n*
آن زن her *adj*	آوازه rumor *n*
آن زن she *pron*	آوردن bring, fetch *v*
آن زن را her *pron*	آویزان کردن dangle *v*
آن مرد he, him *pron*	آویزان کرده hang *v*
آن یکی that *pron*	آیسکریم ice cream *n*
آنان those *pron*	آیسکریم پاپ سیکل popsicle *n*
آناناس pineapple *n*	آیکن icon *n*
آنتن antenna *n*	آینده future *n*
آنجا there *adv*	آینده incoming, coming;
آنسو beyond *prep*	upcoming; forthcoming *adj*
آنلاین online *adj*	آینده next *adv*
آنها they *pron*	آینده نگری foresight *n*
آنها those *adj*	آیه verse *n*
آنها خودشان themselves *pron*	آیینه looking glass, mirror *n*
آه sigh *n*	
آه کشیدن sigh *v*	
آهسته slow *adj*	۱
آهسته آهسته خورد شدن dwindle *v*	
آهسته بروید slow down *v*	
آهسته زدن tap *v*	ابتدایی rudimentary *adj*
آهسته قدم زدن shuffle *v*	ابتدانیه elementary *adj*
آهن iron *n*	ابتکار initiative; innovation *n*
آهن ربا magnet *n*	ابدیت eternity *n*
آهنگ song, tune *n*	ابر cloud *n*
آهنگ مشهور hit *n*	ابرآلود cloudy *adj*
آهنگر blacksmith *n*	ابرقدرت superpower *n*
آهو deer *n*	ابرو eyebrow *n*
آواز بلند loud *adj*	ابری overcast *adj*
آواز خواندن sing *v*	ابریشم silk *n*
آواز خواندن دسته جمعی choir, *n*	ابزار gadget *n*
chorus	ابطال revoke *v*

irrefutable *adj* ابطال ناپذیر	allowance; clearance; *n* اجازه
complication *n* ابهام	permission
apartment, condo *n* اپارتمان	may *modal v* اجازه خواستن
April *n* اپریل	allow, authorize, let, *v* اجازه دادن
room; chamber *n* اتاق	permit
اتاق الماری های قفل دار *n*	let in *v* اجازه دادن به داخل
locker room	coercion, compulsion *n* اجبار
اتاق امتحان کردن لباس *n*	binding; compelling; *adj* اجباری
fitting room	compulsive, mandatory,
bedroom *n* اتاق خواب	obligatory
classroom *n* اتاق درسی	sociable, social *adj* اجتماعی
attic *n* اتاق کوچک	socialize *v* اجتماعی کردن
dining room *n* اتاق نان خوری	restraint; abstinence *n* اجتناب
living room *n* اتاق نشیمن	refrain *v* اجتناب کردن
cubicle *n* اتاقک	shun *v* اجتناب کردن از
integrity; solidarity, *n* اتحاد	inevitable, *adj* اجتناب ناپذیر
unity, alliance	unavoidable
union *n* اتحادیه	ancestor *n* اجداد
link, connection; *n* اتصال	performance *n* اجرا
junction	perform, execute; *v* اجرا کردن
come about; *v* اتفاق افتادن	run up
happen	performer *n* اجرا کننده
incidentally *adv* اتفاقاً	performance *n* اجرای کنسرت
accidental; casual *adj* اتفاقی	symphony *n* اجرای موسیقی
reliance *n* اتکا	executive *n* اجرایی
rely *v* اتکا ورزیدن	summit *n* اجلاس
accusation *n* اتهام	goods, stuff *n* اجناس
trace; efficiency *n* اثر	premises *n* احاطه
print *n* اثر انگشت	encircle, surround *v* احاطه کردن
clue *n* اثر چیزی	combustion *n* احتراق
artwork *n* اثر هنری	reverence, respect; *n* احترام
lease *n* اجاره	tribute

self-respect n احترام به خود	اخبار n news
احترام کردن v respect	اختتامیه n conclusion
احترامات n regards	اختراع n invention
احتکار کردن v hoard	اختراع کردن v invent
likelihood, probability n احتمال	اختصار n abbreviation;
probably, likely, adv احتمالاً	contraction
presumably; possibly	اختصاص دادن v allot
contingency n احتمالی	اختطاف n abduction
potential adj احتمالی	abduct, kidnap v اختطاف کردن
caution; precaution n احتیاط	kidnapper n اختطاف کننده
sensation; sense, n احساس	embezzle v اختلاس کردن
emotion, feeling	friction; disagreement, n اختلاف
احساس بوقوع پیوستن چیزی n	discrepancy
hunch	disruption n اختلال
احساس شرم داشتن n shyness	season, marinate v اخته کردن
احساس کردن v feel	voluntary, optional adj اختیاری
sentiment, feelings n احساسات	dismissal, expulsion n اخراج
passionate; adj احساساتی	expel; lay off v اخراج کردن
sentimental	premonition n اخطار
census; statistic n احصائیه	warn v اخطار دادن
statistical adj احصائیوی	warning n اخطاریه
summon v احضار کردن	ethics, character, moral; n اخلاق
fool, goof, idiot n احمق	manners
fool v احمق ساختن	اخلاقاً morally adv
silly, foolish, stupid, adj احمقانه	ethical, moral adj اخلاقی
idiotic	recent adj اخیر
greeting n احوالپرسی	ادا کردن v utter
greet v احوالپرسی کردن	management, n اداره
revive v احیا کردن	administration; agency
rehabilitate v احیای مجدد کردن	conduct, administer v اداره کردن
extortion n اخاذی	administrator n اداره کننده
extort v اخاذی کردن	administrative adj اداری

continuation *n* ادامه	promote; go up *v* ارتقا کردن
continue, go on, *v* ادامه دادن	hereditary *adj* ارثی
keep on; keep up	reference *n* ارجاع
homage *n* ادای احترام	army *n* اردو
politeness *n* ادب	expedition *n* اردوکشی
literature *n* ادبیات	cheap, inexpensive *adj* ارزان
urine *n* ادرار	value *n* ارزش
urinate *v* ادرار کردن	value *v* ارزش دادن
comprehensive *adj* ادراک	worth *adj* ارزش داشتن
perception *n* ادراک	invaluable *adj* ارزشمند
assertion, claim *n* ادعا	worthwhile *adj* ارزنده
allege, assert, claim *v* ادعا کردن	study, appraisal, *n* ارزیابی
fusion, integration, ادغام	evaluation
merger	screen, look over; *v* ارزیابی کردن
drug, medication, *n* ادویه	appraise, evaluate
medicine	dispatch; forward *v* ارسال کردن
annoy, disturb, *v* اذیت کردن	senior *adj* ارشد
harass	seniority *n* ارشدیت
annoying *adj* اذیت کننده	magenta; purple *n* ارغوانی
harassment *n* اذیت و آزار	data *n* ارقام
will *n* اراده	saw *n* اره
terrain *n* اراضی	chainsaw *n* اره برقی
briefing; *n* ارایه معلومات	saw *v* اره کردن
presentation	jigsaw *n* اره کوچک برقی
communication *n* ارتباط	Europe *n* اروپا
ارتباط برقرار کردن *v*	European *adj* اروپایی
communicate	diagonal *adj* اریب
relate *v* ارتباط دادن	lantern *n* اریکین
resilient *adj* ارتجاعی	from; of *prep* از
altitude, elevation *n* ارتفاع	its *adj* از این
promotion *n* ارتقا	hers *pron* از آن زن
foster; upgrade *v* ارتقا دادن	his *adj* از آن مرد

از طریق via *prep*	از آن مرد his *pron*
از عمق قلب heartfelt *adj*	از آنها their *adj*
از عهده برامدن tackle *v*	از آنها theirs *pron*
از عهده چیزی برامدن afford *v*	از بالا دیدن overlook *v*
از قبل تعیین کردن premeditate *v*	از بین بردن remove; *v*
از قید رها کردن emancipate *v*	dismantle; eliminate,
از کسی whose *pron*	eradicate
از کسی احوال نیامده *adj*	از بین رفتن perish *v*
unheard-of	از پا درامدن succumb *v*
از کسی نمایندگی کردن represent *v*	از پیش اخطار دادن forewarn *v*
از کی whose *adj*	از پیش خبر کردن foreshadow *v*
از گرسنگی مردن starve *v*	از پیش فرض کردن presuppose *v*
از لحاظ روانی psychological *adj*	از جای خود بیرون کردن dislodge *v*
از لحاظ قانونی legally *adv*	از حد تجاوز کردن exceed *v*
از لحاظ مالی financially *adv*	از خط خارج شدن derail *v*
از لحاظ منطقی logically *adv*	از خود own *pron*
از من mine *pron*	از خودگذری devotion *n*
از من my *adj*	از دست دادن miss *v*
از نظر تخنیکی technically *adv*	از دور afar *adv*
از نظر مسلکی professionally *adv*	از دور شنیدن overhear *v*
از نو ساختن refurbish *v*	از راه بدر کردن seduce *v*
از هم پاشیدن؛ fall apart; *v*	از راه دور virtual *adj*
disintegrate; dissipate	از راه دور شدن dive *v*
از هم پاشیده گی disintegration *n*	از راه فرعی گذشتن bypass *v*
از هم جدا کردن rupture *v*	از روی جبر compulsory *adj*
از وسط قطع کردن intersect *v*	از روی راستی truly *adv*
از وقتیکه since *adv*	از زمین بلند کردن lift-off *n*
از یاد خوانی recital *n*	از زیر خاک بیرون کردن unearth *v*
ازآنوقت since *prep*	از شما your *adj*
ازخود راضی cocky; smug *adj*	از شما your, yours *pron*
ازدحام crowd, swarm; *n*	از طرف روز daytime *n*
stampede; traffic	از طریق through *adv*

ازدحام ترافیکی n traffic jam	استحکام n ;reinforcements
ازدحام کردن v swarm	fortitude; granite
ازدواج n marriage, matrimony	استخدام n employment; recruit
ازراه دور adj remote	استخدام کردن v employ, hire,
ازما adj our	recruit
ازما pron ours	استخراج کردن v extract
ازنظر ذهنی adv mentally	استخراج معدن v mine
اژدها n dragon	استخوان n bone
اسارت n captivity	استخوان گونه n cheekbone
اساس n rationale; principle	استدعا کردن v invoke
اساس قرار دادن v base	استدلال adj staunch
اساساً adv basically	استدلال غلط n fallacy
اساسات n basics	استدلال کردن v reason
اساسنامه n charter	استدیو n studio
اساسی adj principal; substantial	استر n lining
اسب n horse	استراتیژی n strategy
اسب کوچک n pony	استراتیژیک adj strategic
اسبق n predecessor	استراحت n rest
اسپرم n sperm	استراحت کردن v rest
اسپری n spray	استعداد n ;caliber, merit
اسپری کردن v spray	aptitude, talent
اسپرین n aspirin	استعفا n resignation
استاد n professor	استعفا دادن v resign, bow out
استاد پوهنتون n lecturer	استعلام n inquiry
استادان پوهنتون n faculty	استعمار n colonization
استبداد n tyranny	استفاده n usage
استبلر n stapler	استفاده شده adj used
استبلر کردن v staple	استفاده کردن v use, utilize
استثمار کردن v exploit	استفاده کننده n user
استثنا n exception	استفراغ کردن v vomit, throw up
استثنایی adj exceptional	استقامت n ;course, direction
	stamina

استقامت کردن v persevere	اشاره n hint; gesture
استقلال n independence	اشاره کردن v hint; imply; point
استماعیه n hearing	اشباع کردن v saturate
استندرد n standard	اشتباه n oversight, error, fault, mistake
استیج نمایش n stage	
استیدیوم n stadium	اشتباه بزرگ n blunder
استیریو n stereo	اشتباه تایپی n typo
استیشن بس n station, bus station	اشتباه کردن v mistake
	اشتراک n participation; subscription
استیشن پولیس n police station	
استیشن تلویزیون و رادیو n station	اشتراک کردن v attend; participate; subscribe
استینسل n stencil	
اسراف کردن v squander	اشتراک کننده n participant
اسطوره n myth	اشتها n appetite
اسفنج n sponge	اشتها آور n appetizer
اسفنجی adj spongy	اشتیاق n eagerness
اسکلیت n skeleton	اشغال شده adj occupied
اسکن کردن v scan	اشغال کردن v occupy
اسکنه n chisel	اشغال نشده adj unoccupied
اسکوتر اطفال n scooter	اشک n tear
اسکی بازی کردن v ski	اشک ریختن v weep
اسکیت بازی n figure skating	اشیا n stuff
اسکیت بازی کردن v skate	اشیای بیکاره n refuse, junk
اسلام n Islam	اصابت n hit
اسلامی adj Islamic	اصالت n nobility
اسلحه n weapon	اصرار n urge
اسلحه گرم n firearm	اصرار ورزیدن v persist
اسم n noun	اصطکاک n friction
اسهال n diarrhea	اصطلاح n expression, term, idiom
اسیر n captive, hostage	
اسیر گرفتن v captivate	اصطلاحات n terminology
اشاره v beckon	اصطلاحنامه n thesaurus

origin n اصل	اطمینان حاصل کردن v ensure
originally adv اصلاً	اطمینان دادن v assure, reassure
modification, n اصلاح	اطو کردن v iron
amendment, correction	اظهار n saying
modify; amend; v اصلاح کردن	اظهار داشتن v state; cite
rectify; reform	اظهار کننده adj assertive
اصلاح کردن متن v edit	اظهار نظر کردن v remark
اصلاح کردن مو v trim	اعانه n contribution
اصلاح مو n haircut	اعتبار n credit; prestige,
اصلاح موی n clipping	reputation; validity,
اصلاحات n reform	authenticity
original; native adj اصلی	اعتبار داشتن از یک تاریخ در گذشته
staple n اصلی	retroactive adj
surplus n اضافه	اعتبار کردن v credit
surcharge n اضافه بها	moderation n اعتدال
overtime n اضافه کاری	protest n اعتراض
add v اضافه کردن	protest v اعتراض کردن
affix v اضافه نمودن	confession n اعتراف
overweight adj اضافه وزن	اعتراف کردن v admit, confess
extra adv اضافی	confessor n اعتراف کننده
redundant; adj اضافی	strike n اعتصاب
additional; plus	اعتصاب کردن v strike
اضطراب n unrest; worry, anxiety	faith n اعتقاد
emergency n اضطراری	اعتماد n confidence, trust
obedience n اطاعت	اعتماد به نفس n self-esteem
اطاعت کردن v abide by, obey	اعتماد کردن v confide, trust
about adv اطراف	اعتنا کردن به v mind
children n اطفال	اعتنا نکردن v brush aside,
fire department n اطفائیه	disregard
inform v اطلاع دادن	addiction n اعتیاد
know-how n اطلاعات	اعتیاد آور adj addictive
اطمینان n certainty, assurance	deployment n اعزام

اعزام کردن v deploy	افسانه n ,myth, fable, fairy tale
اعشاری adj decimal	fiction, legend
اعضای خانواده شاهی n royalty	افسانوی adj fictitious; legendary
اعضای فامیل همسر n in-laws	افسر اردو n major
اعطا کردن v ,award, grant	افسر پولیس n policeman
bestow	افسردگی n depression
اعلام بی تقصیری کردن v absolve	افسرده کردن v depress
اعلام کردن v declare, proclaim	افسرده کننده adj depressing
اعلامیه n ,announcement	افسوس n sigh; pity
proclamation, declaration	افسوس کردن v sigh
اعلان n advertisement	افسون کردن v bewitch
اعلان تجارتی n ;promotion	افشا n exposure
commercial	افشا شده adj exposed
اعلان کردن v advertise; announce	افشا کردن v ,reveal, disclose
اعلان کننده n announcer	divulge
اعلی adj supreme	افشاء n revelation
اعلیحضرت n majesty	افق n horizon
اعمار کردن v build, construct	افقی adj lateral; horizontal
اعمال زور n exertion	اقامت n stay
اغفال n delusion	اقامت کردن v stay
اغلب adv often	اقبال n fortune
افتادن v plummet, drop; fall	اقتدارگرا adj authoritarian
افتتاح n opening, inauguration	اقتصاد n economy
افتتاح کردن v inaugurate	اقتصاد دان n economist
افتخار n honor, pride	اقتصادی adj economic
افراط n excess	اقتصادی بودن adj economical
افراط کردن v indulge; overdo	اقتصادی ساختن v economize
افراطی adj extremist; radical	اقدام n ;action; approach
افزایش n ;raise, increase	measure
increment	اقدام به کار پرخطر کردن v venture
افزایش دادن v ;raise; enhance	اقدام کردن v act
increase	اقلاً pron least

minority *n* اقلیت	divine *adj* الهی
climate *n* اقلیم	divinity *n* الهیات
accordion *n* اکاردیون	till *prep* الی
academy *n* اکادمی	until *conj* الی
acquisition *n* اکتساب	but *conj* اما
exploration *n* اکتشاف	ambulance *n* امبولانس
largely *adv* اکثراً	emperor *n* امپراتور
majority *n* اکثریت	empire *n* امپراتوری
acrobat *n* اکروبات	exam, test *n* امتحان
aquarium *n* اکواریوم	quiz *v* امتحان دادن
if *conj* اگر	try; test *v* امتحان کردن
jaw *n* الاشه	quiz *n* امتحان مختصر
implore; solicit *v* التماس کردن	refusal *n* امتناع
inflammation *n* التهاب	concession; *n* امتیاز
a *a* الف	prerogative; privilege
alphabet *n* الفبا	allowance *n* امتیازات
electronic *adj* الکترونیکی	natural *adj* امرعادی
alcohol *n* الکل	today *adv* امروز
alcoholic *adj* الکلی	today *n* امروز
template, pattern; icon *n* الگو	American *adj* امریکایی
cabinet; closet *n* الماری	tonight *adv* امشب
cupboard *n* الماری ظروف	tonight *n* امشب
locker *n* الماری قفل دار	autograph, signature *n* امضا
bookcase *n* الماری کتاب	sign *v* امضا کردن
wardrobe *n* الماری لباس	possibility *n* امکان
diamond *n* الماس	amenities *n* امکانات برای آسایش
bolt, lightning *n* الماسک	feasible *adj* امکانپذیر
Olympics *n* المپیک	estate *n* املاک
replica *n* المثنی	security *n* امنیت
aluminum *n* المونیم	goods *n* اموال
inspiration *n* الهام	cargo *n* اموال تجارتی
goddess *n* الهه	hope *n* امید

امید کردن v hope	انتقام گرفتن v avenge, retaliate
امیدوار adj hopeful	انتقام گرفتن n revenge
اناتومی n anatomy	انتیبیتیک n antibiotic
انبار n mound, heap, pile, stack; cellar; depot	انجام دادن v accomplish, carry out, do
انبار شدن n backlog	انجام شده adj done
انبار کاه n haystack	انجام شده با دست adj manual
انبار کردن v heap, pile, stack	انجام نشده گذاشتن v skip
انباشتن v pile up	انجمن n association
انبور n pliers; tongs	انجنیر n engineer
انتخاب n choice, pick, selection	انجنیر برق n electrician
انتخاب کردن v nominate, pick, choose, select, elect	انجیر n fig
انتخابات n election	انچ n inch
انترنیت n internet	انحراف n aberration, deviation; detour; diversion
انتشار n release	انحراف v offset
انتظار n expectancy	انحصار n monopoly
انتظار کشیدن v wait	انداختن v throw
انتقاد n criticism; objection	اندازه n scale, gauge; volume, size
انتقاد کردن v criticize; object	اندازه کردن v calibrate; measure
انتقال n transfer	اندازه گرفتن v span
انتقال دادن v relay, transfer; transport, carry; convey, channel	اندازه گیری n measurement
	اندک pron less
انتقال دادن برق v conduct	اندوه n sorrow, grief
انتقال دادن مامورین v shuttle	اندیشیدن v contemplate, ponder
انتقال دهنده n courier	انرژی n power, energy
انتقال دهنده برق n conductor	انزوا n quarantine, isolation
انتقال یافتن v transmit	انسان n human
انتقالات n transportation	انسانی adj human
انتقام n vengeance	انسجام n coordination
انتقام جویی n reprisal	انسداد n blockage; closure

انشعاب ramification n	انگیزه impulse; motive; n
انصاف fairness n	stimulus
انطباق compliance n	انگیزه آور impulsive adj
انعام bonus n	انواع species n
انعام دادن reward v	اهتزاز کردن sway v
انعطاف flexibility n	اهدا donation n
انعطاف پذیر flexible, supple adj	اهدا کردن donate v
انعطاف پذیری flexibility n	اهل جنوب southerner n
انعطاف داشتن flex v	اهل مناطق شمالی northerner n
انعطاف ناپذیر inflexible adj	اهلی tame adj
انعکاس reflection; echo n	اهلی شده domesticated adj
انفجار blast; explosion; n	اهمیت significance, n
outburst	importance
انفرادی sporadic; solo; adj	اهمیت داشتن matter v
individual; solitary	او خودش herself pron
انقباض traction n	او مرد خودش himself pron
انقضا expiration n	اوباش thug, hoodlum n
انقطاع interruption n	اوج climax n
انقلاب revolution n	اوج گرفتن soar v
انقلابی revolutionary adj	اودومیتر odometer n
انقلابی کردن revolutionize v	اوضاع circumstance n
انکار denial n	اوطو iron n
انکار کردن recant v	اوقات تلخی tantrum n
انکار ناپذیر undeniable adj	اوقات فراغت leisure n
انکشاف development n	اولاد offspring, posterity n
انکشاف کردن develop v	اولویت priority n
انگشت finger n	اولویت بندی کردن prioritize v
انگشتر ring n	اولی first adj
انگلیسی English n	اولین قسمت initial n
انگنار artichoke n	اونس ounce n
انگور grape n	اوه oh e
انگیزش animation n	ایالت state n

ایجاد سوراج perforation *n*	بُعدى dimensional *adj*
ایدیتور editor *n*	با with *prep*
ایستاد stagnant, stationary *adj*	با احتیاط carefully; prudent *adv*
ایستاد static *n*	با ادب polite *adj*
ایستاد شدن stand *v*	با اراده single-minded *adj*
ایستادگی کردن stand for *v*	با ارزش worthwhile; worthy *adj*
ایستگاه stop *n*	با استعداد gifted *adj*
ایستگاه بس bus stop *n*	با اعتبار prestigious *adj*
ایکسری X-ray *n*	با افتخار proudly *adv*
ایمیل e-mail (email) *n*	با انرژی energetic *adj*
ایمیل کردن e-mail (email) *v*	با ایمان faithful *adj*
این it, this *pron*	با آنهم however *adv*
این this *adj*	با بالش آراستن cushion *v*
این و آن either *adj*	با باندارژ بستن bandage *v*
اینان these *pron*	با پاس پاس پاک کردن mop *v*
اینجا here *adv*	با پول جورآمد کردن buy off *v*
اینها these *adj*	با تجربه experienced *adj*
ائتلاف کردن pool *v*	با تسمه بسته کردن strap *v*
بی ارزش useless, worthless *adj*	با تفصیل بیان کردن detail *v*
	با توپ بازی کردن bowl *v*
	با تیپ بستن tape *v*
	با جزئیات detailed *adj*
ب	با چوب زدن bludgeon; mug *v*
	با چیغ و فریاد صحبت کردن *v* squeak
بَنر banner *n*	با خلوص sincerely *adv*
بُت idol *n*	با خوشحالی joyfully *adv*
بُت ساختن و پرستیدن idolize *v*	با دست manually *adv*
بُته bush, shrub *n*	با دوام durable, lasting *adj*
بُرج tower *n*	با ذکاوت intelligently *adv*
بُز goat *n*	با ریسمان زدن lasso *v*
بُشکه barrel *n*	با سروصدا noisily *adv*
بُعد dimension *n*	

با صدا غذا خوردن v smack	باد دار bloated adj
با صدای بلند به زمین زدن v bang	باد شده puffy adj
با عیب flawed adj	باد کردن v ;deflate; inflate
با کمال میل willingly adv	wind up
با لایه پوشاندن v pad	باد گرفتن bloat v
با لکنت حرف زدن v stutter	باد و سیلاب زودگذر torrent n
با لکنت گفتن v stammer	بادام almond n
با مثال واضح کردن v exemplify	بادام زمینی peanut n
با محبت loving adj	بادپکه fan n
با محبت پروردن v pamper	باددار puffy adj
با مروت humane adj	بادرایت tactful adj
با مزه tasteful adj	بادرنگ cucumber n
با معنی meaningful adj	بادنجان رومی tomato n
با مهارت skillful adj	بادی windy adj
با نوک انگشت به جان کسی زدن v	بار burden, load n
poke	بار کردن موتر load v
با نوک سوراخ کردن v peck	باران rain n
با هوش ingenious adj	باران شدید rainfall n
باارزش precious, valuable adj	بارانی rainy adj
بااستعداد talented adj	باربری barge n
بااقتدار sovereign adj	باربی کیو barbecue n
بااندیشه thoughtful adj	باردار pregnant adj
باتدبیر tactful adj	باردار شدن conceive v
باتقوا virtuous adj	بارداری pregnancy n
باتلاق swamp n	بارش precipitation n
باثبات stable n	بارش برف snowfall n
باثبات sustainable adj	بارشده loaded adj
باثبات کردن stabilize v	بارکش porter n
باجدیت earnestly adv	بارکود barcode n
باحوصله meek; patient adj	بارندگی downpour n
باختن lose v	باروت gunpowder n
باد wind n	بارور fertile adj

fertility *n* باروری	lever; arm, forearm *n* بازو
rain *v* باریدن	game *n* بازی
thin, narrow, slim *adj* باریک	skate *n* بازی اسکیت
splinter *n* باریکه چوب	bowling *n* بازی بولینگ
open, ajar *adj* باز	baseball *n* بازی بیس بال
openness *n* باز بودن	pool *n* بازی پول
break open *v* باز شدن	tennis *n* بازی تینیس
unlock *v* باز کردن	ice skate *v* بازی روی یخ
unfasten *v* باز کردن کمربند	soccer *n* بازی ساکر
untie *v* باز کردن گره	stalemate *n* بازی شطرنج
market *n* بازار	fencing *n* بازی شمشیر زنی
market *v* بازاریابی کردن	wrestling *n* بازی کُشتی
relay *v* بازپخش کردن	play *v* بازی کردن
kickback; *n* بازپرداخت	cricket *n* بازی کریکیت
reimbursement, repayment	golf *n* بازی گلف
win back *v* بازپس گیری	surfing *n* بازی موج سواری
deter *v* بازداشتن	hockey *n* بازی هاکی
review, go over, *v* بازدید کردن	recycled *adj* بازیافت شده
look through, look into	recover, retrieve; *v* بازیافتن
visitor *n* بازدید کننده	recycle
search *n* بازرسی	toy *n* بازیچه
checkers *n* بازرسی کننده گان	player *n* بازیکن
remodel, *v* بازسازی کردن	golfer *n* بازیکن گلف
reconstruct	playful *adj* بازیگوش
open; unfold, unravel *v* بازکردن	gratefully *adv* باسپاس
unscrew *v* بازکردن پیچ	archaeology *n* باستان شناسی
unbutton *v* بازکردن دکمه	primitive; classical *adj* باستانی
restore *v* بازگرداندن	blissful *adj* باسعادت
comeback, return *n* بازگشت	literate *adj* باسواد
return *v* بازگشت کردن	stale *adj* باسی
survivor *n* بازمانده	splendid, glorious, *adj* باشکوه
loser *n* بازنده	magnificent, majestic

باشنده inhabitant, resident *n*	بالاخره finally *adv*
باطل void *adj*	بالای over *prep*
باطل کردن quash, abrogate, *v*	بالای above *prep*
nullify, undo	بالای چیزی تکیه کردن lean on *v*
باطله waste *adj*	بالش cushion, pillow *n*
باعث شدن result; cause *v*	بالغ grown-up, adult *n*
باعزت dignified *adj*	بالغ mature *adj*
باغ garden; orchard *n*	بالغ شدن به amount to *v*
باغ تاک vineyard *n*	بالکن balcony *n*
باغ وحش zoo *n*	بام roof *n*
باغبان gardener *n*	بانت موتر hood *n*
بافت texture *n*	باند موسیقی band *n*
بافتن knit; weave *v*	بانداژ bandage *n*
بافته شده woven *adj*	بانشاط vivacious *adj*
باقهر صحبت کردن snap *v*	بانک bank *n*
باقی ماندن stick, remain *v*	باهم together *adv*
باقی مانده remnant, residue *n*	باهم یکجا altogether *adv*
باقیمانده left *adj*	باهوش perceptive; conscious *adj*
باقیمانده rest, remainder, *n*	باوجواینکه though *adv*
surplus	باوجود despite *prep*
باقیمانده چیزی stub *n*	باوجود notwithstanding *adv*
باکتریا bacteria *n*	باوجود این nonetheless *adv*
باکره maiden, Miss, virgin *n*	باوجوداینکه however *conj*
باکیفیت prime *adj*	باوجوداینکه notwithstanding *prep*
بال fin; wing *n*	باوجوداینهم nevertheless *adv*
بال بال زدن flutter *v*	باور کردن believe *v*
بالا up *adv*	باورکردنی plausible *adj*
بالا بردن escalate; climb; *v*	باورنکردنی unbelievable *adj*
move up	بایت byte *n*
بالا بردن uptight *adj*	باید shall, must; *modal v*
بالاپوش coat, jacket, overcoat *n*	ought to, should
بالاپوش بارانی raincoat *n*	بایسکل bicycle, bike *n*

بایسکل ران cyclist n	بخشیدن excuse, forgive, v
بایسکل رانی cycling n	pardon; condone; give in
بجز از except prep	بخواب رفتن fall asleep v
بجلک پا ankle n	بخیه stitch n
بجه o'clock adv	بخیه کردن stitch v
بچه boy n	بد gross; bad, evil adj
بچه اندر stepson n	بد چانش unlucky adj
بحث debate, discussion n	بد خلق grouchy, grumpy adj
بحث برانگیز contentious, adj	بد شگون ominous adj
controversial	بداخل into prep
بحث کردن debate, discuss v	بدبخت unlucky; miserable, adj
بحر ocean n	wretched
بحران crisis n	بدبختانه unfortunately adv
بحران اقتصادی recession n	بدبختی adversity, misery, n
بحرانی critical adj	misfortune
بحریه fleet n	بدبو smelly, stinking adj
بخار rash; haze; fumes; n	بدبین cynic n
steam; vapor	بدبین pessimistic adj
بخار دادن fumigate v	بدبینی pessimism n
بخار روی جلد wart n	بدتر worse adj
بخار صورت در جوانی pimple n	بدتر کردن aggravate, worsen v
بخارشدنی volatile adj	بدترین worst adj
بخاری heater; stove n	بدخُلق sullen adj
بخاطریکه because conj	بدخو cranky adj
بخت fortune, luck n	بدخواهی rancor, malice n
بخش portion, sector, part, n	بدخوی moody adj
section, segment; ward;	بدرستی right adv
compartment	بدرفتاری کردن manhandle;
بخشش forgiveness n	misbehave; mistreat v
بخشنده gracious adj	بدرقه کردن chase away v
بخشی از ماشین panel n	بدست آوردن achieve, attain; v
	acquire, get, obtain

بدشکل clumsy; ugly *adj*	برابر اندام fitting *adj*
بدکار wicked *adj*	برابر به ۳۰ گرام ounce *n*
بدمعاش gangster *n*	برابر بودن fit *v*
بدن body *n*	برابر کردن equate *v*
بدنام notorious, infamous *adj*	برابری parity; equation *n*
بدنام کردن defame; denigrate *v*	برادر brother *n*
بدنی bodily *adj*	برادر اندر stepbrother *n*
بدون without *prep*	برادر زاده nephew *n*
بدون احساس senseless *adj*	برادر یا خواهر sibling *n*
بدون آسیب unharmed *adj*	برادرانه brotherly *adj*
بدون چون و چرا unequivocal *adj*	برادری fraternity *n*
بدون حرکت standstill *n*	برازنده graceful *adj*
بدون حرکت still *adj*	برافراشتن hoist *v*
بدون خطر safely *adv*	برافروخته ablaze *adj*
بدون در نظرداشت regardless *adv*	براق glossy *adj*
بدون درز seamless *adj*	برامدگی bulge; splint *n*
بدون ستون فقرات spineless *adj*	برامده hunched *adj*
بدون سروصدا serene *adj*	برامده گی پشت hunchback *n*
بدون شک undoubtedly *adv*	برانگیختن evoke *v*
بدون قسمت تحتانی bottomless *adj*	برای for *prep*
بدون قید freely *adv*	برای کی whom *pron*
بدون کافیین decaffeinated *adj*	برای ما us *pron*
بدون لکه spotless *adj*	برای همیشه forever *adv*
بدون مواد کیمیاوی organic *adj*	برائت acquittal *n*
بدون وقفه nonstop *adv*	برآمده گی hump *n*
بدی evil *n*	برآورد کردن rate *v*
بدیل alternative *n*	برآورده کردن fulfill *v*
بدیل alternative *adj*	برپا کردن set up *v*
بدینوسیله hereby *adv*	برپاکردن step up *v*
بذله گو witty *adj*	برپایی setup *n*
بذله گویی wit *n*	برتر premier; superior *adj*
برابر even, equal *adj*	

excellence; preference; *n* برتری	برطرف کردن *v* resolve
supremacy	برعکس *n* reverse
برتری داشتن *v* excel	برعکس *adj* unlike
برتری یافتن *v* transcend	برف *n* snow
lighthouse *n* برج کنترول کشتی ها	برف باریدن *v* snow
illustrious, *adj* برجسته	برفکوچ *n* avalanche
outstanding; noticeable,	برق *n* electricity
prominent	برق گرفتگی *n* shock
striking; highlight *n* برجسته	برقی *adj* electric, electrical
stand out *v* برجسته بودن	برقی ساختن *v* electrify
indent *v* برجسته کردن	برکنار کردن *v* depose
rise *v* برخاستن	برگ *n* leaf
contrary *adj* برخلاف	برگر *n* burger
opposite *adv* برخلاف	برگرداندن *v* revert; turn in
behavior *n* برخورد	برگزار کردن *v* hold
برخورد احمقانه کردن *v*	برگزیدن *n* excerpt
mess around	برگزیده *adj* favorite
run into *v* برخوردن	برگشت *v* rebound, come back;
some *pron* برخی از	get back
pick; pick up *v* برداشتن	برگشت *n* reversal
tolerant *adj* بردبار	برگشت پذیر *adj* reversible
take away *v* بردن	برگشت ناپذیر *adj* irreversible
bondage *n* برده گی	برگها *n* leaves
assessment *n* بررسی	برملا ساختن *v* reveal
assess *v* بررسی کردن	برملا کردن *v* uncover
sweatpants *n* برزو	برمه *n* drill
brush *n* برس	برمه کردن *v* drill
toothbrush *n* برس دندان	برنامه *n* plan, program;
برس رنگمالی یا نقاشی *n*	platform
paintbrush	برنامه آشپزی *n* recipe
brush *v* برس کردن	برنامه آموزشی *n* training
hairbrush *n* برس مو	برنامه ساختن *v* program

برنامه ساز programmer n	بزرگ كردن raise, amplify v
برنامه سفر itinerary n	بزرگ نشان دادن zoom v
برنامه كمپيوتر program n	بزرگ نمايى كردن magnify v
برنج rice n	بزرگ و مهم monumental adj
برنده winner n	بزرگتر elder n
برنده تمام پول jackpot n	بزرگداشت كردن commemorate v
برنده شدن win v	بزرگسال senior, elderly adj
برهنه bare, naked, nude adj	بزرگى greatness, magnitude n
برهنه شدن، strip, undress, v	بزغاله scapegoat n
take off	بس bus n
بروت mustache n	بست خالى vacancy n
بروت هاى پشك whiskers n	بستر bed n
برونز bronze n	بستر مرگ deathbed n
بريان شده fried adj	بسترى شدن در شفاخانه v
بريان كردن broil; fry; parch v	hospitalize
بريدگى gash; rift n	بسته bundle, package, pack; n
بريدن shear, hack v	pouch; batch
بريده گى cut n	بسته closed adj
بريس هاى دندان braces n	بسته اشيا set n
بريک كردن brake v	بسته بندى شده packed adj
بريک موتر brake n	بسته بندى كردن pack v
بز بز buzz n	بسته را باز كردن unpack v
بز بز كردن buzz v	بسته شدن clog v
بز كوهى antelope n	بسته كارى چوب scaffolding n
بزرگ significant; grave; adj	بسته كردن buckle n
ample, grand, spacious,	بسته كردن tie; block v
sizable, bulky; big, huge,	بسته كردن تسمه يا كمربند v
immense, large	buckle up
بزرگ ساختن enlarge v	بسته كردن كمربند fasten v
بزرگ شدن outgrow; grow up v	بسكويت biscuit, cracker n
بزرگ شده grown adj	بسكويت وافر wafer n
بزرگ شده grown-up n	بسكيتبال basketball n

سفّیcient, enough *adj* بسنده	بطرف جنوب *adv* south
far; much; very *adj* بسیار	بطرف چیزی دیدن *v* look at
lot *adv* بسیار	بطرف خانه *adj* home
many *pron* بسیار	بطرف داخل *adj* inward
great *adj* بسیار بزرگ	بطرف شرق *adj* eastbound
great *adj* بسیار خوب	بطرف عقب *adv* backward
okay *adv* بسیار خوب	بطرف غرب *adv* westbound
faraway *adj* بسیار دور	بطری *n* battery
especially, really; *adv* بسیار زیاد	بطن *n* womb; abdomen
well	بطور اقتصادی *adv* economically
ice-cold *adj* بسیار سرد	بطور آزاد *adv* freely
great *adj* بسیار مهم	بطور آشکار *adv* evidently
multitude *n* بسیاری	بطور آماده *adv* readily
mobilize *v* بسیج کردن	بطور بد *adv* badly
humankind, mankind *n* بشر	بطور برابر *adv* evenly
plate, saucer *n* بشقاب	بطور بی ربط *adv* incoherently
dramatize *v* بشکل درامه در آوردن	بطور بیهوده *adv* vainly
including *prep* بشمول	بطور تصادفی *adv* randomly
optical; visual *adj* بصری	بطور ثابت *adv* constantly
بصورت اجتناب ناپذیر *adv*	بطور جداگانه *adv* separately
inevitably	بطور جزئی *adv* slightly
individually *adv* بصورت انفرادی	بطور چشمگیر *adv* dramatically
intensively *adv* بصورت تشدیدی	بطور خفیف *adv* lightly
بصورت غیر بسنده *adv*	بطور خودکار *adv* automatically
inadequately	بطور رسمی *adv* officially
بصورت کلی آزمایش کردن *v*	بطور سازگار *adv* consistently
explore	بطور سالانه *adv* annually
virtually *adv* بصورت مجازی	بطور سخت گیرانه *adv* sternly
suddenly *adv* بصورت ناگهانی	بطور سنتی *adv* traditionally
toward *prep* بطرف	بطور سنجیده شده *adv* deliberately
upwards *adv* بطرف بالا	بطور شفاهی *adv* orally; verbally
downward *adv* بطرف پایین	بطور ضعیف *adv* poorly

justly *adv* بطور عادلانه	بطورعینی *adv* objectively
naturally; *adv* بطور عادی	بعد از *prep* after
ordinarily	بعد از آن *adv* then, afterward
principally *adv* بطور عمده	بعد از ظهر *n* afternoon
irrationally *adv* بطور غیر منطقی	بعد ازاین *adv* hereafter
unofficially *adv* بطور غیررسمی	بعد ها *adv* later
abnormally *adv* بطور غیرعادی	بعداً *adj* later
illegally *adv* بطور غیرقانونی	بعدی *adj* subsequent, upcoming,
physically *adv* بطور فزیکی	following, next, future
بطور قابل ملاحظه *adv*	بعضی اوقات *adv* sometimes
considerably, notably	بعلاوه *adj* further, more
fully *adv* بطور کامل	بعلاوه *n* plus
widespread *adj* بطور گسترده	بعهده گرفتن *v* undertake
differently *adv* بطور متفاوت	بقاء *n* survival
distinctly *adv* بطور متمایز	بقایا *n* remains
positively *adv* بطور مثبت	بقه *n* frog, toad
briefly; *adv* بطور مختصر	بقیه *n* remnant
precisely	بکار انداختن *v* launch
secretly *adv* بطور مخفیانه	بکار بردن *v* wield; exert
particularly *adv* بطور مشخص	بکس پشتی *n* backpack
بطور مصنوعی خواب کردن *v*	بکس دستی *n* handbag
hypnotize	بکس سفری *n* baggage, luggage,
safely; securely *adv* بطور مصوون	suitcase, briefcase
appropriately *adv* بطور مناسب	بکسک جیبی *n* wallet
coherently *adv* بطور منسجم	بل *n* bill
regularly *adv* بطور منظم	بل دادن *v* bill
temporarily *adv* بطور موقت	بلاک شهری *n* block
half *adv* بطور ناقص	بلاک کانکریتی *n* block
indefinitely *adv* بطور نامحدود	بلامنازعه *adj* undisputed
inappropriately *adv* بطور نامناسب	بلدوزر *n* bulldozer
explicitly *adv* بطور واضح	بلعیدن *v* guzzle, swallow
broadly *adv* بطور وسیع	بلند *adv* aloud

ب

بلند high, lofty; top adj	بند دست wrist n
بلند رفتن surge n	بند مانده stuck adj
بلند شدن get up, stand up; rise, v	بندرگاه harbor, port n
arise; elevate	بندش stuffy adj
بلند کردن heighten; lift v	بندش بینی stuffy adj
بلند گو speaker n	بندش سرک block n
بلند و باریک slender adj	بندل bundle n
بلندپروازی snob n	بنفش رنگ violet adj
بلندگو loudspeaker n	بنیاد origin; base, foundation; n
بلندی top; height n	rationale, principle, premise
بلوط acorn; oak n	بنیادی basic, fundamental adj
بلوغ adolescence, puberty; n	به to prep
adulthood, maturity	به اتفاق آرا unanimous adj
بلی yes adv	به احتمال زیاد potentially adv
بلیارد billiards n	به اساس متر metric adj
بم bass adj	به استثنای excluding prep
بم mine; bomb n	به اشاره فهماندن insinuate v
بم دستی grenade n	به اصطلاح so-called adj
بمانید hang up v	به امید اینکه hopefully adv
بمبار کردن bomb v	به اندازه enough pron
بمپر موتر bumper n	به اندازه کافی adequately adv
بمجرد upon prep	به اندازه یک قاشق spoonful n
بموقع duly adv	به اوج رسیدن culminate v
بنابراین hence, therefore, adv	به آرامی quietly; gingerly adv
thus	به آسانی easily adv
بنابراین so conj	به آنها them pron
بنای تاریخی monument n	به آهستگی slowly adv
بند strap n	به آواز بلند loudly adv
بند استخوان ligament n	به باریکی thinly adv
بند انگشت knuckle n	به برازندگی gracefully adv
بند آب dam n	به بزرگی enormously adv
بند بوت lace, shoelace n	به بلندی high adv

به خواب زمستانی رفتن hibernate v
به داخل inwards adv
به دام انداختن trap v
به دام عشق انداختن enchant v
به درستی duly, correctly, adv properly
به درشتی roughly adv
به رسمیت شناختن recognition n
به روز up-to-date adj
به زحمت ساختن trouble v
به زشتی harshly adv
به زودی shortly, soon adv
به زور forcibly adv
به زور داخل شدن break in v
به زور گرفتن extort v
به زیبایی nicely adv
به ساده گی plainly, simply adv
به ساده گی قابل دید adj eye-catching
به ستوه آوردن pester v
به سختی barely, hardly adv
به سرعت abruptly, fast, adv quickly, swiftly
به سرعت رفتن dash v
به سفتی firmly adv
به سمت شمال north adv
به سوی toward; onto prep
به شجاعت bravely adv
به شدت strongly, highly, adv intensely
به شوخی jokingly adv
به صداقت honestly adv

به بهترین شیوه best adv
به بی احتیاطی carelessly adv
به بی میلی reluctantly, adv unwillingly
به پایین دیدن look down v
به پشت تکیه کردن lean back v
به پهلو sideways adv
به پیش onward adv
به پیش بردن carry on v
به پیش حرکت کردن v move forward
به پیش رفتن proceed v
به تازه گی newly adv
به ترتیب زمان chronological adj
به تصویر کشیدن picture, v portray
به تعقیب after prep
به تعقیب after conj
به تعلیق آوردن postpone v
به تعویق انداختن defer, v suspend; procrastinate; put up
به تلخی bitterly adv
به تواضع humbly adv
به جوش آمدن simmer v
به چالش کشیدن challenge v
به حافظه سپردن memorize v
به حد بلوغ رسیدن mature v
به خاطر آوردن recall v
به خاموشی quietly adv
به خطر انداختن endanger, v jeopardize, risk

به صدای بلند خواندن dictate v	به نامردی cowardly adv
به صدای بلند نام کسی را خواندن v	به نحوی somehow adv
call out	به ندرت scarcely, seldom adv
به صراحت expressly adv	به نرمی gently, smoothly, adv
به صف شدن line up v	softly
به ضمانت رها شدن bail out v	به نظر رسیدن seem v
به طرف راست right adv	به نماینده گی از behalf n
به طریقی someway adv	به هر حال anyway adv
به عجله hastily, hurriedly adv	به هم زدن stir up v
به عصبانیت madly adv	به همه اعلام کردن exclaim v
به عقب رفتن back v	به همین ترتیب likewise adv
به علت because of prep	به هیجان آوردن thrill v
به عوض instead adv	به وحشت انداختن terrorize v
به غمگینی sadly adv	به وقت early adj
به فراخی loosely adv	به یاد آوردن remind v
به فرزندی گرفتن adopt v	به یاد داشتن remember v
به فرض اینکه supposing conj	به یکباره گی once conj
به فصاحت fluently adv	بهانه pretense; excuse n
به کار انداختن run v	بهبود improvement n
به کار بد راضی کردن pander v	بهبود یافتن recuperate v
به کرایه گرفتن lease v	بهتر better adj
به گردش درآوردن circulate v	بهتر است که better adv
به گستاخی rudely adv	بهترین best adj
به لرزه درآوردن vibrate v	بهترین مرد best man n
به مزایده گذاشتن auction v	بهترین نمونه classic adj
به ملایمت gently adv	بهشت heaven, paradise n
به من me pron	بهشتی heavenly adj
به مهربانی kindly adv	بهم ارتباط داشتن correlate v
به موجب آن whereby adv	بهم پیوسته related adj
به موقع timely adj	بهم چسپاندن solder v
به میراث بردن inherit v	بهم خوردن collide v
به نام namely adv	بهم زدن overthrow v

ب

بهم زنی تمرکز n distraction	بی احتیاطی n carelessness
بهم فشردن v clench; compress	بی احساس adj heartless
بو n smell	بی اختیار adj ;indisposed
بو دادن v smell	spontaneous
بوت n footwear, shoe	بی ادب adj impolite
بوت سلیپر n slipper	بی اراده adj aimless
بوت فروشی n shoe store	بی ارزش n trashy
بوتل n bottle	بی ارزش ساختن v depreciate
بودجه n budget; fund	بی ارزشی n depreciation
بودن v be	بی اساس adj ,unfounded
بودن n being	baseless
بودنه n quail	بی اعتبار adj invalid
بورس تحصیلی n ;fellowship	بی اعتبار ساختن v invalidate
scholarship	بی اعتبار کردن v deface; discredit
بوره n sugar	بی اعتباری n disbelief
بوریا n mat	بی اعتماد adj distrustful
بوزینه n ape	بی اعتمادی n distrust, mistrust
بوسه n kiss	بی اعتمادی کردن v ,distrust
بوسیدن v kiss	mistrust
بوفی در رستورانت n buffet	بی انتها adj timeless; infinite
بوکسر n boxer	بی اهمیت جلوه دادن v trivialize
بوکسینگ n boxing	بی آستین adj sleeveless
بولت آهنی n bolt	بی باک adj audacious, intrepid
بوم n owl	بی بنیاد adj unfounded
بوی بد n stink, odor	بی بوی adj odorless
بوی بد دادن v stink	بی پایان adj endless
بوی تعفن n stench	بی پروا adj frivolous; rash
بوییدن v smell, sniff	بی پول adj penniless
بی احترام adj disrespectful	بی تجربه adj inexperienced
بی احترامی n disdain; disrespect	بی تخم adj seedless
بی احتیاط adj ;careless, reckless	بی ترس adj fearless
indiscreet	بی تصمیم adj indecisive

بی تصمیمی *n* indecision	بی خطر *adj* benign
بی تطابق *adj* incompatible	بی خوابی *n* insomnia
بی تفاوت *adj* ;inconsiderate	بی درد *adj* painless
indifferent	بی دفاع *adj* defenseless
بی تفاوتی *n* apathy, indifference	بی ربط *adj* ;inconsistent
بی تکلیف *adj* unassuming	irrelevant, unrelated
بی توجه *adj* oblivious	بی رحم *adj* ,ruthless, merciless
بی ثبات *adj* fickle; unstable	relentless
بی ثباتی *n* instability	بی رحمی *n* atrocity
بی جان *adj* lifeless	بی رنگ *adj* colorless
بی جایی *n* displacement	بی زمان *adj* timeless
بی جرات *adj* shy; wimp	بی سواد *adj* uneducated
بی جراتی *n* shyness	بی سیم *adj* cordless, wireless
بی چون و چرا *adj* indisputable	بی شرم *adj* shameless
بی حد *adj* boundless	بی شمار *adj* countless
بی حرف *adj* speechless	بی صدا *n* consonant
بی حرکت *adj* ,immobile	بی صداقت *adj* dishonest
motionless	بی صداقتی *n* dishonesty
بی حرکت کردن *v* immobilize	بی ضرر *adj* harmless
بی حرمتی *n* dishonor	بی طرفانه *adj* unbiased
بی حس *adj* insensitive; numb	بی عاطفه *adj* callous
بی حسی *n* numbness	بی عدالتی *n* injustice
بی حوصلگی *adj* demented	بی عقل *adj* dumb
بی حوصلگی *n* impatience	بی علاقه *adj* disinterested
بی حوصله *adj* moody; impatient	بی عیب *adj* ;perfect, flawless
بی حیا *adj* ,shameless	spotless; wholesome
impertinent; lewd	بی عیب و نقص *adj* ;blameless
بی حیایی *n* ;indecency	foolproof; impeccable
impertinence	بی عیبی *n* perfection
بی خانه *adj* homeless	بی فایده *adj* wasteful
بی خبر *adj* unaware	بی فکر *adj* mindless
بی خدا *adj* godless	بی قدرت *adj* powerless

ب

بیجا کردن misplace v	بی کفایت incompetent adj
بیدار awake adj	بی کفایتی incompetence n
بیدار شدن wake (up) v	بی کیفیت tasteless; shoddy adj
بیدار کردن wake (up), rouse v	بی گمان unsuspecting adj
بیداری vigil n	بی مانند unique adj
بیر beer n	بی مزه tasteless adj
بیرق flag n	بی معنی pointless, senseless, adj meaningless
بیره gum n	
بیروبار crowded adj	بی مو bald adj
بیروبار کردن crowd v	بی مورد trumped-up; undue adj
بیرون out, outside adv	بی میل distasteful; reluctant adj
بیرون از چیزی افتادن drop off v	بی میل کردن dismay v
بیرون از کشور overseas adv	بی میلی dismay; distaste n
بیرون از منزل outdoor adv	بی ناموس dishonorable adj
بیرون آمدن come out v	بی نزاکتی indecency n
بیرون برآمدن step out v	بی نظم disorganized, messy, adj chaotic
بیرون بردن take out v	
بیرون رو outgoing adj	بی نظمی mess, clutter n
بیرون ریختن emit v	بی نظیمی disorder n
بیرون شدن bow out; get out, v go out, move out	بی نهایت infinitely adv
	بی نیاز well-to-do; needless adj
بیرون شده withdrawn adj	بی هدف aimless adj
بیرون کردن evict, oust; exclude v	بی وفا disloyal, unfaithful adj
بیرون گرا extroverted adj	بی وفایی treason n
بیرونی exterior, external, adj outer, outward	بی وقفه incessant adj
	بیابان wilderness n
بیزار weary; fed up adj	بیان با چهره expression n
بیست twenty n	بیان کردن state, express; v illustrate
بیستم twentieth adj	
بیسواد illiterate adj	بیانیه statement n
بیش از over prep	بیجا ساختن dislocate v
بیش از اندازه excessive adj	بیجا شدن displace v

بیش از این anymore *adv*	بیموقع untimely *adj*
بیش از حد exceedingly *adv*	بین المللی international *adj*
بیش از حد overdone *adj*	بینش intuition *n*
بیش از حد تخمین کردن *v* overestimate	بینظیر unique *adj*
بیش از حد چارج کردن *v* overcharge	بیننده onlooker *n*
بیش از حد رشد کرده *adj* overgrown	بینهایت extreme *adj*
بیش از همه most *pron*	بینهایت extremely *adv*
بیشتر further *adv*	بینی nose *n*
بیشتر از over *adv*	بیهوده pointless, futile, vain *adj*
بیشتر از تعداد معین بودن *v* outnumber	بیهوش unconscious *adj*
بیشتر از حد معمول high *adj*	بیهوش شدن pass out *v*
بیشتر درخشیدن outshine *v*	بیهوشی anesthesia; trance *n*
بیشتر زنده ماندن outlive *v*	بیوگرافی biography *n*
بیشتراً mostly *adv*	
بیشترین most, utmost *adj*	**پ**
بیضوی شکل oval *adj*	
بیطرف impartial, neutral *adj*	پَر feather *n*
بیطرفی neutral *n*	پُر loaded, full *adj*
بیعت allegiance *n*	پُر کردن fill *v*
بیقرار restless *adj*	پُر کردن بین شیرینی filling *n*
بیکار jobless, unemployed *adj*	پُر کردن دندان filling *n*
بیکاری unemployment *n*	پُر کردن سوراخ plug *v*
بیگانه alien; stranger *n*	پُست کارت postcard *n*
بیگانه شده estranged *adj*	پُست هوایی airmail *n*
بیل oar; shovel *n*	پُسته خانه post office *n*
بیل زدن shovel *v*	پُسته رسان postman *n*
بیمه insurance *n*	پُل bridge *n*
بیمه کردن insure *v*	پا foot *n*
	پا برهنه barefoot *adj*
	پا ورقی footnote *n*

ب

پاک کردن v clean; erase; wipe

پاکت n packet

پاکت خط n envelope

پاکی n cleanliness; purity

پاگذاشتن v tread

پالش بوت n shoe polish

پالش کردن v polish

پالیسی n policy

پاندول n pendulum

پانزده n fifteen

پانزدهم adj fifteenth

پانقراس n pancreas

پاها n feet

پای پاک دهن دروازه n doormat

پای حیوان n leg

پایان نامه n thesis

پایپ n pipe

پایپ آب n hose

پایپ برای نوشیدن n straw

پایپ تخلیه آب n drainpipe

پایتخت n capital

پایدار adj constant, steady, sustainable

پایداری n sustenance

پایدل n paddle; pedal

پایدل زدن v paddle

پایدل زدن کشتی v row

پایگاه نظامی n base

پایمال کردن v trample

پایه n pillar; stand

پایه چوبی یا آهنی n post

پایه میز n leg

پابند adj adhesive

پابند بودن v adhere

پاپی n puppy

پاداش n reward, gratuity

پادشاه n king, monarch

پارازیت n parasite

پاراگراف n paragraph

پارامیتر n parameter

پارانتیز n parenthesis

پارچه n slice

پارسل n parcel

پارک n park

پارک تفریحی n theme park

پارک کردن موتر v park

پارکینگ n parking

پارگی n tear

پارلمان n parliament

پاره کردن v mangle; rip, tear

پاره کردن n rip-off

پاره گی n rupture

پاس پاس n mop

پاسپورت n passport

پاستا n pasta

پاسخ n reply

پاسخ دادن v reply

پاسخگو adj responsive

پاشیدن v shed; scatter; splash; sprinkle

پافشاری n urge; persistence

پاک adj pure, clean, neat

پاک سازی v purge

پاک کاری کردن v scour

پ

پذیرایی n reception	پایین below; low adv
پذیرایی کردن v welcome	پایین down; low adj
پذیرش n acceptance;	پایین افتادن v fall down
admittance	پایین آمدن v descend, come
پذیرفتنی adj plausible	down, get down; dip
پر از پریشانی و فشار های روحی adj	پایین تر adj lower
stressful	پایین رتبه adj junior
پر جنب و جوش adj vibrant	پایین رفتن v go down
پر زرق و برق adj flamboyant	پایین منزل پایین adj downstairs
پر سروصدا adj fussy	پایین و بالا رفتن n scroll
پر طراوت adj succulent	پایهٔ پُل n pier
پر کردن v stuff	پتلون کاوبای n jeans
پر کردن داخل چیزی n stuffing	پختن v bake
پر مزیت adj rewarding	پخته adj cooked; ripe
پرارزش adj rewarding	پخته شدن v ripen
پراکندگی v sprawl	پخته شده در خانه adj homemade
پراکنده adj sparse	پخته کردن v ripen; cook
پراگنده adj sporadic	پخش شدن v spread
پراگنده شدن v scatter	پخش کردن v disseminate
پربار adj burdensome	پخش کننده موسیقی n
پرتاب کردن v throw, pitch, cast,	record player
hurl, toss; shove	پخش و نشر کردن v televise
پرتاب کننده توپ n pitcher	پدر n dad, father
پرتحرک adj dynamic	پدر اندر n stepfather
پرتگاه n abyss; bluff	پدرانه adj fatherly
پرچالش adj challenging	پدرسالار n patriarch
پرحرف adj talkative	پدرکلان n grandfather
پرخاطره adj memorable	پدرکلان و مادرکلان n
پرخطر adj precarious	grandparents
پرداخت کردن v disburse	پدری n fatherhood, paternity
پرداختن v pay	پدیده n phenomenon
پرده n curtain, drapes	پذیرا adj receptive

پرده تلویزیون و کمپیوتر screen *n*	پروردن foster *v*
پرده نقش دار tapestry *n*	پرورش دادن nurture *v*
پرزحمت troubled *adj*	پرورش دادن حیوان خانگی pet *v*
پرزه اضافی یا عوضی spare part *n*	پرورش طفل upbringing *n*
پرستار nurse *n*	پرورش کردن raise, rear, foster *v*
پرستار طفل babysitter *n*	پروژه project *n*
پرستاری طفل babysit *v*	پروسه process *n*
پرستاری کردن nurse *v*	پروفیسور professor *n*
پرسروصدا noisy, tumultuous *adj*	پری fairy *n*
پرسشنامه questionnaire *n*	پری دریایی mermaid *n*
پرسونل personnel *n*	پریدن gallop *v*
پرسیدن ask *v*	پریشان worried, distraught *adj*
پرش jump *n*	پریشان کننده distressing *adj*
پرش کردن gallop; jump *v*	پریشانی distress *n*
پرشور passionate; dashing *adj*	پژمرده faded *adj*
پرشی jumpy *adj*	پژمرده شدن fade, languish, *v*
پرقدرت mighty *adj*	wither
پرمصرف costly *adj*	پژوهشگر scholar *n*
پرمنفعت profitable, lucrative *adj*	پس انداز savings *n*
پرنده bird *n*	پس انداز کردن save *v*
پرنده مانند باشه buzzard *n*	پس پرداخت refund *n*
پرنده ماهیخور pelican *n*	پس خانه pantry *n*
پرنفوذ influential *adj*	پس مانده refuse *n*
پرنفوس ساختن populate *v*	پس مانده غذا leftovers *n*
پرهیز restraint *n*	پس منظر background *n*
پرواز flight *n*	پست تر inferior *adj*
پرواز کردن fly *v*	پست فطرت mean *adj*
پروانه moth *n*	پستان breast *n*
پروانه طیاره propeller *n*	پستان داران mammal *n*
پروای چیزی را داشتن care about *v*	پستی scoundrel *n*
پروتین protein *n*	پسر son *n*
پروجیکتور projector *n*	پسر کاکا cousin *n*

back, rear *n* پشت	blink *v* پلک زدن
behind *prep* پشت	leopard; panther; tiger *n* پلنگ
get over *v* پشت سر گذاشتن	jaguar *n* پلنگ خالدار
backstage *adv* پشت صحنه	step *n* پله
dedication *n* پشت کار	pump *n* پمپ
inside out *adv* پشت و رو	pump *v* پمپ کردن
back *v* پشتی کردن	pancake *n* پن کیک
patron, supporter *n* پشتیبان	resort *v* پناه بردن
support, backing *n* پشتیبانی	haven *n* پناهگاه
vindicate *v* پشتیبانی کردن	asylum *n* پناهند گی
cat *n* پشک	cotton *n* پنبه
wool *n* پشم	five *n* پنج
fleece *n* پشم گوسفند	pentagon *n* پنج ضلعی
fuzzy; woolen *adj* پشمی	fifty *n* پنجاه
mosquito *n* پشه	fifty-fifty *adv* پنجاه پنجاه
remorseful *adj* پشیمان	fiftieth *adj* پنجاهم
regret *v* پشیمان شدن	skylight *n* پنجره اتاق
regret, remorse *n* پشیمانی	fifth *adj* پنجم
petroleum *n* پطرولیم	pitchfork, fork; claw; *n* پنجه
pants, trousers *n* پطلون	paw
tray *n* پطنوس	toe *n* پنجه پا
blow *v* پف کردن	bud *n* پندُک
puff *n* پف کردن	swell *v* پندیدن
razor *n* پل ریش	swollen *adj* پندیده
platinum *n* پلاتین	swelling *n* پندیده گی
pliers *n* پلاس	pencil *n* پنسل
plastic *n* پلاستیک	penguin *n* پنگوین
program, plan *n* پلان	unnoticed; covert, *adj* پنهان
plan *v* پلان کردن	hidden
eyelid *n* پلک	conceal, hide *v* پنهان کردن
plug *n* پلک برق	eavesdrop *v* پنهانی گوش کردن
unplug *v* پلک را کشیدن	cheese *n* پنیر

پوش فرنیچر دوزی n upholstery	پهلو به پهلو collateral adj
پوش کتاب n paperback	پهلوی چیزی next to adj
پوشاک n apparel, clothing	پهنا n width
پوشاندن v shield, cover; cap;	پهناور vast adj
coat	پوپنک n mold
پوشانیدن v mask	پوپنک زده moldy adj
پوشانیده n cover-up	پوچ empty adj
پوشت n crust	پوچی n emptiness
پوشش n lining; coverage;	پودر n powder
wrapping	پودر کردن v pulverize
پوشش n camouflage	پودینگ n pudding
پوشیدن v wear	پوز پیچ n hood
پوشیده از ابر overcast adj	پوزبند n mask; muzzle
پوشیده از یخ icy adj	پوزخند n grin
پوقانه n balloon; bubble	پوزخند زدن v grin
پوقانه ساجق n bubble gum	پوست n peel
پول n money	پوست آفتاب خوردگی n suntan
پول بخششی n tip	پوست جلد n skin
پول تحویل داده شده n input	پوست درخت n bark
پول تقاعدی n pension	پوست کردن v peel, skin
پول سیاه n change	پوست میوه n skin
پول گذاشته شده در بانک n deposit	پوست نخود یا لوبیا n hull
پول نقد n cash	پوستر n poster
پول یورو n euro	پوستین n fur
پولیس n cop, police	پوستین دار furry adj
پوند n pound	پوسیدن v corrode; rot, decay
پوهنتون n university; varsity	پوسیده putrid, rotten adj
پویا dynamic adj	پوسیده گی n decay
پی بردن v find out	پوش n top, cover, covering
پی در پی consecutive adj	پوش بالش n pillowcase
پیاده رو n crosswalk; pavement;	پوش چیزی را دور کردن v strip
sidewalk	پوش سیت دوزی n upholstery

پیاده شدن disembark, v	پیچیده complex, intricate adj
dismount, get off	پیچیده گی complexity n
پیاده شطرنج pawn v	پیدا کردن pull up v
پیاده کردن overhaul v	پیرامون surroundings n
پیاز onion n	پیراهن top, shirt n
پیاله cup n	پیراهن بلوز blouse n
پیام message n	پیراهن سپورتی T-shirt n
پیام رسان messenger n	پیراهن ورزشی jersey n
پیام صوتی voice mail n	پیرو follower n
پیام فرستادن از طریق تیلفون text v	پیرو مذهب بودا Buddhist n
پیام کتبی text message n	پیروز victor n
پیامد implication n	پیروز victorious, triumphant adj
پیانو piano n	پیروز شدن بر vanquish v
پیانو نواز pianist n	پیروزی triumph, victory n
پیتزا pizza n	پیش before conj
پیچ بازکن corkscrew n	پیش آمدن come forward v
پیچ خوردن sprain v	پیش بردن تجارت run v
پیچ خورده twisted adj	پیش پرداخت down payment n
پیچ دادن twist v	پیش رفتن go ahead v
پیچ کش screwdriver n	پیش زمینه foreground n
پیچ و تاب دادن warp v	پیشانی brow, forehead n
پیچ و خم maze n	پیشانی ترشی کردن frown v
پیچاندن rewind; wind, wrap; v	پیشآهنگ scout n
bolt	پیشبند apron n
پیچاندن screw n	پیشبینی anticipation; n
پیچانده شده wrapper n	prediction
پیچش scroll; twist n	پیشبینی کردن anticipate, v
پیچک ivy n	forecast, foresee, predict
پیچکاری shot; injection n	پیشتاز lead v
پیچکاری کردن inject v	پیشتاز leading adj
پیچیدگی labyrinth n	پیشدستی کردن preempt v
پیچیدن coil n	پیشرفت advance, progress n

پیشرفت کردن advance, thrive, progress *v*	**پیوند دادن** transplant *v*
پیشرفت ناگهانی breakthrough *n*	
پیشرفته advanced *adj*	# ت
پیشرو forward *adv*	
پیشرو کش کردن pull ahead *v*	**تُشله** marble *n*
پیشکش offer *n*	**تُن** ton *n*
پیشکش کردن offer, present *v*	**تا** till, until *prep*
پیشکی beforehand *adv*	**تا اندازه ای** partially *adv*
پیشکی دادن advance *v*	**تاب خوردن** swing *v*
پیشگام pioneer *n*	**تاب خورده** warped *adj*
پیشگفتار foreword *n*	**تابستان** summer *n*
پیشگویی premonition; oracle *n*	**تابش** radiation; glitter *n*
پیشگویی کردن foretell *v*	**تابع** obedient *adj*
پیشگیرانه preventive *adj*	**تابعیت** citizenship *n*
پیشنهاد proposition, bid, proposal, suggestion *n*	**تابلیت** tablet, pill *n*
پیشنهاد آخر ultimatum *n*	**تابه** casserole *n*
پیشنهاد کردن bid, propose, suggest; prose *v*	**تابوت** coffin *n*
پیشوای مذهبی pastor *n*	**تابیدن** glow *v*
پیشوند prefix *n*	**تاپه** stamp *n*
پیشی گرفتن outdo, outrun, surpass *v*	**تاپه روی جلد** tattoo *n*
پیگرد قانونی کردن prosecute *v*	**تاپه کردن** seal, stamp *v*
پیگیری کردن trace, track *v*	**تاتو** tattoo *n*
پیلوت pilot *n*	**تاثیر** effect, impact *n*
پیمان treaty, pact *n*	**تاثیر کردن** affect, impact *v*
پیمانه gauge *n*	**تاثیر گذار** telling; impressive *adj*
پیمانه کردن gauge *v*	**تاج** crest; crown *n*
پیوستگی bond, conjunction *n*	**تاج گذاری** coronation; crown *n*
پیوستن adjoin; ally, join *v*	**تاجر** businessman, entrepreneur, merchant, trader *n*

تاحدی adv partly, somewhat	تاک انگور n grapevine
تاخیر n delay	تاکاوی n basement
تاخیر کردن v delay, loiter	تاکتیک n tactic
تادیه n payment	تاکید کردن v persist; emphasize, stress; insist, urge
تادیه کردن v pay	تالار کنفرانس n auditorium
تار n thread	تانک تیل n gas station
تار جولا n cobweb	تانک نظامی n tank
تار عنکبوت n web	تانکی n tank
تاریخ n date; history	تاهنوز adv still, yet
تاریخ پرداخت چیزی تیر شده adj overdue	تایپ کردن v type
تاریخ تیر شده adj outdated	تایر n wheel; tire
تاریخ نویس n historian	تایید adj affirmative
تاریخی adj historical	تایید n confirmation, verification
تاریک adj murky, dark	تایید کردن v acknowledge, affirm, verify, confirm, corroborate
تاریک کردن v darken	
تاریکی n dark, darkness; mare	تایید نکردن v disapprove
تازماتیکه v till	تأثیر گذاری n impression
تازه adj latest, recent; fresh	تأثیر گذاشتن v impress
تازه عروسی شده n newlywed	تأسف آور adj regrettable
تازه کار n beginner, novice	تأسفبار adj pathetic
تازه کار adj rookie	تأکید n emphasis
تازه کردن v refurbish; freshen, refresh	تأکید کردن v stick out
	تأیید و امضا n endorsement
تازه وارد n newcomer	تأیید و امضا کردن v endorse
تاسف بار adj deplorable	تب n fever
تاسف خوردن v deplore, regret, lament	تبادله کردن v exchange, trade
	تباشیر n chalk
تاسیس n establishment	تبخیر شدن v evaporate
تاسیس کردن v establish	تبدیل کردن v convert, switch
تاسیسات n installation	تبدیل نمودن هوا v ventilate
تاک n vine	

تبدیلی هوا n ventilation
تبر n axe
تبریک گفتن v congratulate
تبریکی n congratulations
تبرئه کردن v acquit
تبسم n smile
تبسم کردن v smile
تبعه n citizen
تبعید n exile
تبعید کردن v exile
تبعیض n prejudice, discrimination
تبعیض کردن v discriminate
تبلیغات n propaganda, publicity
تبه کار n villain
تب حمام n bathtub, tub
تپش n beat
تپش v throb
تپه n mound, hill
تپه ای adj hilly
تپه دریایی n reef
تثبیت هویت n identification
تجارت n business, commerce, trade
تجارتی adj commercial
تجاوز کردن v encroach; overrun
تجدید کردن v renovate, renew, update; revise
تجدید نظر n revision
تجدید نظر کردن v reconsider
تجربه n experience
تجربه کردن v experience

تجربه و تخصص n expertise
تجزیه کردن v decompose
تجلیل کردن v celebrate, glorify
تجمع n accumulation, gathering, rally, congregation
تجمع ستارگان n constellation
تجمع کردن v congregate, convene
تجملی adj fancy
تجهیز کردن v supply
تجهیز کننده n supplier
تجهیزات n supplies, supply; equipment
تحت البحری n submarine
تحت اللفظی adj literal
تحت اللفظی adv verbatim
تحت تاثیر قرارگرفته adj petrified
تحت تاثیرقراردادن v overshadow
تحت فشار adj strained
تحت کنترول درآوردن v subject
تحرک داشتن v motion
تحریف n distortion
تحریف کردن v distort
تحریک n incitement, motivation; spur
تحریک کردن v incite, instigate, motivate, provoke, stimulate
تحریک کننده adj rousing, stimulating
تحریک کننده احساسات adj touching
تحریم n sanction

تحریم کردن v boycott, sanction

تحسین n admiration

تحسین کردن v acclaim, admire, adore

تحسین کننده n admirer

تحصیل کرده adj educated

تحفه n gift, present

تحقق n fulfillment

تحقیر n contempt

تحقیر آمیز adj degrading, demeaning, derogatory

تحقیر کردن v condescend, demean, humiliate; debase

تحقیق n investigation, research

تحقیق کردن v interrogate; investigate, probe, research

تحلیل n analysis

تحلیل کردن v analyze

تحلیلگر n analyst

تحلیلی adj analytic

تحمل n tolerance

تحمل کردن v bear, endure, tolerate, withstand, put up with

تحمل کن v hold out

تحمیل کردن v impose, inflict; protrude

تحمیل کننده adj pushy

تحمیلی adj imposing

تحول n upheaval

تحویل دادن v deliver; hand over

تحویل دار n teller

تحویل کردن v submit

تحویلی n delivery

تخت پادشاهی n throne

تخت خواب سفری n bunk bed

تخته اطو کاری n ironing board

تخته اعلانات تجارتی n billboard

تخته بازی n board

تخته بازی اسکیت n skateboard

تخته پاک n eraser

تخته تباشیری n chalkboard

تخته چوبی n board

تخته سنگ n boulder; slab

تخته سیاه n blackboard

تخته موج سواری n surfboard

تخته نمرات n scoreboard

تخصص n specialty

تخصص داشتن v specialize

تخصیص n allocation

تخصیص دادن v allocate

تخطی کردن v trespass; violate

تخفیف n discount, rebate

تخفیف دادن v discount

تخلص n pseudonym, nickname; last name, surname

تخلف کردن v trespass

تخلیه n discharge

تخلیه آب n drainage

تخلیه کردن v discharge; evacuate

تخلیه نمودن بار v unload

تخم با رومی و پیاز n omelet

تخم پزی n frying pan; saucepan

تخم دار adj seedy

ت

تخم زراعتی seed n	تراش کردن scrape; scrub v
تخم گذاشتن hatch v	تراشیدن shave v
تخم مرغ egg n	تراکتور tractor n
تخمیر کردن brew v	تراکم congestion n
تخمین estimate n	ترانزیت transit n
تخمین کردن approximate adj	ترانسپورت transportation n
تخمین کردن estimate v	ترانسپورت زیرزمینی subway n
تخمینی roughly adv	تربوز watermelon n
تخنیک technique n	تربیت طفل upbringing n
تخنیکر technician n	ترتیب و تنظیم setup; n
تخنیکی technical adj	composition
تخیل imagination n	ترتیبات arrangement n
تدارک provision n	ترجمان translator n
تدارک کردن procure v	ترجمه interpretation n
تداوم continuity n	ترجمه کردن interpret, translate v
تداوی treatment n	ترجیح دادن prefer v
تداوی امراض روانی psychiatry n	تردید suspicion; indecision, n
تداوی کردن treat v	hesitation
تدبیر tact n	ترس phobia, fear, fright n
تدریجاً eventually adv	ترساندن appall, frighten, v
تدریجی eventual; gradual adj	terrify, horrify, scare, startle;
تدریجی piecemeal adv	daunt, dread; intimidate,
تدفین burial n	scare away
تذکر hint; mention n	ترساننده eerie adj
تذکر دادن hint; mention v	ترسناک appalling, horrible; adj
تر soggy, wet, soaked adj	terrifying, frightening,
تر شدن soak up v	spooky, scary, dreadful,
تر کردن drench, soak v	harrowing; fearful; tardy
ترادف sequence n	ترسو timid adj
ترازو scale n	ترسیدن chicken out; fear v
تراژیدی tragedy n	ترسیده afraid, frightened, adj
تراس terrace n	scared, startled

ت

تزیین decorum n	ترش sour adj
تزیین کردن decorate v	ترش tart v
تزیینات decoration n	ترش tart n
تزیینی decorative adj	ترشی pickle n
تزئین dressing n	ترفیع raise n
تسخیر conquest n	ترق ترق کردن pop v
تسکره برای انتقال مریض n	ترقی خواه progressive adj
stretcher	ترک abandonment; crack n
تسکین solace, relief n	ترک تحصیل dropout n
تسکین دهنده pacifier n	ترک دنیا کرده monk n
تسکین شدن relieve v	ترک کردن leave, desert; quit; v
تسلیت condolences; console n	relinquish
تسلیم دادن submit v	ترک کننده deserter n
تسلیم دشمن شدن capitulate v	ترکیب blend, synthesis, n
تسلیم شدن succumb, surrender v	combination, concoction
تسلیم کردن yield v	ترکیب کردن combine v
تسلیم گرفتن اتاق در هوتل check in v	ترکیبات ingredient n
تسمه strap n	ترکیبی synthetic adj
تسمه پطلون suspenders n	ترکیدن burst, crack v
تسمه گردن حیوانات collar n	ترمامیتر thermometer n
تسهیل کردن facilitate v	ترموستات thermostat n
تسهیلات facilities n	ترمیم کردن repair v
تشخیص recognition; diagnosis n	ترمینل terminal n
تشخیص کردن diagnose; v	ترور کردن assassinate v
recognize	تروریزم terrorism n
تشدید کردن intensify v	تروریست terrorist n
تشدیدی intensive adj	ترویج promotion n
تشریح explanation n	ترویج کردن promote v
تشریح کردن explain v	تریلر trailer n
تشریحی descriptive adj	ترینر trainer n
تشعشع radiation n	ترینر ورزش coach n
تشکر thank you, thanks n	تزلزل ناپذیر adamant adj

تظاهر

تصفیه شده refined *adj*	تشکری کردن thank *v*
تصفیه کردن purify, refine *v*	تشکل انجمن دادن club *v*
تصمیم resolution, decision *n*	تشکیل formation *n*
تصمیم عوض کردن shift *v*	تشکیل دادن form; institute *v*
تصمیم گرفتن decide *v*	تشناب bathroom, lavatory, *n*
تصمیم گیرنده deciding *adj*	restroom
تصمیم نگرفته undecided *adj*	تشنج convulsion, spasm; *n*
تصور کردن depict; imagine *v*	hysteria
تصور و تشخیص کردن چیزی *v*	تشنج کردن convulse *v*
discern	تشنگی thirst *v*
تصویب passage; resolution *n*	تشنه thirsty *adj*
تصویب مجدد reenactment *n*	تشویش pressure; worry *n*
تصویر photograph, image, *v*	تشویش کردن worry, stress out *v*
photo, picture, portrait	تشویق ovation *n*
تصویر بردار photographer *n*	تشویق کردن encourage, *v*
تصویر سایه دارد silhouette *n*	inspire; patronize
تصویر کشیدن figure *v*	تشویق کننده cheerleader *n*
تضاد conflict; contrast *n*	تشویق و تمجید applause *n*
تضعیف روحیه کردن demoralize *v*	تشویقی incentive *n*
تضمین guarantee *n*	تصادف coincidence *n*
تضمین کردن guarantee; *v*	تصادفی coincidental, random *adj*
vouch for	تصادم collision, crash *n*
تضمین کننده guarantor *n*	تصادم کردن crash *v*
تطابق adaptation; alignment; *n*	تصدی enterprise *n*
conformity	تصدیق verification; *n*
تطابق پذیر adaptable *adj*	acknowledgment
تطابق داشتن adapt *v*	تصدیق کردن attest, *v*
تطابق دهنده adapter *n*	authenticate, certify, validate
تطابق کردن comply *v*	تصدیقنامه certificate *n*
تطبیق کردن enforce, implement *v*	تصرف seizure *n*
تظاهر pretense, pretension; *n*	تصریح کردن stipulate *v*
simulation	تصفیه خانه refinery *n*

تعادل equilibrium *n*

تعارفی complimentary *adj*

تعامل داشتن interact *v*

تعاونی cooperative *adj*

تعبیه کردن improvise *v*

تعجب shock, surprise; marvel, *n* wonder

تعجب آور shocking, surprising, *adj* astonishing, breathtaking

تعجب کردن wonder *v*

تعدیل amendment; *n* adjustment

تعریف definition *n*

تعریف کردن define *v*

تعریف و تمجید compliment *n*

تعریق perspiration *n*

تعصب prejudice *n*

تعفن stink *n*

تعقیب کردن stalk, follow, *v* pursue, chase, trace; sue

تعلق داشتن affiliate *v*

تعلیق suspension; suspense *n*

تعلیم و تربیه education *n*

تعمیر building *n*

تعهد drive; pledge, promise, *n* commitment, obligation

تعهد pledge *v*

تعهد کردن promise, vow *v*

تعویض replacement *n*

تعیین کردن determine *v*

تعیین موقعیت locate *v*

تغذی nutritious *adj*

تغذیه nourishment, nutrition *n*

تغذیه کردن feed, nourish *v*

تغلیظ condensation *n*

تغییر change, modification, *n* variation, alteration

تغییر استقامت دادن reverse *v*

تغییر جهت turn *n*

تغییر دادن modify, alter *v*

تغییر در وضعیت shift *n*

تغییر شکل deformity; *n* transformation

تغییر شکل دادن remodel, *v* transform; deform, disfigure

تغییر قیافه disguise *n*

تغییر قیافه دادن disguise *v*

تغییر کردن change *v*

تف انداختن spit *v*

تفاهم understanding *adj*

تفاوت difference *n*

تفاوت داشتن differ, vary *v*

تفتیش inspection *n*

تفتیش کردن screen, check, *v* audit, inspect

تفریح pastime, recreation; *n* sightseeing

تفریح کردن recreate *v*

تفریق subtraction *n*

تفریق کردن subtract *v*

تفسیر gloss; interpretation, *n* paraphrase; commentary

تفصیل detail *n*

تفصیلی formal *adj*

reflection, meditation, n تفكر	تقلبى counterfeit adj
thought	تقليد simulation, imitation; n
تفكر كردن v meditate	mime
separation, n تفكيك	simulate, imitate, v تقليد كردن
segregation	mimic
تفنگ gun n	تقليد كسى را كردن impersonate v
تفنگ دستى handgun n	تقنينى legislative adj
تفنگ ساچمه يى shotgun n	تقوا virtue n
تفنگ ماشيندار machine gun n	تقويت reinforcements n
تفنگچه pistol; rifle n	تقويت كردن uphold; augment, v
تفنگدار gunman n	boost, improve, reinforce
تفويض صلاحيت delegation n	تقويت كننده amplifier n
plea, request; demand n تقاضا	تقويه كردن bolster, strengthen v
plead, beg; v تقاضا كردن	تك تك كردن knock v
demand; request	تكامل يافتن evolve v
retirement n تقاعد	تكاملى evolutionary adj
تقاعد كردن retire v	تكان shock; jolt, bump n
تقدس sanctity n	تكان خوردن rock, wobble; v
applaud, v تقدير كردن	bump
commend; reward	تكان خوردن skirmish n
roughly, almost, adv تقريباً	تكان دادن shock, galvanize; v
approximately, nearly, near	rock, shake, jerk, jolt, wiggle,
share, division n تقسيم	twitch, flick; pulsate, quake
schedule n تقسيم اوقات	تكان دادن سر nod v
hectic adj تقسيم اوقات مصروف	تكان دار bumpy adj
partition n تقسيم بندى	تكان دهنده shocking; adj
share, divide, v تقسيم كردن	poignant; impetuous
hand out	تكان ناگهانى jerk n
culpability, guilt n تقصير	تكت ticket n
distill v تقطير كردن	تكت پوستى stamp; postage n
fraud n تقلب	تكتيكى tactical adj
swindle v تقلب	تكثير duplication n

تلقین n insinuation
تلقین کردن v insinuate
تلگراف n dispenser
تلویزیون n television
تلویزیون کیبلی n cable television
تماس n touch; contact
تماس برقرار کردن v call on
تماس تیلفونی n calling
تماس گرفتن v contact
تماشا کردن v watch
تماشاچی n bystander, spectator
تمام adj entire
تمام n whole
تمام شدن v run out
تمام شده adj finished
تمام نشدنی adj unending
تمام نشده adj unfinished
تمایل n trend, tendency, inclination, leaning, propensity, willingness; preoccupation; sentiment; fantasy; liking
تمایل داشتن v tend
تمثیل n act
تمثیل کردن v act
تمدن n civilization
تمدید n extension
تمدید کردن v extend
تمدید مدت پرداخت v roll over
تمرکز n concentration, focus
تمرکز را برهم زدن v distract
تمرکز کردن v concentrate, focus

تکثیر کردن v duplicate, clone, replicate
تکذیب کردن v refute
تکرار n frequency, recurrence, repetition
تکرار شدن v recur
تکرار کردن v frequent; repeat
تکراری adj repetitive
تکسی n cab, taxi
تکمیل کردن v accomplish
تکمیل کردن n complement; complete
تکنالوژی n technology
تکنولوژی بالا adj high-tech
تکه n scrap; cloth, fabric
تکه برای نقاشی n canvas
تکه تکه adv piecemeal; apiece
تکه کاوبای n denim
تکه کتان n linen
تکیه n reliance
تکیه کردن v lean
تلاش n struggle; effort; quest
تلاش کردن v attempt; struggle
تلاطم n turbulence
تلافی n compensation
تلافی کردن v compensate; make up
تلخ adj bitter
تلخی n bitterness
تلفات وارد کردن v decimate
تلفظ n pronunciation
تلفظ کردن v pronounce

تمرین practice n	تنزل درجه demote v
تمرین برای اجرای نمایش n rehearsal	تنزل قیمت دادن devalue v
تمرین کردن practice v	تنش tension n
تمرین کردن برای اجرای نمایش v rehearse	تنظیم کردن arrange, organize, v manage, regulate; figure out
تمرینات drill n	تنظیم کننده موسیقی composer n
تمرینات ورزشی exercise n	تنفر resentment; disgust, n dislike, hatred
تمساح alligator; crocodile; n whale	تنفر آور repulsive adj
تمسخر آمیز scornful adj	تنفر داشتن abhor v
تمسخر کردن mock, scoff, scorn v	تنفس aspiration n
تمویل کردن fund v	تنفس کردن inhale v
تمویل کننده donor n	تنگ cramped, tight adj
تمیز distinction n	تنگنا strait; pinch n
تمیز دادن distinguish v	تنگه strait; gorge n
تناسب proportion, symmetry n	تنه بدن torso n
تناسب اندام fitness n	تنه درخت trunk n
تناقض contradiction n	تنها only adv
تناقض داشتن contradict v	تنها solo, alone, lonely adj
تناوب frequency n	تنهایی loneliness, solitude n
تنباکو tobacco n	تنور furnace n
تنبان کششی slacks n	تنوع diversity, variety n
تنبان ورزشی sweatpants n	تنومند burly adj
تنبل sluggish; slob; lazy adj	تهداب foundation n
تنبلی laziness n	تهدید blackmail; menace, n threat
تند spicy adj	تهدید کردن threaten v
تند باد gust n	تهمت libel n
تند و تلخ austere adj	تهمت زدن slander n
تند و تیز hot adj	تهیه provision n
تنزل degradation n	تهیه شده provided conj
تنزل دادن degrade v	تهیه کردن provide v

you *pron* تو	توجیه کردن *v* justify, rationalize
توازن *n* coordination; parity;	توجیه نشده *adj* unjustified
symmetry; balance	تورم *n* inflation
تواضع *n* humility, modesty	تورنمینت *n* tournament
توافق *n* consensus	توریزم *n* tourism
توافق پذیر *adj* agreeable	توزیع *n* distribution
توافق کردن *v* agree	توزیع کردن *v* dispense,
توافق نکردن *v* disagree	distribute
توافقنامه *n* agreement	توسط *prep* by
توانا *adj* almighty; able	توسعه یافتن *v* boom
توانستن *modal v* can, could	توسل *n* recourse
توبه کردن *v* repent	توش رنگه *n* crayon
توپ *n* ball	توصیه کردن *v* prescribe
توپ را به کسی پرتاب کردن *v* pass	توطئه *n* plot
توپ که اتومات فیر میشود *n* cannon	توطئه کردن *v* plot
توپخانه *n* artillery	توفان *n* tempest, cyclone, storm
توت *n* berry	توفان برف *n* snowstorm
توت زمینی *n* strawberry	توفان برفی *n* blizzard
توته *n* scrap, bit, slice, chunk,	توفانی *adj* windy, stormy
piece	توقع *n* expectancy, expectation
توته توته شدن *v* shatter	توقع داشتن *v* expect
توته توته کردن *v* dice	توقف *n* suspension
توته چوب *n* chip; wedge	توقف کردن *v* stop; stop by
توته شدن *v* crush	توقیف *n* custody, detention
توته کاغذ *n* slip	توقیف کردن *v* detain; impound
توته کردن *v* shatter; chop, slice	تول بکس موتر *n* trunk
توته های چوب *n* chopsticks	تولد *n* birth
توته یخ *n* ice cube	توله *n* flute
توجه *n* attention, notice	تولید *n* produce
توجه *v* heed	تولید کردن *v* generate,
توجه را جلب کردن *v* mesmerize	manufacture, produce; prod
توجیه *n* justification	تولید کننده *n* generator

ث

تیلفون کردن v call, phone
تیلفون همراه n ,cell phone
mobile phone
تیلیسکوپ n telescope
تیم n team
تیم ورزشی n league
تیوب n tube
تیوری n theory

ث

ثابت adj ,resolute; constant
steady, stable, fixed
ثانوی adj secondary
ثانیه n second
ثبات n sustenance; stability
ثبت n registration
ثبت در کتاب n entry
ثبت صدا n recording
ثبت کردن v log
ثبت کردن رویداد ها v record
ثبت کننده صدا n tape recorder
ثبت معلومات در کمپیوتر v load
ثبت موسیقی v record
ثبت موسیقی n record
ثبت نام n register
ثبت نام کردن v enroll, register
ثبوت n proof
ثبوت شده adj proven
ثبوت کردن v prove

تولید مثل کردن v ,breed
procreate
تولید مجدد n reproduction
تولید مجدد کردن v reproduce
تولید نسل n reproduction
تولید نسل کردن v reproduce
تولیدات n production
تومور n tumor
تونل n tunnel
توهم n delusion
توهین n ,libel; abuse, affront
offense, insult
توهین آمیز adj abusive; offensive
توهین کردن v insult, offend
تیاتر n theater
تیاترسینمایی n movie theater
تیار adj ready
تیپ چسب دار n tape
تیر n arrow
تیرانداز n sniper
تیراندازی n gunfire, gunshot
تیره adj murky
تیز adj ,poignant, sharp; quick
rapid, fast, swift, brisk
تیز کردن v sharpen
تیزاب n acid
تیزکننده n sharpener
تیشه n hatchet
تیغ n razor; blade
تیل n gasoline
تیلر n trailer
تیلفون n phone, telephone

ثروت wealth n
ثروتمند rich, affluent, adj
wealthy

ج

جَو rye n
جا افتاده entrenched adj
جا خالی کردن dock v
جا دادن accommodate v
جابجا شدن budge v
جاده avenue, boulevard n
جادو magic n
جادوآمیز magical adj
جادوگر magician, sorcerer, n
wizard
جادوگری sorcery, witchcraft n
جادویی magic adj
جاذب absorbent adj
جاروب broom n
جاروب برقی vacuum n
جاروب کردن sweep; vacuum v
جاری continuous, ongoing adj
جاری شدن creak; ebb; flow v
جاسوس spy n
جاسوسی espionage n
جاسوسی کردن spy v
جاطلب ambitious adj
جاکت sweater n
جاگزین در وظیفه relieve v

جالب interesting adj
جالی net n
جالی بازی تینیس racket n
جام قهرمانی trophy n
جامد solid adj
جامد solid n
جامد ساختن solidify v
جامعه community, society n
جانبدار biased adj
جانبداری bias n
جانبی lateral adj
جاندار living adj
جانشین substitute; successor n
جانشین شدن substitute v
جانور وحشی wild boar n
جاویدان immortal adj
جای setting, place n
جای باریک و تنگ pinch n
جای خالی vacancy n
جای دیگر elsewhere adv
جای زخم scar n
جای کسی را گرفتن take over v
جایداد property n
جایزه reward, award, prize n
جایگاه مقدس sanctuary n
جبران compensation n
جبران کردن atone; v
recompense; recoup
جبهه front n
جدا apart adv
جدا separate adj
جداً strongly adv

جدا شدن v ;break away	جرقه زدن v sparkle
break up, split up; come apart	جرقه کردن v flash
جدا شده asunder adv	جریان n ;stream; circulation
جدا کردن v ;intercept; split	flow; tide
separate, sever, cut out, take	جریان آب n current
apart; desegregate; detach,	جریان برق n current
disentangle; segregate	جریان عادی n routine
جداسازی segregation n	جریمه n surcharge; fine, penalty
جدال controversy n	جریمه کردن v penalize
جدایی separation; severance n	جزء n ;component; item
جدول table, chart n	جزء کلمه n syllable
جدول معما crossword puzzle n	جزا n punishment
جدی grim, serious adj	جزا دادن v punish
جدید anew adv	جزبه جز نوشتن v itemize
جدید original; new adj	جزر و مد n tide
جذاب adj ,handsome, gorgeous	جزوه معلوماتی n handout
attractive, appealing,	جزیره n island
charismatic; spectacular;	جزئی adj ,petty, trivial; partial
intriguing	slight
جذاب بودن v appeal	جسارت n audacity
جذابیت n allure, attraction, charisma	جست و خیز زدن v tumble
جذامی leper n	جست و خیز کردن v skip
جذب کردن v absorb, assimilate	جستجو n search, navigation
جذبه appeal n	جستجو کردن v ,browse, navigate
جرات nerve n	search, seek, look for; prowl
جرات نکردن v chicken out	جستجو کننده در کمپیوتر n browser
جراحات casualty n	جستجو گر n prowler
جراحت maim v	جستجوگر n explorer
جراحت wound, injury n	جسد n carcass, corpse
جرأت کردن v dare	جسم آویخته n pendulum
جرثقیل crane n	جشن n ,festival, celebration
جرقه spark n	feast, function

جشن مسیحیان Christmas n	جمع کردن amass, collect v
جعبه case n	جمع کردن ارقام sum v
جعل اسناد forgery n	جمع کن برگها rake n
جعل کردن fake, feign, falsify v	جمع کننده collector n
جعل هویت کردن impersonate v	جمع و جور compact adj
جعلی fake, fraudulent adj	جمله sentence n
جغرافیه geography n	جمنازیوم gymnasium (gym) n
جک آب jug n	جمهوری republic n
جگر liver n	جن elf; ghost n
جگرخون blue adj	جنازه funeral n
جلال glory n	جنایت crime; felony n
جلب کردن draw, attract v	جنایتکار criminal; felon n
جلد سوراخ سوراخ porous adj	جنایی criminal adj
جلد کتاب volume n	جنباندن wag v
جلد یا شماره مجله issue n	جنبش movement n
جلسه sitting, meeting, session n	جنبنده wobbly adj
جلو چیزی را گرفتن dodge v	جنبه facet n
جلوگیری prevention n	جنتری calendar n
جلوگیری از آمدن صدا insulate v	جنجال tumult n
جلوگیری کردن avoid, prevent v	جنرال general n
جلیقه vest; life jacket n	جنس good n
جمجمه scalp; skull n	جنسی genial adj
جمع addition; plural n	جنسیت gender, sex n
جمع all adv	جنگ war, warfare n
جمع آوری حاصلات crop v	جنگ تن به تن duel n
جمع آوری کردن populate; v muster	جنگ طلب belligerent adj
جمع آوری مجدد recollection n	جنگ کردن fight v
جمع آوری محصولات harvest v	جنگجو warrior, combatant n
جمع شدن accumulate, v assemble, gather, drift, herd, huddle	جنگسالار warrior n
	جنگل forest; jungle n
	جنگل بارانی rainforest n
	جنگلی wild adj

جوره pair n
جوس juice n
جوش boiling adj
جوش و خروش tempest n
جوشاندن boil v
جوشیدن simmer v
جولاگک spider n
جولای July n
جوی ditch, gutter n
جویا شدن inquire v
جویدن chew, munch v
جیب pocket n
جیرجیرک cricket n
جیرجیری squeaky adj
جیلی jelly n

چ

چُرت nap n
چُرت زدن nap v
چابک brisk; deft adj
چاپ print n
چاپ انگشت fingerprint n
چاپ پا print n
چاپ خوب fine print n
چاپ غلط misprint n
چاپ کردن print v
چاپلوسی adulation, flattery n
چاپلوسی کردن flatter v
چادر veil n

جنوب south n
جنوب شرق southeast n
جنوب غرب southwest n
جنوباً southbound adv
جنوبی south, southern adj
جنوری January n
جهانگرد tourist n
جهانی worldly; global; adj
universal
جهانی شدن globalization n
جهیل بزرگ lake n
جهیل کوچک lagoon n
جو barley n
جواب answer, response n
جواب دادن answer, respond v
جواری corn n
جواری پُله popcorn n
جواز دادن license v
جواز رانندگی license, driver's n
license
جوالی porter n
جوان young, youthful adj
جوانتر youngster n
جوانه زدن sprout v
جوانی youth n
جواهر jewel n
جواهر فروش jeweler n
جواهرات jewelry n
جوراب sock n
جوراب ساق بلند stocking n
جورآمد compromise n
جورآمد کردن compromise v

چارغ خواب n lampshade	چارج برق n charge
چراغ رهنما n beacon	چارچوب n framework
چراغ کنار جاده n lamppost	چارچوب ساخته شده adj built-in
چراگاه n meadow, pasture	چارمغز n walnut
چرب adj greasy	چاشت n noon
چرب کردن v grease, lubricate	چاشنی n sauce
چربی n grease, fat	چاق adj fat, obese; plump
چربی دار adj fatty	چاق کردن v fatten
چرت زدن v doze, snooze; drool	چاق و چله adj chubby
چرخ n wheel	چاقو n knife
چرخ دهنده n twister	چاقو زدن v stab
چرخ کردن گوشت v mince	چاک n slash; slot
چرخان n twister	چاکلیت n chocolate
چرخاندن v spin, rotate; steer;	چالش n challenge
rewind; swivel	چانه زدن v bargain, haggle
چرخش n rotation	چاه n well
چرخش آب n whirlpool	چای n tea
چرخیدن v rotate, spin, revolve,	چاینک n kettle, teapot
whirl; steer	چپ n left
چرک n smear	چپراس دروازه n hinge
چرک شدن v soil	چپس n fries; potato chip
چرک کردن v smear	چپلک n sandal
چرک گوش n earwax	چپن n robe, cloak; gown
چرم n leather	چپن بی آستین n cape
چریدن v graze	چپن حمام n bathrobe
چسب n paste; sticker	چتری n umbrella
چسبناک adj sticky, tacky	چرا adv why
چسپاندن v paste	چراغ n torch; lamp, light
چسپیدن v pester; stick	چراغ پیشرو n headlight
چشم n eye	چراغ ترافیکی n traffic light
چشم انداز n panorama, outlook	چراغ توقف n stop light
چشم بستن v blindfold	چراغ جاده n streetlight

چنگال pitchfork n	چشم بسته blindfold n
چنگال دار gripping adj	چشم بند blind n
چنگک hook n	چشم به راه بودن look forward v
چنین such adj	چشم پوشی کردن ignore v
چه whether conj	چشم پوشیدن از spare v
چه زمانی when conj	چشمک زدن peep; squint, v
چهار four n	wink; twinkle
چهارده fourteen n	چشمگیر resounding adj
چهارراهی crossroads, n	چشمه آب spring n
intersection	چشمه آب گرم geyser n
چهارم fourth adj	چطور how adv
چهل forty n	چک بانکی check n
چوب mill; lumber, wood, n	چک زدن bite v
timber; stick	چک معاش paycheck n
چوب باریک تراش کردن splinter v	چکاندن instill v
چوب بامبو bamboo n	چکش hammer; hammock n
چوب برای زدن چیزی club n	چکش چوبی maul v
چوب پنبه cork n	چکش زدن hammer v
چوب تیر beam n	چکیدن drip, trickle v
چوب رهنمای موسیقی baton n	چلاندن operate v
چوب زیر بغل crutch n	چلپاسه lizard n
چوب سوخت firewood n	چلیپایی cross adj
چوبک دندان toothpick n	چملک wrinkled adj
چوبی wooden adj	چملکی wrinkle n
چوپان shepherd n	چمن lawn, turf n
چوتی braid n	چمن زار prairie n
چوچه اسب colt n	چند few; several pron
چوچه پرنده chick n	چند دانه few adj
چوچه پشک kitten n	چند دستگی ramification n
چوکات frame n	چند رسانه یی multimedia adj
چوکات کردن frame v	چندین several adj
چوکی chair, seat n	چنگ زدن clutch v

wheelchair *n* چوکی تایر دار	fringe
as, since *conj* چونکه	حاشیه ای *adj* marginal
what *adj* چی	حاصل کردن *v* gain
what *pron* چی را	حاصلات *n* crop, harvest
when *adv* چی وقت	حاصلخیز *adj* fertile
chicken pox *n* چیچک	حاصلخیزی *n* fertility
ornamental *adj* چیز زینتی	حاضر *adj* present
grotesque *adj* چیز عجیب و غریب	حاضر شدن *v* show up
prodigy *n* چیز غیرعادی	حاضری *n* attendance
roll *n* چیز لوله شده	حاضرین *n* audience
puree *n* چیز مخلوط شده	حافظه انسان *n* memory
something *pron* چیزی	حافظه کمپیوتر *n* memory
check *n* چیزی را چک کردن	حاکم *adj* prevalent
spot *v* چیزی را دیدن	حاکم منطقه *n* ruler
riddle *n* چیستان	حال آنکه *conj* whereas
scream, shriek *n* چیغ	حالا *adv* now
screech, shriek, yell *v* چیغ زدن	حالت *n* posture, pose; state,
scream *v* چیغ زدن	status; mode, setting
crease, pleat *n* چین خوردگی	حالت بعد از حادثه *adj* traumatic
pleated; riveting *adj* چین خورده	حالت عاجل *n* urgency
crease *v* چین دادن	حامل *n* bearer
channel *n* چینل تلویزیونی	حاملگی *n* pregnancy;
	conception
	حامله *adj* pregnant
ح	حامی *n* patron, sponsor,
	supporter
verdict; warrant *n* حُکم	حبس کردن *v* incarcerate
pilgrim *n* حاجی	حبوبات *n* cereal; oatmeal
accident; incident *n* حادثه	حتمی *adj* indispensable
tragedy *n* حادثه غم انگیز	حتمی الوقوع *adj* inevitable
brim, margin, verge; *n* حاشیه	حتی *adv* even
	حتی اگر *adv* even if

pilgrimage n حج	حرکت داشتن v roam
veil n حجاب	حرکت کردن v proceed; depart
cell n حجره بدن	حرکت های ورزشی v lunge
bulk n حجم	حرمت n reverence; sanctity
byte n حجم فایل کمپیوتری	حروف اول نام n initials
bulky adj حجیم	حروف بزرگ الفبا n uppercase
scope, limit n حد	حروف صدادار n vowel
maximum adj حد اعظمی	حروف کوچک الفبا n lowercase
minimal adj حد اقل	avid; greedy adj حریص
average adj حد اوسط	gobble v حریصانه خوردن
time limit n حد زمانی	party n حزب
contour n حد فاصله	sensation, sense n حس
mediocre adj حد متوسط	sensible adj حس شدنی
speed limit n حد مجاز سرعت	sense v حس کردن
conjecture, guess n حدس	account; arithmetic n حساب
speculate, guess v حدس زدن	bank account n حساب بانکی
speculation n حدس و گمان	debit n حساب دهی
omission n حذف	settle v حساب را تسویه کردن
delete; omit v حذف کردن	حساب هوتل را تسویه کردن v
warmth, heat n حرارت	check out
heat v حرارت دادن	accountable adj حسابده
unlawful adj حرام	envy, jealousy n حسادت
greed n حرص	envy v حسادت کردن
preposition n حرف اضافی در گرامر	perceptive, sensitive, adj حساس
letter n حرف الفبا	tender; susceptible
capital letter n حرف بزرگ	allergy n حساسیت
article n حرف تعریف	allergic adj حساسیتی
the a حرف تعریف در گرامر	courtesy, goodwill n حسن نیت
professional adj حرفه ای	envious, jealous adj حسود
movement, motion n حرکت	bug, insect n حشره
slow motion n حرکت آهسته	pesticide n حشره کش
move, shift v حرکت دادن	fence n حصار

ح

حصار کشی n fencing	حکومت n government
حصه n share	حکومت استبدادی n dictatorship
حصول n acquisition	حکومت کردن v rule
حضور n presence	حل کردن v solve
حفاظت n conservation; protection, safeguard	حلبی n tin
حفاظت کردن v protect	حلزون n snail
حفاظت نشده adj unprotected	حلقه n ring, circle; curl; hoop; reel
حفر کردن v dig, excavate	حلقه کردن v circle; curl
حفظ n retention	حلقه یی adj curly
حفظ الصحه n hygiene	حلیم adj submissive
حفظ کردن v sustain, uphold, maintain; retain	حماقت n stupidity
حفظ و مراقبت n maintenance	حماقت کردن v goof
حق الزحمه n wage	حمام n bath
حق العبور n toll	حمام کردن v bathe
حق حاکمیت n sovereignty	حمایت n support
حق طبع و نشر n copyright	حمایت کردن v support; vindicate
حق قانونی n right	حمایوی adj supportive
حقوقدان n lawyer	حمل شدنی adj portable
حقیر adj lowly	حمل و نقل n carriage, freight, haul, shipment
حقیقت n truth, fact	حمله v assault
حقیقی adj factual, true, truthful	حمله n strike, attack, raid
حک کردن v carve	حمله کردن v strike, attack, invade, raid, charge
حکاکی n engraving	حمله کننده n attacker
حکاکی کردن v engrave	حوصله n mood; patience
حکایت n anecdote	حوض n pond
حکایت کردن v narrate	حوض آببازی n pool, swimming pool
حکم n order	حومه شهر n countryside; suburb
حکم کردن v order	حومه های شهر n outskirts
حکمرانی کردن v govern	حویلی n yard
حکمفرما adj rampant	

ح

خ

خُطبه sermon n

خُلق temper n

خاتمه sequel; end, ending, n
final

خاتمه بخشیدن conclude, end up v

خاتمه دادن terminate v

خار thorn n

خارپشت کوهی porcupine n

خارج abroad adv

خارج از outside prep

خارج بستر outpatient n

خارج قسمت quotient n

خارجی foreign adj

خارجی outsider n

خاردار thorny adj

خارش rash n

خارش دار itchy adj

خارق العاده extraordinary adj

خاریدن tickle; itch v

خاص special, privileged adj

خاصتاً especially, specially adv

خاصیت حیاتی vitality n

خاصیت مقناطیسی magnetism n

خاطرات memoirs n

خاطره memory n

خاک dust; soil n

خاک انداز dustpan n

خاک آلود dusty adj

خاک آلود شدن dust v

حویلی عقب خانه backyard n

حیات lifetime adj

حیات وحش wildlife n

حیاتی crucial, vital adj

حیثیت prestige, reputation n

حیران surprised adj

حیران شده petrified adj

حیران کردن astound v

حیران کننده stunning adj

حیرت prodigy; amazement n

حیرت انگیز surprising, adj
amazing, astounding

حیرت آور marvelous adj

حیرت آورد prodigious adj

حیرت زده کردن stun v

حیله باز foxy adj

حیله گر wily, cunning adj

حیوان animal, beast n

حیوان پستاندار rodent n

حیوان خانگی pet n

حیوان دریایی ده پا prawn n

حیوان صفت vicious adj

حیوان کوچک litter n

څارنوال prosecutor n

خاموشی n ;silence; blackout	خاک پاک کن duster n
clam	خاک شده soiled adj
خانقاه monastery n	خاکستر cinder, ash n
خانگی homely adj	خاکستر ذغال نیم سوز embers n
خانم lady, madam; wife n	خاکستردانی ashtray n
خانم خانه housewife n	خاکی و آبی amphibious adj
خانم صاحب خانه landlady n	خال speck n
خانه home adv	خال سیاه mole n
خانه home, house n	خال های سیاه بر صورت freckle n
خانه جولاگک spider web n	خالص pure, genuine adj
خانه خورد چوبی shed n	خالصانه sincerely adv
خانه زنبود عسل beehive n	خالق creator n
خانه سامان housekeeper n	خاله aunt n
خانه سگ یا پشک kennel n	خالی empty, blank; devoid; adj
خانه کوچک برای حیوانات pen n	hollow; vacant
خانواده household n	خالی کردن deplete, empty; v
خانواده بزرگ extended family n	vacate
خائن traitor n	خام crude; raw adj
خبررسان informer n	خاموش off adv
خبرنامه bulletin n	خاموش out; offline; mute, adj
خبرنگار correspondent n	quiet, silent
ختم over prep	خاموش باش shut up v
ختم کردن end, finish v	خاموش شدن die out v
خجالت embarrassment n	خاموش شده extinct adj
خجالت shameful adj	خاموش کردن smother, stifle, v
خجالت آور embarrassing adj	suffocate, muffle, snub; shut
خجالت زده embarrassed adj	off, switch off, turn off
خجالت شدن embarrass v	خاموش کردن حریق extinguish v
خجالت کشیدن cringe v	خاموش کردن صدا mutual adj
خجل self-conscious adj	خاموش کننده حریق n
خجلت embarrassment n	fire extinguisher
خدا حافظ goodbye e	خاموش کننده صدا muffler n

bye *e* خداحافظ	خرس *n* bear
farewell *n* خداحافظی	خرگوش *n* hare, rabbit
God *n* خداوند	خرمهره *n* charm
service *n* خدمت	خروج *n* emission, exhaust; exit
minister; serve *v* خدمت کردن	خروس *n* rooster
butler, servant, maid; *n* خدمتگار	خریدار *n* buyer
janitor	خریداری *n* shopping; purchase
donkey *n* خر	خریداری کردن *v* order, purchase,
spoil; break down *v* خراب شدن	shop
botch; debunk; *v* خراب کردن	خریدن *v* buy
demolish, wreck; deteriorate;	خریطه *n* pouch, bag, sack
vandalize	خریطه یی *adj* baggy
vandal *n* خرابکار	خزان *n* fall, autumn
charade; *n* خرابکاری	خزنده *n* reptile
demolition, vandalism	خزه *n* moss
sabotage *n* خرابکاری قصدی	خزیدن *v* slither, crawl, creep
sabotage *v* خرابکاری کردن	خساره *n* loss
wreckage *n* خرابی	خستگی *n* boredom; exhaustion,
scratch *n* خراش	fatigue
scratch, graze *n* خراشیدگی	خستگی ناپذیر *adj* tireless
scratch *v* خراشیدن	خسته *adj* strained; weary, tired,
superstition *n* خرافات	bored
melon *n* خربوزه	خسته باب *n* nut
expense *n* خرج	خسته شدن *v* bore
crab; cub; lobster *n* خرچنگ	خسته کردن *v* exhaust, tire
shred *v* خرد کردن	خسته کن *adj* dull, boring
petty *adj* خرده	خسته کننده *adj* exhausting,
shred *n* خرده	tedious, tiresome
rubble *n* خرده سنگ	خسته میوه *n* pit
retailer *n* خرده فروش	خسر *n* father-in-law
retail *n* خرده فروشی	خسربره *n* brother-in-law
crumb *n* خرده یا توته	خسک *n* flea

stingy *adj* خسیس	equator *n* خط استوا
hiss *v* خش خش کردن	ridge *n* خط الراس
debris *n* خش و خاشاک	groove *n* خط باریک دراز
diamond; brick *n* خشت	stripe *n* خط خط
block *n* خشت کانکریتی	striped *adj* خط دار
bricklayer *n* خشتمال	racetrack *n* خط دوش
dry *adj* خشک	hyphen *n* خط ربط
drain *v* خشک شدن	railroad *n* خط ریل
dry *v* خشک کردن	coastline *n* خط ساحلی
dryer *n* خشک کن	route, trajectory *n* خط سیر
drought *n* خشکسالی	ruler *n* خط کش
dry-clean *v* خشکه شویی کردن	tangent *n* خط مماس
dried *adj* خشکیده	scribble *v* خط ناخوانا
irate *adj* خشگمین	foul *adj* خطا
infuriate *v* خشگین کردن	foul *n* خطا در ورزش
rampage *v* خشم	mistaken *adj* خطا کردن
wrath, fury, outrage, *n* خشم	address *v* خطاب کردن
rage	danger, hazard, peril, risk *n* خطر
fierce; furious; *adj* خشمگین	borderline *adj* خطر مرزی
outrageous	dangerous, *adj* خطرناک
enrage, *v* خشمگین کردن	hazardous, perilous, risky
exasperate	down *adj* خفه
furiously *adv* خشمگینانه	smother, stifle, *v* خفه کردن
rough, violent; crusty; *adj* خشن	strangle, suffocate, choke
tough; crass; hoarse, harsh	stifling *adj* خفه کننده
mother-in-law *n* خشو	fair, moderate *adj* خفیف
aggression, violence *n* خشونت	opening, gap *n* خلا
aggressive *adj* خشونت آمیز	out *adj* خلاص شده
trait *n* خصوصیت	summary *n* خلاصه
hostility *n* خصومت	debrief, recap, *v* خلاصه کردن
hostile *adj* خصومت آمیز	summarize
line *n* خط	unconventional *adj* خلاف عُرف

خلاف واقعیت *trumped-up adj*	خواب دیدن *v dream*
خلاق *creative adj*	خواب کوتاه کردن *v nap*
خلاقیت *creativity n*	خواب مصنوعی *hypnosis n*
خلای قانونی *loophole n*	خواب و خیال هنگام خواب *dream n*
خلع سلاح *unarmed adj*	خواب وحشتناک *nightmare n*
خلع سلاح کردن *disarm v*	خوابیدن *sleep v*
خلق کردن *create v*	خوابیده *asleep adj*
خلقت *creation n*	خوار شمردن *despise v*
خلوت *privacy n*	خواستار *willing adj*
خلوص *purity n*	خواستگاری *courtship n*
خلوص نیت *sincerity n*	خواستگاری کردن *court,*
خلیج *gulf n*	*propose to*
خم شدن *bend down, bend, v*	خواستن *want v*
bow; crouch; recline	خوانا *legible adj*
خم شده *inclined; bent adj*	خواندن *read v*
خم کردن *incline v*	خواندن *reading n*
خم کردن بدن *squat v*	خوانش *reading n*
خمیر *batter v*	خواننده *reader n*
خمیر *paste; dough n*	خواه *whether conj*
خمیرکردن *knead v*	خواهد *shall; should; will modal v*
خمیرمایه *yeast n*	خواهد بود *would-be adj*
خنثی کردن *defuse v*	خواهد شد *would modal v*
خنجر *dagger n*	خواهر *sister n*
خنده *laugh, laughter n*	خواهر اندر *stepsister n*
خنده آور *ridiculous, comical, adj*	خواهرزاده *niece n*
funny, laughable	خوب *all right, fine, good, adj*
خنده دار *hilarious adj*	*well*
خندیدن *chuckle, giggle, laugh v*	خوب یاد گرفتن *master v*
خنک *chill n*	خوبی *goodness n*
خواب *dream; nap n*	خود *self n*
خواب *sleep n*	خود آگاه *self-conscious adj*
خواب آلود *drowsy, sleepy adj*	خود را به کسی رساندن *catch up v*

خود شما yourself pron	خوش لباس، stylish, adj
خودخواه boastful, selfish adj	well-dressed
خودخواهی selfishness n	خوش مزه delicious adj
خودداری کردن abstain v	خوش منظر، picturesque, adj
خودش itself pron	scenic
خودکار auto n	خوش نداشتن dislike v
خودکار، automated, adj	خوش نما good-looking adj
automatic	خوشایند pleasant adj
خودکشی کردن suicide n	خوشبخت fortunate, lucky adj
خودما ourselves pron	خوشبو fragrant adj
خودنمایی flaunt v	خوشبو کننده deodorant n
خودنمایی ostentatious adj	خوشبویی fragrance; incense n
خودنمایی کردن show off v	خوشحال، elated, glad, happy, adj
خوراک سرپایی snack n	jolly, jovial, pleased
خورد petite adj	خوشحال کننده gratifying, adj
خورد ضابط lieutenant; n	pleasing
sergeant	خوشحالی pleasure, happiness n
خوردسال juvenile adj	خوشنودی satisfaction n
خوردسن young adj	خوشه bunch n
خوردن ingest, devour, eat v	خوشی delight; festivity n
خوردنی edible adj	خوشی کردن rejoice, cheer, v
خورشیدی solar adj	exult
خوش merry adj	خوف phobia; hang-up n
خوش اخلاقی mannerism n	خوفناک horrific adj
خوش آمدید welcome n	خوک hog, pig n
خوش آمدید گفتن welcome v	خوک آبی seal n
خوش برخورد folksy, sociable, adj	خوک وحشی boar n
affable, well-behaved	خون blood n
خوش بین optimistic adj	خون آشام vampire n
خوش بینی optimism n	خون بها ransom n
خوش داشتن like v	خونخوار bloodthirsty adj
خوش ساختن delight, please v	خونریزی کردن bleed v

خ

خونسردی composure n	**د**
خونین bloody adj	
خویشاوند relative n	دُم حیوان tail n
خویشتن گرای introvert adj	دُهل drum n
خیاشنه sister-in-law n	داخل in adv
خیاط seamstress, tailor n	داخل آمدن come in v
خیال phantom, illusion n	داخل بردن take in v
خیالی imaginary adj	داخل چیزی افتادن drop in v
خیانت larceny; treason, n	داخل رفتن go in v
treachery, betrayal	داخل شدن enter, get in v
خیانت کردن betray v	داخل شدن به محل کار log in v
خیانتکار treacherous adj	داخل کردن insert; admit v
خیرات handout, charity n	داخل کشور inland adj
خیرخواه benevolent adj	داخله admission n
خیرخواهی benevolence n	داخلی civil, domestic; inner, adj
خیره blurred, dazed, dim adj	internal
خیره دیدن stare v	داخلی ساختن domesticate v
خیره ساختن dim v	داخلی شده domesticated adj
خیره شدن daze, gaze v	دادن relay; give; hand in v
خیره کردن blur v	دادوبیداد rampage v
خیره کننده dazzle v	دادوبیداد rowdy adj
خیریه charitable adj	دارا بودن own v
خیز زدن bounce, spring v	دارالیتام orphanage n
خیز و جست hop v	دارای finance n
خیز و جست leap n	دارای خال های سیاه روی صورت adj
خیز و جست کردن leap v	freckled
خیزش rise n	دارای شخصیت حقوقی adj
خیلی lot, much pron	corporate
خیلی ذکی brilliant adj	دارای طرح و دیزاین sketchy adj
خیلی سیاه pitch-black adj	دارای کمبود deficient adj
خیمه tent n	دارایی asset n

دارچین cinnamon n	دایر کردن شماره تیلفون dial v
داس sickle n	دایرة المعارف encyclopedia n
داستان story, tale n	دایف کردن در آب dive v
داستان عاشقانه romance n	دایمی perennial, permanent adj
داش oven n	داینسور dinosaur n
داشتن have v	دایه midwife n
داغ hot adj	دچار نفس تنگی asthmatic adj
داکتر doctor, physician n	دچار وسوسه کردن tempt v
داکتر امراض روانی psychiatrist n	دخالت کردن meddle v
داکتر جراح surgeon n	دختر daughter; gal, girl n
داکتر حیوانات veterinarian n	دختر اندر stepdaughter n
داکتر دندان dentist n	دخل پول piggy bank n
دالر dollar n	دخول insertion; entry n
دام snare, trap n	دخول مجدد reentry n
داماد bridegroom, groom; n	دخیل involved adj
son-in-law	دخیل بودن engage, involve v
دامن lap; skirt n	در at prep
دامن کوتاه miniskirt n	در ابتدا initially, primarily adv
دامنه hem n	در اطراف around prep
دامنه تپه hillside n	در امتداد along prep
دانا wise adj	در این اواخر lately, recently adv
دانایی wisdom n	در این روزها nowadays adv
دانش knowledge n	در آغاز قرار دادن initial v
دانش آموز learner n	در آغوش گرفتن cuddle, v
دانشکده college n	embrace, hug
دانه کمسایی dice n	در آنجا there pron
دانه های برف snowflake n	در بالا above adv
داور judge; umpire n	در بالای over adv
داور مسابقات referee n	در بانک پول گذاشتن deposit v
داوطلب volunteer n	در بر داشتن contain v
داوطلبانه voluntary adj	در برابر versus prep
دایپر diaper n	در بلندی up prep

د

در بوتل ریختن v bottle	**در زیر قرار گرفته** underlying adj
در بیرون outside adj	**در سراسر** across adv
در بیرون از منزل outdoors adv	**در سراسر دنیا** globally adv
در بین between adv	**در سراسر دنیا** worldwide adj
در پایین down adv	**در سیاه آب گیر مانده** swamped adj
در پهلوی beside prep	**در صف آوردن** v range
در تقاضای بلند demanding adj	**در عقب** after prep
در تماس بودن interactive adj	**در عقب** behind adv
در تماس نزدیک closely adv	**در عمق** in depth adv
در تنگنا قرار گرفتن v pinch	**در عمق** in-depth adj
در چاراطراف whereabouts n	**در عوض** instead prep
در حال حاضر currently adv	**در عین زمان** meanwhile adv
در حال مرگ dying adj	**در فاصله معین بین هم قرار دادن** v
در حالت تعلیق pending adj	space out
در حالت تعلیق suspense n	**در فلم تمثیل کردن** v shoot
در خواب غُریدن v snore	**در قطی نگهداری شده یا کنسرو** adj
در داخل aboard adv	canned
در داخل in, inside prep	**در قید** cramped adj
در داخل خانه indoors adv	**در کدام جای** somewhere adv
در درجه نخست foremost adj	**در کمپیوتراز یک متن به متن دیگر**
در دریا overboard adv	**رفتن** scroll v
در دو نسخه خوشتن v duplicate	**در کمین بودن** v lurk
در رابطه به concerning, prep	**در کنار** alongside prep
regarding	**در کنج گذاشتن** v corner
در زباله انداختن v dump	**در گوش کسی گفتن** v whisper
در زیر below, beneath; prep	**در مجموع** overall adv
down	**در مرکز قرار دادن** v center
در زیر under adv	**در مضیقه** hard adv
در زیر آب underwater adv	**در معرض خطر** endangered adj
در زیر چیز خط کشیدن v underline	**در معرض گذاری** exposure n
در زیر چیزی underneath prep	**در معرض واقع شدن** dispose v
در زیر زمین underground adv	**در مقابل** against, versus prep

د

در مقایسه به than prep	درجه یک classy adj
در مورد about prep	درحال استفاده شدن occupied adj
در میان across; amid, prep	درخت tree n
among, between	درخت بید willow n
در نزدیکی nearby adj	درخت خرما palm n
در نظر گرفتن account for v	درخت ناجو pine n
در هرجای wherever conj	درخشان flashy, glowing adj
در هنگام while n	درخشش gleam n
در هوا گشت زدن hover v	درخشش آفتاب sunshine n
در وسط middle adj	درخشنده brilliant, shiny adj
در یک رشته تحصیل کردن major v	درخشیدن blink; shine v
in, minor	درخواست plea, appeal n
دراز long adj	درخواست کردن appeal, plead; v
دراز چوکی bench n	apply
دراز کشیدن lie, lay v	درخواست کننده applicant n
دراز کشیده oblong adj	درخواستی petition; application n
دراز مدت long-term adj	درد ache, pain n
درامه drama n	درد مفاصل arthritis n
درایت tact n	درد ناگهانی pang n
درایف کمپیوتر drive n	درداخل within prep
درآمد earnings n	دردسر ساز troublesome adj
درب منزل doorstep n	دردناک painful, sore adj
دربست کرایه کردن charter v	درز seam n
درج insertion n	درس lesson n
درج کردن file v	درس دادن teach v
درجریان during prep	درساحل ashore adv
درجن dozen n	درست all right, alright adv
درجه grade, level n	درست right, correct; fixed; adj
درجه بندی کردن grade v	orthodox
درجه حرارت temperature n	درست است okay adj
درجه صدا volume n	درست کردن correct, fix, mend; v
درجه هوا degree n	devise

د

precision; validity *n* درستی	درهمین نزدیکی ها *adv* nearby
throughout *prep* درسراسر	درو کردن حاصلات *v* reap
rough, coarse *adj* درشت	دروازه *n* door; gate
within *prep* درظرف	دروازه بالکن *n* patio
meantime *adv* درعین زمان	دروازه بعدی *adj* next door
otherwise *adv* درغیرآن	دروازه دخولی *n* entrance
otherwise *adv* درغیرآنصورت	دروازه عقبی *n* backdoor
perception *n* درک	دروغ *n* fib, lie
understand, catch *v* درک کردن	دروغ گفتن *v* lie
on, comprehend, perceive,	دروغگو *adj* liar
realize; apprehend	درون *adv* inside
apprehensive *adj* درک کننده	درون مرزی *adv* inland
where *conj* درکجا	درونی *adv* internally
doorway *n* درگاه	درونی *adj* subjective
clash *v* درگیر شدن	دریا *n* river; sea
clash *n* درگیری	دریا زده *adj* seasick
therapy *n* درمان	دریاچه *n* bay
helpless *adj* درمانده	دریاچه سرپوشیده *n* cove
therapist *n* درمانگر	دریافت کردن *v* receive
publicly *adv* درمحضر عام	دریایی *adj* marine
expose *v* درمعرض قرار گرفتن	دریبل زدن *v* dribble
as *prep* درنتیجه	دریخچال گذاشتن *v* refrigerate
valley *n* دره	دریشی *n* suit
canyon *n* دره بزرگ	دریغ داشتن *v* spare
quarterly *adj* درهر سه ماه یکبار	دزد *n* burglar, robber, thief
tangle *n* درهم پیچیدن	دزد ادبی یا هنری *n* pirate
intertwine *v* درهم تنیده	دزدانه *adj* stealthy
breakdown *n* درهم شکستن	دزدکی *adj* stealthy
smash *v* درهم کوبیدن	دزدی *n* hold-up, burglary,
sloppy *adj* درهم و برهم	robbery, theft
mix-up *n* درهم و برهمی	دزدی ادبی یا هنری *n* piracy
hang around *v* درهمانجا باشید	دزدی از فروشگاه *n* shoplifting

د

دزدی کردن v burglarize, steal	دستمال n handkerchief
دزدیدن v rob; snitch	دستمال کاغذی n napkin; tissue
دژ n fort	دستمال گردن n scarf
دست n hand	دسته n lever, handle
دست آورد n accomplishment, achievement	دسته بندی n assortment
دست برداشتن v desist	دسته بندی کردن v, categorize, classify
دست به دست کردن چیزی v pass around	دستی adj manual
دست پاچگی n panic	دسمبر n December
دست پاچه شدن v overwhelm	دسیپلین n discipline
دست تکان دادن v wave	دسیسه n conspiracy
دست خط n handwriting	دشمن n enemy
دست زدن v touch	دشمنی n animosity; feud
دست ساخته adj handmade	دشوار adj difficult
دست کشیدن از v give up	دشواری n difficulty
دست کم گرفتن v underestimate	دعا n blessing
دست نشانده n puppet	دعا کردن v pray, bless; invoke
دستبند n bracelet, cuff	دعوا کردن v contend
دستبند v handcuff	دعوت کردن v invite
دستخط n script	دعوتنامه n invitation
دسترسی n access; reach	دعوی n quarrel
دسترسی داشتن v access	دعوی حقوقی n lawsuit
دستشوی n basin, sink	دعوی کردن v dispute, quarrel
دستکاری n manipulation	دعوی یی adj quarrelsome
دستکاری کردن v manipulate	دفاع n defense
دستکش n glove	دفاع خودی n self-defense
دستکول زنانه n purse	دفاع کردن v defend
دستگاه نشراتی n broadcaster	دفتر n office
دستگیر دروازه n doorknob, knob	دفتر اسناد رسمی n notary
دستگیر کردن v arrest, capture	دفتر مرکزی n headquarters
دستگیره کتاره n handrail	دفتر نماینده گی n branch office
	دفترچه یادداشت n pad

دلداری دادن v console

دلربا charming, enchanting adj

دلسرد despondent, adj disenchanted

دلسرد ساختن v discourage

دلسرد شده dejected adj

دلسرد کردن v dishearten

دلسرد کننده discouraging adj

دلسردی discouragement n

دلسوز caring, sympathetic adj

دلسوزی compassion n

دلک پا calf n

دلکش glamorous adj

دلگرم کننده encouraging adj

دلهره آور daunting adj

دلیر valiant, bold adj

دلیری boldness n

دلیل point, reason n

دموکراتیک democratic adj

دموکراسی democracy n

دنبال کردن v track

دنباله trail n

دنباله دار comet n

دنباله داشتن v trail

دندان dental adj

دندان tooth n

دندان آسیاب molar n

دندان دردی toothache n

دندان فیل ivory, tusk n

دندانها teeth n

دندانهای مصنوعی dentures n

دنده بیسبال bat n

دفتری clerical adj

دفع کردن v perspire; defray; fend; foil; repel, repulse

دفع کننده repellant n

دفع مایعات emission n

دفن کردن v bury

دقت scrutiny; precision, n accuracy

دقیق stringent; subtle; adj accurate, exact, meticulous, scrupulous

دقیقاً right, accurately, adv exactly, definitely

دقیقه minute n

دکان store n

دکشنری dictionary n

دکمه لباس button n

دکمه ماشین button n

دگرگونی variation; conversion n

دگرمن colonel n

دل ربودن v charm

دلال middleman; auctioneer n

دلالت کردن v implicate, signify

دلبدی nausea n

دلپسند delightful adj

دلتنگ lonesome adj

دلتنگ وطن homesick adj

دلچسب hearty adj

دلخراش dismal adj

دلخواه arbitrary; ideal adj

دلخواه favorite n

دلداری consolation n

universe, world n دنیا	دوبار بررسی کردن v double-check
worldly adj دنیایی	دوبار کلیک کردن v double-click
ten n ده	دوباره again adv
rural, rustic adj دهاتی	دوباره استفاده کردن v reuse
villager n دهاتی	دوباره انجام دادن v redo
gag v دهان بستن	دوباره آوردن v bring back
gag n دهان بند	دوباره بردن v take back
nozzle; crater n دهانه	دوباره پر کردن v refill, replenish
terror n دهشت	دوباره پرداختن v repay, pay back
terrorist n دهشت افگن	دوباره تادیه کردن v reimburse
terrorism n دهشت افگنی	دوباره تنظیم کردن v ;rearrange
farmer; peasant n دهقان	reorganize
corridor; lobby n دهلیز	دوباره جمع آوری کردن v recollect
tenth adj دهم	دوباره جوان کردن v rejuvenate
mouth n دهن	دوباره چاپ کردن n reprint
grimace n دهن کجی	دوباره چارج کردن v recharge
decade n دهه	دوباره خلق کردن v recreate
two n دو	دوباره دادن v give back
hesitant adj دو دل	دوباره دور دادن v turn back
waver v دو دل بودن	دوباره رفتن v go back
hesitate v دو دله بودن	دوباره روشن کردن v reboot
bilingual adj دو زبانه	دوباره زمان بندی کردن v
pair n دو شخص مرتبط بهم	reschedule
twice adv دو مرتبه	دوباره ساختن v rebuild
drugstore, pharmacy n دواخانه	دوباره شروع کردن v resume
twelve n دوازده	دوباره ظاهر شدن v reappear
twelfth adj دوازدهم	دوباره عیار کردن v reset
pharmacist n دواساز	دوباره کوچیدن v move back
last v دوام کردن	دوباره متحد شدن v reunite
everlasting adj دوامدار	دوباره نواختن n replay
penicillin n دوای پنسیلین	دوباره هموار کردن v resurface
twice adv دوبار	دوباره یکجا شدن n reunion

دوتایی double, dual *adj*	دوزخ hell *n*
دوجانبه mutually *adv*	دوزنده seamstress; sewer *n*
دوجانبه reciprocal *adj*	دوست buddy, fellow, friend, *n*
دوچند ساختن double *v*	mate
دوخت stitch; sewage *n*	دوست پسر boyfriend *n*
دوختن sewing *n*	دوست داشتنی beloved; *adj*
دوختن stitch; sew *v*	likable, lovable; lovely
دود smoke *n*	دوست داشتنی crony *n*
دودکش بخاری chimney *n*	دوست دختر girlfriend *n*
دودلی half-hearted *adj*	دوست شدن befriend *v*
دور aloof, distant *adj*	دوستانه amicable, friendly *adj*
دور off *prep*	دوستی friendship *n*
دور out, away, far *adv*	دوسیه folder *n*
دور انداختن discard, junk, *v*	دوسیه کاغذی file *n*
scrap, throw away	دوش run *n*
دور خوردن turn *v*	دوشک mattress *n*
دور دادن turn, turn over *v*	دوشیزه maiden, Miss *n*
دور زدن go around *v*	دوکان shop *n*
دور شدن go away *v*	دوکان جواهر فروشی *n*
دور کردن remove; banish *v*	jewelry store
دور مسابقه lap *n*	دوگانگی twin *n*
دور نگهداشتن keep out *v*	دولفین dolphin *n*
دور و بر around *adv*	دوم second *adj*
دوران circuit; cycle *n*	دومی second *adv*
دوران کردن cycle *v*	دونده runner *n*
دوران نوزادی infancy *n*	دونفری نواختن duet *n*
دورانی cyclical *adj*	دوهفته forthright *adj*
دوربین binoculars *n*	دویدن race, run, jog *v*
دورتر farther *adv*	دیاگرام diagram *n*
دوره یی circular *adj*	دیالوگ dialog *n*
دورویی hypocrisy *n*	دیامتر caliber, diameter *n*
دوری کردن elude *v*	دبییت کارت debit card *n*

د

دیوار کشیدن دراتاق n partition	دیپلوم diploma n
دیوار نویسی n graffiti	دیپلوم تحصیلی degree n
دیواره rim n	دیپلومات diplomat n
دیوانگی n frenzy, insanity, lunacy, madness	دیپلوماتیک diplomatic adj
دیوانه mad, crazy, lunatic adj	دیپلوماسی diplomacy n
دیوانه madman n	دیتابیس database n
دیوانه وار insane, maniac adj	دیجیتال digital adj
	دید چشم sight, eyesight, vision n
	دیداری visual adj
ذ	دیدگاه peephole; perspective n
	دیدن see, look, view v
	دیدن از مناظر sightseeing n
ذائقه savor v	دیدنی spectacular adj
ذائقه taste, flavor n	دیر tardy, late adj
ذبح کردن slaughter v	دیرباور skeptical adj
ذخیره stockpile, stock n	دیرشده belated adj
ذخیره آب reservoir n	دیروز yesterday adv
ذخیره کردن save, stock, store v	دیزل diesel n
ذخیره گاه trunk; warehouse, storage n	دیسک disc; disk n
ذغال coal n	دیسک درایف disk drive n
ذغال سنگ charcoal n	دیکتاتور dictator n
ذغال کردن char v	دیکتاتوری dictatorial adj
ذکاوت intelligence n	دیکور décor n
ذکی bright, intelligent adj	دیگ pan n
ذهن mind n	دیگدان fireplace n
ذهنی subjective; mental adj	دیگر another; else; other adj
ذهنیت mentality n	دین religion n
ذوب شدن melt v	دین دار devout adj
ذینفع beneficiary n	دینامیت dynamite n
	دینی religious adj
	دیو giant n
	دیوار wall n

راز موفقیت key n
رازداری secrecy n
راست direct adv
راست upright adj
راست شده erect adj
راست کردن straighten v
راضی satisfied, content adj
راضی ساختن satisfy v
راضی کردن consent v
راکت rocket n
راکد stagnant adj
راکد static n
راکون raccoon n
رام docile, tame adj
رام شده subdued adj
رام کردن lure; subdue, tame v
ران پا thigh n
راندن ride; drive v
رانده outcast adj
راننده driver n
راننده لاری trucker n
راننده موتر chauffeur n
راه way n
راه انداختن trigger v
راه بند block n
راه بندان jam n
راه بیرون رفت outlet, way out n
راه پیمایی march n
راه حل remedy, solution n
راه دادن yield v
راه دخول way in n
راه فرعی bypass n

ر

رُک frank adj
رُک گویی candor n
رُک و پوست کنده candid adj
رُک و راست blunt, frankly, adj
straightforward
رنج و پلاس wrench n
را the a
رابر rubber n
رابطه link n
رابطه اجتماعی تامین کردن v
socialize
رابطه بین اشیا relation n
رابطه دادن link v
رابطه عاشقانه relationship n
رابطه فامیلی relation n
رابطه نزدیک rapport n
راجع کردن refer v
راحت relaxed, comfortable; adj
placid; convenient; cuddly
راحت شدن relax v
راحت کردن ease v
راحت کننده relaxing adj
راحتی relaxation; relief, n
comfort; convenience
رادار radar n
رادار striped adj
رادیاتور radiator n
رادیو radio n
راز mystery, secret n

راه کوتاه shortcut n	رد refusal; rejection n
راه و چاره means n	رد پا track, footprint n
راهب monk n	رد کردن deny, disprove, rebut, v
راهبه nun n	rebuff, refuse, reject,
راهپیمایی procession n	repudiate, veto
راهپیمایی کردن march v	رد کردن پیشنهاد turn down v
راهرو aisle; driveway; n	رد مرز deportation n
hallway; isle	رد مرز کردن deport v
راهزن bandit n	ردپا trace n
راهکار mechanism n	رده range n
راهگذر passer-by n	ردیف queue, row n
رای poll, vote n	رزالت scoundrel n
رای دادن vote v	رزمنده fighter n
رایگان free adj	رژیم regime n
ربط relevance n	رژیم غذایی diet n
ربط داشتن concern v	رژیم غذایی گرفتن diet v
ربطی relative adj	رساله brochure, leaflet n
رتبه rank n	رساله معلوماتی pamphlet n
رتبه بندی rating n	رسامی drawing n
رتبه بندی کردن rank v	رسانه ها media n
رجوع کردن refer v	رستگاری redemption n
رحم womb n	رستوران کوچک diner n
رحم mercy n	رستورانت tavern, restaurant n
رحمت clemency, grace n	رسم کردن draw v
رحیم merciful adj	رسم کشیدن draw v
رخ دادن occur v	رسم گذشت parade n
رخصت شدن از کار log off v	رسم و رواج tradition, custom n
رخصت کردن dismiss v	رسماً formally adv
رخصتی holiday, vacation n	رسمی formal, official, adj
رخصتی هفته weekend n	solemn
رخنه breach n	رسمی ساختن officiate v
رخنه کردن penetrate v	رسمیات formality n

رقابت n competition, rivalry	رسوا notorious adj
رقابت کردن v compete	رسوایی n disgrace, scandal
رقابتی adj competitive	رسید n receipt
رقاص n dancer	رسیدگی کردن v reach; handle
رقاصه n ballerina	رسیدن v reach, arrive
رقاصی n dancing	رشته n strand
رقص n dance	رشته تحصیلی domain, field, n
رقص بلیت n ballet	major
رقصیدن v dance	رشته ورزشی n course
رقم n figure	رشد کردن v grow, mature,
رقیب challenger, competitor, n	flourish
rival	رشوه n bribe
رقیق ساختن v dilute	رشوه دادن v bribe
رکن n column	رشوه گیری n bribery
رکود adj downturn	رضاکار n volunteer
رکود v slump	رضاکاری کردن v volunteer
رگ n vein	رضایت n satisfaction; consent;
رمرور v review, look into	euphoria
رمز n code; password	رضایت بخش adj satisfying
رمزی کردن v mystify	رطوبت n humidity, moisture
رنج n suffering, agony	رعد و برق n thunder,
رنج آور adj agonizing;	thunderbolt
displeasing	رفاقت n company
رنج کشیدن v suffer	رفاه n welfare; opulence
رنجاندن v displease	رفت و آمد زیاد adj haunted
رنجش n resentment	رفت و آمد زیاد کردن v frequent
رنجیدن از v resent	رفت و برگشت کردن v commute
رنگ n color, dye, paint, ink	رفتار treat; conduct, n
رنگ ارغوانی adj purple	demeanor
رنگ آبی n blue	رفتن v depart, go
رنگ بنفش n violet	رفتنی adj volatile
رنگ پرنتر n cartridge	رفیق n pal

lurid; pale *adj* رنگ پریده
complexion *n* رنگ پوست
gray *adj* رنگ خاکستری
yellow *n* رنگ زرد
green *n* رنگ سبز
red *adj* رنگ سرخ
gold *adj* رنگ طلایی
paint, color, dye *v* رنگ کردن
beige *n* رنگ کریمی
cream *adj* رنگ کریمی
pink *n* رنگ گلابی
ring *n* رنگ مسابقه
orange *n* رنگ نارنجی
tan *n* رنگ نخودی
silver *adj* رنگ نقره یی
painter *n* رنگمال
colorful *adj* رنگه
redeem *v* رها ساختن
rid of *v* رها شدن از
leave, drop out; *v* رها کردن
release, unleash, let out;
relinquish, abandon, forsake,
let down
residential *adj* رهایشی
abandonment; *n* رهایی
salvation
let go *v* رهایی
disillusion *n* رهایی از خواب و خیال
rid *v* رهایی یافتن از
monastic *adj* رهبانی
leader *n* رهبر
conductor *n* رهبر آرکستر

leadership *n* رهبری
lead *v* رهبری کردن
mortgage *n* رهن
guide *n* رهنما
guide *v* رهنمایی کردن
usher *n* رهنمایی کردن
guidance *n* رهنمود
stoic *adj* رواقی
psychologist *n* روانشناس
psychology *n* روانشناسی
head for *v* روانه شدن
mental; psychic *adj* روانی
fox *n* روبا
robot *n* روبات
ahead *adv* روبرو
face *v* روبرو شدن
sheet, bedspread *n* روجایی
phantom; soul *n* روح
clergy *n* روحانی
spirit *n* روحیه
cheer up *v* روحیه دادن
bowel, colon, gut, *n* روده
intestine
guts *n* روده و شکمبه
day *n* روز
increasing *adj* روز افزون
tomorrow *n* روز بعد
Thursday *n* روز پنجشنبه
yesterday *n* روز پیش
birthday *n* روز تولد
Friday *n* روز جمعه
Wednesday *n* روز چهارشنبه

روز دوشنبه Monday n	روغنی oily adj
روز سه شنبه Tuesday n	روک drawer n
روز شنبه Saturday n	رول role n
روز کاری weekday n	رومانتیک romantic adj
روز مذهبی ایستر Easter n	روند trend n
روز های اوج خوشبختی heyday n	رونق boom n
روز هفته weekday adj	رونق کردن thrive v
روز یکشنبه Sunday n	رونمایی کردن unmask v
روزمره daily adv	رونویسی کردن transcribe v
روزمره routine adj	روی face n
روزنامه newspaper n	روی on prep
روزنه peephole n	روی پاک towel n
روزه گرفتن fast v	روی چیز را دور دادن flip v
روش manner, methodology n	روی چیزی دست زدن touch on v
روشن bright, vivid, light; adj	روی چیزی متمرکز ماندن stick to v
explicit; online	روی چیزی نزاع نشده باشد adj
روشن objective n	undisputed
روشن on adv	روی ذغال بریان کردن charbroil v
روشن ساختن lighten v	روی هم رفته overall adj
روشن شدن kindle v	روی هم قرار گرفتن overlap v
روشن فکر open-minded adj	رویا dream n
روشن کردن brighten, v	رویا پردازی کردن daydream v
enlighten, illuminate; light,	رویارویی encounter n
ignite, switch on, turn on	رویاندن سبزیجات vegetation n
روشنایی brightness; lighting n	رویداد event, affair, happening n
روشنایی خیره glimmer n	رویه کردن behave v
روشنایی روز daylight n	روییدن grow v
روشنفکر broadminded adj	ریاضت austerity n
روشنی beam n	ریاضی math n
روغن oil n	ریاضیات mathematics n
روغن زیتون olive oil n	ریتم rhythm n
روغن کاری lubrication n	ریختاندن spill v

ریختن v shed; spill, leak, pour	**ز**
ریزرف n reservation	
ریزرف شده adj reserved	
ریزرف کردن v book, reserve	زادگاه n hometown
ریزش n cold, flu; outpouring; spill	زاغ n crow
ریزه adj petite	زانو n knee
ریزه n shred	زانو زدن v kneel
ریزه کردن v shred	زاویه n angle
ریسمان n rope; string	زایمان n maternity
ریسمان اسب n lasso	زائد adj superfluous, redundant, extra
ریسمان برای ریسمان بازی adj jump rope	زائر n pilgrim
ریسمان سگ n leash	زباله n dump
ریسمان کشی n draw	زباله سوز n incinerator
ریش n beard	زبان n language, tongue
ریش دار adj bearded	زبان طیاره n flight attendant
ریشخند کردن v coax	زبان عامیانه n slang
ریشه n root	زحمت n trouble
ریشه کن کردن v uproot	زحمت کشیدن v toil
ریکارد ورزشی n record	زحمتکش adj hard-working
ریکشای اطفال adv stroller	زخم n wound, sore, ulcer
ریگ n sand	زخم خشک شده n scab
ریگ روان n quicksand	زخمی adj wounded, hurt, injured
ریگمال n sandpaper	زخمی کردن v traumatize; injure
ریل n station; rail; train	زدن v beat, hit, spank
ریمل مژه و ابرو n mascara	زره n armor
ریموت n remote control	زراعت n agriculture
رییس n chairman	زراعتی adj agricultural
رئیس n director; dean	زرافه n giraffe
رئیس پوهنتون n chancellor	زردآلو n apricot
رئیس جمهور n president	زردک n carrot

زردی yellow adj	زنجیر chain n
زردی تخم yolk n	زنجیرک zipper n
زرنگ shrewd; smart adj	زنجیرک را باز کردن unzip v
زشت gross, disgusting, adj	زنخ chin n
hideous; heinous; harsh;	زندان jail, prison n
awkward	زندانی prisoner n
زگنال تیلفون signal n	زندانی بودن confinement n
زگنال دادن signal v	زندانی کردن imprison, jail v
زلزله earthquake n	زندگی life n
زمان era, time n	زندگی کردن live, live off v
زمان بندی کردن schedule v	زنده alive adj
زمان سنج timer n	زنده دل lively adj
زمخت clumsy adj	زنگ bell, buzzer n
زمرد emerald n	زنگ خطر siren, alarm n
زمزمه murmur n	زنگ خطر آتش fire alarm n
زمزمه کردن hum, murmur v	زنگ دروازه doorbell n
زمستان winter n	زنگ زدگی rust n
زمین terrain, ground, land; n	زنگ زدن corrode; ring v
Earth	زنگ زدن آهن rust v
زمین شناسی geology n	زنگ زده rusty adj
زمین هموار plateau n	زهر poison, venom n
زمینی terrestrial adj	زهرآلود poisonous adj
زن woman n	زهری toxic adj
زن بیوه widow n	زهری ساختن poison v
زن تاجر businesswoman n	زهریات toxin n
زن جادوگر witch n	زوال decadence; n
زن یا دختر سبزه brunette adj	deterioration
زنان women n	زوج couple n
زنانه female; ladylike adj	زوج couple n
زنانه گی feminine adj	زود باور gullible adj
زنبور bee; wasp n	زود رس precocious adj
زنجبیل ginger n	زودشکن brittle adj

ز

زیربغل armpit n

زیرپوشی underwear n

زیرخانه basement n

زیردریایی submarine n

زیرزمینی bunker n

زیرزمینی underground adj

زیرسن underage adj

زیرک shrewd, astute, sharp; adj subtle

زیرنویس فلم subtitle n

زیست شناسی ecology n

زین اسب saddle n

زینتی ornament n

زینه ladder, stepladder; n staircase

زینه ها stairs n

ژ

ژل gel n

ژن gene n

ژنیتیکی genetic adj

ژورنال صحی journal n

ژورنالیست journalist n

زودگذر fleeting adj

زور push; strain n

زورگو bully n

زورگویی کردن bulldoze v

زورگیری کردن mugging n

زولانه handcuffs n

زیاد many adj

زیاد more pron

زیاد too; much; pretty; so; adv very

زیاد بودن abound v

زیاد طول کشیدن outlast v

زیادتر more adv

زیاده رو indulgent adj

زیادی excess n

زیادی superfluous adj

زیارت pilgrimage; shrine n

زیان evil; damage; n disadvantage

زیان آور damaging, adj detrimental

زیان رساندن damage v

زیبا picturesque, beautiful, adj nice, pretty

زیبا ساختن beautify v

زیبایی beauty n

زیبایی پسند aesthetic adj

زیتون olive n

زیر bottom n

زیر under prep

زیر و بمی صدا pitch n

زیرآب underwater adj

س

سُرب n lead

سابقه n past; precedent

ساجق n gum

ساحل n beach, coast, shore

ساحل دریا n seashore

ساحلی adj coastal

ساحه n zone, area

ساختار n structure

ساختگی n fake, sham

ساختگی adj phony

ساختمان n structure

ساختن v fabricate, forge, make, concoct; compose

ساخته دست بشر adj man-made

ساخته شده adj composed

سادگی n simplicity

ساده adj simple, plain; unassuming

ساده کردن v simplify

ساده یا غریب adj humble

ساری adj contagious

ساری n epidemic

سازگار adj conformist; consistent

سازگاری n consistency

سازمان n organization

ساس n sauce

ساسج n sausage

ساعت n hour

ساعت دستی n watch

ساعت دیواری n clock

ساعت زنگ دار n alarm clock

ساعت وار adv clockwise; hourly

ساق پا n shin

ساقه n stalk, stem

ساقه نبات n stalk

ساکت adj still

ساکت برق n socket

ساکت کردن v hush

ساکن n inhabitant, resident, occupant

ساکن adj stationary

ساکن بودن v inhabit

سال n year

سال کبیسه n leap year

سالانه adj annual

سالانه adv yearly

سالخورده adj aged

سالخورده n old age

سالسا n salsa

سالگرد n anniversary

سالم adj sane; wholesome; intact

سالون n salon, hall, lounge

سالون رقص n ballroom

سالون شهر n city hall

سالون شهری n town hall

سانتی میتر n centimeter

ساندویچ n sandwich

ساندویچ مکسیکویی n taco

سانسور n censorship

site *n* سایت انترنیتی	spring *n* سپرینگ
other *pron* سایر	then *adv* سپس
science *n* ساینس	sport *n* سپورت
scientist *n* ساینس دان	sporty *adj* سپورتی
shadow *n* سایه	star *n* ستاره
overshadow *v* سایه انداختن	astronomer *n* ستاره شناس
awning *n* سایه بان	astrology *n* ستاره شناسی
eyeshadow *n* سایه چشم	star *n* ستاره هنری
shady *adj* سایه دار	ovation; *n* ستایش
shade *n* سایه رخ	commendation, praise
pulverize; gnaw *v* ساییدن	praise *v* ستایش کردن
basket *n* سبد	satellite *n* ستلایت
green *adj* سبز	tyranny *n* ستم
green *adj* سبز و خُرم	praiseworthy *adj* ستودنی
grass *n* سبزه	pillar *n* ستون
broccoli *n* سبزی براکولی	column *n* ستون روزنامه
spinach *n* سبزی پالک	vertebra, *n* ستون فقرات
vegetarian *n* سبزی خور	backbone, spine
celery *n* سبزی کرفس	quarrelsome *adj* ستیزه جو
vegetable *n* سبزیجات	sticker *n* ستیکر
light *adj* سبک	bounty *n* سخاوت
style *n* سبک	generous *adj* سخاوتمند
lifestyle *n* سبک زندگی	generosity *n* سخاوتمندی
old-fashioned *adj* سبک قدیمی	hard, strenuous, strict; *adj* سخت
lightweight *n* سبک وزن	crusty
dandruff *n* سبوسک	hardware *n* سخت افزار کمپیوتر
gratitude *n* سپاسگزاری	harden, toughen *v* سخت کردن
shield *n* سپر	squeamish; stern *adj* سخت گیر
shield *v* سپر شدن	rigor; stern *n* سخت گیری
entrust, hand in *v* سپردن	strict, stringent *adj* سختگیر
elapse *v* سپری شدن	rigorous *adj* سختگیرانه
spend *v* سپری کردن	

سختی difficulty, hardship; *n* tenacity	سرخ شدن blush *v*
سخنرانی speech *n*	سرخکان measles *n*
سد barrier *n*	سرخوردن glide *v*
سر head *n*	سرد cool, chilly, cold *adj*
سر تپه hilltop *n*	سرد خانه mortuary *n*
سر زدن come over *v*	سرد کردن chill, cool *v*
سراپا thorough *adj*	سرد کننده radiator; cooler *n*
سراشیب upside-down *adv*	سرد کننده هوا draft *n*
سراشیبی slope; precipice *n*	سردرد migraine, headache *n*
سرانجام lastly *adv*	سردرگمی quandary *n*
سرایت کردن penetrate, *v* permeate	سردی cold, chill *n*
	سرزمین اصلی mainland *n*
سرایت مرض plague *n*	سرزنده vivacious *adj*
سرآشپز chef *n*	سرزنش کردن censure, rebuke, *v* reproach, scold
سرباز veteran *n*	
سربازی اجباری conscript *n*	سرش glue *n*
سربالایی uphill *adv*	سرش کردن glue *v*
سرپایینی downhill *adv*	سرشیب steep *adj*
سرپرست foreman *n*	سرطانی cancerous *adj*
سرپناه shelter *n*	سرعت rate, velocity, speed *n*
سرپناه دادن shelter *v*	سرعت بخشیدن accelerate *v*
سرپوش lid *n*	سرعت دهنده accelerator *n*
سرپوش بوتل cap *n*	سرعت گرفتن speed *v*
سرپوش بوتل واین plug *n*	سرفه cough *n*
سرپوشیده indoor *adj*	سرفه کردن cough *v*
سرپیچ کردن squirt *v*	سرقت larceny, heist *n*
سرپیچی کردن defy *v*	سرک road, street *n*
سرچپه upside-down *adv*	سرک فرعی lane *n*
سرچشمه گرفتن originate *v*	سرک ناهموار ragged *adj*
سرحال livid *adj*	سرکس circus *n*
سرخ red *n*	سرکشی defiance *n*
	سرکه vinegar *n*

س

سركه سيب cider n	سروكار داشتن با چيزى يا شخصى v deal
سركوب كردن v repress, suppress	سروى survey n
سرگردان stranded adj	سروى كردن survey v
سرگردان vagrant n	سرويس هاى برقى tram n
سرگردان بودن wander v	سريال تلويزيونى series n
سرگرم ساختن entertain v	سريع swift, quick, rapid, adj prompt, speedy; agile
سرگرم كردن amuse v	سريع السير express adj
سرگرم كننده amusing, adj entertaining, fun	سزاوار deserving adj
سرگرمى pastime, amusement, n entertainment, hobby	سزاوار بودن deserve v
سرگين dung n	سست frail; slack; sleazy adj
سرمازدگى frostbite n	سست كردن slacken v
سرمايه capital n	سستى frailty n
سرمايه دار tycoon n	سطح surface n
سرمايه گذار investor n	سطح شيب دار ramp n
سرمايه گذارى investment n	سطحى superficial adj
سرمايه گذارى كردن finance, v invest	سطل bucket, pail n
سرمعلم principal n	سطل كثافات garbage can, n wastebasket
سرمقاله editorial n	سعادت prosperity; bliss n
سرمه يى navy blue n	سعادتمند well-to-do adj
سرميزى tablecloth n	سفارت embassy n
سرنج پيچكارى syringe n	سفارش پُستى mail order n
سرنخ clue n	سفارش كردن recommend v
سرنگون شدن plummet; topple v	سفارشنامه recommendation n
سرنوشت destiny, fate n	سفارشى ساخته شده adj custom-made
سرنوشت ساز fateful adj	سفت tense, firm, stiff, sturdy adj
سرود hymn n	سفت tight adv
سروصدا clamor; cuss v	سفت شدن curdle v
سروصدا clash, noise; fuss n	سفت يا محكم كردن stiffen v
سروصدا كردن fuss v	

سفتی stiffness n	سگ کوچک puppy n
سفتی عضلات stretch n	سگرت cigarette n
سفر expedition, journey, trip n	سگرت کشیدن smoke v
سفر دریایی کردن voyage n	سلاته salsa n
سفر دوطرفه round-trip adj	سلاد salad n
سفر زمینی drive n	سلام hello, hi e
سفر زندگی odyssey n	سلامت عقل sanity n
سفر کردن travel, trip v	سلب صلاحیت کردن disqualify v
سفید white adj	سلحشور gladiator n
سفید کردن bleach, whiten v	سلسله sequence, series; n
سفید کننده bleach n	dynasty
سفیدی white n	سلسله کوه ها range n
سفیدی تخم egg white n	سلسله مراتب hierarchy n
سفیر ambassador n	سلطنت reign n
سقط کردن abort v	سلطنت کردن reign v
سقف اتاق ceiling n	سلطنتی regal adj
سقوط fall; downfall; drop n	سلطه sovereignty n
سقوط slump v	سلطه گر domineering adj
سقوط کردن collapse; v	سلف predecessor n
fall through	سلمان barber, hairdresser n
سکته stroke n	سلندر cylinder n
سکتور sector n	سلول زندان cell n
سکرتر secretary n	سمارق mushroom n
سکه change, coin n	سمبول symbol n
سکه ۲۵ سنتی quarter n	سمبولیک symbolic adj
سکه ۵ سنتی nickel n	سمبولیک ساختن symbolize v
سکه ده سنتی dime n	سمستر semester n
سکوت silence n	سمنت cement n
سکونت اختیار کردن dwell v	سن age n
سکونت داشتن reside v	سنا senate n
سگ dog n	سناتور senator n
سگ آبی beaver n	سناریو scenario n

سنتی traditional *adj*	سهم گرفتن *v* contribute
سنجاق *n* pin	سهم گیرنده *n* contributor
سنجاق کردن *v* pin	سهمگیری, *n* participation,
سنجش *n* measurement	involvement
سنجیدن *v* measure, rate,	سهمیه *n* quota
calibrate; deliberate	سهولت *n* ease
سنجیده *adj* deliberate	سوء استفاده *n* misuse
سنجیده حرف زدن *v* articulate	سوء استفاده کردن *v* abuse
سند *n* document	سوء تغذی *n* malnutrition
سندان *n* anvil	سوء تفاهم شدن *v* misunderstand
سنگ *n* stone, rock	سوء هاضمه *n* indigestion
سنگ پشت *n* tortoise, turtle	سوابق *n* background
سنگ ریزه *n* gravel	سوابق تحصیلی و کاری *n*
سنگ سرامیک *n* ceramic	qualification
سنگ قبر *n* gravestone	سوار بر *adv* aboard
سنگ مرمر *n* marble	سوار بر دیسک *n* (DJ) disc jockey
سنگ معدنی *n* ore	سوار شدن *v* ride; board, mount
سنگ مقبره *n* tombstone	سواری *n* ride
سنگ نوشته *n* inscription	سوال *v* query
سنگر *n* trench	سوال *n* question
سنگریزه *n* pebble	سوال برانگیز *adj* questionable
سنگی *adj* rocky	سوال کردن *v* question
سنگین *adj* grave; cumbersome, heavy	سوپ *n* soup
سنگین تر بودن از *v* outweigh	سوختگی *n* burn
سنگینی *n* heaviness	سوختن *v* burn
سه *n* three	سود *n* interest
سه پایه *n* tripod	سودمند *adj* beneficial, conducive; instrumental
سه ضلعی *n* triangle	سوراخ *n* burrow; hole, leak, puncture; leakage; piercing
سه گانه *adj* triple	
سهل *n* facility	سوراخ بینی *n* nostril
سهم *n* quota	سوراخ حیوانات *n* den

سوراخ دکمه buttonhole n	سیاه آب swamp n
سوراخ کردن، punch; perforate, v pierce	سیاه چاه dungeon n
سوراخ های روی صورت pore n	سیاهی black adj
سوزاندن char, scorch, scald; v cremate	سیاهی grime n
سوزن needle n	سیب apple n
سوزن سوزن شدن tingle v	سیت set n
سوغات souvenir n	سیر garlic n
سوق دادن propel v	سیر تکامل evolution n
سوگند pledge, oath n	سیر علمی field trip n
سوگند کردن pledge v	سیر کردن roam v
سوگند یاد کردن swear v	سیر نشدنی insatiable adj
سوگواری کردن mourn v	سیزده thirteen n
سوم third adj	سیستم system n
سوهان کردن ناخن file v	سیستم تنفسی ماهی gill n
سوهان ناخن file n	سیستم ثبت ارقام database n
سویچ switch n	سیستم ثبت فروشات register n
سی thirty n	سیستم گرم کننده heating n
سیاح tourist n	سیستماتیک systematic adj
سیاحت tourism; tour n	سیف safe n
سیاحت کردن explore v	سیگار pipe; cigar n
سیار mobile adj	سیل بردن flood v
سیاره planet n	سیلاب flood n
سیاره اورانوس Uranus n	سیلی زدن slap v
سیاره زحل Saturn n	سیم wire n
سیاره عطارد Mercury n	سیم پیچ را باز کردن unwind v
سیاره مشتری Jupiter n	سیمفونی symphony n
سیاره نپتون Neptune n	سینت penny, cent n
سیاستمدار politician n	سینما cinema n
سیاسی political adj	سینه بند bra n
سیاه black n	

س

ش

شُپ کردن v sip	شاهدخت n princess
شُش n lung	شاهراه n freeway, highway
شُل adj sleazy	شاهکار n feat; masterpiece
شاخ n horn	شاهی n kingdom; monarchy
شاخ n horn	شاهی adj royal
شاخک n tentacle	شاهین n hawk
شاخه درخت n branch	شاور n shower
شاخه کوچک n twig	شاید adv probably, maybe, perhaps
شاد adj merry, festive	شایستگی n competence
شاداب adj succulent; lush	شایسته adj competent
شادی n monkey	شایع adj rampant, widespread
شادی کردن v rejoice; revel	شایعه n rumor, hearsay
شاعر n poet	شایعه پراکنی n gossip
شاعری n poetry	شایعه پراکنی کردن v gossip
شاکی n plaintiff	شب n night
شاگرد n pupil, disciple, student	شب بخیر e good night
شاگرد کار آموز n apprentice	شب پرک n butterfly
شام n evening	شب پرک چرمی n bat
شامپو n shampoo	شب زنده داری n vigil
شامل بودن v comprise; entail	شب عید n eve
شامل ساختن v include	شب گذشته adv last night
شانزده n sixteen	شب هنگام n nighttime
شانه n comb; shoulder	شب هنگام adv overnight
شانه بالا انداختن v shrug	شبانه adj nightly; nocturnal
شانه کردن v comb	شباهت n likeness, resemblance, similarity
شاه بلوط n chestnut	شباهت داشتن v resemble
شاهانه adj royal	شبکه n mesh, network
شاهد n witness	شبکه اجتماعی n social network
شاهد عینی n eyewitness	شبنم n dew
	شبه جزیره n peninsula

شبیه similar adj	شدید grim, stark; chronic; adj
شبیه ساختن simulate v	rigorous, strenuous; acute,
شپش lice, louse n	drastic, intense, severe
شپشی lousy adj	شدید ساختن intensify v
شپلاق whistle n	شدیداً badly adv
شپلاق کردن whistle v	شراب wine n
شپلیدن squeeze v	شراب ساختن distill v
شتاب haste; velocity n	شراکت partnership n
شتاب hustle v	شرایط circumstance, terms n
شتاب زده hasty adj	شربت syrup n
شتاب کردن hasten v	شرح gloss; description; n
شتر camel n	discretion
شترمرغ ostrich n	شرح با تصویر illustration n
شجاع valiant, brave, adj	شرح دادن describe v
courageous, gallant	شرشره cascade n
شجاعانه daring adj	شرط requirement; bet n
شجاعت bravery, courage n	شرط بستن bet v
شخص one; person n	شرق east n
شخص اجتماعی folksy adj	شرقاً east adv
شخص بیرونی outsider n	شرقی east, eastern adj
شخص پیاده pedestrian n	شرکت enterprise, company, n
شخص خارجی foreigner n	firm
شخص زنده live adj	شرکت سهامی corporation n
شخص سرگرم کننده entertainer n	شرکت کننده participle n
شخص کم دل wimp n	شرکت هوانوردی airline n
شخص محترم gentleman n	شرم shame n
شخصی own, personal, adj	شرم آور bashful adj
private	شرمنده shameful; ashamed adj
شخصیت character, personality n	شرمنده ساختن shame v
شدت intensity n	شرمنده شدن blush v
شدن become v	شروع start, kick off n
شدنی workable, feasible adj	شروع به کار کرده set out v

ش

شروع کردن launch, begin, v	شغل آزاد self-employed n
embark, start	شفا یافتن heal v
شریان artery n	شفاخانه hospital n
شریر villain n	شفاف clear, transparent; lucid adj
شریر wicked adj	شفاف crystal n
شریف noble adj	شفاهی oral, verbal adj
شریک accomplice; partner n	شفایاب convalescent adj
شریک تجارت shareholder n	شفایافتن recover v
شریک ساختن share v	شفت کاری shift n
شریک شدن pool v	شفتالو peach n
شریم shrimp n	شفقت clemency, mercy n
شست انگشت thumb n	شقیقه temple; sideburns n
شستشو کردن flush v	شک suspicion, doubt n
شستشوی مغزی brainwash v	شک داشتن reservation n
شستن wash v	شک کردن doubt, suspect v
شش six n	شکار prey; hunting n
ششم sixth adj	شکار کردن hunt v
شصت sixty n	شکارچی hunter n
شطرنج chess n	شکاف seam; slash; slot, n
شعار motto, slogan n	crevice, slit, split
شعار دادن chant n	شکاف باریک crack n
شعاع radius; ray n	شکاف بزرگ chasm n
شعبده باز juggler n	شکاف کردن slash, slit v
شعبده بازی کردن juggle v	شکافتن split v
شعبه unit, department; ward n	شکایت complaint, grievance n
شعر verse, poem n	شکایت کردن complain v
شعر ترانه lyrics n	شکر sugar n
شعله آتش flame n	شکرگذار grateful, thankful adj
شعله ور شدن flare n	شکست setback n
شعله ور شدن flare up v	شکست دادن defeat v
شعور consciousness n	شکست ناپذیر invincible, adj
شغل career, occupation n	unbeatable

ش

شکستگی wreckage; fracture n	شمشیر sword n
شکستگی در کشتی shipwreck n	شمع candle n
شکستن snap, break v	شمعدانی candlestick n
شکستنی breakable adj	شنا swimming n
شکسته broken adj	شناخته شده well-known adj
شکل form, figure, shape n	شناسایی کردن identify v
شکل دادن model, shape v	شناور afloat adv
شکم belly, tummy n	شناور swimmer; buoy n
شکنجه torment v	شناورشدن float v
شکنجه torture n	شنونده listener n
شکنجه کردن torture v	شنیداری audio adj
شکننده؛ frail, fragile; adj	شنیدن hear v
shattering	شنیدنی audible adj
شکوه glory, splendor n	شنیع heinous adj
شگفت انگیز prodigious, adj	شهاب آسمانی asteroid n
stupendous	شهاب سنگ meteor n
شگفت آور fabulous adj	شهادت testimony n
شگوفه blossom v	شهادت دادن testify v
شگوفه کردن bloom v	شهادت دروغ perjury n
شگون omen n	شهامت dare n
شل کردن loosen v	شهر city, town n
شلاق lash, whip n	شهرت fame n
شلاق زدن lash, whip; lash out v	شهردار mayor n
شما you pron	شهروند ارشد senior citizen n
شمار محدود handful n	شهری urban adj
شمارش count n	شهزاده prince n
شمارش مجدد recount n	شهوت lust n
شمارش معکوس countdown n	شهوتی lustful adj
شمال wind; north n	شواهد evidence n
شمال شرق northeast n	شوخ playful, witty; brat; adj
شمالی north, northern adj	naughty
شمردن count v	شوخ طبع humorous adj

ش

humor *n* شوخ طبعی
joke, prank; fun *n* شوخی
hoax *n* شوخی فریب آمیز
joke, kid *v* شوخی کردن
salty *adj* شور
shake; stir *v* شور دادن
council *n* شورا
mob, gang, cluster; *n* شورش
uprising, rebellion, riot
revolt *v* شورش
rebel, riot *v* شورش کردن
rebel *n* شورشی
revolting *adj* شورشی
rebel *v* شوریدن
zest *n* شور و شور
enthusiasm *n* شوق و علاقه
ominous *adj* شوم
husband *n* شوهر
item, object, thing; good; *n* شی
substance
slope *n* شیب
slanted, inclined *adj* شیب دار
lion; milk *n* شیر
nursery *n* شیرخوارگاه
tap, faucet *n* شیردهن نل
sap *n* شیره
milky *adj* شیری
sweet *adj* شیرین
lollipop *n* شیرین چوشک
sweeten *v* شیرین ساختن
deli; dessert, candy *n* شیرینی
pastry, sweets *n* شیرینی باب

glass *n* شیشه
windshield *n* شیشه پیشروی موتر
mischief *n* شیطنت
mischievous *adj* شیطنت آمیز
charm *v* شیفته کردن
stylish *adj* شیک
posh *adj* شیک و عصری
outbreak *n* شیوع
break out *v* شیوع کردن
style *n* شیوه
tactic *n* شیوه جنگ

ص

soap *n* صابون
landlord *n* صاحب خانه
export; issue *v* صادر کردن
exporter *n* صادر کننده
straight, honest *adj* صادق
glossy *adj* صاف
clear *v* صاف کردن
strainer *n* صاف کننده
strainer *n* صافی
morning *n* صبح
breakfast *n* صبحانه
brunch *n* صبحانه دیر
hang on, hold up *v* صبر کن
talk *n* صحبت
chat, talk *v* صحبت کردن
monologue *n* صحبت یکنفری

صحت health n	صرفاً merely adv
صحتمند healthy adj	صرفه جو thrifty adj
صحرا desert n	صرفه جویی frugal adj
صحن حویلی courtyard n	صرفه جویی providence n
صحن مزرعه farmyard n	صریح unequivocal, adj
صحن مکتب یا پوهنتون campus n	clear-cut, outspoken
صحنه scene n	صعود ascend v
صخره cliff n	صغیر minor n
صد hundred n	صف range; queue n
صدا beep v	صفاکار cleaner n
صدا sound, tone, voice; n	صفایی cleanliness n
racket	صفت adjective n
صدا دادن sound v	صفحه page n
صدا در گوش ring n	صفحه انترنیتی website n
صدا کردن call v	صفحه شماره ها dial n
صدا کردن زاغ crow v	صفحه گسترده در کمپیوتر n
صداقت honesty n	spreadsheet
صدای بم bass n	صفر zero n
صدای تیلفون dial tone n	صفرا bile n
صدای چسپیدن cling v	صفینه spaceship n
صدای زنگ تیلفون ringtone n	صلاحیت authority n
صدای زیر یا باریک tenor n	صلح peace n
صدای مرغابی کشیدن quack v	صلح آمیز peaceful adj
صدف shellfish n	صلیب cross n
صدف خوراکی oyster n	صلیب دوگانه double-cross v
صدف دریایی seashell n	صلیبی cross adj
صدم hundredth adj	صمیمی amicable, cordial, adj
صدمه رساندن hurt v	wholehearted; intimate, near
صراف cashier n	صمیمیت intimacy n
صرف only adv	صنایع دستی craft n
صرف mere; sole adj	صندوق box n
صرف نظر کردن renounce v	صندوق پُستی mailbox n

ص

ضخیم ساختن v thicken
ضد n opposite
ضد آب adj waterproof
ضد آتش adj fireproof
ضد زنگ زدگی adj rust-proof
ضد زهر n antidote
ضد صدا adj soundproof
ضد عفونی کردن v disinfect
ضدمرمی adj bulletproof
ضرب prep times
ضرب الاجل n deadline
ضرب کردن v multiply
ضرب و شتم n mayhem
ضربان n beating
ضربان v throb
ضربان قلب n heartbeat
ضربه n, stroke, blow, flap, knock, pat
ضربه آهسته n tap
ضربه زدن v jab
ضربه مغزی n concussion
ضرر n harm
ضرر رساندن v harm
ضرورت n, urgency, necessity, need
ضرورت داشتن v need
ضروری adj, indispensable, essential, necessary
ضریب n quotient
ضعف n weakness
ضعف کردن v faint

صندوق چوبی crate n
صندوق دریافت پیام inbox n
صندوق ذخیره گاه chest n
صندوق سینه chest n
صندوق مصوون برای پول safe n
صندوق یخ icebox n
صندوقچه bin n
صندوقچه جواهرات casket n
صنعت industry n
صنعتگر craftsman n
صنف class n
صنف اول first class adj
صنف درسی class n
صوتی vocal; acoustic adj
صورت face n
صورت حساب invoice, tab n
صیقل polish n
صیقل کردن polish v

ض

ضُعف کردن v pass out
ضامن n sponsor
ضایع شدن v spoil
ضایع کردن v waste
ضایعات n waste
ضبط کردن v confiscate; forfeit
ضبط کردن v tape
ضخامت n thickness
ضخیم adj thick

ص

ضعیف powerless, faint, *adj* feeble, meager, weak; slack	طبیعی natural, organic *adj*
ضعیف underdog *n*	طراح designer *n*
ضعیف کردن slacken, weaken *v*	طراوت refreshment *n*
ضعیفی weakness *n*	طراوت بخش refreshing *adj*
ضمانت bail; warranty *n*	طرح plan, concept, scheme, *n* layout, outline, blueprint, design, sketch, plot; pattern; platform
ضمانت کردن sponsor; warrant *v*	
ضمنی implicit *adj*	
ضمیر در گرامر pronoun *n*	طرح بندی layout *n*
ضمیمه attachment; enclosure *n*	طرح ساختمان floor *n*
ضمیمه شده attached *adj*	طرح قانون legislate *v*
ضمیمه کردن attach; enclose *v*	طرح کردن design, scheme, *v* plan, outline, sketch, project
ضمیمه نشده unattached *adj*	
ضیافت banquet *n*	طرز برخورد attitude *n*
ضیق tight *adj*	طرز تفکر ideology *n*
	طرزالعمل procedure *n*
	طرزالعمل ها guidelines *n*
ط	طرف side *n*
	طرف چپ left *adv*
	طرف راست right *adj*
طاعون pest; plague *n*	طرف راست right *n*
طاقت last *n*	طرف مخالف opposition *n*
طاقت فرسا grueling; *adj* overbearing	طریقه way *n*
طاقچه ledge; rack, shelf *n*	طعمه prey, bait *n*
طالع بین astrologer *n*	طعنه irony, sarcasm, satire *n*
طاووس peacock *n*	طعنه آمیز ironic, sarcastic *adj*
طبقه class, caste *n*	طغیان کردن overflow *v*
طبقه پایین downstairs *adv*	طفل baby, child, kid *n*
طبی medical *adj*	طفلانه childish *adj*
طبیعت nature *n*	طفولیت childhood *n*
طبیعتاً naturally *adv*	طلا gold *n*
	طلاق divorce *n*

ظرف n tank, container, pot; dish	طلاق دادن v divorce
ظرفیت n capacity	طلای سفید n platinum
ظروف n utensil	طلایی n blonde
ظروف چینی n porcelain	طلایی adj golden
ظروف نقره یی n silverware	طلسم n charm; mascot
ظریف adj susceptible; tender, delicate; elegant	طلوع آفتاب n sunrise
ظلم n cruelty; oppression	طناب n cord
ظلم کردن v oppress	طوطی n parrot
ظهور کردن v emerge	طول n span, length
	طولانی adv long
	طولانی کردن v lengthen; prolong
	طویل adj lengthy
ع	طویله n barn
	طی کردن v go through
عابر n pedestrian	طی مراحل اداری n paperwork
عاجز adj shy	طی مراحل کردن v process
عاجل n emergency	طیاره n aircraft, airplane, plane
عاجل adj pressing, urgent	طیاره جیت n jet
عادت n habit	
عادت داشتن idiom used to	
عادت کردن v acclimatize, accustom	**ظ**
عادتی adj habitual	
عادلانه adj fair, just; transparent	
عادلانه n right	ظالم adj ruthless, cruel
عادی adj regular, normal, ordinary	ظالم n tyrant; leech
عازم شدن v set off	ظاهر n appearance; outside
عاشق n lover	ظاهر شدن v appear
عاشقانه n romance	ظاهراً adv allegedly, apparently
	ظاهراً ساده adj simple
	ظاهری adj superficial; pretentious
	ظرافت n delicacy, elegance; nuance

عجیب bizarre, strange; adj extravagant	عاشقانه romantic adj
	عاطفه affection n
عجیب و جالب quaint adj	عاطفی emotional adj
عجیب و غریب creepy; exotic, adj peculiar, weird	عاق کردن disown v
	عاقبت consequence n
عجیب و غریب oddity n	عاقل sane, wise adj
عدالت fairness, justice n	عالم یهودی rabbi n
عدد figure, digit, number n	عالی exquisite, incredible, adj splendid, sublime, supreme, awesome, excellent, fantastic, super, wonderful
عدد تاق odd adj	
عدد جفت even adj	
عدس lentil n	
عدل bale n	عام substandard adj
عدم امکان impossibility n	عام فهم simple adj
عدم بلوغ immaturity n	عامل factor n
عدم تایید disapproval n	عامه public adj
عدم تحمل intolerance n	عاید earnings, income, n proceeds, revenue
عدم تطابق incompatibility n	
عدم توازن imbalance n	عایق کاری insulation n
عدم فعالیت malfunction n	عایق کاری کردن insulate v
عدم مساوات inequality n	عبادت meditation n
عدم مصوونیت insecurity n	عبادت کردن meditate; worship v
عذاب suffering, doom; hassle n	عبادتگاه یهود synagogue n
عذاب torment v	عبارت phrase n
عذاب آور excruciating adj	عبور passage, crossing; n transition
عذاب دادن hassle v	
عذاب کشیدن agonize v	عبور از cross out v
عذرخواهی pardon n	عبور کردن pass; cross v
عربی Arabic adj	عبوری transit n
عرصه sphere, arena; aspect n	عبوس sullen adj
عرض latitude; width n	عتیقه antique n
عرفانی mystic adj	عجله haste, hurry n
عرق sweat n	عجله کردن hurry, rush v

ع

sweaty *adj* عرق آلود	modern *adj* عصرى
perspiration *n* عرق بدن	modernize *v* عصرى ساختن
perspire, sweat *v* عرق کردن	supper *n* عصریه
bride; daughter-in-law *n* عروس	muscle *n* عضله
jellyfish *n* عروس دریایی	member *n* عضو
wedding *n* عروسی	organ; limb *n* عضو بدن
married *adj* عروسی شده	stoic *adj* عضو مکتب رواق
marry, wed *v* عروسی کردن	membership *n* عضویت
unmarried *adj* عروسی نشده	cologne, perfume, scent *n* عطر
wide *adj* عریض	sneeze *n* عطسه
petition *n* عریضه	sneeze *v* عطسه زدن
mourning *n* عزادارى	majesty *n* عظمت
dignity *n* عزت	enormous, giant, *adj* عظیم
dignify *v* عزت بخشیدن	massive, tremendous
resolution *n* عزم	colossal *adj* عظیم الجثه
determination *n* عزم و اراده	infection *n* عفونت
close, dear *adj* عزیز	infectious *adj* عفونی
sweetheart *n* عزیز	infected *adj* عفونی شده
departure *n* عزیمت	eagle *n* عقاب
troops *n* عساكر	back *n* عقب
soldier *n* عسکر	back *adv* عقب
veteran *n* عسکر سابق	fall back *v* عقب افتادن
honey *n* عسل	back out *v* عقب برآمدن
love *v* عشق ورزیدن	setback *n* عقب گرد
staff *n* عصا چوب	fall behind, get *v* عقب ماندن
sap; extract *n* عصاره	behind
nerve *n* عصب	backward *adj* عقب مانده
mad, frantic *adj* عصبانی	hold-up, hindrance *n* عقب مانی
madden *v* عصبانی کردن	back away *v* عقب نشینی
anger *n* عصبانیت	recess *n* عقب نشینی
nervous *adj* عصبی	withdraw, *v* عقب نشینی کردن
era *n* عصر	back down, recede, retract

ع

withdrawn *adj* عقب نشینی کرده	علامه اپاستراف *n* apostrophe
back, rear *adj* عقبی	علامه تقسیم *v* divide
obsession *n* عقده روحی	علامه جمع *prep* plus
obsess *v* عقده کردن	علامه ستاره *n* asterisk
wisdom *n* عقل	علامه کامه *n* comma
common sense *n* عقل سلیم	علامه گذاشتن *v* brand
rational *adj* عقلانی	علامه ندائیه *n* exclamation
belief *n* عقیده	علامه نقطه *n* period
barren, sterile *adj* عقیم	علاوتاً *adv* furthermore
sterilize *v* عقیم کردن	علاوه بر *prep* besides
photographer *n* عکاس	علاوه براین *adv* moreover
photography *n* عکاسی	علت *n* cause
photograph *v* عکس	علف هرزه *n* weed
reaction *n* عکس العمل	علف هرزه را چیدن *v* weed
react *v* عکس العمل کردن	meadow *n* علفزار
X-ray *n* عکس برقی	science *n* علم
snapshot *n* عکس فوری	economics *n* علم اقتصاد
shot *n* عکس یا فلم	politics *n* علم سیاست
hiccup *n* عکک زدن	astronomy *n* علم نجوم
remedy *n* علاج	academic; scientific *adj* علمی
enthusiastic, fond, *adj* علاقمند interested	put away *v* علیحده کردن
interest *v* علاقمند ساختن	against *prep* علیه
interest, fondness, *n* علاقمندی passion	mansion *n* عمارت بزرگ
emblem *n* علامت	purposely *adv* عمداً
exclamation *n* علامت تعجب	chiefly, mainly *adv* عمدتاً
checkmark *n* علامت صحه	principal, chief, main, *adj* عمده major
mark down *v* علامت گذاری کردن	staple *n* عمده
minus *n* علامت منفی	intentional *adj* عمدی
marker, symbol, mark, *n* علامه sign, symptom	lifetime *adj* عمر
	short-lived *adj* عمر کوتاه
	depth *n* عمق

ع

عمل practice; act n

عمل متقابل interaction n

عمل متقابل کردن counteract v

عمل یا کردار deed n

عملکرد بهتر outperform v

عمله طیاره crew n

عملی practical adj

عملی کردن wield v

عملیات operation n

عملیات جراحی surgery n

عملیات کردن operate v

عملیه تقسیم در ریاضی division n

عملیه ضرب multiplication n

عمه aunt n

عمودی erect, vertical adj

عموماً generally adv

عمومی substandard; general adj

عمومی ساختن generalize v

عمیق abysmal, deep, adj
profound

عمیق کردن deepen v

عمیقاً deeply adv

عنصر element n

عنعنه tradition n

عنعنوی traditional adj

عنکبوت spider n

عنوان heading n

عهد treaty n

عوارض جانبی side effect n

عواقب fallout n

عوض replacement n

عوض کردن swap, replace v

عوضی spare adj

عوعو کردن bark v

عیادت visit n

عیادت کردن visit v

عیار کردن program, adjust, v
customize, set

عیب flaw, blemish, defect n

عیبی defective adj

عیبی ساختن defect v

عینک eyeglasses, glasses n

عینک آببازی goggles n

عینک آفتابی sunglasses n

عینک زانو kneecap n

عینک فروشی optician n

غ

غده tumor n

غر زدن growl; mumble v

غرش roar n

غرش rumble v

غرغر کردن grumble; grunt v

غریدن rave; roar v

غار cave, cavern n

غارت loot n

غارت pillage v

غارت کردن loot, plunder, v
ransack

غافل ignorant adj

غالب dominant adj

غالب شدن v overcome	غصب کردن v seize
غایب adj absent	غصه خوردن v grieve
غبار n haze, fog, mist	غضب n wrath
غبار آلود adj hazy, misty	غفلت n ignorance; neglect
غبارآلود adj foggy	غفلت شده adj neglected
غذا n diet, food, meal	غفلت کار adj delinquent
غذا تهیه کردن v cater	غفلت کردن v neglect
غذا خوردن v dine	غلام n slave
غذای اصلی n entree	غلامی n slavery
غذای آماده n fast food	غلبه n domination
غذای بحری n seafood	غلبه کردن v, dominate,
غذای عصرانه n supper	overpower
غذای متنوع n cuisine	غلط v misconstrue
غرامت n dues	غلط adj phony, erroneous, false,
غرب n west	wrong
غرباً adv west	غلط تفسیر کردن v misinterpret
غربال کردن v sift	غلط محاسبه کردن v miscalculate
غربی adj west, western	غلط هجا کردن v misspell
غرغره کردن v guzzle	غلظت n density
غرفه n stall, booth	غله n grain
غرفه بزرگ n grandstand	غلیظ adj dense
غرفه فروش اخبار n newsstand	غلیظ ساختن v condense
غرق شدن v capsize, drown,	غم n sorrow
dunk, inundate, sink	غم انگیز adj bleak, ghastly, gory,
غرق شدن n deluge	tragic
غرق شده adj sunken	غم و اندوه n anguish, gloom
غروب n dawn; dusk	غمشریکی n empathy
غروب آفتاب n sundown, sunset	غمگین adj unhappy, gloomy,
غرور n arrogance, vanity	sad, somber
غریب adj poor	غمگین کردن v sadden
غریبانه adv poorly	غمگینی n sadness
غریزه n instinct	غنی adj rich

ع

غنى ساختن enrich v	غيرقابل تحمل intolerable, adj unbearable
غنيمت spoils n	غيرقابل تصور unthinkable adj
غوطه خوردن plunge v	غيرقابل تقسيم indivisible adj
غوطه كردن immerse v	غيرقابل توضيح inexplicable adj
غوطه ور شدن duck; submerge v	غيرقابل خواندن illegible adj
غوطه ورى immersion n	غيرقابل دسترس inaccessible adj
غوغا turmoil adj	غيرقابل ديد invisible adj
غوغا uproar, tumult n	غيرقابل علاج incurable adj
غول پيكر gigantic adj	غيرقابل كنترول uncontrollable adj
غيابت absence n	غيرقابل لمس untouchable adj
غير محبوب unpopular adj	غيرقابل محاسبه incalculable adj
غير محتمل improbable adj	غيرقابل مقاومت irresistible adj
غيراخلاقى immoral adj	غيرقانونى unlawful, illegal adj
غيرانسانى inhuman adj	غيركافى inadequate adj
غيرت zeal n	غيرمترقبه unexpected
غيرتمند zealous adj	غيرمتعارف unconventional adj
غيررسمى informal, unofficial adj	غيرمحتمل unlikely adj
غيرشخصى impersonal adj	غيرمستقيم indirect adj
غيرصحى unhealthy adj	غيرمسلكى unprofessional adj
غيرصميمى insincere; adj unfriendly	غيرمسوول irresponsible adj
غيرضرورى unnecessary adj	غيرمصمم undecided adj
غير عادلانه unfair adj	غيرمصوون insecure; unsafe adj
غير عادى abnormal, eccentric adj	غيرمعمول odd, uncommon, adj unusual
غيرعملى impractical adj	غيرممكن impossible adj
غيرفعال passive; inactive adj	غيرمنطقى unreasonable, adj illogical, irrational
غيرقابل اشتباه unmistakable adj	غيرمنظم irregular adj
غيرقابل اعتماد unreliable adj	غيرموثر ineffective adj
غيرقابل بخشش inexcusable adj	غيرواقعى unreal adj
غيرقابل پيشبينى unforeseen, adj unpredictable	
غيرقابل تجزيه inseparable adj	

غ

ف

factory *n* فابریکه
mill *n* فابریکه کاغذ
conqueror *n* فاتح
victorious *adj* فاتح
catastrophe, disaster *n* فاجعه
disastrous *adj* فاجعه بار
yawn *v* فاجه کشیدن
graduate *v* فارغ شدن
ranch *n* فارم بزرگ
dairy farm *n* فارم لبنیات
farming *n* فارمداری
putrid; degenerate *adj* فاسد
worst *n* فاسد
degenerate *v* فاسد شدن
perishable *adj* فاسد شدنی
corrupt *v* فاسد کردن
distance *n* فاصله
mileage *n* فاصله پیموده شده
long-distance *adj* فاصله دور
green bean *n* فاصلیه
refuse *n* فاضله
unqualified *adj* فاقد شرایط لازم
omen *n* فال
family *n* فامیل
mortal *adj* فانی
fiber *n* فایبر
benefit *v* فایده کردن
file *n* فایل کمپیوتر
football *n* فتبال

conquer *v* فتح کردن
intrigue *n* فتنه
federation *n* فدراسیون
federal *adj* فدرال
beyond *adv* فراتر
transcend, overstep *v* فراتر رفتن
roomy; loose *adj* فراخ
loose *v* فراخ کردن
call *n* فراخوان
summon *v* فراخواندن
runway *n* فرار
elude, escape, flee, *v* فرار کردن
run away, get away
evade *v* فراربخاطر نجات
scare away *v* فراردادن
castaway; fugitive *n* فراری
parachute *n* فراشوت
graduation *n* فراغت
forget *v* فراموش کردن
unforgettable *adj* فراموش نشدنی
forgetful *adj* فراموشکار
amnesia *n* فراموشی
supplier *n* فراهم کننده
procure *v* فراهم نمودن
plentiful *adj* فراوان
abundance, plenty *n* فراوانی
individual *n* فرد
suspect *n* فرد مشکوک
tomorrow *adv* فردا
erosion *n* فرسایش
send; ship *v* فرستادن
sender *n* فرستنده

erode v فرسودن	plunge v فرورفتن
rotten; decrepit, adj فرسوده	crumble v فروریختن
worn-out	sale; sellout n فروش
rot; wear down v فرسوده شدن	shop n فروشگاه
floor n فرش اتاق	seller n فروشنده
furnish v فرش کردن اتاق	saleswoman n فروشنده زن
angel n فرشته	salesman n فروشنده مرد
angelic adj فرشته ای	quench v فرونشاندن
chance, opportunity n فرصت	shriek, scream, shout, n فریاد
suppose, assume, v فرض کردن	howl, outcry
presume, deem, reckon	wail v فریاد
supposing conj فرضاً	scream v فریاد زدن
hypothetical adj فرضی	shout v فریاد کشیدن
premise, hypothesis n فرضیه	trick, deceit, deception; n فریب
secondary adj فرعی	enticement, gimmick
distinction n فرق	bluff, cheat, v فریب دادن
differentiate v فرق گذاشتن	deceive, defraud, delude,
battalion, regiment; cult n فرقه	dupe, entice, mortify, trick
command, decree n فرمان	deceitful adj فریبکار
command v فرمان دادن	swindler, cheater n فریبکار
admiral, commander n فرمانده	fraud n فریبکاری
order n فرمایش خریداری	swindle v فریبکاری
pudding, custard n فرنی	con man n فریبنده
furniture n فرنیچر	deceptive, devious; adj فریبنده
dent n فرو رفتگی	enticing
quell v فرو ریختن	physics n فزیک
dent; ram v فروبردن	physical adj فزیکی
submissive; modest adj فروتن	corruption, depravity n فساد
sell v فروختن	festival n فستیوال
sold-out adj فروخته شده	cancellation n فسخ
descend v فرود آمدن	cancel v فسخ کردن
dip n فرورفتگی	fossil n فسیل

فشار tension, pressure; push *n*	فقط همین حالا just *adv*
فشار آوردن push *v*	فقیر impoverished *adj*
فشار دادن؛ push; pressure; *v* wring	فکاهی joke *n*
فشار روحی یا فزیکی stress *n*	فکتور factor *n*
فشار یا جراحت وارد شده strain *n*	فکر mind *n*
فشردن squeeze, press *v*	فکر کردن think *v*
فشرده compact *adj*	فلاکت adversity *n*
فشرده summary *n*	فلتر filter *n*
فشرده سازی compression *n*	فلتر کردن filter *v*
فشرده کردن compact *v*	فلج cripple *adj*
فشرده موضوع outline *n*	فلج paralysis *n*
فصاحت eloquence *n*	فلج شدن paralyze *v*
فصل season *n*	فلج کردن cripple *v*
فصل بهار spring *n*	فلز nickel; metal *n*
فصل کتاب chapter *n*	فلزی metallic *adj*
فصلی seasonal *adj*	فلسفه philosophy *n*
فصیح fluent *adj*	فلسفی philosophical *n*
فضا perimeter; room, space *n*	فلش درایف flash drive *n*
فضانورد astronaut *n*	فلش کمره flash *n*
فضای خالی بین اشیا space *n*	فلم film, movie *n*
فعال active *adj*	فلمبرداری کردن film *v*
فعال بودن perform, work *v*	فن method, technique *n*
فعال کردن activate *v*	فنری bouncy *adj*
فعالیت activity *n*	فهرست catalog *n*
فعالیت کردن function *v*	فهرست اشیا directory *n*
فعل verb *n*	فهرست بندی کردن catalog *v*
فعلی current *adj*	فهرست کتب bibliography *n*
فقدان lack *n*	فهرست لغات glossary *n*
فقر poverty *n*	فهرست مطالب index *n*
فقره item *n*	فهمیدن grasp, see, *v* understand, know, figure out
فقط merely, just, only; alone *adv*	فواره fountain *n*

ف

فوتوكاپی photocopy n	قوی adj strong, powerful, forceful; tough, vigorous, potent, boisterous

ق

قُطری diagonal adj
قُله كوه peak n
قابل اجرا workable, applicable adj
قابل احترام respectable adj
قابل استطاعت affordable adj
قابل استفاده useable adj
قابل اعتبار valid, credible, reliable adj
قابل اعتماد dependable, trustworthy adj
قابل انعطاف pliable adj
قابل باور believable adj
قابل بحث debatable adj
قابل بخشش forgivable adj
قابل پرداخت payable adj
قابل پیشبینی predictable adj
قابل تبدیل شدن convertible n
قابل تحسین admirable; adorable adj
قابل تحمل bearable, tolerable adj
قابل تطابق compatible adj
قابل تقسیم divisible adj
قابل تقلید exemplary adj

فوراً immediately, instantly adv
فوران eruption n
فوران كردن erupt v
فورمه form n
فورمول formula n
فوری immediate adj
فوری instant n
فوق العاده incredible, wonderful, phenomenal, superb, terrific adj
فولاد steel n
فولاد وغیره mill n
فیته lace; strip; ribbon n
فیته رابری rubber band n
فیته لاستیكی band n
فیر تفنگ shot n
فیر كردن shoot v
فیروزه یی cyan n
فیس fee n
فیس پوهنتون tuition n
فیشن fashion n
فیصد percent n
فیصدی percentage n
فیصله كردن settle v
فیل elephant n
فیل دریایی walrus n
فیلسوف philosopher n
فیلمرغ turkey n
فینالیست finalist n
فیوز برق fuse n
قوه جاذبه gravity n

adjustable *adj* قابل تنظیم	قابلیت دید *n* visibility
substantial, sizable; *adj* قابل توجه	قات کردن *v* bind; fold; tuck
striking, noteworthy,	قاتل *n* assassin, killer, murderer
remarkable	قاچاق کردن *v* smuggle
detachable *adj* قابل جدا شدن	قاچاقبر *n* smuggler
avoidable *adj* قابل جلوگیری	قادر *adj* almighty; capable
combustible *n* قابل حریق	قادر ساختن *v* enable
legible *adj* قابل خواندن	قاره *n* continent
understandable *adj* قابل درک	قاره یی *adj* continental
curable *adj* قابل درمان	قاز *n* goose
attainable *adj* قابل دریافت	قاشق *n* spoon
free, open, *adj* قابل دسترس	قاشق چای خوری *n* teaspoon
accessible	قاشق نان خوری *n* tablespoon
available *adj* قابل دسترسی	قاشق و پنجه *n* cutlery
visible *adj* قابل دید	قاضی *n* judge, magistrate
inhabitable *adj* قابل رهایش	قاطر *n* mule
praiseworthy *adj* قابل ستایش	قاطعیت *n* certainty
habitable *adj* قابل سکونت	قافیه در شعر *n* rhyme
flammable *adj* قابل سوخت	قافیه ساختن *v* rhyme
washable *adj* قابل شستن	قاق *adj* crispy, crunchy
understandable *adj* قابل فهم	قالب *n* cast, template
acceptable *adj* قابل قبول	قالب *v* mold
tangible, palpable *adj* قابل لمس	قالب بندی *n* format
manageable *adj* قابل مدیریت	قالیچه *n* rug
comparable *adj* قابل مقایسه	قالین *n* carpet
considerable, *adj* قابل ملاحظه	قاموس *n* thesaurus
notable	قانع *adj* satisfied
midwife *n* قابله	قانع ساختن *v* satisfy
ability, capability *n* قابلیت	قانع شدن برای *v* settle for
credibility *n* قابلیت اعتبار	قانع کننده *adj* satisfying; convincing
compatibility *n* قابلیت تطابق	قانون *n* act, law, rule
availability *n* قابلیت دسترسی	قانون اساسی *n* constitution

ق

قانون شکن outlaw *n*	قدم footstep *n*
قانونگذار lawmaker *n*	قدم زدن stroll, walk *v*
قانونگذاری legislation *n*	قدیمی primitive, ancient, *adj*
قانونی lawful, legal *adj*	antiquated, archaic
قانونی ساختن legalize *v*	قرابت relationship *n*
قایق canoe; yacht *n*	قرارداد settlement; contract *n*
قبر grave *n*	قرارداد بستن contract *v*
قبرستان cemetery, graveyard *n*	قراردادن place, pose *v*
قبرغه rib *n*	قرائت کردن recite *v*
قبض constipated *adj*	قربانی victim *n*
قبل ago, before *adv*	قربانی دادن sacrifice *n*
قبل از before *prep*	قربانی کردن victimize *v*
قبل از چیزی واقع شدن precede *v*	قربانی کردن حیوان sacrifice *n*
قبلاً already; formerly, *adv*	قرص loaf *n*
previously	قرص نان loaf *n*
قبلی preceding, former, *adj*	قرض debt *n*
previous, prior	قرض دادن lend *v*
قبول کردن accept, concede *v*	قرض دهنده creditor *n*
قبولی acceptance *n*	قرض گرفتن borrow *v*
قبیله caste; tribe *n*	قرضدار debtor *n*
قپیدن grab, snatch, catch *v*	قرضدار بودن owe *v*
قتقتک tickle *n*	قرضه loan *n*
قتقتک دادن tickle *v*	قرضه دادن loan *v*
قتل homicide, killing, murder *n*	قرضه را پرداختن pay off *v*
قتل عام massacre *n*	قرطاسیه stationery *n*
قحطی famine *n*	قرعه کشی raffle *n*
قد بلند tall *adj*	قرقره pulley *n*
قد کوتاه short *adj*	قرن century *n*
قدرت power, might, strength *n*	قرنطین quarantine *n*
قدرت نفوذ leverage *n*	قرون وسطی medieval *adj*
قدردانی appreciation *n*	قریب الوقوع imminent, *adj*
قدردانی کردن appreciate *v*	impending

ق

قضاوت غلط کردن v misjudge	قریه n village
قضاوت کردن v judge	قریه نشین n villager
قضیه n proposition	قسط n installment
قضیه محکمه n case	قسم n type
قطب n pole	قسم خوردن v swear
قطب نما n compass	قسماً adv partly
قطبی adj polar	قسمت n ,compartment, part
قطره باران n raindrop	,proportion, section, segment
قطری adj diagonal	portion
قطع n severance	قسمت آخر کوچه بسته است n
قطع رابطه کردن v break off	dead end
قطع شدن v disconnect	قسمت بالا adj upstairs
قطع کردن v ;cut, cut off	قسمت برامدگی پای اسب n hoof
intercept; amputate	قسمت پیش برامده کشتی n bow
قطع کردن سبزه v mow	قسمت پیشرو adj front
قطع موقت جریان برق n glitch	قسمت تحتانی adj bottom
قطعه n fragment	قسمت داخلی adj inside, interior
قطعه بازی n deck	قسمت سریال n episode
قطعه زمین n lot, plot, patch	قسمت کردن v part
قطعه کردن v patch	قسمت کشالۀ ران n groin
قطعه موسیقی عاشقانه n serenade	قسمت نخست n lead
قطعی adj definitive	قسمتی از سرمایه شرکت n stock
قطی n tin; can	قشر n hull, shell; crust
قطی بازکن n can opener	قصاب n butcher
قطی کثافات n trash can	قصد n intention
قطی کوچک n canister	قصد داشتن v intend
قفس n cage	قصداً adv purposely
قفل n lock; padlock	قصداً خراب کردن v sabotage
قفل دروازه n latch	قصدی adj intentional
قفل ساز n locksmith	قصر n castle, palace
قفل کردن v lock	قصه n tale, story
قفل کردن ساختمان v lock up	قضاوت n verdict, judgment

ق

قلب heart n
قلب شکستگی heartbreak n
قلب شکسته heartbroken adj
قلبه کردن زمین plow v
قلعه fort n
قلعه نظامی fortress n
قلقلک یا قتقتک ticklish adj
قلم pen n
قلم توش marker n
قلمرو territory n
قمار زدن gamble v
قمارخانه casino n
قناعت بخش satisfactory adj
قناعت دادن convince v
قناعت داده نشده unconvinced adj
قناعت دهی persuasion n
قندیل chandelier n
قندیل یخ icicle n
قهر bitter, angry adj
قهرمان champion, champ; n hero; knight
قهرمانانه heroic adj
قهرمانی heroism n
قهوه coffee n
قهوه ای maroon adj
قهوه تیره سیاه espresso n
قهوه خانه café n
قو swan n
قوچ ram n
قورت gulp n
قورت کردن ingest, gulp v
قوس parenthesis n

قوس باز و بسته bracket n
قوطی package n
قول دادن handshake n
قوله کشیدن howl v
قومی ethnic adj
قوه force n
قوه مقننه legislature n
قیاس analogy n
قیام uprising n
قیچی scissors n
قیچی کردن shear v
قید adverb n
قیدک clip n
قیر tar n
قیرشده asphalt n
قیماق cream n
قیماق دار creamy adj
قیمت price n
قیمتی expensive, pricey adj
قیود شب گردی curfew n

ک

کُره sphere n
کُروی spherical adj
کُشتی گرفتن wrestle v
کُشتی گیر wrestler n
کُند blunt, dull; sluggish adj
کُند کردن dull v
کابین cabin n

کابین طیاره cockpit n	کارگر معدن miner n
کاپی کردن copy v	کارمند employee; officer n
کاپی گرفتن back up v	کارمند اطفائیه firefighter, n
کاپی گرفتن backup n	fireman
کاتب clerk n	کارمند رسمی official n
کار work n	کارمندان staff, personnel n
کار داوطلبانه کردن volunteer v	کاروان caravan n
کار ساختمانی construction n	کاری را شروع کردن v
کار کردن work v	get down to
کار های روزمره chore n	کاریکاتور caricature n
کار های محوله errand n	کاستن deduct v
کارا professional n	کاسه bowl n
کارا proficient; efficient adj	کاشتن plant, sow; implant v
کاراته karate n	کاشی tile n
کارآموز intern v	کاغذ paper n
کارآموز trainee n	کاغذ تشناب toilet paper n
کاربرد use n	کاغذ کاک cardboard n
کارت card n	کاغذ یادداشت notepaper n
کارت را در ماشین زدن swipe v	کاغذپران kite n
کارت رای دهی ballot n	کاغذپیچ را باز کردن unwrap v
کارتون cartoon n	کافی sufficient, adequate, adj
کارخانگی homework n	enough
کارخانه housework n	کافیین caffeine n
کارخانه شراب سازی brewery, n	کاکا uncle n
winery	کاکاو cocoa n
کارخانه کشتی سازی shipyard n	کاکتوس cactus n
کارشناس احصائیه statistician n	کالا merchandise n
کارشناس محیط زیست n	کالج college n
environmentalist	کالوری calorie n
کارفرما employer n	کام palate n
کارگاه بافندگی loom n	کامل complete; perfect; adj
کارگر labor; worker n	thorough

completely; quite *adv* كاملاً	book *n* كتاب
outright *adj* كاملاً	ledger *n* كتاب ثبت
cram *v* كاملاً پر كردن	log *n* كتاب ثبت معلومات
brand new *adj* كاملاً جديد	textbook *n* كتاب درسی
prosperous *adj* كامياب	guidebook, *n* كتاب رهنما
pass *n* كامياب شدن در امتحان	handbook; workbook
prosperity *n* كاميابی	manual *n* كتاب رهنما
canal *n* كانال	bible *n* كتاب مقدس
channel *n* كانال آب	booklet; notebook *n* كتابچه
contour *n* كانتور	checkbook *n* كتابچه چک بانكی
canteen *n* كانتين	journal, diary *n* كتابچه يادداشت
candidate *n* كانديد	library *n* كتابخانه
concrete *n* كانكريت	librarian *n* كتابخانه دار
kangaroo *n* كانگرو	bookkeeper *n* كتابدار
congress *n* كانگريس	bookstore *n* كتابفروشی
hay *n* كاه	porch *n* كتاره پيشروی خانه
cut; decline *n* كاهش	category *n* كتگوری
downturn *adj* كاهش	litter, garbage, trash *n* كثافات
devaluation *n* كاهش ارزش	filth, dirt *n* كثافت
decline, decrease, *v* كاهش دادن	multitude *n* كثرت
diminish, mitigate, reduce,	squalid, dirty, filthy; *adj* كثيف
cut back	nasty
lettuce *n* كاهو	crooked, curved; italics *adj* كج
steak *n* كباب	slanted *adj* كج شده
grill; roast *v* كباب كردن	distort; tilt *v* كج كردن
dove; pigeon *n* كبوتر	where *adv* كجا
gray *n* كبود	potato *n* كچالو
bruise *n* كبود شده گی پوست	yam *n* كچالوی شيرين
bruise *v* كبود كردن	which *adj* كدام
cupcake *n* كپ كيک	somebody *pron* كدام كسی
captain *n* كپتان	which *pron* كدام يكی
capsule *n* كپسول	pumpkin *n* كدو

کدو squash *v*	کسی که عمداً آتش میزند *n* arsonist
کدوچه zucchini *n*	کسی که میسازد *n* maker
کر کردن deafen *v*	کش دار elastic *adj*
کر کننده deafening *adj*	کش کردن drag, pull; stretch *v*
کراچی cart *n*	کشت cultivation *n*
کراچی دستی trolley; *n*	کشت کردن cultivate *v*
wheelbarrow	کشتن kill, murder *v*
کراچی که توسط حیوانات کش میشود	کشتی ark, boat, boat, ship, *n*
sled; sleigh *n*	vessel
کرامت dignity *n*	کشتی بادی sailboat *n*
کرایه rent *n*	کشتی جنگی battleship *n*
کرایه دادن rent *v*	کشتی ران sailor *n*
کرایه طیاره airfare *n*	کشتی رانی sail *n*
کرایه گرفتن rent *v*	کشتی رانی کردن row; cruise, *v*
کرایه موتر fare *n*	sail
کرایه نشین tenant *n*	کشتی یا قایق raft *n*
کردن do *v*	کشش stretch; traction *n*
کرکس vulture *n*	کششی elastic *adj*
کرگدن rhinoceros *n*	کشف جرایم uncover *v*
کرم cabbage; worm *n*	کشف کردن detect, discover; *v*
کرم ابریشم caterpillar *n*	decipher
کره زمین globe *n*	کشف کننده detector *n*
کریدیت credit *n*	کشفی detective *n*
کریدیت کارت credit card *n*	کشفیات discovery *n*
کریسمیس Christmas, X-mas *n*	کشمش raisin *n*
کریم دندان toothpaste *n*	کشمکش کردن bustle *v*
کریم ضد آفتاب sun block *n*	کشنده deadly, fatal, lethal *adj*
کسر deficit; deduction; *n*	کشور country *n*
fraction	کشیدن eject *v*
کسر کردن deduct *v*	کشیش clergyman *n*
کسوف و خسوف eclipse *n*	کف پا sole *n*
کسی one; someone *pron*	کف دریا foam *n*

ک

کف دست palm n	کلید پایین low-key adj
کف روی آب را گرفتن skim v	کلید دروازه key n
کف زدن applaud, clap v	کلید وسایل موسیقی key n
کف کردن صابون lather n	کلیسا church n
کف کشتی deck n	کلیسای جامع cathedral n
کفاره atonement n	کلیسای کوچک chapel n
کفتریا cafeteria n	کلیشه stereotype n
کل entire adj	کلیک کردن click v
کل whole n	کلینیک clinic n
کلاً entirely adv	کم low, little, minimal adj
کلاسیک classic n	کم little adv
کلالی pottery n	کم آب dehydrated adj
کلاه hat n	کم آب شدن dehydrate v
کلاه آهنی helmet n	کم کردن alleviate, lessen, v
کلاه بردار crook n	minimize, cut down
کلاهبردار swindler n	کم کم sparingly adv
کلاهبرداری scam n	کم کم از هم جدا شدن drift apart v
کلب club n	کم وزن underweight adj
کلبه cottage; shed, hut, shack n	کمال perfection n
کلتور culture n	کمان bow, arch n
کلتوری cultural adj	کمان رستم rainbow n
کلچ موتر clutch n	کمایی کردن earn v
کلچه cookie n	کمبود scarcity, shortage, n
کلچه مربا دار pie n	deficiency
کلکین window n	کمبودی deficit, shortcoming n
کلمه word n	کمپ camp n
کلمه به کلمه verbatim adv	کمپ زدن camp v
کلمه یا عبارت در سخنرانی n	کمپاین campaign n
figure of speech	کمپاین کردن campaign v
کلونیا cologne n	کمپل blanket n
کلی generic adj	کمپیوتر computer n
کلید بند key ring n	کمپیوتر کوچک tablet n

کمتر fewer, less; minus *adj*	کنایه metaphor *n*
کمترین least *adj*	کنترول control *n*
کمترین minimum *n*	کنترول کردن control *v*
کمر waist *n*	کنج corner *n*
کمربند belt *n*	کنجکاو inquisitive, curious *adj*
کمربند ایمنی safety belt *adv*	کنجکاوی curiosity *n*
کمربند چوکی seat belt *n*	کندن pluck *v*
کمرنگ شدن wane *v*	کنده چوب log *n*
کمره camera *n*	کنده یخ glacier, iceberg *n*
کمک aid, help *n*	کنری canary *n*
کمک بلاعوض grant *n*	کنسرت concert *n*
کمک خیریه دولت welfare *n*	کنفرانس conference *n*
کمک کردن support, aid, assist, *v* help	کنیسه synagogue *n*
کمک کننده helper *n*	که that *conj*
کمکی auxiliary *adj*	کهکشان galaxy *n*
کمود تشناب toilet *n*	کهن classic *n*
کمونیزم communism *n*	کهنه rag *n*
کمونیست communist *adj*	کهنه stale, old, shabby *adj*
کمیاب rare, scarce, *adj* infrequent	کهنه شدن wear out *v*
کمیت quantity *n*	کوبیدن pound *v*
کمیته committee *n*	کوپون coupon, voucher *n*
کمیدی comedy *n*	کوتاه short *adj*
کمین کردن stalk *v*	کوتاه کردن trim, shorten *v*
کمین گرفتن ambush *v*	کوتاه مدت short-term *adj*
کنار آمدن get along, get by *v*	کوتاه نویسی shorthand *n*
کنار رفتن sidestep *v*	کوتاهی brevity *n*
کنار گذاشتن sidestep, leave *v* out, put aside	کوچ sofa; coach *n*
کناره گیری کردن retreat, step *v* down	کوچ فرنیچر couch *n*
	کوچ کشی move *n*
	کوچ کشی کردن move *v*
	کوچک lesser, minor, small, *adj* little, tiny

ک

کوک کردن v tune	little pron کوچک
کوما n coma	minor n کوچک
کومه n cheek	shrink v کوچک شدن
کوه n mountain	belittle v کوچک شمردن
کوهنوردی n climbing; hike	downsize v کوچک کردن
کوهنوردی کردن v hike	less adv کوچکتر
کی pron who	least adv کوچکترین
کیبل n cable	lane, alley n کوچه
کیبورد n keyboard	gypsy n کوچی
کیچپ v ketchup	compost n کود برای نباتات
کیسه بری n pickpocket	fertilize v کود دادن
کیفیت caliber, quality	manure n کود زراعتی
کیک n cake	zip code n کود منطقه
کیله n banana	code n کود نرم افزار
کیلوگرام (kilo) n kilogram (kilo)	coat hanger n کودبند
کیلومتر n kilometer	hanger n کودبند لباس
کیلووات n kilowatt	coup n کودتا
کیمیا n chemistry	toddler n کودک نوپا
کیمیادان n chemist	childcare, daycare n کودکستان
کیمیاوی adj chemical	fertilizer n کودکیمیاوی
کینه n rancor, spite; grudge	blind v کور کردن
کینه جو adj vindictive	broiler, grill n کوره کباب
کینه دل adj spiteful	heel n کوری پا
کیهانی adj cosmic	urn n کوزه
گودال n cavity, pothole, trench	pitcher n کوزه آب
	diligent, industrious adj کوشا
	struggle n کوشش
	strain, try, strive v کوشش کردن
	tug v کوشیدن
	meatball n کوفته
	stitch n کوک
	stitch v کوک زدن

گ

گُدام n warehouse	
گُدی n doll	

گپ کسی را قطع کردن interrupt v	گُرده kidney n
گَچ گیری cast n	گُرگ wolf n
گدا beggar n	گُل flower n
گذار transition n	گُل سر قبر wreath n
گذاشتن put v	گُل میخ tack, thumbtack n
گذر pass, passage n	گُل یاسمن jasmine n
گذرگاه pass n	گُم missing adj
گذشته past adj	گُم شده lost adj
گذشته از aside adv	گُم کردن lose v
گذشته از past prep	گُنگ vague adj
گراف graph n	گِرد round adj
گرام gram n	گِل clay; mud n
گرامر grammar n	گِل آلود muddy adj
گرامی داشتن cherish v	گاراج موتر garage n
گرانولا granola n	گارسون waiter n
گرچه although, though conj	گارسون زن waitress n
گرچه even though adv	گاز gas n
گرد گُل pollen n	گاز پانسمان gauze n
گرد آوردن amass v	گاز تفریحی برای اطفال swing n
گردآوری collection n	گاز خوردن swing v
گردباد hurricane; tornado n	گالوانیزه کردن galvanize v
گردش circulation; walk n	گام step, pace; stair n
گردش بیرون از شهر outing n	گام برداشتن pace, stride v
گردشگاه promenade n	گام به گام step-by-step adv
گردن neck n	گام گذاشتن step v
گردنبند necklace; pendant n	گاه گاهی occasionally adv
گرسنگی hunger, starvation n	گاهی ever adv
گرسنه hungry adj	گاو cow n
گرفتار شدن entangle v	گاو نر bull, ox n
گرفتگی eclipse n	گاوچران cowboy n
گرفتگی عضلات cramp n	گاومیش bison; buffalo n
گرفتن grab, seize, take v	گپ زدن speak v

گرفتن مواد سوخت refuel v	گزینه option n
گرم warm adj	گژدم scorpion n
گرم شدن thaw v	گستاخ cheeky, insolent, rude adj
گرم کردن warm v	گستاخی rudeness n
گرم کننده thermostat n	گسترش دادن branch out v
گرم کننده نان toaster n	گسستن rupture v
گرم و نرم cozy adj	گشاد loose adj
گرما warmth n	گشت و گذار tour, excursion n
گرمازدگی heatstroke n	گفتار مغایر paradox n
گرمسیر tropical adj	گفتگو converse n
گرمکاری warm up v	گفتن utter, say; tell v
گره knot n	گفته saying n
گره خورده tangled adj	گل بنفش violet n
گرو mortgage n	گل پیاز bulb n
گروپ light bulb n	گل سرخ rose n
گروپ چراغ bulb n	گل لاله tulip n
گروپ دستی flashlight n	گل مروارید daisy n
گروه cluster; gang, mob, n group	گل میخک carnation n
گروهی gregarious adj	گلابی pink adj
گرویدن gravitate v	گلبرگ petal n
گریپ فروت grapefruit n	گلپی cauliflower n
گریزان elusive, evasive adj	گلخانه nursery, greenhouse n
گریس grease n	گلدان flowerpot, vase n
گریه cry n	گلدوزی embroidery n
گریه کردن cry, sob v	گلدوزی کردن embroider v
گزارش report n	گلساز florist n
گزارش دادن report v	گلگون rosy adj
گزارشگر reporter n	گلگیر fender n
گزمه patrol n	گله flock, herd n
گزنده stinging adj	گله گاو cattle n
گزیدن sting v	گلو throat n
	گلوی کسی را فشردن strangle v

گوشت بره n lamb	گماشتن v appoint, designate
گوشت خوک n ;bacon; ham; pork	گمان n assumption
lard	گمان کردن v speculate, suppose
گوشت گاو n beef	گمراه adv astray
گوشت گوساله n veal	گمراه adj perverse, misguided
گوشت میوه n pulp	گمراه کردن v seduce; mislead
گوشکی n headset	گمراه کننده adj ;misleading
گوشکی تیلفون n ,earphones	sinister
headphones	گناه n sin
گوشه نشین n hermit	گناه کردن v sin
گوشواره n earring	گنبد n dome
گوگرد n match	گنج n treasure
گول در فتبال n goal	گنجشک n sparrow
گول کیپر n goalkeeper	گندم n wheat
گوناگون کردن v diversify	گندیدن v fester
گونه n sort	گنس adj dizzy
گونه ها n species	گنگ adj dumb, speechless
گوهر n gem	گهواره n cradle, crib
گوینده n teller	گواکامول n guacamole
گیاه n plant, herb	گواهی n testimony
گیاه جعفری n parsley	گواهی دادن v testify
گیاه شناسی n botany	گودال سرپوشیده n pitfall
گیتار n guitar	گوره خر n zebra
گیج شده adj puzzled	گوریلا n gorilla
گیج کردن v ,baffle, bewilder	گوزن n reindeer
confound	گوزن شمالی n reindeer
گیج کننده adj puzzling	گوساله n calf
گیج کننده ذهن adj mind-boggling	گوسفند n sheep
گیجی n distraction; confusion	گوش n ear
گیر انداختن v entangle	گوش دادن v listen
گیر موتر n gear	گوش دردی n earache
گیرا n tongs; grip	گوشت n flesh, meat

لب lip n

لب دریا bank n

لباس robe; costume, garment, n
dress, outfit

لباس آببازی swimsuit n

لباس آببازی زنانه bikini n

لباس پوشاندن clothe v

لباس پوشیدن dress, dress up v

لباس جالی دار see-through adj

لباس حمام bathing suit n

لباس خواب; nightgown; n
pajamas

لباس شویی laundry n

لباس مخصوص uniform n

لباسها clothes n

لبخند smile n

لبسیرین lipstick n

لبلبو beetroot n

لبنیات dairy n

لبه hem, fringe, brim; margin, n
rim, edge, verge; ridge; spike

لبه پیاده رو curb n

لبه دار edgy; spiky adj

لپ تاپ laptop n

لجاجت کردن grouch v

لجباز obstinate adj

لجن زار marsh n

لجوج grouchy; stubborn adj

لحاف quilt n

لحظه moment n

لحظه به لحظه momentarily adv

لحیم کردن solder v

گیره clip; clamp n

گیرۀ کاغذ paperclip n

گیلاس glass n

گیلاس آب mug n

گیلن gallon n

لمس کردن feel, touch v

ل

لابراتوار laboratory n

لاتری lottery n

لاری truck n

لاری که موتر را انتقال میدهد n
tow truck

لاری کوچک van n

لاشتک موی bun n

لاشه carcass n

لاغر thin, underweight, adj
lean, skinny; flimsy

لاغر شدن atrophy v

لاف زدن boast, brag v

لالایی lullaby n

لایتر سگرت lighter n

لایزر laser n

لایسنس license n

لایسنس پلیت license plate n

لایه strand; layer n

لایه بالش pad n

لایه دار padded adj

لایه گذاری padding n

ل

clot *n* لخته خون	elevator, escalator *n* لفت
enjoyment, gusto, joy *n* لذت	literally *adv* لفظاً
enjoyable, joyful *adj* لذت بخش	title *n* لقب
enjoy, relish *v* لذت بردن	lecture *n* لکچر
wobbly, shaky *adj* لرزان	lecture *v* لکچر دادن
rattle *v* لرزاندن	falter *v* لکنت زبان پیدا کردن
quiver *v* لرزش	blot *v* لکه
vibration, tremor *n* لرزش	smear, stain; speck *n* لکه
thrill; vibration *n* لرزه	stain *v* لکه دار شدن
vibrate, flicker, shiver, *v* لرزیدن	tarnish *v* لکه دار کردن
shudder, tremble	smear *v* لکه کردن
language *n* لسان	kick *n* لگد
list *n* لست	kick *v* لگد زدن
inventory *n* لست اجناس	run over *v* لگد مال کردن
list *v* لست نوشتن	hip *n* لگن خاصره
slippery; smooth *adj* لشم	touch *n* لمس
smooth *v* لشم کردن	lame *adj* لنگ
tenderness *n* لطافت	limp *n* لنگ
favor *n* لطف	anchor *n* لنگرکشی
please *e* لطفاً	dock *n* لنگرگاه
curse *n* لعنت	limp, stagger *v* لنگیدن
curse *v* لعنت کردن	accent; dialect *n* لهجه
vocabulary *n* لغات	supplies, supply *n* لوازم
slide *v* لغزاندن	cosmetic *n* لوازم آرایشی
lapse *n* لغزش	gear *n* لوازم ورزش و کار
slip *n* لغزش یا خطا	beans *n* لوبیا
slippery *adj* لغزنده	sign *n* لوحه
slither, slide, slip, *v* لغزیدن	banner *n* لوحه تکه یی
stumble	lotion *n* لوشن
revoke *v* لغو	deluxe *adj* لوکس
quash, repeal, *v* لغو کردن	luxury *n* لوکس
abolish, call off	roll *v* لول دادن

لوله roll n
لوله کردن roll v
لیاقت چیزی را ندارد adj
undeserved
لیبل label, tag n
لیبل زدن label v
لیتر liter n
لیسانسه bachelor n
لیسه high school n
لیسیدن lick v
لیگ league n
لیلام sale n
لیلیه dormitory n
لیمو lemon n
لیموی سبز lime n
لین wire n
لین تیلفون line n
لینز lens n
لینز کمره را عیار کردن focus v
مانع barrier, barricade, n
hurdle, obstacle, impediment,
obstruction, bottleneck,
drawback, hitch
مهربان warm, affectionate, adj
mellow, sweet; humane,
compassionate, kind,
merciful; pitiful

م

مُبلغ مذهبی missionary n
مُد fashion n
مُد روز fashionable, trendy adj
مُدل model n
مُدل مو hairstyle n
مُدل موتر make n
مُرکب compound n
مُسکن درد painkiller n
مُفسر commentator n
مُقصر guilty adj
مُلا priest n
مُهر کردن seal v
مُهر کردن کاغذ stamp out v
مُهر یا تاپه seal n
ما we pron
ما را us pron
ماجرا adventure n
ماحول environment n
مادر mom, mother n
مادر اندر stepmother n
مادرکلان grandmother n
مادرکیک beetle; cockroach n
مادری maternal adj
مادری motherhood n
ماده substance n
ماده پاک کننده cleanser n
ماده کیمیاوی chemical n
مادی گرایی materialism n
مار snake n

مار بزرگ serpent n	مالی financial adj
مارپیچ spiral, winding adj	مالیات پذیر deductible adj
مارچوبه asparagus n	مالیخولیا melancholy n
مارشال marshal n	مالیدن rub v
مارکیت بزرگ supermarket n	مالیه tax n
ماساژ massage n	ماما uncle n
ماساژ کردن massage v	ماندن stay v
ماساژ کننده masseuse n	ماندنی lingering adj
ماست yogurt n	مانع دخول آب watertight adj
ماستر master n	مانع شدن bar, hinder, inhibit, v
ماسک پوشیدن masquerade v	hold back
ماشه trigger n	مانند as adv
ماشین engine, motor, machine n	مانند like prep
ماشین اسکنر scanner n	مانند such as idiom
ماشین تایپ type writer n	مانور maneuver n
ماشین چاپ press, printer n	مانیتور کمپیوتر monitor n
ماشین حساب calculator n	مانیکور manicure n
ماشین ظرف شوی dishwasher n	ماه month n
ماشین فوتوکاپی photocopier n	ماه اکتوبر October n
ماشین قطع سبزه lawnmower n	ماه آگست August n
ماشین کاپی copier n	ماه جون June n
ماشین کالاشویی washing machine n	ماه روزه Lent n
ماقبل preceding adj	ماه سپتمبر September n
ماقبل تاریخ prehistoric adj	ماه عسل honeymoon n
مال shopping mall n	ماه فبروری February n
مال تجارتی merchandise n	ماه مارچ March n
مالته orange adj	ماه می May n
مالته orange, citrus, tangerine n	ماه نومبر November n
مالداری livestock n	ماهانه monthly adv
مالک owner n	ماهر deft, expert, skilled, adj
مالک بودن possess v	versed
مالکیت ownership n	ماهر master n

م

fish *n* ماهی	مبتلا شدن *v* afflict
fishy *adj* ماهی بوی	pressing *adj* مبرم
tuna *n* ماهی تونا	amount *n* مبلغ
sardine *n* ماهی ساردین	basis *n* مبنا
salmon *n* ماهی سلمون	hazy, vague, imprecise, *adj* مبهم
cod *n* ماهی کاد	obscure, opaque; ambiguous;
cannibal *n* ماهی همگون خوار	nuclear
essence *n* ماهیت	sorry *adj* متاسف
fisherman *n* ماهیگیر	nerve; poise *n* متانت
fish *v* ماهیگیری کردن	remaining *adj* متباقی
fluid, liquid *n* مایع	aggressor *n* متجاوز
microchip *n* مایکروچیپ	petrified *adj* متحجر شده
microscope *n* مایکروسکوب	ally *n* متحد
microphone *n* مایکروفون	united *adj* متحد
microwave *n* مایکروویف	unify, unite *v* متحد کردن
mile *n* مایل	animate *v* متحرک کردن
willing *adj* مایل	tolerant *adj* متحمل
mayonnaise *n* مایونیز	sustain, incur, *v* متحمل شدن
reference *n* مأخذ	undergo
mission *n* مأموریت	amaze *v* متحیر ساختن
disappoint *v* مأیوس کردن	stunning *adj* متحیر کننده
disappointing *adj* مأیوس کننده	authority, specialist, *n* متخصص
swap *v* مبادله کردن	specialist, expert
champion; combatant *n* مبارز	delinquent *adj n* متخلف
combat, fight *n* مبارزه	tape measure متر برای اندازه گیری
battle, combat *v* مبارزه کردن	synonym *n* مترادف
blessed *adj* مبارک	congested *adj* متراکم
exaggerate, *v* مبالغه کردن	interpreter *n* مترجم شفاهی
overstate	indecisive *adj* متردد
vulgar *adj* مبتذل	progressive *adj* مترقی
مبتلا به مرض روانی پارانویا *adj*	derelict, deserted, *adj* متروک
paranoid	desolate

متمایز distinct, distinctive *adj*	متریک metric *adj*
متمایل oriented; *adj* predisposed, prone	متشکل بودن از consist *v*
متمایل شدن gravitate *v*	متشنج hysterical *adj*
متمدن ساختن civilize *v*	متضاد ambivalent, *adj* conflicting
متمرکز کردن centralize *v*	متضرر victim *n*
متن context; text *n*	متضرر ساختن victimize; *v* undermine
متناقض contradictory, *adj* repugnant	متضرر نشده unharmed *adj*
متناوب alternate, staggering *adj*	متعاقب subsequent; *adj* consequent
متناوب کردن alternate *v*	متعاقباً consequently *adv*
متناوباً alternatively *adv*	متعجب surprised *adj*
متنفر disgusted; hateful *adj*	متعجب ساختن shock, surprise, *v* astonish
متنوع assorted, diverse, *adj* varied	متعدد multiple, numerous *adj*
متهم کردن charge, accuse; *v* incriminate	متعصب defiant; fanatic *adj*
متوازن balanced; *adj* symmetrical	متعلق بودن belong *v*
متوازن کردن balance *v*	متعلقات belongings *n*
متواضع humble *adj*	متعهد committed *adj*
متوجه mindful *adj*	متغیر variable *adj*
متوجه شدن notice *v*	متفاوت different *adj*
متوجه شدن چیزی spot *v*	متفرق شدن disperse *v*
متورم bloated *adj*	متفرقه miscellaneous *adj*
متوسط average *n*	متفکر thoughtful *adj*
متوسط medium *adj*	متقابل reciprocal *adj*
متوسطه intermediate *adj*	متقابلاً conversely *adv*
متوسل شدن resort *v*	متقاعد ساختن persuasion *n*
متوقف ساختن cease; stall *v*	متقاعد نشده unconvinced *adj*
متوقف کردن check; *v* discontinue, halt	متقلب crooked *adj*
	متکبر conceited *adj*
	متکی reliant *adj*

متولد born *adj*	مجموعاً totally *adv*
مثال example, instance *n*	مجموعه sum, total *n*
مثانه bladder; cyst *n*	مجهز ساختن equip *v*
مثبت positive *adj*	مجهز کردن supply *v*
مثل like *adj*	مجهول passive *adj*
مثل parable *n*	مجوز authorization *n*
مثمر constructive, fruitful, *adj* productive	محاسب accountant *n*
مجادله altercation *n*	محاسبه calculation *n*
مجادله کردن cope *v*	محاسبه کردن calculate, compute *v*
مجازات chastisement *n*	محاصره blockade, siege *n*
مجازات کردن chastise *v*	محاصره کردن besiege *v*
مجازی virtual *adj*	محافظ bodyguard *n*
مجاورت proximity, vicinity *n*	محافظت guard *n*
مجبور ساختن con *v*	محافظت کردن guard *v*
مجبور کردن force *v*	محافظوی conservative *adj*
مجدداً تأکید کردن reiterate *v*	محبت affection, love *n*
مجذوب کردن fascinate *v*	محبوب darling, popular; *adj* decent
مجرا opening; aqueduct; duct *n*	محبوبیت decency *n*
مجرد single, unmarried *adj*	محبور obliged *adj*
مجروح wounded *adj*	محتاط alert *n*
مجروح کردن strain *v*	محتاط close, careful, *adj* cautious, discreet, wary
مجسم کردن embody; visualize *v*	محترم شمردن esteem *v*
مجسمه statue, sculpture *n*	محتمل contingent; probable *adj*
مجسمه ساز sculptor *n*	محتوا content *n*
مجلس assembly *n*	محدود pent-up; finite *adj*
مجلس سنا senate *n*	محدود ساختن restrict *v*
مجلل lavish, luxurious, *adj* sumptuous	محدود کردن bound, confine, *v* constrain, curb; curtail, limit
مجله magazine *n*	محدوده boundary, limitation *n*
مجموع total, whole *adj*	محدوده زمانی span; time limit *n*
مجموع ارقام فرعی subtotal *n*	

محدودیت constraint, n	محكومیت ;sentence, conviction
restriction	condemnation n
محراب altar n	محل spot, site n
محرک stimulant n	محل پارکینگ parking lot n
محرم confidant n	محل خریداری تکت تیاتر n
محرمانه confidential adj	box office
محرمیت privacy n	محل خوابیدن و نشستن در فضای باز
محروم deprived adj	terrace n
محروم کردن deprive v	محل دفن کثافات landfill n
محرومیت deprivation n	محل سکونت residence n
محسور کردن mesmerize v	محل کار workshop n
محسوس sensible; tangible adj	محل نصب وسایل نجومی n
محصل سال اول freshman n	observatory
محصول output, product n	محل نگهداری زنبور عسل hive n
محض sole; mere adj	محله parish n
محضاً صرفاً solely adv	محله فقیرنشین slum n
محفل party n	محله یهودی نشین ghetto n
محفل رقص ball n	محلول solution n
محفل گرفتن party v	محلی local adj
محقق scholar; researcher n	محموله consignment n
محکم secure, sturdy, firm, adj	محو شدن fade; vanish v
solid, stiff, rigid	محو کردن obliterate v
محکم tight adv	محور axis; axle n
محکم بستن chain v	محوطه premises n
محکم زدن slam v	محول کردن delegate v
محکم کردن solidify; clinch; v	محیط perimeter n
tighten	محیط اطراف surroundings n
محکم گرفتن grasp, grip; clip v	محیط زیست environment n
محکمه court, courthouse n	مخاطره venture n
محکوم به doomed adj	مخالف adversary, opponent n
محکوم کردن condemn, v	مخالف dissent v
denounce; convict, sentence	مخالف opposite adj

مخالف بودن oppose v | مداخله کردن، interfere, v

مخالفت کردن antagonize v | intervene

مختصات coordinate n | مداخله گر nosy adj

مختصر short, brief, concise; adj | مدار orbit n

precise | مداری clown n

مختصر کردن abbreviate; v | مدافع defendant; defender n

abridge | مدال medal n

مختصر نویسی shorthand n | مداوم persistent adj

مختل کردن disrupt; impair v | مدت period, term, duration n

مختل کننده disruptive adj | مدعی plaintiff; contender n

مختلف various adj | مدغم کردن integrate v

مخرب pernicious adj | مدنظر گرفتن consider v

مخرج outlet, vent n | مدنی civic adj

مخروط cone n | مدیر manager n

مخزن آب cistern n | مدیریت management n

مخفی clandestine, secret, adj | مدیریت غلط کردن mismanage v

undercover | مذاکره negotiation n

مخفی کردن camouflage v | مذاکره کردن negotiate v

مخفیانه secretive adj | مذکر male n

مخفیانه حرکت کردن sneak v | مذهب religion n

مخفیگاه hideaway n | مذهب بودا Buddhism n

مخلص sincere adj | مذهبی religious adj

مخلوط mixture n | مراجعه recourse n

مخلوط شده scrambled adj | مراجعه کردن haunt v

مخلوط کردن mix, blend, mash, v | مراسم ceremony n

scramble; season; shuffle | مراسم مذهبی ritual n

مخلوط کن mixer n | مراعت کردن regard v

مخلوط کننده blender n | مراقب watchful adj

مخلوق creature n | مراقبت care; surveillance n

مخمل velvet n | مراقبت صحی healthcare n

مخملی plush adj | مراقبت کردن care, look after v

مداخله interference n | مراقبت کردن از care for v

مراقبت کننده *n* caretaker	مرچه *n* ant
مربا *n* jam	مرحله *n* step, stage, phase, milestone
مربای نارنج *n* marmalade	مرحله نهایی مسابقات *n* showdown
مربع *n* square	مرد *n* guy, man
مربوط *adj* concerned; relevant	مرد بیوه *n* widower
مربوط به ادویه *adj* medicinal	مردانگی *n* manliness
مربوط به آب *adj* aquatic	مردانه *adj* male, masculine, virile
مربوط به آواز *adj* vocal	مردانه وار *adj* manly
مربوط به تعلیم و تربیه *adj* educational	مردم *n* folks, people
مربوط به دفتر *adj* clerical	مردم عام *n* public
مربوط به شرایط *adj* circumstantial	مردم غرب نشین *adj* westerner
مربوط به صورت *adj* facial	مردم یک محله *n* parishioner
مربوط به محیط زیست *adj* environmental	مردمک چشم *n* pupil
مربوط به معاهده *adj* conventional	مردمی *adj* grassroots
مربوط به موسیقی *adj* musical	مردن *v* die
مربوط به میلودی یا نغمه *adj* melodic	مردن از اثر برق *v* electrocute
مربوط به نسل *adj* genetic	مردنی *adj* mortal
مربوط به ورزش *adj* sporty	مرده *adj* dead, deceased
مربوط بودن به *v* depend	مرده شوی خانه *n* mortuary
مربوطه *adj* respective	مردها *n* men
مربی *n* instructor	مرز *n* border, frontier
مرتبان *n* jar	مرسوم *adj* customary
مرتبط *adj* related; pertinent; relative	مرض *n* disease
مرتکب شدن *v* commit	مرض جذام *n* leprosy
مرتکب شده *v* perpetrate	مرض سرطان *n* cancer
مرجانی *n* coral	مرض سگ دیوانه *n* rabies
مرچ *n* chili, pepper	مرض شکر *n* diabetes
مرچ دلمه *n* bell pepper	مرض ملاریا *n* malaria
	مرطوب *adj* soggy, wet, damp, humid, moist

م

مرطوب کردن v ;dampen	مزاحم شدن v intrude
moisturize	مزاحمت n disturbance; nuisance
مرغ n chicken	مزاحمت کردن v perturb
مرغ خانگی n poultry	مزایده n auction
مرغ دریایی n seagull	مزخرف adj ludicrous; trashy
مرغ ماکیان n hen	مزخرف n nonsense
مرغابی n duck	مزد n wage
مرغزار در بیابان n oasis	مزد روزانه n ration
مرکز n center, hub	مزد روزانه دادن v ration
مرکز خریداری n, shopping mall,	مزدحم adj crowded
mall	مزرعه n field; farm
مرکز شهر n downtown	مزمن adj chronic
مرکزی adj central	مزه n flavor, taste
مرگ n death, demise	مزه v savor
مرگ و میر n mortality	مزه دار adj tasty
مرموز adj mysterious	مزه کردن v taste
مرمی n bullet	مزین کردن v emboss
مرهم n balm, ointment	مژه n eyelash
مروارید n pearl	مس n copper
مرور n review	مسابقات ورزشی n tournament
مری n esophagus	مسابقه n race, contest, racing
مریخ n Mars	مسابقه دادن v race
مریض adj ailing, ill, sick	مسابقه دهنده n contestant
مریض n patient	مسابقه ورزشی n match
مریض روانی n psychopath	مسابقه ورزشی یا سرگرمی n event
مریض شکر adj diabetic	مساعدت n assistance
مریض کردن v sicken	مسافر n, passenger, traveler,
مریض کننده adj sickening	voyager
مریضی n, ailment, illness,	مسافرت n travel
sickness	مسافرت رایگان n hitchhike
مزاج n mood, temper	مسافرخانه n inn, motel
مزاحم n intruder	مساوات n equality

م

مساوی equal *adj*	مسطح flat *adj*
مساوی کردن close, shut *v*	مسکن dwelling *n*
مستارد mustard *n*	مسکن سربازان barracks *n*
مستبد tyrant, despot *n*	مسکن گزینی settlement *n*
مستبدانه despotic *adj*	مسکه butter *n*
مستثنی کردن waive *v*	مسلح armed *adj*
مستحکم robust; concrete *adj*	مسلح کردن arm *v*
مستحکم کردن fortify *v*	مسلط prevalent *adj*
مستری mechanic *n*	مسلک career, profession *n*
مستریح restful *adj*	مسلکی professional *n*
مستطیل rectangle *n*	مسلکی professional *adj*
مستطیلی rectangular *adj*	مسلماً undoubtedly *adv*
مستعمره colony *n*	مسلمان Muslim *adj*
مستعمره کردن colonize *v*	مسوده draft *n*
مستعمل used *adj*	مسوده را ترتیب کردن draft *v*
مستقر شدن settle down *v*	مسوول accountable, *adj*
مستقر کننده settler *n*	responsible, liable
مستقل independent *adj*	مسوول پذیرش receptionist *n*
مستقیم through *prep*	مسوولیت burden, liability, *n*
مستقیم upright; straight, *adj*	responsibility
direct	مسیحی Christian *adj*
مستقیماً directly, straight *adv*	مسیحیت Christianity *n*
مستلزم بودن require *v*	مسیر route, track, path; *n*
مستند documentary *n*	way in
مستند سازی documentation *n*	مسیر اصلی mainstream *n*
مسجد mosque *n*	مسیر برای گردش trail *n*
مسخره ridiculous *adj*	مسیر عبور ریل railway *n*
مسخره کردن ridicule *v*	مسئله issue *n*
مسدود کردن jam *v*	مشابه like *conj*
مسرت pleasure *n*	مشابه same *pron*
مسرور cheerful *adj*	مشابه similar, alike, identical, *adj*
مسرور delighted *v*	same

مشاجره argument *n*
مشاجره کردن argue *v*
مشاهده observation *n*
مشاهده کردن behold, observe *v*
مشاور adviser, aide, *n*
consultant, counselor
مشاور رهنما guidance counselor *n*
مشت fist *n*
مشت زدن punch *v*
مشتاق ardent, eager, fervent *adj*
مشتاق بودن yearn *v*
مشترکاً jointly *adv*
مشتری client, customer *n*
مشتریان clientele *n*
مشتعل ablaze *adj*
مشتق derivative *adj*
مشتق کردن derive *v*
مشخص significant; *adj*
particular, specific
مشخص کردن denote, pinpoint, *v*
specify
مشخصاً specifically *adv*
مشخصات یک شخص profile *n*
مشخصه characteristic *adj*
مشخصه quality *n*
مشروب liquor *n*
مشروط conditional *adj*
مشروع legitimate *adj*
مشعل torch *n*
مشغله preoccupation *n*
مشغول busily *adv*
مشقت hardship *n*

مشکل hard, tough *adj*
مشکل problem *n*
مشکل برانگیز problematic *adj*
مشکل پسند choosy *adj*
مشکوک fishy, suspicious; *adj*
precarious, doubtful,
dubious; unclear
مشکوک skeptic *n*
مشمول conclusive *adj*
مشمول inclusive *adv*
مشهور famous, renowned *adj*
مشوره tip, advice, *n*
consultation, counseling
مشوره دادن counsel, advise *v*
مشوره کردن consult *v*
مصاحبه interview *n*
مصاحبه کردن interview *v*
مصارف expenditure *n*
مصالح باب condiment *n*
مصالح جات seasoning, spice *n*
مصالح دار spicy *adj*
مصالحه compromise *n*
مصالحه compromise *v*
مصرف consumption; cost *n*
مصرف expense *n*
مصرف بیش از حد دوا overdose *n*
مصرف داشتن cost *v*
مصرف کردن spend; consume *v*
مصرف کننده consumer *n*
مصروف busy *adj*
مصمم resolute, decisive, *adj*
determined

مصنوعی adj synthetic, artificial
مصوون adj secure, safe; immune
مصوون از خطا adj infallible
مصوون نگهداشتن v secure
مصوونیت n immunity; safety
مصیبت n affliction, ordeal, tribulation, calamity
مضر n detriment
مضر adj pernicious, harmful, noxious
مضطرب adj worried, anxious
مضمون n subject, theme, topic, matter, course
مضمون خنده n laughing stock
مطابق adj corresponding
مطابق به prep per
مطابق عصر فعلی adj up-to-date
مطابقت داشتن v conform, match; correspond
مطالبه پول v charge
مطالبه کردن پول n charge
مطالعه n study
مطالعه کردن v study
مطبوعات n press
مطرح شدن v come up
مطرح کردن v bring up
مطرود adj outcast
مطلب n theme, topic
مطلب را حذف کردن v slur
مطلع n informant
مطلع بودن v beware

مطلع ساختن v notify
مطلق adj absolute; abstract
مطلقاً adv absolutely
مطلوب adj congenial, favorable, desirable
مطلوب و بی عیب adj model
مطمئن adj certain, confident, sure
مطمئناً adv surely
مطیع adj docile
مظاهره n demonstration
مظلوم adj oppressed
معادل adj equivalent
معاش n payment, pay, salary
معاشقه کردن v flirt
معاصر adj contemporary
معاصر n contemporary
معاف adj exempt
معاف کردن v waive
معافیت n immunity, exemption
معالجه n treat; treatment, cure
معالجه کردن v treat, cure
معامله n bargain, deal, transaction
معامله تجارتی v barter
معامله گر n dealer
معاهده n convention
معاوضه کردن v interchange
معاون n assistant; vice
معاینه n checkup, examination
معاینه داکتر n physical
معاینه کردن v examine

معبد temple n
معتاد addicted adj
معتاد مواد مخدر drug addict n
معتبر valid, authentic; adj authoritative
معتدل mild, moderate adj
معتقد convinced; adj opinionated
معجزه miracle n
معجزه یی miraculous adj
معدن سنگ quarry n
معدنی mineral n
معده stomach n
معذرت pardon; apology n
معذرت خواستن apologize v
معرفی introduction n
معرفی کردن introduce v
معشوقه sweetheart n
معصوم immaculate; adj innocent
معصومیت innocence n
معضله problem n
معطر aromatic, scented adj
معطل شدن linger v
معطل شونده lingering adj
معطل کردن postpone v
معطل کردن چیزی long for v
معکوس opposite prep
معکوس reverse n
معلق pent-up; pending adj
معلم teacher, tutor n
معلول handicapped adj

معلولیت handicap n
معلوم شدن seem v
معلومات information n
معلومات دادن brief v
معما mystery, riddle, puzzle n
معمار builder n
معمول common, typical, adj usual
معمولاً normally, usually adv
معنوی spiritual adj
معنی meaning n
معنی داشتن mean v
معیار norm n
معیارها criteria n
معیاری standard n
معیاری standard adj
معیاری ساختن standardize v
معیشت livelihood n
معین definite adj
معیوب flawed, defective; adj disabled
معیوبیت disability n
مغاره cave n
مغاره ساختن cave in v
مغازه مواد غذایی grocery store n
مغالطه fallacy n
مغرور arrogant, proud adj
مغز brain n
مغشوش confused adj
مغشوش کردن confuse v
مغشوش کننده confusing adj
مغلق complicated adj

مغلق ساختن complicate v	مقدم بودن precede v
مغلوب كردن defeat v	مقدماتى preliminary; primary adj
مفتش inspector n	مقدمه preface, prologue n
مفرط extreme adj	مقرره regulation n
مفسد corrupt adj	مقصد intention n
مفصل joint n	مقصد سفر destination n
مفقود missing adj	مقصر culprit n
مفكوره thought, idea, opinion n	مقصر بودن perpetrate v
مفلس broke adj	مقناطيسى magnetic adj
مفهوم concept n	مقياس scale n
مفيد profitable, helpful, useful adj	مقيد bound adj
مقابل opposite adj	مكاتبه correspondence n
مقابله confrontation n	مكار tricky, wily, sly adj
مقابله كردن confront; contrast v	مكالمه conversation n
مقاله article, essay n	مكالمه كردن converse v
مقاوم persistent; hardy adj	مكان site n
مقاومت resistance n	مكتب school n
مقاومت كردن resist v	مكتب ابتدائيه elementary school n
مقايسه comparison n	مكتوب letter n
مقايسه كردن compare v	مكث كردن pause v
مقبره tomb n	مكر ruse n
مقبول handsome; cute adj	مكرر regular, frequent adj
مقدار amount, quantity n	مكروب germ n
مقدار زياد bulk, mass n	مكروبى شدن infect v
مقدار زياد most adv	مكروبى شده infected adj
مقدار كم handful n	مكرونى macaroni n
مقدار مصرف دوا dosage n	مكعب cube n
مقدار معلوم و مشخص parameter n	مكعبى cubic adj
مقدس holy, sacred adj	مكلف obliged, obligated adj
مقدس saint n	مكلف ساختن obligate v
	مكمل complete adj

مکیدن suck v	مملو laden adj
مگراینکه unless conj	ممنوعیت prohibition n
مگس fly n	من I pron
ملاحظه consideration, regard n	من خودم myself pron
ملازم attendant; custodian n	منازعه dispute n
ملاقات visit n	مناسب appropriate, adj
ملاقات کردن see, visit; meet v	reasonable, expedient; fit,
ملاقه ladle n	suitable; proper
ملامت کردن blame v	مناسبت occasion n
ملامتی blame n	منافق hypocrite n
ملایم lenient; mild, mellow, adj	منبع resource; source n
gentle	منتج شدن result v
ملایم و مهربان soft adj	منتشر شدن spread, diffuse v
ملایمت leniency; smoothness n	منتشر کردن release, post v
ملت nation n	منتظر await v
ملخ grasshopper n	منتظر چیزی بودن hold on to; v
ملکه empress, queen n	stick around
ملکیت property, possession n	منتقد critic n
ملی national adj	منتقل کردن hand down v
ملی سرخک radish n	منجمد کردن refrigerate v
ملیت nationality n	منحرف perverse adj
ممانعت ban n	منحرف شدن deviate, digress, v
ممپلی peanut n	stray, veer
ممتاز best n	منحرف شده disoriented adj
ممتاز distinguished, adj	منحرف کردن deprave; divert v
privileged	منحل کردن disband; dissolve v
ممثل actor n	منحنی curve n
ممثل زن actress n	منزل اول ground floor n
ممثل کمیدی comedian n	منزل بالا upstairs adv
ممکن might modal v	منزوی secluded adj
ممکن possible adj	منزوی کردن isolate v
ممکن بودن may modal v	منسجم coherent adj

outdated *adj* منسوخ	منفی کردن *v* subtract
منسوخ شده *adj* obsolete	منقار *n* beak
منشور *n* mandate	منقار مرغابی *n* bill
منشی *n* secretary	منقضی شدن *v* expire
منصرف شدن *v* withdraw	منی *n* sperm
منصرف کردن *v* dissuade	مهاجر *n* ,emigrant, immigrant
منصفانه *adv* fairly	migrant; refugee
منطبق *adj* compliant; matching	مهاجرت *n* refuge; immigration
منطبق ساختن *v* align	مهاجرت کردن *v* ,emigrate
منطق *n* logic	immigrate, migrate
منطقه *n* borough; region	مهاجم *n* invader
منطقوی *adj* regional	مهار کردن *v* restrain
منطقی *adj* rational, logical	مهارت *n* skill
منظره *n* ,panorama, spectacle	مهارت را تقویت کردن *v* brush up
sight, view, prospect;	مهتاب *n* moon
landscape, scenery	مهربانی *n* kindness
منظم *adv* neatly	مهره *n* vertebra
منظم *adj* regular; organized, tidy	مهم *adj* ,significant, serious
منظم کردن *v* sort, sort out	important; chief
منظور کردن *v* approve	مهمات جنگی *n* ammunition
منظوری *n* acknowledgment; approval	مهمان *n* visitor, guest
منع کردن *v* ;ban, forbid, prohibit	مهمان کردن *v* treat
obstruct	مهمان نوازی *n* hospitality
منعکس کردن *v* reflect	مهماندار *n* host
منفجر شدن *v* explode	مهماندار زن *n* hostess
منفجر کردن *v* blow up, detonate	مهمترین *adj* prime, paramount
منفجر کننده *n* detonator	مهندس *n* architect
منفرد *adj* single	مهندسی *n* architecture
منفعت *n* advantage, gain	مو *n* hair
منفی *prep* minus	مو چینک *n* tweezers
منفی *adj* negative	مواجه شدن *v* ,come across
منفی *n* subtraction	encounter, run into

مواد material *n*	مودب respectful *adj*
مواد انفجاری dynamite *n*	مودبانه politely *adv*
مواد سوخت fuel *n*	مودیم modem *n*
مواد ضد عفونی کننده *n*	مورد پسند استفاده کننده *adj*
disinfectant	user-friendly
مواد غایطه stool *n*	مورد پیگرد قانونی قرار دادن sue *v*
مواد غذایی groceries *n*	مورد توجه قرار نگرفته *adj*
مواد لباس شویی detergent *n*	unnoticed
مواد مخدر drug *n*	مورد ضرب و شتم beaten *adj*
مواد منفجره explosive *adj*	موزایک mosaic *n*
موازی parallel *adj*	موزه boot *n*
مواظب mindful, considerate *adj*	موزیم museum *n*
مواظب باش watch out *v*	موس کمپیوتر mouse *n*
مواظب بودن look out *v*	موسس founder *n*
موافقت کردن comply *v*	موسسه institution *n*
موتر automobile, car *n*	موسمی seasonal *adj*
موتر پیکپ pickup *n*	موسیقی music *n*
موتر را با ریسمان کش کردن tow *v*	موسیقی دان musician *n*
موتر های لینی streetcar *n*	موسیقی راک rock *n*
موترسیکل motorcycle *n*	موسیقی و رقص waltz *n*
موثر effective; proficient *adj*	موش mouse, rat *n*
موثریت effectiveness; *n*	موش خرما squirrel *n*
proficiency	موشگافی scrutiny *n*
موج wave; surge *n*	موضوع subject, theme, topic, *n*
موج بزرگ tidal wave *n*	matter
موج دار ripple *n*	موضوع را خلاصه بیان کردن *v*
موج ریز microwave *n*	outline
موج سواری کردن surf *v*	موضوعی topical *adj*
موجب سقوط شدن bring down *v*	موطلایی blonde *adj*
موجدار wavy *adj*	موعظه sermon *n*
موجودیت existence *n*	موفق successful *adj*
مودار hairy *adj*	موفق شدن prosper, succeed *v*

م

میدان ورزشی n court; field	موفقانه successfully adv
میراث n inheritance, heritage,	موفقیت success n
legacy	موقت provisional, temporary adj
میز n table; counter; desk	موقعیت location n
میز آرایش n dresser	موقف place, position, post n
میز پذیرش n reception	موم wax n
میزایل n missile	مومن believer n
میعاد n term	مومیایی mummy n
میکانیزم n mechanism	مومیایی کردن v embalm
میگرین n migraine	مونوگراف برای دریافت دیپلوم n
میل n mile	thesis
میل شدید به n craving	مونولوگ monologue n
میل لنگ n crank	موهم پرستی superstition n
میله n picnic	موی چتری مانند bangs n
میله آهنی n bar, rod	موی مصنوعی wig n
میله بیرق n flagpole	مؤدب courteous adj
میله خم شده n crowbar	مؤلف author n
میله های بزرگ بر سر کشتی n mast	مؤنث female n
میلودی n melody	میانبر shortcut n
میلی گرام n milligram	میانجی mediator n
میلی متر n millimeter	میانجی گری کردن v mediate
میلیارد n billion	میانه روی moderation n
میلیاردر n billionaire	میتر برق meter n
میلیون n million	میتودی methodical adj
میلیونر adj millionaire	میخ nail n
میمون n monkey	میخ چوبی stake n
میمون شامپانزی n chimpanzee	میخ کوبیدن v nail
مین n mine	میخانه tavern, bar n
میناتوری n miniature	میخانه دار bartender n
مینوی غذا n menu	میدان بازی playground n
میوه n fruit	میدان بازی گلف golf course n
میوه آووکادو n avocado	میدان هوایی airfield, airport n

میوه یی fruity *adj*
نهر creek *n*

ن

نا امید desperate *adj*
نا امیدی despair *n*
ناامید helpless, hopeless *adj*
ناآشنا unfamiliar *adj*
نابالغ immature *adj*
نابرابر unequal *adj*
نابرابری disparity *n*
نابغه genius *n*
نابه هنگام untimely *adj*
نابود کردن annihilate, *v* exterminate
نابینا blind *adj*
نابینایی blindness *n*
ناپاک squalid, impure *adj*
ناپایا unsteady *adj*
ناپدید شدن disappear *v*
ناپدیدی disappearance *n*
ناپسند obscene *adj*
ناتکمیل incomplete *adj*
ناتوان incapable, unable *adj*
ناتوان invalid *n*
ناتوان ساختن incapacitate *v*
ناتوانی inability *n*
ناچیز trivial, insignificant, *adj* paltry

ناچیز پنداشتن underestimate *v*
ناحیه zone, district *n*
ناحیه یک ایالت county *n*
ناخالص impure *adj*
ناخن nail *n*
ناخن انگشت fingernail *n*
ناخن پنجه پا toenail *n*
ناخوش unhappy *adj*
ناخوشایند grim, unpleasant, *adj* awful
نادان silly, foolish, stupid *adj*
نادر rare, infrequent *adj*
نادرست inaccurate, *adj* incorrect, untrue, wrong
نادیده گرفتن overlook; slur *v*
ناراحت uncomfortable, *adj* uneasy; upset
ناراحت ساختن frustrate, irritate *v*
ناراحت کردن perturb, upset *v*
ناراحت کننده disturbing; *adj* inconvenient; irritating, obnoxious
ناراحتی unrest; discomfort; *n* frustration
ناراضی disgruntled, *adj* dissatisfied
نارییل coconut *n*
نازک lean; crisp *adj*
ناسازگار incoherent *adj*
ناسالم unfit *adj*
ناسپاس ungrateful *adj*
ناشر publisher *n*

ungrateful *adj* ناشکر	نام نویسی کردن *v* ;enlist
unbroken *adj* ناشکسته	matriculate
anonymity *n* ناشناس	نامثبت *n* negative
anonymous *adj* ناشناس	نامحدود *adj* unlimited
deaf *adj* ناشنوا	نامرتب *n* slob
due *adj* ناشی از	نامرد *n* coward
observant *adj* ناظر	نامرغوب *adj* inferior
supervisor *n* ناظر	نامزد *adj* engaged
unjust *adj* ناعادلانه	نامزد *n* fiancé
belly button, navel *n* ناف	نامزد کردن *v* nominate
disobedient *adj* نافرمان	نامزدی *n* engagement
disobedience *n* نافرمانی	نامساعد *adj* bland
disobey *v* نافرمانی کردن	نامشروع *adj* illicit
faulty *adj* ناقص	نامطلوب *adj* ,adverse
pear *n* ناک	unfavorable, undesirable
inefficient *adj* ناکارا	نامطمئن *adj* uncertain, unsure
insufficient *adj* ناکافی	نامعقول *adj* ;unreasonable
fail, go under *v* ناکام شدن	absurd
failure *n* ناکامی	نامعلوم *n* anonymity
unspeakable *adj* ناگفتنی	نامعلوم *adj* uncertain, unknown
precipitate *v* ناگهان واقع شدن	نامعین *adj* indefinite
sudden *adj* ناگهانی	نامناسب *adj* ,unreasonable, unfit
groan *n* ناله	improper, inappropriate,
wail *v* ناله	unsuitable
groan; whine *v* ناله کردن	نامنظم ساختن *v* mess up
moan *v* ناله کشیدن	نامه *n* mail, letter
title, name *n* نام	نامه الکترونیکی *n* (email) e-mail
first name *n* نام اول	نامه الکترونیکی فرستادن *v* e-mail
brand *n* نام تجارتی	(email)
maiden name *n* نام خانوادگی	نامه رسان *n* mailman
pseudonym *n* نام مستعار	نامه فرستادن *v* mail
registration *n* نام نویسی	نامه هرزه *n* spam

نامهربان unkind adj

ناموافق dissident adj

ناموفق unsuccessful adj

نامیدن name v

نان bread n

نان برگر bun n

نان بریان شده toast n

نان چاشت lunch n

نان چپاتی burrito n

نان شب dinner n

نانوا baker n

نانوایی bakery n

ناهموار rocky; ragged, adj jagged, uneven

ناهوار rugged adj

ناوقت late adv

ناوقت tardy adj

ناول novel n

ناول نویس novelist n

ناوه chute n

نبات plant n

نبرد battle n

نبض pulse n

نبودن lack v

نبوغ ingenuity n

نپذیرفتن refute v

نت و بولت nut n

نتوانستن cannot v

نتیجه outcome, result, n output; sequel

نتیجه برعکس گرفتن backfire v

نتیجه گیری deduce v

نتیجه گیری کردن infer v

نجابت nobility n

نجات salvation n

نجات دادن save, rescue, salvage v

نجات دهنده savior n

نجات دهنده در حوض آببازی n lifeguard

نجات یافتن survive v

نجات یافته survivor n

نجار carpenter n

نجاری carpentry n

نجوا whisper n

نجوا کردن whisper v

نجومی astronomic adj

نجیب noble adj

نخ thread, yarn n

نخ دندان floss n

نخ کردن thread v

نخست first adv

نخستین initial adj

نخود pea n

نخیر no adj

نخیر not adv

ندرت scarcity n

ندرتاً rarely adv

نرخ rate n

نرخ تخمینی دادن quotation n

نرخ دادن quotation, quote n

نرم fluffy, spongy, soft; lenient adj

نرم افزار کمپیوتر software n

نرم کردن mellow; soften v

نرم کننده conditioner n

نرم کننده laxative *adj*	نشاط آور *adj* ;exhilarating
نرمش leniency *n*	jubilant
نرمی smoothness *n*	نشان *n* emblem, badge, logo
نزاع quarrel, brawl; strife *n*	نشان دادن *v* ,feature
نزده nineteen *n*	demonstrate, indicate, show
نزدیک close *adj*	نشان دادن روی دیوار *v* project
نزدیک close *adv*	نشان دهنده *n* indicator
نزدیک near *prep*	نشان دهنده موقعیت *n* cursor
نزدیک بین nearsighted, *adj*	نشانه *n* ,symptom, mark
shortsighted	indication, token
نزدیک بینی myopic *adj*	نشانی کردن *v* check, mark
نزدیک شدن approach *v*	نشایسته starch *n*
نزدیکی proximity, vicinity *n*	نشر کردن *v* air, publish
نزول descent *n*	نشرات broadcast *n*
نژاد race *n*	نشرات زنده live *adj*
نژاد پرست racist *adj*	نشرات کردن *v* broadcast
نژاد پرستی racism *n*	نشریه publication *n*
نژادی ethnic *adj*	نشست sitting *n*
نسبت ratio *n*	نشست طیاره landing *n*
نسبت به than *conj*	نشست کردن بر زمین *v* land
نسبت دادن attribute *v*	نشستن sit *v*
نسبتاً rather *adv*	نشه drunk *adj*
نسخه edition, version *n*	نصاب تعلیمی curriculum *n*
نسخه اصلی original *n*	نصب کردن *v* ,paste; erect, set up
نسخه الکترونیکی کتاب *n* e-book	install; step up
نسخه خطی manuscript *n*	نصب کردن خیمه *v* pitch
نسخه داکتر prescription *n*	نصف half *adj*
نسخه نمایشی demo *n*	نصف کردن *v* halve
نسل *n* ;breed; descendant	نصواری brown *n*
generation	نطفه sperm *n*
نسل شناسی gene *n*	نظارت *n* ,oversight, surveillance
نسیم breeze *n*	supervision

monitor, oversee, v نظارت کردن	silver n نقره
supervise, preside	role n نقش
military n نظامی	part n نقش در فلم
overview n نظر اجمالی	mirage n نقش روی آب
according to prep نظر به	scheme, sketch, map n نقشه
comment v نظر دادن	flaw, imperfection, n نقص
poll n نظرسنجی	shortcoming
point, tip, view, notion, n نظریه	violate v نقض کردن
thought, comment, feedback	spot, dot n نقطه
order n نظم	peak n نقطه اوج
mint n نعنا	viewpoint n نقطه نظر
melody n نغمه	copy n نقل
hate n نفرت	paraphrase; quote v نقل قول
despicable, adj نفرت انگیز	quote n نقل قول
detestable, gruesome, odious	relocate v نقل مکان کردن
detest, hate, v نفرت داشتن	نکات مهم را نشانی کردن v
loathe	highlight
resent v نفرت کردن	necktie, tie n نکتایی
breath; ego n نفس	point n نکته
exhale n نفس بیرون کشیدن	writing n نگارش
asthma n نفس تنگی	glance, look n نگاه
breathe v نفس کشیدن	glance v نگاه انداختن
gasp, wheeze v نفسک زدن	glare n نگاه خیره
benefit, profit n نفع	glimpse n نگاه سریع
influence; intrusion n نفوذ	glare n نگاه قهر آمیز
permeate, infiltrate v نفوذ کردن	looks n نگاه ها
population n نفوس	concern n نگرانی
exquisite adj نفیس	curator, guardian, n نگهبان
nag v نق زدن	warden
painter n نقاش	nanny n نگهبان طفل
painting n نقاشی	bridesmaid n نگهبان عروس
paint v نقاشی کردن	retention; hold n نگهداری

نگهداری کردن conserve v	model, sample, n نمونه
نگهداشت conserve n	specimen
نگهداشتن keep, preserve; v	نمونه یک نشریه copy n
withhold	disgraceful adj ننگین
نل آب آتش نشانی fire hydrant n	nine n نه
نلدوان plumber n	no adv نه
نلدوانی plumbing n	nor conj نه
نم نم باران drizzle n	نهایی definitive, ultimate, adj
نم نم باران باریدن drizzle v	final
نماز prayer n	نهایی کردن finalize v
نماز خواندن pray v	نهر آب stream n
نمایان کردن feature v	نهم ninth adj
نمایش spectacle, display, n	نهنگ shark n
show, play	نو ساختن renovate v
نمایش از قبل preview n	نواختن موسیقی play v
نمایش اوپرا opera n	نوار strip n
نمایش دادن display, exhibit v	نوازش کردن caress v
نمایش طنزیه revue n	نوازنده وایلین violinist n
نمایش کمیدی farce n	نواسه grandchild n
نمایشگاه exhibition, fair; n	نواسه پسر grandson n
gallery	نواسه دختر granddaughter n
نمایشی symbolic, adj	نوآوری novelty n
demonstrative; dramatic	نوبت turn n
نمایندگی از کسی representation n	نوبت دادن turn up v
نماینده agent, delegate, n	نوت دالر bill n
representative	نوت های موسیقی note n
نماینده گی delegation n	نوجوان adolescent, juvenile, n
نمد ساخته شده از پشم felt n	teenager
نمره grade, score n	نوجوان teenage adj
نمره گرفتن در بازی score v	نوجوانی boyhood n
نمک salt n	نود ninety n
نمکی salty adj	نور gleam n

نور افكن spotlight n	نيرنگ، trick n
نور آفتاب sunlight n	نيرنگ باز tricky adj
نوراني luminous adj	نيرو strain n
نورگير skylight n	نيرومند potent, powerful; adj husky
نورم norm n	
نوری optical adj	نيروها troops n
نوزاد infant, newborn n	نيروی انسانی manpower n
نوسازی renovation n	نيروی دريايی navy n
نوسان كردن sway, fluctuate v	نيزل nozzle n
نوستالژی nostalgia n	نيزه dart, harpoon, spear n
نوشابه refreshment, n beverage, drink	نيزه انداختن dart v
	نيش bite; fang; sting n
نوشابه گازدار soda n	نيش زدن sting; nibble; prick v
نوشتن write v	نيش زننده stinging adj
نوشته شده written adj	نيشكر cane n
نوشيدن drink v	نيكر shorts n
نوشيدن به سلامتی كسی toast v	نيكر آببازی swim trunks n
نوشيدنی drinkable adj	نيكوكار benefactor n
نوع form; sort, type, kind n	نيكی goodness n
نوع بازی lacrosse n	نيلون nylon n
نوك point, tip n	نيم پخته rare adj
نوك انگشت fingertip n	نيم گرم tepid adj
نوك پا tiptoe v	نيمه half n
نوك تيز sharp adj	نيمه دل half-hearted adj
نوك دار pointed adj	نيمه روز midday n
نوك زدن peck v	نيمه روشن twilight n
نوك سينه nipple n	نيمه شب midnight n
نوك نيزه spearhead v	نيمه شفاف see-through adj
نويسنده writer n	نيمه عميق shallow adj
نياز requirement n	نيمه كاره halftime n
نياز داشتن require v	نيمه گرم lukewarm adj
نيازمند destitute, needy adj	

و

و and conj

و غیره etcetera adv

وابستگی affiliation; n dependence

وابسته dependent adj

وابسته به جراحی surgical adj

وابسته به قانون اساسی adj constitutional

وابسته به کتاب مقدس biblical adj

واپس نگری hindsight n

واجد شرایط eligible, qualified adj

واجد شرایط بودن qualify v

واحد unit n

واحد اندازه گیری pint n

واحد اندازه گیری یارد yard n

واحد پول currency n

واحد پیمایش pint n

واحد طول یا متر meter n

وادار کردن coerce, compel, v induce, lobby, persuade; oblige

وادار کننده persuasive adj

وادی valley n

وارث heir n

وارث زن heiress n

وارخطا embarrassed adj

وارد کردن import v

واژگون کردن overturn v

واژگونی reversal n

واسطه middleman n

واسطه نقلیه vehicle n

واسکت نجا vest

واضح clear, explicit, frank, adj obvious; distinct; vivid

واضح و پرقدرت graphic adj

واضحاً clearly, obviously adv

واعظ preacher n

وافر abundant adj

وافر wafer n

وافل waffle n

واقع در located adj

واقع در جای situated adj

واقعا really adv

واقعاً actually, indeed adv

واقعبین down-to-earth adj

واقعبینانه realistic adj

واقعی actual, real adj

واقعیت truth, reality n

واکسین vaccine n

واکسین کردن immunize, v vaccinate

واکنش تند backlash n

واگذار کردن entrust; assign; v give out

واگون wagon n

وال valve n

وال نل آب valve n

والا prominent; sublime adj

والدین parent n

والی governor n

والیبال volleyball n

وانمود کردن v pretend	ورقه نمرات در مکتب n report card
وبلاگ n blog	ورکشاپ n workshop
وبلاگ نویس n blogger	ورود n admittance; arrival
وجد زده adj ecstatic	ورودی adj incoming
وجدان n conscience	وزارت n ministry
وجه وصفی در گرامر n participle	وزن n weight
وجود داشتن v exist	وزن در خواندن آهنگ n rhythm
وجوه n funds	وزن زیاد n heaviness
وحشت n terror, horror; brutality	وزن کردن v weigh
وحشتناک adj formidable; grisly;	وزیر n minister
horrendous, terrible	وسایل n appliance
وحشی n barbarian	وسط n center, middle
وحشی adj wild; brutal, savage,	وسطی n mediocrity
ferocious	وسعت n latitude, scope,
وحشی شدن v brutalize	breadth, extent; expansion
وحشیانه adj atrocious, barbaric	وسعت دادن v expand
وخیم adj dire, tense	وسوسه n temptation
وخیم تر adv worse	وسوسه انگیز adj tempting
وخیم ترین adv worst	وسیع adj wide, vast, broad,
وراثت n inheritance	extensive; roomy
ورزش n sport	وسیع ساختن v broaden, widen
ورزش بوکس v box	وسیعاً adv widely
ورزش جمناستیک n gymnastics	وسیله n device, instrument
ورزش کردن v exercise, work out	وسیله برقی n signal
ورزش یوگا n yoga	وسیله کار n tool
ورزشکار n athlete, sportsman	وسیله هدایت طیاره n rudder
ورزشکار جمناستیک n gymnast	وصل کردن v connect
ورزشکار دوش n runner	وصیت n will
ورزشی adj athletic	وصیت نامه n testament
ورشکسته adj bankrupt	وضاحت n clarification; clarity
ورق المونیمی n foil	وضاحت دادن v clarify
ورق کاغذ n sheet	وضع n pose

وضع خطرناک predicament *n*	وقف کردن dedicate, devote *v*
وضع غیرعادی abnormality *n*	وقفه recess, break, interval *n*
وضع مالیات levy *v*	وقوع occurrence *n*
وضعیت state, condition, *n*	وکالت کردن advocate *v*
situation; setting, mode;	وکیل مدافع attorney *n*
posture	ولایت province *n*
وضعیت دشوار jam, mess, *n*	ولتاژ برق voltage *n*
dilemma	ولخرجی کردن squander *v*
وضعیت فزیکی shape *n*	ولگرد stray *adj*
وطن homeland *n*	ونیلا vanilla *n*
وطندوست patriotic *adj*	ویبسایت website *n*
وطندوستی patriot *n*	ویتامین vitamin *n*
وظیفه position, post, *n*	ویدیو video *n*
employment, assignment,	ویدیو گیم video game *n*
duty, job, task	ویران کردن destroy, devastate, *v*
وعده promise *n*	ravage, ruin
وعده کردن promise *v*	ویرانگر destructive, *adj*
وعده ملاقات appointment *n*	devastating
وعده ملاقات گذاشتن date *v*	ویرانی desolation, *n*
وعظ دینی کردن preach *v*	destruction, devastation,
وفات شدن pass away *v*	havoc, ruin
وفادار loyal *adj*	ویروس virus *n*
وفاداری allegiance, fidelity, *n*	ویژگی trait *n*
loyalty	ویژه special *adj*
وقار dignity, poise *n*	ویژه گی significance; feature *n*
وقت early *adv*	ویلدینگ کردن weld *v*
وقت time *n*	ویلدینگکار welder *n*
وقت را معین کردن time *v*	
وقت شناس punctual *adj*	
وقت معین در سال season *n*	
وقت نان چاشت lunchtime *n*	
وقف شده dedicated *adj*	

هردو both *adj*	
هردوی both *pron*	
هرروز everyday *adj*	
هرزمانی whenever *adv*	
هرشخص everybody *pron*	
هرکدام each *pron*	
هرکس anybody; everyone *pron*	
هرکسی anyone *pron*	
هرگز never *adv*	
هرم pyramid *n*	
هروقت whenever *conj*	
هریک either *adv*	
هریکی any *adv*	
هریکی each *adj*	
هزار thousand *n*	
هزار سال millennium *n*	
هسته core *n*	
هشت eight *n*	
هشت پا octopus *n*	
هشتاد eighty *n*	
هشتم eighth *adj*	
هشدار دادن alert *v*	
هشدار دهنده alarming *adj*	
هضم کردن digest *v*	
هفت seven *n*	
هفتاد seventy *n*	
هفتم seventh *adj*	
هفته week *n*	
هفته وار weekly *adv*	
هفده seventeen *n*	
هک کامپیوتر hack *v*	
هکتار acre *n*	

ه

هات داگ hotdog *n*	
هارن horn *n*	
هارن کردن honk *v*	
هارن موتر horn *n*	
هاضمه digestion *n*	
هیپنوتیزم hypnosis *n*	
هتک حرمت کردن desecrate *v*	
هجا syllable *n*	
هجده eighteen *n*	
هجدهم eighteenth *adj*	
هجوم invasion *n*	
هجی spell, spelling *n*	
هجی کردن spell *v*	
هدایات directions, instruction *n*	
هدایت دادن direct, instruct *v*	
هدف goal, objective, purpose, *n* target	
هدف aim *n*	
هدف قراردادن aim *v*	
هدیه دادن give away *v*	
هذیان گفتن hallucinate *v*	
هر any; every *adj*	
هرآنچه whatever *pron*	
هرآنکس whoever *pron*	
هرج و مرج chaos *n*	
هرجا anywhere; everywhere *adv*	
هرچه whatever *adj*	
هرچیز everything *pron*	
هرچیزی anything *pron*	

هکر hacker v

هلیکوپتر helicopter n

هم اتاقی roommate n

هم درجه peer n

هم درجه بودن peer v

همانند سازی cloning n

هماهنگ کردن coordinate,
harmonize v

هماهنگ کننده coordinator n

هماهنگی harmony n

همآیش summit n

همبرگر hamburger n

همبستگی unity, solidarity n

همتا peer, counterpart n

همجوار adjacent, adjoining adj

همچنان too, also adv

همخوان corresponding adj

همدردی sympathy n

همدردی کردن relate, sympathize v

همدست ally, accomplice n

همدلی empathy n

همراه companion n

همراه با with prep

همراهی companionship n

همراهی کردن accompany v

همزمان simultaneous adj

همزمان بودن coincide v

همزمان ساختن synchronize v

همزیستی coexist v

همسایگی neighborhood n

همسایه neighbor n

همسر spouse n

همسران wives n

همصنفی classmate n

همکار associate v

همکار collaborator, colleague, n
teammate

همکار fellow adj

همکاری collaboration, n
cooperation

همکاری کردن collaborate, v
cooperate

همگام ساختن synchronize v

همگرایی کردن converge v

همه all adj

همه کاره versatile adj

هموار smooth, even, flat adj

هموار کردن spread, flatten, v
level; pave

همواره invariably adv

همیشگی habitual; perennial adj

همیشه always adv

هندسه geometry n

هنر art n

هنر آمیزش رنگها collage n

هنر گرافیک graphic adj

هنرمند artist n

هنرمند مشهور celebrity n

هنری artistic adj

هنگام while conj

هنوز yet conj

هوا air n

هوا دادن ventilate v

هوا دهی ventilation n

هوابند airtight *adj*
هواپیما ربا hijacker *n*
هواپیما ربایی hijack *v*
هواپیمایی aviation *n*
هواداران fan *n*
هوانورد aviator *n*
هوایی overhead *adj*
هوتل hotel *n*
هوس fad *n*
هوس چیزی کردن whim *n*
هوس کردن crave *v*
هوش conscience *n*
هوشیار alert, attentive, *adj*
sober; clever
هویت identity *n*
هی hey *e*
هیاهو commotion *n*
هیبت کردن awe *n*
هیجان thrill, excitement *n*
هیجان آور exciting, thrilling *adj*
هیجانی excited *adj*
هیجانی کردن excite *v*
هیچ any *pron*
هیچ neither *adv*
هیچ no *e*
هیچ none *prep*
هیچ nothing *n*
هیچ جا nowhere *adv*
هیچ یک neither *pron*
هیچکدام neither *adj*
هیچکس no one, nobody *pron*
هیچیک nothing *pron*

هیولا monster *n*
هیولایی monstrous *adj*
هیئت panel *n*
هیئت داوران jury *n*

ی

یا either *pron*
یا or *conj*
یادداشت record, annotation, *n*
notation, memo
یادداشت کردن note *v*
یادداشت مختصر note *n*
یادداشت نوشتن annotate *v*
یادگاری memento *n*
یازده eleven *n*
یازدهم eleventh *adj*
بازنه brother-in-law *n*
یاغی rebel *n*
یافتن find *v*
یاقوت ruby *n*
یالان cape *n*
یاور helper *n*
یأس disappointment *n*
یتیم orphan *n*
یخ ice *n*
یخ بستن freeze *v*
یخ را آب کردن defrost *v*
یخ زده freezing, frigid, frozen *adj*
یخبندان frost *n*

یخچال n freezer; refrigerator
یخمالک n slide
یخن n collar
یخنی n broth
یخنی گوشت n gravy
یخنی گوشت و سبزیجات n stew
یقیناً adv surely, certainly
یک a an
یک adj one
یک پارچه n lot
یک جانبه adj unilateral
یک چهارم حصه n quarter; quart
یک روز adv someday
یک کسی pron oneself
یک مقدار adj some
یکبار adv once
یکبار مصرف adj disposable
یکپارچگی n integrity
یکجا adv together
یکجا با adv along
یکجا شدن v get together
یکجا نمودن v merge
یکدسته adv single-handed
یکسان adj akin; uniform
یکسانی n uniformity
یکنواخت adj monotonous
یکنواختی n uniformity

یکنوع آله بازی n joystick
یکنوع توت سرخ n raspberry
یکنوع چتنی n mustard
یکنوع حیوان شبه موش خرما n raccoon
یکنوع خربوزه n cantaloupe
یکنوع خزنده n tarantula
یکنوع خسته n hazelnut
یکنوع خوراک در صبحانه n granola
یکنوع سمارق n fungus
یکنوع عفونت گوش n mumps
یکنوع غذای دریایی n shrimp
یکنوع غله n rye
یکنوع کلچه n waffle
یکنوع کیک n pancake
یکنوع مار بزرگ n python
یکنوع ماهی چهارکنج n squid
یکنوع یاقوت کبود n sapphire
یکی دیگر pron another; each other
یکی کردن v unify, unite, consolidate
یهودی n Jew
یهودی adj Jewish
یهودیت n Judaism
یونیفورم n uniform
ییخ زده adj frosty